The Moral Dimensions of Intellectual Property Rights

For Shireen
and
Ryan, Dayna and Thomas

The Moral Dimensions of Intellectual Property Rights

Steven Ang

Nanyang Technological University, Singapore

Edward Elgar

Cheltenham, UK • Northampton, MA, USA

Published by
Edward Elgar Publishing Limited
The Lypiatts
15 Lansdown Road
Cheltenham
Glos GL50 2JA
UK

Edward Elgar Publishing, Inc.
William Pratt House
9 Dewey Court
Northampton
Massachusetts 01060
USA

A catalogue record for this book
is available from the British Library

Library of Congress Control Number: 2013944957

This book is available electronically in the ElgarOnline.com Law Subject Collection, E-ISBN 978 1 78254 668 9

ISBN 978 1 78254 667 2

Typeset by Columns Design XML Ltd, Reading
Printed and bound in Great Britain by T.J. International Ltd, Padstow

Contents

v

Preface and acknowledgements

The Moral Dimensions of Intellectual Property Rights explores the various aspects of IPRs in which moral evaluation and claims play a role. According to R.M. Hare, in *The Language of Morals* (1952) and *Freedom and Reason* (1963), moral concepts and reasoning are characterized by the universalization of prescriptions. Universalization links the various dimensions in a way that rationally forces us to revise the moral basis of the various claims we make for, about and of IPRs, and ultimately provides grounds for their reform. This requires a foundational set of moral principles to work. Our expectation that moral principles and values must serve to guide us, and resolve conflict between us, with objective rational force, provides the basis for adopting such a set of fundamental prescriptions.

These sum up in the equal right to freedom and well-being as the ultimate basis for moral evaluation of our institutions. An implication of this right is that property in IPR systems must be balanced with participation rights (moral and legal) of the public to a public domain which allows individuals to have access to, and use, objects of intellectual property. This work explores this inter-connectedness through the following: justification of IPRs based on this equal right to freedom and well-being; explanation of the function of, and justification for, the presence of moral concepts and terms in national and international IPR rules; the commitments implied by use of these moral ideas for our obligations in respect of the way we enjoy, exploit and enforce our IPRs, and, ultimately, our duty to reform IPRs in ways that respect the participation rights implied by this principle.

I was able to complete this work in large part owing to the inspiration, support and encouragement afforded me by my supervisors at the Centre for Commercial Laws at Queen Mary (University of London), Professors Michael Blakeney and Spyros Maniatis. I am also indebted to Victor Yeo and Erin Goh, who at various times over the long gestation of this project were Heads of my Division, and to Professor Gillian Yeo, who was the Acting Dean at Nanyang Business School of Nanyang Technological University. Most of all I would like to thank my wife, who patiently endured all the travails of being the spouse of a PhD researcher for an inordinate period of time.

And I give thanks to God, faith in whom sustained me through doubts and uncertainties.

Abbreviations

ACTA	Anti-Counterfeiting Trade Agreement (draft text dated 2 October 2010)
Berne Convention or 'Berne'	Berne Convention for the Protection of Literary and Artistic Works
CBAC	Canadian Biotechnology Advisory Committee
CEO	Chief Executive Officer
CSR	Corporate Social Responsibility
DMCA	Digital Millennium Copyright Act
ECHR	European Convention for the Protection of Human Rights and Fundamental Freedoms 1950
ECJ	European Court of Justice
EPC	European Patent Convention
EPO	European Patent Office
EU	European Union
FAO	UN Food and Agriculture Organization
FTA	Free Trade Agreement
GURTs	Genetic Use Restriction Technology (for genetically modified living things)
HRA	Human Rights Act 1998 (UK)
ICESR	International Covenant on Economic, Social and Cultural Rights
IIPA	International Intellectual Property Alliance
IP	Intellectual Property
IPRs	Intellectual Property Rights
LDCs	least-developed countries
NGOs	Non-Governmental Organizations
PGC	(Gewirth's) Principle of Generic Consistency
PTO	Patent and Trademark Office
TMs	Technological Measures (for the restriction of access to or control of digital copyright material)

TRIPS	Agreement on Trade Related Aspects of Intellectual Property Rights
UDHR	Universal Declaration of Human Rights, UN, 1948
UK	United Kingdom of Great Britain
UN	United Nations
UPOV	International Convention for the Protection of New Varieties of Plants
US	United States of America
USTR	US Trade Representative
WCT	WIPO Copyright Treaty, 1996
WIPO	World Intellectual Property Organization
WPPT	WIPO Performances and Phonograms Treaty, 1996
WTO	World Trade Organization

Table of cases

Table of legal instruments

1. The idea of the moral dimensions of IPRs

1.1 THE RIDDLE IN THE RULES

Ideas are born free; and everywhere are in chains. If one may be forgiven the conceit of paraphrasing J.J. Rousseau's famous opening,[1] the reference is not altogether inappropriate given that the central subject matter of this work is the nature of the moral basis for rights in ideas and the implications of this for the way these institutions should be structured. Ideas, the object of intellectual property laws, are by their nature free;[2] in fact, more naturally free than human beings since they are not capable of tangible restraint once released to the public: it is by laws that they are enchained, not by the actual binding up of ideas themselves, but by restrictions placed upon human persons as to their use. Ideas are controlled through the restrictions we place on ourselves. Though not all types of idea are subject to intellectual property laws, through the workings of international intellectual property conventions, such rules are present in the national laws of countries in virtually every corner of the globe.[3]

Intellectual property rights are legal rights over various types of idea and intangible constructs, the central ones typically giving private persons ownership rights to exclude others in certain ways from uses of aspects of these ideas.[4] Amongst these are *copyright* and related rights,

---

[1] Rousseau, *The Social Contract* (1762), G.D.H. Cole (trans.), Bk 1 §1: 'Man is born free; and everywhere he is in chains'.

[2] A feature recognized since some of the earliest English judicial observations on copyright e.g.: Yates J in *Millar v. Taylor* (1769) 4 Burr. 2303 at 2378–9, 'Ideas are free', though he notes only after publication: 'But whilst the author confines them to his study, they are like birds in a cage, which none but he can have a right to let fly ...'; Lord Camden in *Donaldson v. Beckett*, (1774) 2 Bro. 129, 4 Burr. 2408, '[S]cience and learning are in their nature *public juris*, and they ought to be as free and general as air and water.'

[3] See Ch. 5.

[4] A more detailed description of these rights is given in Ch. 4.

which are rights of reproduction, performance in public and communication to the public, amongst others, over literary and artistic works and other expressive creations, which include music and dramatic and movie productions, but which may also include utilitarian items like computer programs and compilations of data. *Patents* are state grants for a limited period giving their owners rights to the making and use of inventions. *Trade mark* laws give registered owners exclusive rights to certain uses of signs associated with their goods or services. Also associated with these, as intellectual property, are certain rights over the dissemination and use of information that is not publicly available that are protected by *trade secrets* legislation and, in common law systems, under the *action for breach of confidence*. This list is not comprehensive. But it gives paradigmatic examples of intellectual property ('IP'), or intellectual property rights ('IPRs').

The idea of a 'moral dimension', as it is used here, embraces the fact that the central rules of IPRs – which define the conditions of their existence or acquisition, their extent and their exercise – employ moral terms and ideas.

A critical riddle raised by the presence of moral terms and concepts in IPR related rules: What do they mean? This question quickly spins into further questions: Is this a matter of the speaker's intentions? How do the speakers intend themselves to be understood when they use moral terms in their instructions, agreements and commands? What do *we* mean when we use such terms? Can the speakers intend results and conclusions they did not expect when making the utterance? Have moral terms any objective meaning? Are they mere ciphers into which the party with the power to enforce its interpretation may write his own meaning? This inquiry is important to anyone concerned about IPRs as institutions because a cursory investigation soon reveals that they are framed and qualified in terms of, constrained by and legitimized by, rules in which moral terms and concepts play central and critical roles. Moral – that is, normatively evaluative – concepts are present in IPR and related rules by express use of moral terms in IPR rules, and when such rules use overtly technical terms and ideas which require moral judgements to give them at least part of their content, or when they use factual criteria where the classification of phenomena into factual categories requires a morally laden assessment. And they are present in the same way in empowering or limiting ancillary laws like the common law policy, in competition laws and constitutional and human rights laws.

The most significant legal basis for the worldwide expansion and reach of IPRs as social institutions today is the Agreement on Trade Related Aspects of Intellectual Property Rights (the 'TRIPS Agreement' or

'TRIPS') which every World Trade Organization ('WTO') member state must accept and observe. Albeit a product of realpolitik in international trade negotiations,[5] the negotiators at the Uruguay round of the General Agreement on Tariffs and Trade ('GATT') found it necessary to couch some of TRIPS' key provisions in ethical terminology. Its clause on its 'Objectives' (Article 7) speaks of 'the *mutual advantage* of producers and users of technological knowledge and in a *manner conducive to social and economic welfare*, and to *a balance of rights and obligations*'; and that on its 'Principles' (Article 8) declares that appropriate measures 'may be needed *to prevent the abuse of intellectual property rights* by right holders or resort to practices which *unreasonably* restrain trade or adversely affect the international transfer of technology' (emphasis added). The words 'balance of rights and obligations', 'appropriate measures', 'abuse of intellectual property rights' and 'unreasonably' in relation to trade restraint and adverse effects on international transfer of technology, presume and entail – if they are to be given meaningful content – a background set of principles which justify IPRs. How are we to understand them? Do they mean whatever each person chooses them to mean? Yet, these words and their entailed principles set the context for interpreting the rest of the TRIPS provisions.[6]

The other key provisions, defining the range and limits of the IPR protection to be afforded, are the exceptions and limitations allowed under TRIPS. Most notable are what have come to be called the 'three-step tests', of which Article 13 for copyright is one.[7] This sets out the conditions for permissible exceptions to, and limitations on, copyright exclusivity. Namely, they must (1) be confined to 'special cases' which (2) 'do not conflict with a normal exploitation of a work' and (3) 'do not unreasonably prejudice the legitimate interests of the right holder'. The key terms in these conditions invite one to construct a normative background of general justification for IPR exclusivity against which 'special cases' can be distinguished and 'normal exploitation' identified. In copyright laws, the aspect of the subject matter that the right extends to is captured by the notion of the idea–expression dichotomy expressed in Article 9(2) of TRIPS and echoes section 102(b) of the US Copyright Act.[8] Although the distinction is not an overtly moral one, its application forces the judges and legal systems to choose between giving some content to the notion of unprotectable ideas and hence make evaluative

---

[5] See Ch. 5 at §5.2.
[6] See Ch. 5 at §5.3.1.
[7] See Ch. 5 at §5.3.2.
[8] See Ch. 4 at §4.3.2.

decisions about the limits of the realm of copyright, or hollowing out the concept until it becomes an empty mantra, dutifully noted and then passed over for some more substantive principle. For copyright, the more generally significant of the provisions which expressly use moral terms in the national laws are the fair use defences and limitations based on public interest or policy, although these are circumscribed to greater or lesser degrees by the other conditions required by the laws.[9] Just when a use or dealing is 'fair', and how public policy is constructed by the courts, are questions involving at least some moral evaluation.

In the patent regime, there are obvious moral provisions. Article 27(2) of the TRIPS Agreement *allows*, but does not require, WTO member states to 'exclude from patentability inventions, the prevention within their territory of the commercial exploitation of which is necessary to protect *ordre public* or morality'.[10] This accommodates the bar against patentability to which the European Patent Convention members are subject under Article 53(a), and EU members are subject under Article 6 of the Biotechnology Directive.[11]

Such terms are also imbedded in the hearts of the other two main TRIPS IPR regimes that will be considered here. The notion of unfair competition underpins trade secrets protection in civil law systems,[12] and, in common law systems, the test for the circumstances importing an obligation of confidence relies on the judgement of the reasonable man in equity[13] or some other formulation in which the general concept of justice is employed, for example whether it be 'just in all the circumstances that [the recipient of the information] should be precluded from disclosing the information to others'.[14] And so also in the notion of honest commercial practice an ethical test for unfair competition underpins trade mark protection.[15]

Such ethical terms and concepts are also in the ancillary empowering and limiting laws. Examples include the constitutional provisions that sanction the creation of IPRs (or some of them), such as Article 1 section 8 of the US Constitution,[16] and the common law on which the entirety of

---

[9]   See Ch. 4 at §4.3.4.

[10]   See Ch. 4 at §4.7.

[11]   EU Directive 98/44/EC of 6 July 1998. Cf. §§4.7.2 & 4.7.3.

[12]   See Ch. 4 at §4.2.2.

[13]   See *Coco v. A.N. Clark* [1968] F.S.R. 415 (UK).

[14]   *Attorney General v. Guardian Newspapers (No. 2)* [1988] 3 All E.R. 545 per Lord Goff at 658. See Ch. 4 at §4.2.4.

[15]   Art. 10*bis*(3) Paris Convention for the Protection of Industrial Property. See Ch. 4 at §4.5.2.

[16]   See Ch. 8 at §8.2.2.

some IPRs (breach of confidence action) rests,[17] and on which others have occasional recourse for defences based on implied licences or public policy.[18] Besides the laws empowering the making of these rights, another important set of ancillary laws would be competition laws. The notion of 'abuse', such as abuse of dominant position under the EC Treaty,[19] would be empty without a notion of the legitimate purpose justifying the creation of IPRs. Ethical concepts would also impinge on the IPR system through human and fundamental rights laws circumscribing international and national laws. These include the free speech and expression guarantees of the US First Amendment as well as those under Article 10 of the European Convention for the Protection of Human Rights and Fundamental Freedoms ('ECHR').[20] What do they mean, and how do they get their content?

1.2 KEY CONCEPTS

1.2.1 Hare and Universal Prescriptivism

The idea, a 'hunch', that will be pursued and elaborated in this work is that the answers to be found in a certain meta-ethical theory, that of R.M. Hare, will be especially illuminating.[21] The argument will be that to maintain morality as an institution that does what common beliefs about its character hold that it does, the logic of Hare's analysis of moral meanings ultimately leads us, if we do indeed take prescriptivism seriously, to maintain certain principles as the foundation for all moral reasoning and argument. Certain aspects of the meaning of moral terms are determined by convention and usage, and are not generally controversial. They have either a positive or negative connotation and are accordingly used to commend or condemn. They have a typical range, types of subject matter or relations to which they are appropriate. Examples are: 'good' or 'evil' and 'right' or 'wrong'. These examples are terms of the most general types of commendation or disapprobation. Other moral terms are of more limited or specialized application, for

---

[17] See Ch. 4 at §4.2.4.
[18] See Ch. 7 at §7.3.2.
[19] Art. 82 of the Treaty Establishing the European Community (1957). See Ch.7 at §7.3.3.
[20] See Ch. 8 at §8.2.2.
[21] This theory is elaborated by Hare in a lifetime of works (including 1952, 1963, 1981, 1997) cf. §§1.4 & 2.2 herein.

example: 'just', 'legitimate', 'fair', 'reasonable'; or, even more so, 'cruel' and 'humane'. The aspect of a moral term that is most often the subject of controversy is the *grounds*, or conditions, upon which such commendation or disapprobation is to be applied.

R.M. Hare's thesis of universal prescriptivism suggests a two-part solution. The grounds are *prescribed* by the person making the ethical assessment but, in order for them to qualify for the character of being moral rather than some other kind of prescription, the prescription must be in terms which are *universalizable*: that is, in terms that do not contain reference to particular individuals and which the user can accept as applying to any situation satisfying those terms, including those in which he were to occupy in turn each of the envisaged roles. This two-part solution seeks to do several things. First, it explains the content of moral terms in a way that accounts for why this content has force for the user; that is, explain why it is compelling, or at least has some weight on the user's decision making, even if not ultimately prevailing. It has such force, according to universal prescriptivism, because the adoption of the prescription entails some commitment to it. Secondly, it explains how, despite the fact that the adoption of any prescription involves voluntary subscription on the user's part, the process of making judgements is subject to rational inquiry. It remains open to rational inquiry in that one may ask if the grounds are in universal terms and whether the user would still find such a judgement acceptable if the principle in it, so universalized, were to apply to other situations where he will occupy each of the roles involved. Thus, reason plays a substantial role in determining the ultimate grounds of action, and is not – as in the Humean account of morals – left to clarifying means–ends relationships, with ends as the ultimate desiderata of action beyond the reach of reason.[22] Thirdly, it explains how morality is objective: we can act on any judgement we want, but it is logically impossible (given the definition of 'moral') to treat these as 'moral judgements' unless their grounds are framed in universal terms.

1.2.2 Searle's Theory of the Construction of Social Reality

The second conceptual foundation for the 'hunch' being explored here is that IPRs are 'institutions' that may be understood in terms of John R.

---

[22] Hume (2000), Bk 3, Pt 1, §1, p. 302, and at Pt 1, §2: '[S]ince vice and virtue are not discoverable merely by reason, or the comparison of ideas, it must be by means of some impression or sentiment they occasion, that we are able to mark the difference betwixt them.'

Searle's account of institutions and social reality:[23] that is, that they are socially constituted by rules having the logical form 'X counts as Y, in C'. Searle elaborates this basic idea to give an account of various aspects of our social reality, including language, law and even moral ideas like the institution of promising.[24]

Searle builds his account of social reality on four elements: the assignment of function, collective intentionality, constitutive rules and 'the Background'. He notes that even some objects that we regard as physical things have a social aspect in that part of their identity depends on functions that are observer relative. For example, an object with the appropriate physical features is a screwdriver because people assign to it the function of fixing or unfixing screws. Such functions are assigned intentionalities, that are imputed to people, which constitute the world as we experience it. 'Intentionality' is 'a capacity of the mind to represent objects and states of affairs in the world other than itself' to which may be directed beliefs, desires, attitudes, and so on.[25]

Searle says there can be *collective* intentionality – that is, such beliefs, desires and intentions can be *shared*. This is not the same thing as two or more people coincidentally having the same mental state, as in A and B each saying 'I intend' about the same thing in the same way; rather, the intentionality is capable of being shared, as in A or B saying '*We* intend …'.[26] This work will later argue that the conditions under which people are able to say '*we* intend' impose substantive constraints on the content that may come within the concepts of law and morality. The third element Searle relies on for his account of social reality is the idea of 'constitutive rules', that characteristically take the form of 'X counts as Y, in context C'. By such rules, X is conferred a new collectively recognized status (Y) to which a status function is attached. The '"counts as" formula is a function which is attached by way of collective intentionality, where the status and the accompanying function go beyond the sheer brute physical functions that can be assigned to physical objects'.[27] Thus, there can be iterations of institutional facts upon institutional facts. For example, 'a certain sort of promise as X can count as a contract Y, but to be a promise is already to have a Y status-function at a lower level'.[28]

---

23 Searle (1995).
24 *Ibid*, Ch. 2–5.
25 *Ibid*, pp. 6–7.
26 *Ibid*, pp. 23–6.
27 *Ibid*, p. 44.
28 *Ibid*, p. 80.

People need not consciously use the rules because their use does not require that people *follow* them. Rather, Searle suggests, though people sometimes learn these rules, they mostly develop abilities, dispositions and capacities in relation to these rules without learning or internalizing them. This is his 'thesis of the Background: Intentional states function only given a set of Background capacities that do not themselves consist of intentional phenomena.'[29] By 'capacities' he means 'abilities, dispositions, tendencies and causal structures generally'.[30] This is an important concept for the idea of morality that will be developed in this work and will be explained further in Chapter 2 (at §2.4.8).

1.2.3   Searle and Hare Combined

Searle's constitutive rule can be applied to a recounting of Hare's theory to educe the logical structure of universalized prescriptivism. The evaluative assertion or comment (the consequent, q, of the 'if p then q' moral premiss) that is the prescriptive element in the meaning of a moral term is the 'counts as Y' function. The 'X … in C' condition identifies the facts (X) and attending circumstances (C) where this evaluation is appropriate (the antecedent of that premiss). Universalization, then, is the abstracting away of direct and indirect personal identifiers from the 'X … in C' so that the same evaluation would have to be made in all other cases of the relevantly same *type* of 'Xs … in Cs'.

Put in terms of Searle's social function, morality is part of social reality as created by social functions but not part of the brute reality of the world. The insight that Searle's social function enables us to make is an explanation of how morality can be real in the way all our social institutions are real: it requires us to have the intentionality assigning prescriptive values (the commendation or disapprobation) to the factual conditions, and making those prescriptions shared to the extent that we share a collective intentionality to that effect. On its own, this explanation leads to a conventional account of morality as a social institution and is compatible with meta-ethical scepticism about the objectivity of moral norms or values, since social conventions can be arbitrary and depend on whether we participate and share in them. However, the combination of Hare's insight as to universal prescriptivism and Searle's social function enables us to suggest and develop a middle possibility, between a purely conventional prescriptive basis for moral norms and values and theories

---

[29]   *Ibid*, p. 129.
[30]   *Ibid*, p. 129.

that their objectivity lies in their being (natural or intuitively perceived non-natural) facts that bind us as a matter of cognition. This middle possibility is that, given the work that we want them to do, moral norms and values have a certain conceptual character – they are universalized prescriptions – and this feature sets constraints on the content of the conventions we have that we can at the same time maintain are conventions generating moral norms and values. The next chapter will argue that the very project of morality as a social institution created according to Searle's constitutive rule, leads one to certain minimum substantive moral ideas. If this reply is correct then the fact that moral norms as institutional facts are contingent on collective intentionality for their existence does not mean that they are entirely arbitrary, dependent only on either agreement or the acceptance that the use of power can compel. What may be done by way of collective intentionality in instituting moral norms would be limited (though, perhaps, not wholly determined) by the concept of moral norms themselves.[31]

This means asking: What kind of principle underpins the moral judgements we accept? There may be many candidates for the job: for a single action may be justified by a multitude of initial premisses. Though the 'convention' cannot be simply read off some historical event but must be reconstructed in this fashion, it will be suggested that Hare's account, coupled with the *modus tollens* implication to be explained below, will enable one to give an account of this reconstruction project for morals.

1.2.4   The Logical Implications of Universal Prescriptivism

These logical properties enable one to use the practical syllogism:

$$\text{If } p \text{ then } q; \text{ it is } p, \text{ therefore } q.$$

Here q is the prescriptive, and p is the salient set of features constituting the grounds contained in the major premiss of a moral argument. Note that the practical syllogism concludes not with an indicative statement, which can be true or false, but with a prescription. (Here, q = one ought

---

[31]   Although Searle (1995 at pp. 46–7) describes social reality as conventionally constructed, he also indicates that this does not mean that the status functions assigned by collective intentionality are arbitrary: 'The sorts of functions and statuses that can be assigned by the Y term, therefore, are seriously limited by the possibilities of having functions where the performance of the function contains an element that can be guaranteed simply by collective agreement or acceptance.'

to do *x*; or, where the term is an evaluative one like 'good' – this means that in case *p*, *q* has an ought-to-be-pursued quality or other approving or disapproving attitude related to the evaluative term.) Hence, the value of the syllogism lies not in a guarantee that one cannot proclaim or believe in the major premiss and *p*, and then fail to do *q*. It does not provide such a guarantee, as one may nevertheless fail to do *q*, by reason of being weak, hypocritical or illogical.

The real significance of the practical syllogism lies in the *modus tollens* of the argument. If one affirms not-*q* and admits *p* is the case, one cannot at the same time affirm the major premisses: if *p* then *q*. One cannot *justify* the failure to do the act required by the prescriptive principle when the relevant circumstances are present and still with logical consistency affirm the principle in the major premiss. What is logically impossible is not the doing of the forbidden act but the affirmation, simultaneous with that act, of the principle that forbids it.[32]

R.M. Hare's universalization thesis has consequences for the IPR system. IPR laws, and laws empowering or limiting IPR laws, do use moral terms or terms which are loaded with moral connotations. The hypothetico-deductive method stemming from the *modus tollens* implication of the syllogistic argument provides *some* content that enables moral discussion to go on in these situations by excluding moral premisses that are incompatible with the other moral commitments of the participants in the debate, even if it does not unequivocally and obviously determine one right answer. In the fact that in any real social system the participants are committed by Searle's (re)construction of social reality to a vast matrix of interlocking institutions, there is the potential that, where these institutions share moral underpinnings (i.e. moral norms are some of the institutional facts that directly or indirectly underpin the critical *X*s in the 'X counts as Y in C' formula for these institutions), the space of choice between principles that are really open to the participants is much narrower than most would think. For one thing, *if any moral norms as institutional facts are relied on*, either to justify further institutions or as components in their constitutional rules (and it will be argued that both are the case for the IPR system), then the rejection of all moral claims (nihilism) cannot be consistently maintained.

---

[32]   Which Hare compares with Karl Popper's falsifiability test for scientific theory: see Hare (1963) §6.2 pp. 87–90 and (1981) §1.3 pp. 10–15 and §4.1 pp. 65–8 described as a linguistic hypothetico-deductive method for arriving at the meaning of moral terms. Cf. §2.2.2 below.

1.3   A LOOK AHEAD TO THE MORAL DIMENSIONS OF IPRS

The suggestion here is that the IPR system or systems are such interlocking social institutions and that, given implicit commitments required for maintaining these institutions as social facts, some moral commitments have already been made by those who implement, accept or rely on these institutions. Hence, unless we wish to withdraw such reliance, we are *objectively* committed to the universalization of certain norms that limit our room for manoeuvre in moral argument and reasoning. This dilemma is 'objective' in the sense that it is rationally binding for us, irrespective of our beliefs. This is true even though the entire project of moral institution is ontologically subjective. We can choose to abandon morality as a project of reasoned guidance of our choices, or we can rely on it. But this entails a commitment to implicitly necessary concepts that we can avoid only on pain of illogicality or hypocrisy – which would be to abandon the project. We can have our cake, or we can eat it: though there is a choice, the *condition* of exercising it cannot be avoided.

The relation that IPRs bear to all of this is that they are institutions requiring justification themselves and are creatures of law: they have a moral dimension of justification. This is the subject of Chapter 3. As already noted above (§1.1), moral terms and concepts play a critical role in some of the central rules determining the existence and extent of IPRs. The argument will be that, given the nature of morality and the way moral ideas work, their presence in at least some of these rules is an essential part of the justification of the institutions. This is the moral dimension of design, and will be the subject of Chapter 4, as regards national IP laws and Chapter 5 for the international IP laws. There is also a moral dimension to the interpretation of laws and the concept of law. This is dealt with in Chapter 6. We also ask moral questions of and demand moral responses from those who enjoy, exploit and seek to enforce IPRs. This is the moral dimension of exercise of IP rights and is the subject of Chapter 7. Finally, our commitments as a result of the various moral claims we want to make in each of these dimensions also carry implications for the reform of the institutions in the national and international political fori as well as other legal avenues for rule change. Reform is also a moral dimension of IPRs. This is Chapter 8. The conclusion, Chapter 9, restates the main findings of this work, and points out some of its prescriptions.

Moral terms and concepts that are the basis of these institutions, and the nature of the competing claims of owners and other users, should be built into the core rules of IPRs. These core rules would be those stipulating the conditions for their acquisition, the range and strength of the rights acquired and any exceptions to them, and limitations on their duration. As IPRs are creations of positive law, it is possible for legislators to cast these key rules in purely descriptive or technical, and non-evaluative terms. However, where mainly descriptive language is used, as is largely the case with most of the rules relating to conditions of acquisition, two tendencies result:

1.   Greater reliance is placed on the remaining core rules (in most cases, these would be the exceptions and defences) for adaptation of the institution and this quest for justification.
2.   Apparently technical terms and ideas are used and interpreted in ways that tend to reflect this need for adjustment and this aspiration towards justification. This is reflected in the treatment of core ideas like 'inventive step' or 'non-obviousness' in patent laws, and the idea–expression dichotomy, 'originality' as a requirement of acquisition of protection and substantiality of use in determination of infringement in copyright laws.

The key moral ideas that these institutions express and should seek to further are:

3.   The promotion of individual liberty by extending creators' control over certain types of ideas of their own compete with the interests of non-owners in their own freedom to use these ideas for their own purposes, and this competition should be resolved by a balance of rights which is to be struck by reference to the criterion of degree of needfulness for action.[33]
4.   The application of the foregoing criterion should normally respect the closer connection authors or inventors would have over their own creations for the purpose of expressing their individual personalities and, hence, would require that they should be given control, albeit a limited one, over such ideas.
5.   The general balance of rights stemming from (1) and (2) must yield in favour of non-owners' access to a basic interest in freedom and well-being where the criterion of necessity for action would favour the non-owner's claim. For example, where the access is necessary

---

[33]   Cf. §2.5.1 for Gewirth's criterion of needfulness for action.

for the purpose of exercising or enjoying the right of freedom of speech, or to nutrition and health.

6. The argument based on the necessity for control which enables creators to express their personhood also provides grounds for ensuring that they retain access to certain aspects of their creations despite alienating the IPRs in them. These may be safeguarded by rules giving access to all, and by other rules giving the creators special rights. This argues also that some of these rights of access or retained control should be inalienable. The latter would form the basis for the moral rights of authors and inventors.

7. The paucity of evaluative terms in the limitations in the institutions' core rules, and failure of officials to interpret the rules with sufficient sensitivity to the underlying moral basis for the institutions' justification, put pressure on society to express that moral basis through the other moral dimensions. These are the dimensions of exercise and reform. Therefore, the key rules of the laws relating to those dimensions – the common law, competition law, and constitutional and human rights laws – should also employ moral terms and concepts which reflect the intention to ensure that these institutions should be justifiable.

The upshot is that non-holders of IPRs have moral entitlements to access to aspects of IP objects which correlate with the moral obligation of owners to acknowledge a fair share in such resources. This means that non-holders have *moral* rights to the promotion of a public domain; a moral right that is allowed expression in the law of IPRs and related ancillary laws by the moral terms and concepts that are built into them. Ultimately, if the laws governing IPRs and their exercise do not adequately reflect this non-holders' right to a public domain, the justification of IPRs requires their reform, and the acknowledgement of this is the responsibility of all, especially those who would hold and assert IPRs, in the dimension of reform.

1.4 THE LITERATURE ON THE MORAL DIMENSIONS OF IPRS

Depending on how one defines the scope of this work, there is either nothing that quite precedes it, or there is too much to be encompassed in a work of reasonable length. References to writings on these matters are made in the relevant chapters of this work, though it must be at once admitted that they are selective. To keep this work within a manageable compass, it focuses on the implications of universal prescriptivist meta-ethics on the inter-working of morality in these dimensions that is the primary subject of the study.

The core ideas of R.M. Hare's universal prescriptivism are set out in *The Language of Morals* (1952) and *Freedom and Reason* (1963), which he defended and developed upon in *Moral Thinking* (1981). A critique of these is made in the next chapter (at §§2.2.2–2.3). He returns to these themes in chapters of various published volumes, including *Sorting Out Ethics* (1997), which helpfully contains a complete bibliography of his writings to that year, and *Objective Prescriptions and Other Essays* (1999), which revisits the basic ideas in the initial chapters 'Objective Prescriptions' (Ch. 1), 'Prescriptivism' (Ch. 2) and 'Imperatives, Prescriptions, and their Logic' (Ch. 4).[34] The latter book also contains one essay by Hare with a direct bearing on business ethics, Ch. 18 ('One Philosopher's Approach to Business and Professional Ethics'), though it does not say anything about IPRs. A convenient starting point for canvassing the diverse responses to Hare's mature theory would be *Hare and His Critics: Essays on Moral Thinking* (1988),[35] which contains the examination of various philosophers on various aspects of his theory as well as his rebuttal.

Literature on the moral aspects of IPRs fall mainly into three categories: those concerned with the moral and public policy grounds for denying or limiting IP protection, those dealing with the ethics of exploiting IPRs, and works on the justification for IPRs. A collection of contributions reflecting the range of these can be found in Bently and Maniatis, *Intellectual Property and Ethics* (1998). The first group grapples with the moral issues surrounding the grant of patents in biotechnology and includes Mills, *Biotechnological Inventions* (2010), and Resnik, *Owning the Genome* (2004). Unsurprisingly, there is a large literature on the European Patent Convention's Article 53(a) and European Biotechnology Directive Article 6 *ordre public* and morality ground of exclusion, including the foregoing works and numerous articles.[36] Of these, Moufang, 'Patenting Genes, Cells and Parts of the Human Body?' (1994), which explores the intersect between patent law and ethics as regards

---

[34] An online bibliography of his writings and writings on Hare's ethical philosophy may be located at http://www.utilitarian.net/hare/ (last accessed 4 April 2011).

[35] Seanor and Fotion (eds.) (1988).

[36] E.g. Moufang (1994), Warren (1998), European Group on Ethics in Science and New Technologies (2002), Warren-Jones (2006), Thomas and Richards (2004), Laurie (2004), Sommer (2008).

biotechnological inventions, approaches the spirit of the present work in his resort to the principles and values that underpin the patent law, in particular the value of freedom that underpins the various justifications offered for the patent institution (property, reward, incentive and disclosure or contract theories) and human dignity; though the present work seeks to identify a broader and fundamental principle underpinning all IPRs.

The *ordre public* and morality exclusion and similar prohibitions are a small part of, and almost incidental to, this work, though this is the first issue one usually thinks of at the mention of IP and ethics. This is dealt with at §4.7, where reference is made to Beyleveld and Brownsword's *Mice, Morality and Patents* (1993), where the grounding of the European Patent Convention's ('EPC's') 'morality' prohibition in the ECHR's fundamental rights is situated within a more general thesis about the nature of morality which arrives at a similar conclusion. The present work, however, addresses the nature of the moral ideas underpinning all provisions of IPRs given their nature and what we want them to do. This, of course, has implications for how we understand and justify the *ordre public* and morality exclusions, but this work is not primarily concerned with these types of restriction. Works on the ethics of IP exploitation are on the increase given a trend towards acknowledgement of corporate social responsibility ('CSR') in business studies and practice, and the public reaction to the globalization of IP with TRIPS implementation that has focused around the impact of patents on patients' access to medicines. Some of these works are making their way into standard business texts and references. These include: De George, 'Intellectual Property and Pharmaceutical Drugs' (2005), Werhane and Gorman, 'Intellectual Property Rights, Moral Imagination, and Access to Life-Enhancing Drugs' (2005), and Smith and Duncan, 'GlaxoSmithKline and Access to Essential Medicines' (2009). This issue is considered at §8.4, though the subject of this work is not CSR but something more fundamental in that it focuses on the meta-ethics that underpins all ethical argument, including those in the CSR literature.

The list of writings on the justification of IPRs is too voluminous for the scope of a single work, hence the strategy adopted herein has been to focus on a key thought that runs through the thesis, which is the implications of universalization on the way morality works as it runs through the various dimensions on IPRs. This has not itself been the subject of academic treatment. In view of this, reference is made only to some of the major recent works on the theories of justification of IPRs in as far as they set up the background to or illuminate points in this investigation.[37] Selected works on the justification of IPRs are referred to in Chapter 3 on the justification and the justice of IPRs but one very significant acknowledgement must be made here. In *A Philosophy of Intellectual Property* (1996), Peter Drahos makes various suggestions for an instrumentalist theory of intellectual property with a normative character that sceptically treats IPRs as privileges and which also imposes duties on the right-bearers to responsibly exercise and enforce their rights in a way that reflects the purposes for which those privileges are given.[38] His theory is anti-proprietarian and seeks an instrumentalism that is driven by humanist moral values. Though the terminology used and moral theory developed in this present work are non-instrumental, Drahos suggests this alternative route in *A Philosophy of Intellectual Property* when he observes:

> There might also be a non-instrumental way of establishing the existence of the duties we are considering here … [T]he non-instrumental route would involve linking duties to the existence of power. Intellectual property is a sovereignty mechanism. The holder of intellectual property occupies a station of power. Connected to this station are a set of duties that dictate that the power be exercised in a responsible way.[39]

The present thesis owes much in spirit and inspiration to that thought. Indeed, it is devoted to tracking the linkages between legal rights in IPRs

---

[37]   Merges' *Justifying Intellectual Property* (2011) was published after this work was mainly completed but deserves a special mention here as it seeks to ground 'mid-level' IP principles (efficiency, non-withdrawal (from the public domain), proportionality and dignity) in the 'fundamental theories' of Locke, Kant and Rawls. The present work covers, if seen very broadly, overlapping territory with Merges' but focuses on the way morality itself works in the various dimensions of IPRs and, as will be pointed out in Chapter 3 (§3.1), argues that even the justifications based on Locke and Rawls and others assume a still deeper (more basic) level of fundamental principles. Merges' reliance on Kantian autonomy and location of IPRs as institutions governed by Rawls' principles of justice make some of his conclusions on justification parallel those espoused here based on the equal right to freedom and well-being. But the latter concept and the use here of Gewirth's criterion of needfulness for action (see §2.5.1) as a means of choosing between competing liberty claims means (as I think the reader will see) that the claims of non-owners will be given stronger recognition, which I think is more true to both Kant and Rawls. The present project is also different in identifying the various moral dimensions as the means by which adjustments in recognition of this underlying justificatory tension between owners' and public rights are effected in IPR systems.

[38]   Drahos (1996), ch.9, pp. 199–228.

[39]   *Ibid*, 221.

and the moral duties of various actors and claimants – owners, the public, officials and judges, and legislators – that have to do with such systems.

1.5 A NOTE ON METHODOLOGY

1.5.1 Reflective Equilibrium

This is a work of philosophical inquiry, where the central characteristic is clarification and analysis of fundamental concepts, in particular as regards the nature of ethics and the implications of the answer to this question as it is applied in an exploration of the role of moral ideas in various aspects of IPRs as social institutions. The methodology that is thus applied is that mode of inquiry that John Rawls describes as the search for a 'reflective equilibrium'.[40]

A key problem for ethical inquiry concerns how one may defend one's conclusions about the principles and values one uses without assuming these outright from the beginning. If these are to be subject to investigation and defence as well, the question is, how do we know where to begin? The search for reflective equilibrium begins with present practices – a description of personal convictions for an individual, or accepted social institutions and practices for a community – from which one infers the necessary supporting principles of these convictions or institutions. These are tested for the decisions the individual or the society would have to make if they were to be applied to new and different situations, to see if the required conclusions remain acceptable. One may find oneself bound to accept conclusions that one would not have initially embraced, or to reject, revise or refine the principles with which the search commenced. The reformulated principles are then re-applied to existing convictions and practices and yet other situations, with the procedure repeated until an equilibrium accommodation between principles and practices is reached. In his critique of Rawls' method, Ronald Dworkin refines the procedure into a 'constructive model' (which he later uses so productively in his account of legal interpretation) for moral theory formulation which he describes as 'a two way process; we move back and forth between adjustments to theory and adjustments to conviction until the best possible fit is achieved.'[41]

This methodology is required by universal prescriptivism described above (§1.2.1), which Hare describes as a hypothetico-deductive method

---

[40] Rawls (1999) at pp. 18–19 and 42–5.
[41] Dworkin (1977) in ch. 6, pp. 150–83 at 164.

(§1.2.4).[42] This is employed in Chapter 2 of this work, which explores a theory of morality and moral meaning. It begins by identifying commonly accepted characteristics of moral propositions: that they are objective, are subject to rational investigation and provide rational guidance as to actions. These are not taken as unassailable truths but as initial points of departure which may be revised if this is made necessary by the theory of morality we are driven to embrace in the search for an explanation and defence of these expectations. That inquiry eventually leads to what will here be called the fundamental prescriptions and the equal right to freedom and well-being.

The broad structure of this entire work reflects this dialectical search for reflective equilibrium. At the outset, in this chapter (§1.1), it identifies the presence of moral terms and concepts in central IP rules, and asks the questions: What do they mean? How do they get that meaning? What is the nature of such meanings? This leads to the meta-ethical exploration and exposition of Chapter 2. There is, thus, one movement from practice and institution to theory. In the next iteration of the procedure, the resultant theory is applied to the question of the justification of the institution in Chapter 3: this both examines the nature of existing IPRs and develops a theory of their justification. The conclusions about that justificatory theory are then applied to explaining and examining a feature (the role of moral concepts) in the central structures of IPRs in national laws (Chapter 4) and in the international IP system (Chapter 5). The critique of these institutions leads to a review of the role of morality in legal interpretation and the idea of law itself in Chapter 6. The theory as to the aspiration of the law therein developed is then applied to an explanation of how this supplies the moral background for ancillary laws (the common law public policy and competition laws) which are used to ameliorate potential abuses of IPRs (Chapter 7). The practical limitations of these in turn lead us to the implications for the reform of IPRs in Chapter 8. Thus, the application of the methodology of reflective equilibrium to the moral dimensions of IPRs traverses an arc from existing features of existing IPRs to reform of the institutions with which it began.

1.5.2   The IP Laws

The variety of IPRs and traditions from which they spring, and of national systems in which they are represented, presents a problem for this work: one must be highly selective. In this, some aid is provided by

---

[42]   Hare (1981) §4.1 at pp. 65–8.

the intention that the exploration to be made herein is of such regimes and their aspects that have the widest global significance and impact. The focus will be on those categories of IPRs that are mandated by the TRIPS Agreement because observance of these is required of all WTO members; and TRIPS (and the parts of international IP conventions it incorporates) now sets the virtually worldwide minimum standard for IP protection. However, of the types of IPRs required by TRIPS, only the four that are most paradigmatic of IP are considered: protection of undisclosed information (protection under trade secrets laws and the action for breach of confidence), copyright, patents and trade mark protection. As they cover the main part of the spectrum of ideas over which IPRs range – private (non-public) information, literary and artistic and related productions, inventions and commercial signs – the thematic concerns these raise should shed light on those of the others as well.

More problematic is selection from amongst the numerous national systems and the legal traditions they represent. Again, the main guide is the intention to consider the features that are of widespread international significance. To keep the scope of the work within humanly manageable range, the focus will be mainly on US and UK examples, with references to EU models and some civil law cases. The US has been by far the strongest driver of the internationalization of IPRs since the commencement of the Uruguay Round of GATT leading to the adoption of TRIPS in 1994, and is factually important even as it departs from much of the world in certain aspects (e.g. in its more generic fair use defence for copyright, cf. §4.3.4). The UK's common law and statutory models for copyright, patent and trade marks still exert an immense influence on its many former colonies and dominions. The EU, through its harmonizing Directives, not only sets the standard for its member states but is a source of innovations that has a worldwide impact. These systems are the most influential as models for the rest of the world.

Finally, even within this circumscribed set of systems, this work has to be highly selective as to the rules, structures and features of each law that are to be dealt with because the object is to consider only the most important and characteristically significant features of these regimes. This focus on the central rules of IPRs is made not just for reasons of economy but to fulfil the object of the work: an exploration of the moral dimensions of IPRs as institutions with a worldwide significance. It is not every detail of even influential systems that matter, for these may be subject to change and reform, but the major structures and the main alternatives to them.

1.6 THE WAY FORWARD

This work will traverse a long arc from existing moral ideas in IPRs (the present chapter), through an examination of the idea of morality itself (Chapter 2), to an application of this to the justification of IPRs (Chapter 3) and an exploration of the implications of this to the design of national IPR regimes (Chapter 4) as well as the international IP legal framework (Chapter 5), and the implications of moral theory for the theory of legal interpretation and law (Chapter 6), a consideration of what this means for the morality of the way such rights are to be exercised (Chapter 7) and, ultimately, what it says about the need to reform our presently evolving systems of IPRs (Chapter 8). The central thesis is that moral terms and ideas in core IP rules and in adjacent laws serve both justificatory functions and function as transformative resources for the adaptation and reform of IPRs as institutions.

A word of caution may be necessary here in order that the foregoing will not promise too much, and more than a work of this kind can deliver. Its focus is on the role of moral ideas and the way they work in this system and what they require. What they require, though, may be satisfied in a number of different ways. It acknowledges a role for politics and other social processes in the shaping of legal institutions and, indeed, recognizes how power influences can limit the effectiveness of moral considerations. Indeed, it is the near overwhelming presence of economic and trade influences in the shaping of IPRs that makes the focus on their moral dimensions appear somewhat quixotic; but the persistence of the moral dimensions in the face of these is a major theme, as is their role as a resource for both the motivation and facility for reform as an important, albeit often neglected, feature of IPR systems. IPRs are chains for ideas; if these chains are to be defensible, we must understand the morality of their justification, and be willing to embrace the reforms that this justification may demand.

2. Moral terms, moral meaning and morality

2.1 THE KEY QUESTION

R.M. Hare's account of moral terms in language focuses on how a person who is applying moral concepts to a specific situation arrives at a conclusion as to what ought to be done. The questions at the beginning of the previous chapter, about the meaning of moral terms in laws, require us to turn this around and ask: What do we mean by the moral terms when we use them in *general instructions*? In other words: What is their intended meaning from a law maker's viewpoint?

The answer may be somewhat surprising. The implication of universal prescriptivism is that, if the legislators intend such terms to operate as *moral* terms, and not merely as code for a conventionally or otherwise denoted set of descriptive conditions, they must intend that the person directed to use them (judges and subjects) should understand them as requiring the adoption of prescriptions on grounds for action of the relevant types which can be universalized in a manner that is consistent with their other commitments or obligations they ought also to uphold. Whilst the legislators may have entertained certain notions about the expected application of such terms, they may, nevertheless, be taken to have intended the use of a process of reasoning that can result in judgments with quite a different outcome. Another way of putting this is that, with the use of moral terms in general instructions, there can be a difference between the intended meaning and the intended outcome. This raises the question of which intention the recipients of such instructions (judges and subjects in the case of laws) ought to fulfil.

One way of dealing with this possibility is to treat moral terms in such rules as having meaning only as codes denoting a set of descriptive conditions – either conventionally accepted, or those the legislators actually had in mind. Whilst it is possible for legislatures to intend such a denotation, it is better generally to take legislators and makers of agreements to use such words as they are ordinarily used, and, thus, to intend such terms to work as moral terms, with all this logically implies.

The merit of applying Hare's insights on universal prescriptivism to the intended meaning of such instructions is that the parties can be understood to mean that prescriptions of grounds for the relevant types of action should be made by addressees – subject to such prescriptions being universalizable in a manner consistent with the other obligations they are expected to uphold. Even in the face of wide divergences of expectations as to outcomes, the parties can be understood to have done more than agree to disagree: the moral terms do not merely paper over the cracks in unity but present an intention that solutions should be subject to a rational process of inquiry. The promise of universal prescriptivism is that it can generate, from our understanding of purely formal and widely accepted characteristics of what we hold as moral principles and values, substantive conclusions about what is morally required. Does universal prescriptivism deliver on this promise? This chapter suggests that it does but only after adaptation of Hare's own solution. To understand why, we have to review Hare's project.

2.2   A RE-EXAMINATION OF HARE'S THEORY

2.2.1   Meta-ethics' Problematic Triangle

Our commonsense understanding of a concept may be mistaken or wrong-headed but it must be the starting point under the method of reflective equilibrium (§1.5.1) for any explanatory theory, if the theory is to be about the practice. Thus, a satisfactory meta-ethical theory must explain why, and account for how, moral norms are commonly expected to possess three features, or provide compelling reasons for holding one or more of these expectations to be mistaken. It must account for the motivational force of the norms: the ought-to-be-pursued or ought-to-be-done quality associated with a finding that their grounds are present. It must account for their rationality: show how and why such norms are open to reasoned questioning and inquiry. And it must explain their objectivity: their ability to retain some characteristics irrespective of our subjective preferences and what we choose to believe about them. Summed together, the common conception of moral truths is that they have objective rational force. The relevant meta-ethical theory must explain, or explain away, these expectations. Hare has spent a lifetime arguing that universal prescriptivism gives a better account of these features of morality than other generic meta-ethical theories. These other generic meta-ethical theories are naturalism, intuitionism and scepticism.

Naturalism is the view that the meanings of moral norms are constituted by the truth conditions for their application. It founders against the rock of G.E. Moore's 'open question' argument[1] – one can ask of a descriptive criterion on which we apply a moral norm, say, that it is wrong *per se* to cause pain without justification, if it is really 'wrong'. One might disagree with the moral judgement of one who asks that question but must admit that he has not made a simple error of language about the meaning of the moral term. The question is non-tautologously meaningful because we treat the moral term as requiring a judgement that identifies something that operates in a supervenient fashion on the facts. We can agree about the facts but disagree about the moral signification we give to them; therefore the application of moral terms involves something more than identifying the relevant facts.

There is another powerful objection to naturalism, one recognized in the famous passage in Hume's *Treatise* wherein he observes that one should pay careful attention to how moral arguments transit from 'is' to 'ought' propositions. This is often abbreviated as: one may not derive 'ought' from 'is'. More carefully, one cannot derive 'ought' conclusions, from pure 'is' premisses.[2] This brings us back to the point about the supervenience of morality: there must be something extra to the facts that leads us to the moral conclusion that something ought to be done, avoided or pursued. Although naturalism accounts for our expectations that moral norms be subject to rational investigation and be objective by making their existence and nature questions of fact, it fails to account for their motivational force. G.E. Moore's open question argument, and the observation that the moral trait is supervenient on the factual basis, led him to a different answer: one apprehends non-natural facts which are supervenient on the natural ones. The faculty by which this cognition is achieved is intuition. J.L. Mackie raises two arguments against such non-natural facts: the argument from relativity (the theory is wrong because people differ in the practices they regard as right or wrong, for

---

[1]   Moore (1959), at ch. 2, pp. 37–58.

[2]   Hume (2000), Bk. 3, Pt. 1, §1, p. 302: 'In every system of morality, which I have hitherto met with, I have always remark'd, that the author proceeds for some time in the ordinary way of reasoning, and establishes the being of a God, or makes observations concerning human affairs; when of a sudden I am surpriz'd to find, that instead of the usual copulations of propositions, is, and is not, I meet with no proposition that is not connected with an ought, or an ought not. This change is imperceptible; but is, however, of the last consequence. For as this ought, or ought not, expresses some new relation or affirmation, 'tis necessary that it shou'd be observ'd and explain'd …'.

example monogamy versus polygamy); and the argument from queerness (it postulates strange facts unlike any other entity we accept because it requires a non-sensory cognitive faculty, and hence creates unnecessary entities without providing a convincing reason for accepting them).[3] Both objections are weak. Differences between the practices of peoples can be reconciled with shared moral principles at a more abstract level that takes into account differences in contexts, including history and culture.[4] The queerness of the faculty required to detect the non-natural facts posited by intuitionism is not an argument against their existence, if there really is no other explanation for the phenomenon and people do have genuine experiences of such cognition. Mackie's explanation is that the assumption of objectivity of moral norms is a mistake, albeit one so commonly held that it defines what we mean by 'morality' in language. On this argument, moral grounds do not exist at the level of meta-ethical query, though this does not prevent one from subjectively holding beliefs and attitudes at the normative level, or being able to investigate their adoption as empirical facts of the subjective beliefs and attitudes of any group of persons. But as an 'error theory' would prevail only if there are no other plausible accounts for moral meaning, Hare's account must prevail over Mackie's unless refuted.

According to Hare, intuitionism, in as far as it suggests that moral qualities are facts that are the subject of cognition, would be mistaken not because of the relativity or queerness of norms but because they are conceptually evaluations we make supervenient upon natural and social facts.[5] One may add that this does not require us to deny that we may have natural responses to facts that are virtually universal, perhaps resulting from evolutionary pressures on our species.[6] This form of intuitionistic moral theory – perhaps allowing for revision of our intuitive responses to arrive at a reflective equilibrium[7] – would be compatible with universal prescriptivism. However, the problem is that people's intuitions, even amongst those whose views have arrived at reflective equilibrium, may diverge. Then, taking our intuitions as definitive of right and wrong commits us to moral relativism, thereby treating the parties as not really disagreeing but asserting different things – what is right or wrong for themselves not being necessarily the same for the

---

[3]   Mackie (1990), ch. 1, pp. 15–49.

[4]   See Hare (1981), ch. 4, §4.9 at p. 85: '[V]ariations in moral codes reflect primarily different ways of life rather than different perceptions'.

[5]   *Ibid*, ch. 4, §4.6–4.9 at pp. 78–86.

[6]   See Wright (1994) and Ridley (1996).

[7]   See §1.5.1.

others.[8] The problem with this, as Hare and others (e.g. A.J. Ayer[9]) have observed, is that it mischaracterizes our approach to moral disputes: the parties are not asserting different things that pertain only to themselves but intend to assert that the other is wrong. Thus, our common conception of morality commits us to the idea that moral norms and values have the quality of objectivity that enables us to engage in such disputes meaningfully. Intuitionism as an account of the meaning of moral terms treats this disagreement as one resulting from a difference in language and usage: that is, we have such different definitions of 'evil' or 'wrong' or 'good' and so on that we are not really disagreeing but talking about different things. Hare's thesis allows one to say the disputants are talking about the same thing because they agree about the scope and character of terms like 'good', 'fair' and 'just', but have differences about the grounds of their application.

Intuitionism is correct, though, in suggesting that there must be something extra to the facts to which naturalism refers that justifies the application of a moral term. It is just mistaken that that something extra is an experience. Hare's answer is not that there are non-natural facts separate from the described criteria but, instead, we make prescriptions that operate superveniently upon those facts. The argument that will be developed later in this chapter (at §§2.3–2.4), taking the thesis beyond Hare's theory, is that upholding universalizability as a requirement of the moral norms and values we conventionally make (prescribe) leads us to a core set of minimum and fundamental principles. Before we critique Hare though, it will be helpful to situate Hare's thesis in relation to a third major meta-ethical approach: moral scepticism. Some versions of this branch of meta-ethical thought essentially rest on the dilemma identified by Hume already mentioned. 'Oughts' cannot be derived from pure 'is' findings. Hence, the investigation of facts cannot produce an ultimate foundation for norms – not even if the 'fact' one finds is a universally held 'ought' proposition: say, let us assume, all societies recognize at some level that the humanity in each person ought to be respected. Even if empirically proven, it is nevertheless subject to the open question test, or, as Hare pithily gives as the retort of anyone who does wish to repudiate it: '[S]o what?'[10] Social acceptance of norms explains their existence as an anthropological fact but does not rationally

---

[8]   Hare (1997), ch. 5, pp. 82–102.

[9]   Though, unlike Hare, he explains the assertion as intended to produce an emotive effect: Ayer (2006), ch. 6, pp. 104–26.

[10]   Hare, (1999), p. 4: 'One can think that something is wrong, but then go on to say "Yes, it is wrong: so what?" This is one reason why this way of solving

explain its prescriptivity. On the other hand, reason – in Hume's sense of reason as means–end rationality – cannot supply the motivation that gives moral norms their putative force, because reason operates only when ends have been adopted.[11] Thus, according to Hume, 'reason is, and ought only to be the slave of passions'.[12]

Moral sceptics are thus left with some form of conventionalist account of norms and values as social facts, and either an irrationalist account of their own commitment to any norm, or the adoption of nihilism. Hume grounds his account of ethics in one's natural (though weak) capacity for sympathy and conventions (for the protection of property) developing out of mutual convenience. Emotivists[13] explain the meaning of moral norms in terms of the intended conditioning that assertion and repetition may produce in others, rather than in any capacity of the concept to appeal to the reason of others. And Mackie locates them in the conventions we make.[14] But none of these, or other strains of scepticism, are able to account for why any of these conventions, even if existing, ought to be maintained or developed or reformed in any way, without tautologously having to fall back on a norm or value which, according to them, has force and existence only as a convention.

Hare's thesis is an attempt to confront and transcend this problem. The prescriptive element in universal prescriptivism concedes the man-made character of values. But the universalization requirement acts as a constraint on the range and type of prescriptions that one may at the same time prescribe and treat as *moral* norms. Of course, this leaves the possibility that one may choose not to prescribe *moral* but other types of norm. However, so long as one wants to act on the idea of morality, the logical relationship between the idea of universalization and the prescriptions we can make that are compatible with it, has a rational bite. Hence, the rationally objective character of norms stems from the conceptual necessity of universalization, and the motivational force of those ideas stems from the premiss that one wants, in some way, to rely on morality as such. It is necessary to ask, though: Does Hare's thesis achieve what he claims for it?

---

the problem will not do.' See also Hare (1981) at §§4.2 and 4.3, pp. 68–75 at 71–2; and (1997) para. 6.8 at p. 119.

[11]   Hume (2000), Bk. 3, pp. 293–306.
[12]   *Ibid*, Bk. 2, Pt. 3 §3, p. 266.
[13]   The leading proponent of which is C.L. Stevenson, see Hudson (1983), ch. 4, pp. 107–54.
[14]   Mackie (1990), ch. 5, pp. 105–24.

2.2.2 A Critique of *The Language of Morals* and *Freedom and Reason*

R.M. Hare claims that, though 'The thesis of universalizability itself ... is still a logical thesis',[15] it is nevertheless able to generate substantive conclusions about other situations relevantly similar to the one about which a moral judgement has already been made. Much, however, depends on just how the 'relevantly similar' circumstances[16] to which the previous judgement must be universalized are identified. Requiring exactly identical details would nullify the individual judgement and commitment as a source of guidance for future cases because there are no repeats without some form of generalization. The specification that the similarity required must be 'relevant' is meant to exclude differences as to persons and incidental details that one *ought to* ignore in deriving the principle. But here, already, we are using normative criteria to discriminate between features that are relevant and those that are not. Hence, the critique goes,[17] universalization as a purely formal concept is too weak to sustain the claims Hare makes for it, and any adaptation of it to make it so work must make further moral judgements whose validity may be in issue. Hare's initial characterization of universalization seems to be susceptible to this attack because his original account of universalization in *The Language of Morals* (1952) relied on the descriptive meaning of the grounds chosen for any moral judgement. And, in *Freedom and Reason* (1963) he claims:

> [b]ecause of universalizability, a person who makes a moral judgement commits himself, not merely to a meaning rule, but to a substantial moral principle. The thesis of universalizability itself however, is still a logical thesis ... By a 'logical' thesis I mean a thesis about the meanings of words, or dependent solely upon them. I have been maintaining that the meaning of the word 'ought' and other moral words is such that a person who uses them commits himself thereby to a universal rule. This is the thesis of universalizability.[18]

From this purely logical thesis, he argues, one can draw substantive moral principles *but only once one does make a moral judgement*:

---

[15] Hare (1963), p. 30.
[16] *Ibid* at p. 33.
[17] Some such critiques of Hare's early works are reviewed in Hudson (1988), ch. 2, pp. 9–23 at §2.2, pp. 10–15.
[18] Hare (1963), p. 30.

> Offences against the thesis of universalizability are logical, not moral ...
> [T]he logical offence here lies in the *conjunction* of two moral judgements,
> not in either one of them by itself ... What the thesis does forbid us to do is
> to make different moral judgements about actions which we admit to be
> exactly or relevantly similar.[19]

The attraction of his thesis is the suggestion that from the purely logical
character of moral terms having the characteristic of universalizability,
which does not itself contain substantive moral content, the thesis is
'capable of very powerful employment in moral argument when combined with other premisses'.[20] However, the usefulness and power of
such grounds depend very much on the width and scope of the application of the principles we derive from the application of the concept of
universalization. In this respect, he makes an important distinction
between 'universality' and 'generality':

> Now universalism is not a doctrine that behind every moral judgement there
> has to lie a principle expressible in a few general terms; the principle, though
> universal, may be so complex that it defies formulation in words at all. But if
> it were formulated and specified, all the terms used in its formulation would
> be universal terms.[21]

The problem with this definition is that, if the version of universalization
permits the principle that is to be derived from a judgement to be
specifically limited to the most narrow generic features of the case at
hand – the degree of specification being restricted only in that 'proper
names and other singular terms are excluded'[22] – then the principle that
can be strictly obtained by universalization would be so specific as to be
hardly applicable to new situations except to identical cases.

When Hare says 'exactly *or relevantly similar*',[23] the latter qualification introduces an equivocation. Once it is allowed that universalization
is not specifically limited to the narrowest universal types possible which
describe the situation under judgement, but that the judgement's principle
must include elements that are relevantly similar, we must in the process
of universalization make choices about which levels of and which types
of generalization are permissible and appropriate. Such choices are not

---

[19]   *Ibid*, pp. 32–3. Emphasis is Hare's.
[20]   *Ibid*, p. 35.
[21]   *Ibid*, p. 39. See Hare (1981), p. 41.
[22]   Hare (1963), p. 219.
[23]   *Ibid* at p. 33.

logically determined, since it is only the most specific universal descriptions that are so determinable, if at all. This confronts Hare with the dilemma of condemning his universalizability thesis to a degree of specificity that would make it mostly irrelevant to moral arguments about new cases (which, *ex hypothesi*, must be different in some way) or of modifying the idea of universalizability to include some degree of generalization – already suggested by his allowing that the derived principle should apply to 'relevantly similar' cases. The problem is: How is the latter to be allowed without arbitrariness or the use of further moral principles?

In reply to this type of criticism, Hare assays two answers. The first relies on what may be called the hypothetical *ad hominem* case. That is, the key limitation against the moral judgements we can make are not the other judgements about different types of situation that we have or do make, but the moral judgement we would make in an instance exactly the same as the one at hand except that the judgement maker now substitutes him- or herself as the object of the action in question, and the question that is asked is: Can he or she then accept the principle of action proposed as a moral one?[24] Hare is careful to point out that the objection on which he is relying is not a prudential one: not a fear that others would do the same to one. Rather, the point is a logical one: if one cannot honestly accept the same principle applying to one when the roles are reversed (as it would even if the principle is very specific except for the reference to individuals), then one cannot accept it as a *moral* principle, given that universalizability is a requisite of moral norms, because one would not be applying the prescription as one that is universalized.

The pivotal point of this argument emerges on focusing on what it means to have a hypothetical situation that is *exactly the same except for the role substitution*. Does the similarity have to include the characters and preferences of the individuals concerned? If the hypothetical role substitution includes not just the assumption of the parties' external situation but also their personal preferences and characteristics (these include risk aversion, conservatism, degree of compassion, etc.), then the role substitution procedure becomes a direction to ignore some of the most basic features by which we identify ourselves. Why would the choice of this unrecognizable entity have any force for any of us? And, why would its commitments bind us? Further, it would not resolve the essential differences between the parties. A's original preferred principle

---

[24]   *Ibid*, ch. 6, pp. 86–111.

would be inconsistent with B's preferred principle which, on reversal of roles, judge A would have to accept as his own, and *vice versa*. Hare initially attempts to answer this form of critique with his distinction between a 'liberal' and a 'fanatic'.[25] The fanatic is indistinguishable from the liberal in respect of the form of their moral argument; it is in the *content* of their norms that they differ and the liberal is ultimately, when confronted with a conflict of ideals and basic preferences that require the positing of incompatible principles, a preference maximizing utilitarian.

In *Freedom and Reason* (1963) Hare seems willing to accept that the pure logic of the universalization test cannot arbitrate between the two types of views and consoles himself with the thought that 'true fanatics [those that are genuinely able to apply the universalization test even if their own interests are prejudiced] are relatively few, and would have no power at all to harm, were it not for their ability to mislead, and thus win the support of, large numbers of people who are not themselves fanatics'.[26] In *Freedom and Reason* Hare admits this is as far as the test may take us.[27]

2.2.3   A Critique of *Moral Thinking*

In *Moral Thinking* (1981) Hare tries to defend a substantive thesis, building on but not abandoning the formal meta-ethical theory of universal prescriptivism. He argues that, if we can assume perfect and comprehensive command of logic and of the facts (a supposition which he calls the 'Archangel's' viewpoint), 'they would constrain so severely the moral evaluations that we make, that in practice we would be bound all to agree to the same ones'.[28] The logic of universalization alone would not achieve this result but, if it were combined with the intention to act on substantive moral premises that complies with this requirement *when choosing and framing the terms of the principles we adopt*, one would be led by that logic to a utilitarianism that maximizes total preferences at what he calls the 'critical level' of moral thinking.

The 'critical level' of moral thinking is a mode of evaluation where we attempt to make choices about our principles of action after having taken into account every relevant consideration. Hare's 'principles' can be elaborately specific though framed in universal terms. Thus, they would, if necessary, contain exceptions and limitations for every conceivable

---

25   *Ibid*, pp. 177–8.
26   *Ibid*, p. 185.
27   *Ibid*, pp. 184–5.
28   Hare (1981), p. 6.

objection. Such principles would be most perfectly comprehended by his Archangel. He does not contend that such perfect reasoning is humanly possible but that reasoning about such principles at the critical level would be superior to the more general principles we adopt at a more intuitive level of moral thinking, and hence enables us to choose between two conflicting general principles or decide when a general principle chosen at the intuitive level ought to be over-ridden. Moral reasoning at the critical level employs act utilitarianism, which maximizes total preferences because 'the requirement to universalize our prescriptions, which is itself a logical requirement if we are reasoning morally, demands that we treat *other people's* prescriptions (i.e. their desires, likings, and in general, preferences) as if they were our own'.[29]

Hare's account of the 'critical level' of moral thinking, thus, concedes that universalization of principles requires some generalization of their terms and that the choice of how to generalize those terms, requires moral evaluations in turn and cannot be derived by pure logic from the descriptive features of the matter being evaluated.[30] He then applies the universalization test to deciding on the criterion by which we select and frame the terms of our principles at the critical level. This requires that we do not favour our own moral preferences over those of others; instead, each is to be treated equally. Logically, then, all these preferences are to be summed up, and the decision is to choose a principle ('rule' is a better term because the idea of a rule, unlike that of a principle can accommodate exceptions and conditions) that maximizes those preferences. The universalization test, at the critical level of moral thinking, allow extensions only to situations of exact similarity. It is also this viewpoint which is used to judge which of the more general *'prima facie* principles' are to be adopted at the working intuitive level, and when they are to be over-ridden by other considerations.

An objection to this is that it ignores the natural separateness of individuals. This is John Rawls' most basic criticism of utilitarianism.[31] Such utilitarianism ignores the fact that a gain (in terms of preferences satisfied) to others is not thereby a gain to one; and a loss to one is not compensated for (as far as that individual is concerned) by a gain to others except under an assumption of altruism wherein the identity and individualism of each person is erased altogether and replaced by an identification with the aggregate population itself. Such a moral argument

---

[29]   *Ibid*, pp. 16–17, italics are Hare's; see also pp. 94–6 and ch. 6, pp. 107–16.

[30]   *Ibid*, p. 63.

[31]   Rawls (1999), §5, pp. 19–24 and §30, esp. at pp. 163–7.

may appeal to a rational being that is an aggregate of each individual. However, this aggregated being does not exist. Moral arguments are made, ultimately, to individuals. A second objection is that the decision procedure adopted by Hare in *Moral Thinking* does not account for how the commitment thus made has any force. The point Hare makes in *Freedom and Reason* (1963) is that we are logically free to choose the principles on which we act. But the choice to adopt them as *moral* grounds of action requires a will to universalize them and subject their selection to the test of universalizability. The principles so chosen have force for us because such a procedure is *per se* a *commitment by us* to those principles. The later extreme version of this procedure applied in *Moral Thinking*, however, requires us to make this selection of principle from a standpoint that obliterates our recognizable selves from this hypothetical being that is making the selection and commitment. If we cannot identify with this being, how can its commitments have any force for us once we resume the mantle of our actual selves?

A potential utilitarian response to this is to concede the factual separateness of persons but argue, as Hare does, that one ought in reason to act as if there were no such separation. Much depends on the nature of the 'ought' used in this rebuttal. If it is a moral 'ought', then we have a substantive principle that others who disagree with it may reject unless there are further grounds for accepting it as a premiss. Hare tries to argue, instead, that it follows purely formally from the idea of universalization. He argues that if other persons with other preferences and situations are different from one only in that they are not oneself, and universalization requires us to ignore that kind of distinction (personal identifiers), then we are led to the conclusion that we have to (i.e. we logically ought to) treat the preferences and situations of others on an equal footing with our own.[32] Even if this is accepted, however, it does not follow that all preferences must then be aggregated whilst ignoring the fact that the preferences are divergent ones of different individual persons. Equality requires concern for each individual's plight, including their differences.

Two things may be observed about Hare's procedure. First, he now accepts that the universalization of the terms of rules (or 'principles' as he calls them) requires decisions about the form of generalizations to make that are necessarily evaluative. Of any judgment leading to action, one has – in order to identify the principle at work – to decide which features are relevant, what to generalize, what degree of generalization to

---

[32]   Hare (1981), ch. 6, pp. 107–16.

accept, what qualifications and restrictions to admit. Hence, the principles we use in practice (at 'the intuitive level') are themselves chosen according to higher or more fundamental moral criteria. One way to do this is to treat each such evaluative decision as itself a moral judgement involving the use of a principle that (as a moral one) has to be universalized. These may, in turn, be chosen according to even higher (and even more fundamental) principles or rules. There is, thus, in every practical moral judgement, an hierarchy of principles. Hare's earlier work (most notably in *The Language of Morals* (1952) and *Freedom and Reason* (1963)) treats moral argument and thinking as a process of uncovering or reconstructing this hierarchy, and adjusting our choices about this hierarchy with our choices about our actions in practice, for a fit between them.

The second observation we may make about the development of his philosophy in *Moral Thinking* (1981), is that Hare short-circuits this process at the level of 'critical thinking'. When Hare argues that one should treat the preferences of others on an equal footing with our own, he is assuming that there are no intermediate grounds for choosing between our two positions. This assumption brushes aside other competing candidates for background fundamental principles, by arguing that his form of utilitarianism *ought* to be supreme at the level of critical thinking. If it is not true that there are no other possible principles by which the positions of persons may be distinguished, then Hare can no longer claim that the move, using this argument, to the preference maximizing criterion is a purely formal one. Moreover, this second step actually abandons the project of prescribing principles. There is no content to the 'principle' he adopts at this level: instead, he says one should maximize the content that everyone wants.

Hare argues that, as there is no content, he is correct in claiming that he has taken a formal and not substantive step. But there are two very substantive features to this step. First, it requires one to ignore the separateness of individuals not as a fact but as a normative choice. Secondly, it abandons the project of prescribing principles for universalization that we began with in favour of aggregating preference. He tries to reconcile the two by treating the goal of maximizing total preferences as a principle.[33] But this disguises a very significant difference between this 'principle' and the rules or principles with which he began his argument. The latter have content, in the form of criteria, and hence it makes sense to speak of universalizing those criteria by stripping them of personal

---

[33]   *Ibid.*

identifiers and applying the result universally. Hare's ultimate 'principle' at the level of critical thinking has no such criteria, or, rather, is a criterion that uncritically sums the criteria of everyone. As observed already, this involves the moral choice of disregarding other candidates for fundamental moral criteria. It also violates the terms upon which his analysis began. The universalization thesis tries to be plausible on the basis that every term that describes something has a natural width of application determined by its definition. Hence, when we say a principle guiding action applies in a specific case because certain grounds for that principle are present, one can speak sensibly requiring the same action in all other situations where the same grounds are present. Hare's preference utilitarianism cannot rely on this relationship of concept to cases because his 'principle' has no core concept to universalize. Neither can he rely on the 'principles' as applied at the 'critical level' because these (though framed in universal terms) involve highly specific qualifications and conditions which are determined by his ultimate criterion. On the other hand, the principles at the 'intuitive level' are only *prima facie* guides used in moral teaching. These guides are subject to evaluation and modification according to preference utilitarianism at the 'level of critical thinking' when we deal with specific situations. Hence, where the former might naturally be universalized to a new situation, the evaluation at the critical level of moral thinking might justify a new exception or qualification. This last would appear *ad hoc* except that Hare would argue that principles at the 'intuitive level' are *prima facie* in any case and that it is only at the critical thinking level, where all things can be fully considered, that the principle is properly described. This, however, only reinforces the point that his theory ultimately abandons the universalization of *principles* that people prescribe. For this, Hare has substituted the prescribing of the sum of everyone's preferences. Although he has reached this by universalization, it is not the universalization of any principle, and the choice to abandon principles, is a value choice. The point is not that these other candidates can be established without adopting some irreducibly moral stance; rather, it is that neither can Hare's preference utilitarianism. Prescriptivism in operation is premissed unavoidably on one or more such fundamental moral choice. It cannot work without substantive evaluative choices.

Is the moral sceptic, then, right? Is reason, then, incapable of providing ultimate grounds for morality as this requires ultimate substantive premises that are neither founded on reason nor derivable from the formal concept of morality? It seems this viewpoint has several bases. The first is what has been called Hume's Law on the basis of the famous but rather Delphic passage in his *Treatise*:[34] that one may not derive an 'ought' proposition from purely 'is' premises. The argument from this is that no amount of empirical verification generating purely 'is' statements may produce grounds for why one 'ought' to do anything, and, as moral norms are 'ought' propositions, fact finding cannot prove them. This is true even if fact finding establishes what 'ought' propositions people do hold. This anthropological datum merely describes what people think they ought to do, and may even be grounds for predicting what they will do, but is not grounds for what they really ought to do. This is because, as observed above, the concept of morality makes the latter an open question: even in the face of commonly accepted 'oughts', one can logically and sensibly ask if one really ought to act accordingly. Morality is supervenient in this way because we demand of this concept that it provides a reason that appeals to our reason but it is a feature of reasoning that it may always re-examine its premises and ask for justification. This 'open question' consequence is the second primary basis for moral scepticism.

This leads some moral sceptics, like Hume, to stay firmly on the 'is' side of the is/ought chasm, and reject the common understanding of moral norms for factual descriptions of inclinations and conventions. This, though, falls prey to the problems that beset all descriptivist theories: however accurately a theory may describe what the conventional or natural inclination 'is', it is subject to the open question challenge: Why should one obey? Others, like, Ayer, hold the expectation of rational binding grounds to be correct as an account of our normal understanding of moral concepts but argue that these concepts are meaningless because they do not have truth conditions that are verifiable.[35] It follows that the 'open question' argument is misconceived as being founded on a mistake about the possibilities of the concept of morality. One, then, either has to restrict oneself to first order descriptivism, or posit some moral norms for adoption or adopt an essentially nihilist position. Out of the wreckage of this sceptical attack, Hare's initial theory seems to point a way forward for a theory of rational moral grounds that will be advanced in the next section. But it is not Hare's solution in *Moral Thinking* (1981).

---

[34] Cf. n. 2 above.
[35] Ayer (2006), ch. 6, pp. 104–26.

2.3 TAKING PRESCRIPTIVISM SERIOUSLY

2.3.1 A Fresh Start for Universal Prescriptivism

Instead of Hare's solution, relying on preference maximization as the ultimate criterion for framing principles, the thesis to be advanced here is that we can retain much of the elements of Hare's thesis, and make a new start taking into account some of the observations that emerged from the foregoing discussion. These elements include the prescriptivist nature of norms and values, and universalizability as the test of their moral character, and the lessons here learned: that universalization requires generalization of descriptive terms, the very choice and framing of which requires moral choice. Hare's insight into the two levels of moral thinking remains valuable. There is the 'intuitive level' where principles are *prima facie* guides to action (operating as rules of thumb for moral teaching and as general guides for action) that, however, are subject to more elaborate conditions and exceptions when considered at the critical (all things considered) level of moral thinking. The critical level has its own, internal, two-step procedure whereby the framing of the elaborated principles (or, more appropriately, 'rules') is subject to a further normative test. It is only the nature of this last test (albeit important to Hare's mature thesis in *Moral Thinking* (1981)) which is here disputed. In addition, there are the insights contributed by moral sceptics, most notably Hume: that one may not derive 'ought' conclusions from pure 'is' premisses, that reason in the restricted form of means–end rationality is unable to assist us in deriving ultimate ends as guides to conduct, and that, in order to be an efficient force on our conduct, the consideration must begin with a desire, something we want.[36]

One conclusion we may be tempted to draw from moral sceptic critique could be Mackie's suggestion that our idea that norms and values are 'objective' is a mistake, albeit a convenient and useful fiction.[37] This, however, should be accepted only if there is no other theory that will account for our commonly accepted expectation that norms and values have force for us, are susceptible to rational inquiry and clarification, and are objective – in the sense of being independent of our preferences. Scepticism allows, however, that there can be conventional norms and values identifiable in a first order (anthropological and empirical) inquiry.

---

[36] Hume (2000), see nn. 11 & 12 above and text.
[37] Mackie (1990).

This allows us to use Searle's[38] social function ('X counts as Y, in C') as a way of explaining how prescriptions work: prescriptions or evaluative directions are the '*Ys*' that we conventionally attribute to certain facts ('*Xs*') in circumstances ('*Cs*'). This last suggests a way around Mackie's 'error theory' whilst taking note of Hume's observation that practical reason must begin with a desire. The suggestion begins with the question: What if one of the things that we *in fact want*, is to rely on, and make claims on the basis of, principles that are grounded as far as possible on prescriptions justified by rational inquiry? In other words, what system of morality would we get if we take universal prescriptivism seriously?

2.3.2 Fundamental Prescriptivism and its Procedure

Taking prescriptivism seriously begins with recognizing that the act of prescribing a moral norm in Hare's account of use of moral concepts involves intentionality assigning a status function ('counts as Y') to certain universalized features of a situation ('X ... in C'), and that this is a contribution to the making of social reality[39] (cf. §1.2.2). For this status function to be social, the intentionality must be a collective one, intended to be shared: '*we* intend that' in these kinds of facts and circumstance, one ought to do Y (or other evaluative prescription). This recognizes that moral norms, as such status functions, are not brute facts (i.e. existing independently of minds) but are made by people having the required collective intentionality. The implication of universal prescriptivism though, is that the kind of evaluative functions that can be assigned to particular situations are not arbitrary. For *moral* status functions to be effectively assigned, the requirements of universal prescriptivism must be met; and for them to be assigned *collectively*, the conditions for such collective intentionality must be met.

To take prescriptivism seriously, then, is to identify these requisite conditions, and to acknowledge that making morality work requires implicit commitments to these conditions. To 'take prescriptivism seriously' is to recognize the hierarchy of background values and principles (which is recognized in Hare's two levels of moral thinking) that each moral judgement implies, and to subject these to the requirement of universalization. It, however, is also to reject Hare's ultimate solution of a resort to preference utilitarianism at the 'level of critical thinking'. The possibility of such a level of moral thinking is a useful device for

---

[38]   Searle (1995), cf. §§1.2.2 & 1.2.3 above.
[39]   *Ibid.*

analysing the hierarchy of principles, but utilitarianism itself ultimately rejects the use of any principle with substantive content and is, as such, an abandonment of the universalization of prescriptions. The critiques of meta-ethical sceptics do show that, at least to some extent, morality is invented (Mackie, 1990). This does not prevent them from being part of social reality as an institution underpinned by the logical structure identified by Searle: that 'X counts as Y, in C'. A meta-ethical sceptic like Mackie need not dispute this, for he does not deny that morality exists as social practice, and that first order moral propositions are embraced as social facts. He denies that in the second (meta-ethical) order of inquiry, there are objective truths about ethics. However, such a sceptic goes wrong if he thinks that the content of what can be 'invented' is wholly arbitrary. It must be subject to universalization, and therefore it must have prerequisites or be quite a different thing from moral rules altogether. Thus, there is the possibility of a minimum, logically necessary core content of morality. To take prescriptivism seriously is to make commitments to what is necessary to make morality as a project of universalizing prescriptions work.

The institution of morality is the result of coordinative efforts with a common point: to establish universalizable prescriptions (rules) which are a response to a desire that these may serve as ultimate grounds which appeal with objective force to our reason in providing guidance for actions and in the resolution of disputes between agents. Any account of the concept of morality must start with the premiss that morality is expected to serve these purposes, for such are the common expectations that we have of the idea. The account need not hold that these expectations can be realized. Hence, sceptical conceptions of ethics are not ruled out by definition. But sceptics must explain why this expectation is mistaken. The following section will argue, though, that universal prescriptivism leads us to a set of prescriptions ('fundamental prescriptions' or 'FPs') which we are rationally bound to accept as the ultimate basis for justifying other moral rules. This will be called 'fundamental prescriptivism'. The key, though, is that we must *want*, as an ultimate desire, to base our moral claims on grounds that respect reason as far as reason is capable of providing guidance in such matters.

2.4 FUNDAMENTAL PRESCRIPTIONS AND EQUAL FREEDOM AND WELL-BEING

2.4.1 The First FP – The Principle of Rationality

The desire to base our moral claims on grounds that respect reason, as far as reason is capable of providing guidance in such matters, is a condition that satisfies the Humean observation that the motivational force of practical reason presupposes a desired object.[40] Reason may identify the means necessary to achieve the posited object – by establishing matters of fact and in determining whether 'ought' propositions are consistent with one another as a matter of logic – but it is the desire for the object that explains the motivation that requires these means. This observation of Hume's is at the root of scepticism about the capacity of reason alone to identify ultimate grounds for ethics. But the desire to ground our moral claims in reason is a special, pivotal kind of object: for it paradoxically gives motivating force to impartial considerations. It should be noted that this desire has to be an ultimate one. That is, its goal is one that is desired for its own sake. But it need not be a paramount, or even a superior desire: one may want something for its own sake even if other desires are given priority. The point is, when it is given up because of an incompatibility with a higher priority, something is sacrificed, and not merely negated because a rational inquiry has revealed that we do not really want that thing after all. There is a loss because we do want it for its own sake and, because there is a loss, the objective and all its entailed implications have force, even if that force can be over-ridden.

If we have that desire, and reasoning leads us to the recognition that prescriptions must be willed but they must also, in order to be moral prescriptions, be cast in universal terms which themselves are selected according to more fundamental evaluative prescriptions, and, as these too must be willed, we are led finally to the realization that we must make fundamental willed prescriptions as the ultimate criteria for all further moral rules. Moral reasoning climbs up tiers of prescriptions, like a pyramidal chandelier, supported by higher, more general and more vital rungs of prescriptions, reaching for the ultimate hook from which the entire edifice hangs. But the moral sceptics are right in that this ultimate supporting premise does not exist independently of someone willing it to be so. Where the moral sceptics would be wrong, however, is if they contend that this gives us a reason to reject the rational grounding of

---

[40] Hume (2000), Bk. 3, Pt. 1, §1, see discussion above at §2.2.1.

ethics. Since reason leads to the recognition that willed fundamental prescriptions are necessary to making any moral claim that is objective in that it is based on grounds that would rationally exist independently in respect of our own particular desires, save that we admit at least one desire – to ground our claims in reason as far as reason can provide guidance – we have a reasoned basis for willing at least one fundamental prescription:

> The Principle of Rationality: *We ought to will, as grounds for our moral claims against others for social cooperation, principles which can be justified by reason as far as reason is capable of providing guidance in such matters.*

This, though, will lead us to the prescription of other fundamental principles.

2.4.2   The Second FP – The Principle of Freedom

If we want to make any moral claims at all, it is because we have at least some projects that are to us worthwhile and because at least some cooperation from others is necessary to the realization of our projects. To achieve any project, the capacity to act is a necessity. This requires effective freedom: not only liberty from legal restraint (formal liberty corresponding with the liberties associated with Rawls' first principle in his theory of justice,[41] which is discussed later at §3.2.3), but also the conditions and capabilities that enable one to exercise and enjoy those liberties (the social goods that are the subject of Rawls' second principle) because it is the ability to realize our projects and not the formal liberty to pursue them that we would value as agents. Therefore, a rational examination of the conditions for taking prescriptivism seriously, and realizing morality as an institution in social reality that we must will into existence, leads us to accept a second fundamental prescription:

> The Principle of Freedom: *The liberty to have and realize purposes, and such well-being as is necessary to enjoy and exercise that liberty, are to be valued and ought to be promoted and protected.*[42]

---

[41]   Rawls (1999). See Sen (1999, 2009) for capabilities as freedom.

[42]   A debt to Gewirth's Principle of Generic Consistency is acknowledged here (see §2.5.1), though herein, instead of his ethical monism, a cluster of principles is taken to be fundamental; for a critique of his ethical monism, see Singer (1984).

2.4.3   The Third FP – The Principle of Personhood

The third fundamental prescription is:

The Principle of Personhood: *Each human individual is to be respected as a person capable of bearing rights and duties necessary to establishing a moral framework.*

This rejects utilitarianism as a fundamental moral criterion because of Rawls' separateness-of-persons critique[43] of that form of ethics. This is because we make moral appeals ultimately to individual rational agents – other human individuals. Although the human individual is the fundamental unit of appeal, the principle does not claim that individual freedom trumps obligations to others: it is as persons capable of bearing both rights *and duties* that he or she is to be respected. The principle flows from the recognition that the appeal to reason is for the purpose of establishing the collective intentionalities necessary to establishing a moral framework. Since reason leads us to recognize that prescription is necessary if we want to make any moral claim to cooperation from others, and this intentionality must be a collective one (in the form, 'We intend ...'), it also leads us to accept both that cooperation in creating a moral community with correlative rights and obligations amongst its members is necessary, and that this appeal to cooperation is made ultimately to the individual agents that are potential members of that community. The claims for cooperation in morality as an institutional project are made ultimately and irreducibly to individual persons. This gives every*one* a rational reason to prescribe for the respect of all human individuals as persons. The principle of rationality, with the realization that this prescription is a necessary condition for a scheme of morality, logically leads us to will this fundamental prescription.

2.4.4   The Fourth FP – The Principle of Equality

The principles of rationality, freedom and personhood taken together lead us to will a fourth fundamental prescription:

The Principle of Equality: *Each human individual, in the scheme of morality, is to be treated as an equal person and of equal value.*

---

[43]   Rawls (1999) at §5, pp. 19–24 and §30, pp. 163–5. See above at §2.2.3.

This is because the second of the foregoing principles requires us to positively value freedom but the very rationalist scepticism that led us to deny any naturally objective norm or value would have led us to the conclusion that we have, at this fundamental level of moral inquiry, no moral reason (though we may have personal and partial ones) to favour our own personal freedom, or those of any particular other person or category of persons, over others. We must will the promotion of the freedom of all persons as equals because reason tells us we have no valid grounds for distinction at this level of moral thinking and the Principle of Rationality commands that we ought to allow ourselves to be guided by it as far as it is capable of providing reasoned guidance in such matters. Can we reverse the point, and argue that, neither does reason tell us that we cannot make distinctions at this level? This would ignore the second principle, which follows from reason's discovery that effective freedom, liberty and the well-being necessary to realizing that liberty, are to be valued. This would be true of the freedom of everyone, and be unlimited unless positive grounds are found for limiting this principle. That ground is found in the inability of reason to identify grounds for rational distinction at this level of moral rule making. The implication is that the Principle of Freedom is given full rein for each and every person until his or her sphere of freedom begins to encroach disproportionately on that of others. The effect is that maximum liberty (and well-being necessary to enjoy that liberty) is to be promoted subject to an equal liberty and well-being for all.

2.4.5   The Fifth FP – The Principle of Moral Transparency

The Principle of Rationality also requires us to respect the conditions that are necessary to the exploration, challenge and examination of our moral claims and the basis for them, because we have admitted that morality is a social institution that we have to freely cooperate in exercising collective intentionality to maintain. Opaqueness and restrictions on thought and expression about such matters, even if they challenge the currently accepted edifice, impede such free cooperation. To this extent openness, honesty, and freedom of speech and expression are necessary. Hence, it is rationally necessary to will the fifth fundamental prescription:

> The Principle of Moral Transparency: *In matters relating to the institution of morality and claims about it, openness, honesty, and freedom of speech and expression are to be promoted and protected.*

Note, the freedom of speech supported here is of narrower scope than the general freedom of speech that would be part of the Principle of Freedom.

2.4.6 The Sixth FP – The Principle of Cooperation

However, we encounter the realization that these principles are – in their abstract form – under-determinative: their application to particular situations may generate a number of reasonable alternative outcomes. This is where it is important to remind ourselves that such a scheme of morality, as a social institution, requires all participants – people who do make moral claims upon one another – to cooperate in maintaining collective intentionalities making this moral scheme part of our social reality. Thus, reason also leads us to accept that cooperation in giving moral principles, as basic institutions, a determinate form is a prerequisite of such an institution. This includes coordinating our moral judgements where reasonable and taking into account past moral decisions by others that are relevant to institutions that we still intend to maintain. This gives us a reason to will the sixth fundamental prescription:

> The Principle of Cooperation: *We ought to act in good faith in accordance with the best understanding of these fundamental principles that is universalizable in a manner consistent with the institutions and practices that we hold that we ought to keep; and to accept the decisions of others which we cannot reasonably reject as incompatible with these fundamental prescriptions.*

The first part of this principle (that we ought to act in good faith in accordance with the best understanding of these fundamental principles) borrows from Dworkin's defence for his version of the objectivity of morality.[44] The second (accepting the decisions of others we cannot reasonably reject) adapts a test of contractualism advocated by Thomas Scanlon, who suggests, 'An act is wrong if its performance under the circumstances would be disallowed by any system of rules for the general regulation of behaviour which no one could reasonably reject as a basis for informed, unforced general agreement.'[45]

The possibility of plural reasonable moral outlooks and the implication of this for a political framework for cooperation is the subject of John Rawls' *Political Liberalism* (1993). He locates his solution in a political

---

[44] Dworkin (1996).
[45] Scanlon (1982) at p. 110.

conception of justice. He argues that, even amongst reasonable comprehensive religious or ethical doctrines with irreconcilable differences between them, there will be an overlapping of reasonable consensus which enables them to at least agree on the principles of justice he initially proposed in *A Theory of Justice*[46] as governing the framework for cooperation. Amartya Sen advocates a different solution to the problem of moral plurality, embracing the viewpoint of Adam Smith's impartial spectator so that, when making moral decisions, one should endeavour "'to examine our own conduct as we imagine any other fair and impartial spectator would examine it'".[47] Though there can be a 'considerable divergence between differing impartial views', he argues that this would still yield agreement on incomplete rankings of priorities which, though partial, enable us to cooperate on matters of justice.

Both Rawls and Sen are concerned, in these works, with the concept of justice and principles of public cooperation, and, hence, may content themselves with the realm of reasonable agreement. It is different, though, when an individual, whether acting on personal matters or as an official in public matters, has to make a specific decision on which morality has a bearing. He has to combine both respect for the possibility of reasonable plurality with the necessity of deciding (for, even to decide not to decide is a decision) between moral options. The Principle of Cooperation acknowledges this plurality of reasonable realizations of even the above fundamental prescriptions and builds into them a duty to respect reasonable differences, but takes prescriptivism seriously by requiring that a best understanding of the fundamental prescriptions should be sought in good faith. Its rationale for such an attitude is morality as a cooperative social project.

2.4.7   The Equal Right to Freedom and Well-being

Together, these principles are summed generally in the principle of an

> Equal Right to Freedom and Well-being: *Every human individual in any basic social arrangement with others is entitled to cooperation, and obliged to reciprocate that cooperation, in a scheme of universalized moral rules that support social institutions promoting and protecting the liberty of each human*

---

[46]   Rawls (1999); his principles are discussed in the next chapter at §3.2.3.

[47]   Sen (2009), see esp. ch. 6, pp. 124–52 and ch. 9, pp. 194–207; quotes from p. 124, quoting from Adam Smith, *The Theory of Moral Sentiments,* T Cadell: London (extended version, 1790), republished Clarendon Press: Oxford, 1976, III, i, 2.

individual as an equal person to have and realize his or her own purposes, and that support the claims to well-being necessary to enjoy that liberty, to the extent that such purposes are consistent with an equal freedom for all.

This cooperation extends to preferring a moral scheme and its institutions that offer greater total practical freedom over those which offer lesser, and to preferring that which offers the greatest total practical freedom over the others, where these preferences are compatible with respecting each human person as an equal in the moral scheme.

This statement owes deep debts to Gewirth's Principle of Generic Consistency. It also builds on Kant's 'Kingdom of Ends'[48] and the Universal Declaration of Human Rights (see below at §2.5). To avoid awkward reiterations of this formulation, this right will generally be referred to below as the principle of an 'equal right to freedom and well-being'.

2.4.8   The Reality of Morality

We are now able to address these questions: If morality aspires to embodiment as a social institution rather than a brute fact in the fabric of the world, and if social institutions are constituted (as J.R. Searle argues they are) by conventions for institution creating functions having the form 'X counts as Y, in C',[49] why aren't the norms of morality wholly arbitrary? Why isn't our conventional understanding of morality and its requirements, save in terms of conflict with another convention, logically beyond question? And why, in cases of such conflicts, are they not to be regarded as essentially irresolvable by reason? The answer lies in the characteristics that we *want* the institution of morality to have. Under-lying the conventions for various moral rules is a *meta*-convention about their character: that they should have force operating on our motivation, that this force appeals to and is governed by reason, and is objective. This meta-convention can be rejected in theory but the argument that will be made in the following chapters is that we keep having to rely on it if we want to maintain complex social institutions like IPRs. Because of various things that we want such institutions to do, or various things we want to do with them, we find ourselves always wanting to rely on moral claims having this character, even when they are in conflict with other, perhaps more dominant, or urgent wants. As a result, morality, though conventional, has unavoidable characteristics.

---

[48]   Kant (1996), pp. 37–108 at 83–9 [4: 433–40].
[49]   Searle (1995); discussed herein at §1.2.2.

Is there a contradiction between the claim that this meta-convention is to be constructed and the assertion that it exists as part of social reality? Surely it either exists or has to be constructed, but cannot be both? What exists as social facts are practices where we make moral claims upon one another on the basis that these claims have the characteristics of force, rationality and objectivity. The fact that we want these claims to be based on reasons that have these characteristics is a contingent one, but unavoidable given various institutions we uphold and cooperate in maintaining and make claims upon one another to cooperate in maintaining – amongst these, IPRs. It is what is rationally required by this desire – once we have investigated what is needed to make universal prescriptivism do this work – that is constructed. But this is real and objective as well because what is to be constructed is a rationally necessary part of the reality we maintain and continue to rely on.

Another way to explain this is to call on Searle's account of 'the Background'.[50] Whilst it is possible to conceive of the social aspects of our reality in terms of operations of Searle's constitutive rules, this account will have to address two quite immediate objections. First, that the operation of these rules gets too complex in even simple social interactions to be rules that people actually use. Secondly, though attempts are sometimes made to codify these rules (e.g. grammar for languages), they are often not expressed and, if people are not even aware of using these rules, his theory must discharge an explanatory burden as regards how it is then possible for people to have and maintain continuously a collective intentionality assigning status functions under such rules. The answer Searle gives to these objections is that the use of such rules does not require that people *follow* them. Rather, people mostly develop abilities, dispositions and capacities in relation to these rules without learning or internalizing them. He argues:

> The basic idea ... is that one can develop, one can evolve, a set of abilities that are sensitive to specific structures of intentionality without actually being constituted by that intentionality. One develops skills and abilities that are, so to speak, functionally equivalent to the system of rules, without actually containing any representations or internalizations of those rules.[51]

This is what he calls his 'thesis of the Background: Intentional states function only given a set of Background capacities that do not themselves

---

[50] *Ibid*, p. 129; see discussion at §1.2.2.
[51] *Ibid*, p. 142.

consist of intentional phenomena.'[52] By 'capacities' he means 'abilities, dispositions, tendencies and causal structures generally'.[53] Searle argues[54] that the constitutive rules of our social reality causally condition the abilities and capacities a person develops in the Background. Hence, 'he has acquired those unconscious dispositions and capacities in a way that is sensitive to the rule structure of the institution'.[55] It appears, then, that our social reality can be analysed in terms of the functions that are assigned to things, even social things, a large part of which are and depend on there being institutions and social facts constituted by hierarchies and iterations of rules having the form 'X counts as Y, in C'. And these form the logical substructure of our social reality that can be consciously discovered (or reconstructed) by such analysis. Furthermore, once, with Searle, we reject the requirement that one has to *consciously* accept or follow the formula 'X counts as Y, in C' and say that even 'in the very evolution of the institution the participants need not be consciously aware of the form of the collective intentionality by which they are imposing functions on objects'[56] – presumably because the intentionality is to be inferred by the dispositions it shapes – we are driven to the conclusion that the function is really constructed *post hoc*. Or, more accurately, it is reconstructed by a kind of reverse engineering by reasoning, where one asks: What kinds of rule having the form 'X counts as Y, in C' would account for and, in the case of moral norms, justify the disposition at hand?

When we attempt to apply this theory to morality and its relationship to law, and to the IPR system especially, a critical question that arises is the extent to which the relevant constitutive rules are contingent, or are constrained by the very concept of moral norms and principles. Hare's ethical theory would suggest that they are constrained by the nature of prescriptivism, subject to the requirement of universalization. The discussion in this chapter has taken this line of thought further, to the fundamental prescriptions that are the prerequisites of taking universal prescriptivism seriously. The FPs exist because we act on and maintain, in first order practice, moral propositions which imply a critical level of moral thinking: that is, on the assumption that they can be defended or justified at that level, and would be open to revision if not. And, at the

---

52   *Ibid*, p. 129.
53   *Ibid*, p. 129.
54   *Ibid*, p. 131.
55   *Ibid*, p. 144.
56   *Ibid* at p. 47.

critical level of moral thinking, we are led to the rational necessity of prescribing the FPs as a guide to our prescriptions.

A different objection may note that the entire argument is contingent on a desire that we want to make moral claims to justify our actions, and claims for cooperation, on the basis of norms that have force, are rational and objective. But, so the objection may go, even if we have such a desire, this is not an ultimate desire. It is desired because we desire something else: for example, life, pleasure, power. As they are means to an end, a rational person (i.e. one who chooses effective means to ends) would give them up when in conflict with the end. Even if some people do desire to act in a moral way as an end in itself, this would be a minority and often such a desire would be subordinate in priority to other ends. However, these propositions do not have to be negated in order to uphold the reality and force of the fundamental principles. It is not claimed here that these have a force on our motivations that is superior to all other forces. It is merely claimed that they have a kind of force, and this discussion has sought to identify its nature and logical implications. Even if the desire for such a moral basis is the result of pursuing some further desire, or is subordinate to other motivations, it remains true that the desire for a rational, objective morality with force on our motivations is a desire for something that is conceptually ultimate. That is, we begin with wanting, for reasons that are rooted in personal projects and purposes, to be able to appeal for the cooperation of others in maintaining certain social institutions, like IPRs, and hence wanting morality with its characteristic operation upon principles with objective rational force. The former are superior, and supply the motive for the latter. But once we want to call on morality as an institution with objective rational force, however we come to so want it, we cross a Humean Rubicon from 'is' to 'ought'; from a brute fact of a desire to a logically required commitment to a system of ideas which make normative demands of us. This is because our wanting to rely on morality, as a resource that has objective rational force, has implications.

It implies further background prescriptions – and, if the thesis in this chapter is correct, the fundamental prescriptions – which, if they conflict with the end we started with, would logically require that we review our various desires and give up one or the other. That we have to give up one or the other indicates that this morality has a content that is independent of our desires, and hence is objective. The fact that they can be rationally investigated satisfies the criterion of rationality. And the fact that something or other has to be given up is proof of its rational force. (Of course, it is possible for someone to continue to pursue an inconsistent ultimate end, and yet *profess* a desire to act on a moral basis, but this is a different thing from *actually* doing both. The latter is, *ex hypothesi*, logically impossible given the characteristic of universality. Cf. §1.2.4.) Of course, the fact that the commitment is logically required, does not mean that we do make those commitments. But the logical connection puts us into a bind. Thus, the prerequisites of universal prescriptivism have a force for us, even if we choose to give up acting on a moral basis in a particular instance, because there is a loss imposed by the logical character of the concept – an ultimate desire, albeit a weaker one, has to be given up. This logical substructure for any given society can be said to be objective in the sense that it would be true even for an observer adopting an external (anthropological) viewpoint of the practices of a group or subgroup whose behaviour conforms to it[57] because it would correctly describe the logical substructure for that group or subgroup though he himself does not accept those premises. And it remains objective in the foregoing sense, even though this would not (in fact cannot) be true if *no one's* behaviour logically implies acceptance of it, as it requires at least implicit intentional states assigning functions by someone.[58] Though this substructure is constructed by analysis, it is real and can be said to exist because it has causal effects on the knowledge and capacities we have in the Background.

The claim that morality has a rationally objective logical substructure is what distinguishes this theory from moral relativism. Relativism rejects the proposition that there can be morally binding rules or principles except as between parties that mutually accept them.[59] This work concedes that moral rules gain social force when accepted, and that the idea of morality requires that we cooperate in embodying morality as a social institution. But it also maintains that prior to, and independent of, such acceptance, there are rationally objective foundational principles on which that social institution rests and by which it is evaluated. Morality is a transcendental reality of reason which aspires to social embodiment.

---

[57] This is epistemically objective: *ibid*, pp. 7–13.
[58] This would be ontologically subjective: *ibid*, pp. 7–13.
[59] E.g. Harman (2000), see esp. ch. 2, pp. 20–38, and ch. 3, pp. 39–57.

2.5   FUNDAMENTAL PRESCRIPTIVISM AND OTHER THEORIES

2.5.1   Gewirth – A Debt and Some Differences

The ideas here borrow greatly from Alan Gewirth's development of the idea of the Principle of Generic Consistency ('PGC'). The equal right to freedom and well-being follows the PGC in valuing freedom and well-being. He arrives at the PGC by steps of reasoning from propositions which he argues a 'prospective purposive-agent' cannot deny.[60] He begins with the idea that freedom and well-being are necessary for action, 'Hence [the prospective purposive agent] must also accept (4) "I must have freedom and well-being" where this "must" is practical prescriptive … .' He then goes on a chain of reasoning, which will not be entered into here because this work is not intended as a critique of Gewirth, to arrive at the conclusion: '[E]very agent must accept (9) "I have rights to freedom and well-being because I am a prospective-purposive agent."' Because these are necessary conditions of action and successful action in general, and every agent 'logically must hold that he has the generic rights, since otherwise he would be in the position of accepting that he normatively need not have what he has accepted that he normatively must have'. He generalizes this to: 'All prospective purposive agents have rights to freedom and well-being.' His PGC then states: '*Act in accord with the generic rights of your recipients as well as yourself.*'

Each of the stages of his argument has been the subject of much critique and commentary.[61] The argument in this chapter arrives at what appears to be the same, or similar, conclusion by a different route because this work seeks to emphasize one type of contingency. Given the conclusion Gewirth is seeking to support, this argument rests not just on the assumption of a prospective purposive agent but on the additional condition that such an agent wants to ground his or her claims in reason rather than assertions of power. It is not only the desire to reason but also to make, as far as it is possible, reason the basis of our claims upon one another, that one is taken from the conclusion that one should want freedom and well-being, to the idea that one should *claim* a right to

---

[60]   Gewirth (1996) distils the argument himself at pp. 16–19, advanced earlier in Gewirth (1978).

[61]   For an extensive survey of these critiques and a defence of Gewirth, see Beyleveld (1991).

freedom and well-being. The desire to rest the argument on reason leads one to abjure coercion in favour of a *rights* claim, the underlying logic of which is that others should respect it because of its nature and not some other, external, reason. As Gewirth argues that therefore there *is* such a right, he must show why and how the desire to make such a *claim* brings about the right. If the agent wants to have the claim respected because it is a *moral* principle, then Hare's analysis of the conceptual character of norms would lead one to conclude that it must be universalized and the agent, if he or she wants to make a moral claim, must be willing to have it universalized. This commitment to universalization takes us to the equal right to freedom and well-being, or PGC.

Now, it is because every prospective purposive-agent *who desires to ground his or her claims in reason as far as possible* is led logically to the PGC, that it can be said that the right exists for him or her, because of the logical commitments given the desire, and for every other such agent with such desires because they too have to make the same logical commitments. This *conditional* proposition, that such a principle would exist for such agents given the desire to ground their claims in reason as far as possible, is a conceptual truth whatever one chooses to believe. In this sense, the right is independent of individual minds (though not independent of all minds), and can claim objective existence. Even for those who take a moral sceptical position and reject the desire to ground their substantive moral claims in reason, this conditional proposition is logically undeniable; it is just that if they choose – and they are free to so choose – not to commit to the condition, then they would not acknowledge the consequent. But the moral sceptic's rejection of all desire to ground moral claims as far as possible on reason comes with its own costs: moral claims must be given up, or they must ultimately be enforced by the use of power (which would not, by definition, be moral force). If the moral sceptic's rejection is not absolute, in that he seeks to ground some substantive moral claims in reason and others in power, then an inconsistency is admitted which allows the counter-argument: to the extent that there is commitment to the former, why does the logical commitment to the fundamental prerequisites of prescriptivism not, then, lead to a rejection of all claims based *purely* on power?

The desire to ground moral claims in reason itself cannot be true or false. Though the statement that someone has such a desire is verifiable or deniable, that is a different thing. In the nature of the thing, one either chooses to have it, or not. Either branch of the choice, though, must be paid for with the coin of its respective logical commitments. In this way, ethical reasoning presents us with truths (in the form of choices and conditions to the choices) about how institutions can be built, which are independent of what we prefer or would like to believe. Hence, these truths yield objective, rational and action guiding principles. The account leading to the equal right to freedom and well-being given in the preceding subsection is to be preferred because it makes explicit the contingency of the desire to ground moral claims in reason as a premiss. The choice is open, and it clarifies the objective conditions to which such choice is subject. Otherwise, though, this work intends to rely on the applications of the principle Gewirth makes central in *The Community of Rights* (1996). In particular, it will use the implication he draws from this, that one has claims not only to negative liberty but also positive claims on resources that enable one to enjoy as fully as possible the value of the formal liberty. As argued above in relation to the Principle of Freedom (§2.4.2), a person making a fundamental prescription has no rational grounds to prescribe rights to a formal liberty where this is not accompanied by the ability to enjoy them. Therefore, valuing liberty and well-being as a combined concept is to be preferred to John Rawls' theory giving lexical priority to the first principle relating to liberties over the second distributive principle for social goods.[62]

Gewirth also introduces a rational test for a tie breaker instead of a lexical ranking of types of principle. Some means of tie breaking is necessary because it is plain that different people may raise claims to social goods necessary to well-being on conflicting principles that cannot be satisfied in the same case. He suggests that, instead of Rawls' lexical prioritizing of principles, one should apply a 'criterion of degrees of needfulness for action'.[63] This says: 'When two rights are in conflict with one another, that right takes precedence whose object is more needed for action.'[64] This is not an *ad hoc* solution, for it ultimately grounds on the idea that when one has to make normatively based distinctions about when two cases are relevantly alike or dis-similar, one has to rely on background principles, and that this process ultimately leads one to the fundamental prescription that one should advance and respect the equal right to freedom and well-being of persons. This favours increasing capabilities for action, and therefore practical liberty. Our concern and respect for the equality of each human person gives priority, where there is conflict, to the claim to a right that promotes or protects the basis of action that is more needful. Though the conclusions are largely congruent, Fundamental Prescriptivism has another significant difference with

---

[62]   Rawls (1999), §11, pp. 52–6.
[63]   Gewirth (1996), p. 45.
[64]   *Ibid.*

Gewirth. His 'ethical monism', attempting to resolve all moral conflict by reference to a single supreme moral principle, has been criticized as being workable only by employing 'covert and unexamined' further principles.[65] Gewirth can rightly respond that his principle 'has a complex structure that reflects the generic features of action and rights-claims that derive from those features',[66] whilst insisting that a single ultimate criterion is necessary to resolve moral conflict. The approach adopted in this work makes the same point with a different focus: there is one ultimate criterion for prescriptions at the critical level of moral thinking but it comprises a plurality of fundamental principles.

2.5.2 The Kantian Categorical Imperative

The fundamental prescription that one should respect *and* promote the freedom and well-being of each rational individual as equal persons is, on the argument made here, a hypothetical imperative: it is a prescription that must be accepted *if* one wants to ground moral claims in reason as far as possible. Though a hypothetical imperative, this prescription is in substance very much a rephrasing of Kant's categorical imperative. The connection is hardly surprising for R.M. Hare too claims a Kantian kinship for his theory, though he rather paradoxically arrives at a utilitarian bedrock principle.[67] The present projection from Hare's original thesis in this work, which arrives at a more Kantian principle, is actually more faithful to the idea of universal prescriptivism. The appearance of a flat contradiction with Kant in the claim that the principle is a hypothetical imperative is illusory. Kant's principle is a categorical law for *pure rational beings* who are autonomously prescribing action guiding rules (maxims) for themselves.[68] For such beings, the desire to ground their moral claims in reason is a given proviso. The

---

[65] Singer (1984), pp. 23–38, quote at 38.

[66] Gewirth (1984), pp. 192–255, quote at 253.

[67] Hare (1963), pp. 123–4; and (1997), ch. 8, pp. 147–65.

[68] Kant (1996), p. 77 [4:426]: 'The question is therefore this: is it a necessary law *for all rational beings* always to appraise their actions in accordance with such maxims as they themselves could will to serve as universal laws?' Foot (1978, quote at p. 163) argues that morality is a system of hypothetical rather than categorical imperatives which a good man accepts because he wants to, not because he has a duty to observe them, arguing that 'it makes no sense to say that "we have to" submit to the moral law, or that morality is "inescapable" in some special way'. However, this type of argument merely shifts the focus of inquiry to what we mean by, and our basis for acclaiming that a person is, 'good' or 'virtuous', but the task of identifying a basis for the moral labels remains.

point of the fundamental prescriptivism is that on such a proviso, the equal right to freedom and well-being is a necessary law.

Kant propounds a single paramount law expressible in three forms. His first formulation of the categorical imperative is: '[a]ct only in accordance with that maxim through which you can at the same time will that it become a universal law' or 'Act as if the maxim of your action were to become by your will a universal law of nature.'[69] In the idea of willing maxims into universal law, Kant's conception of morality allows for much of morality to be contingent on someone's willing, an intentionality, hence being 'made' or posited. But the requirement of universalization[70] is a constraint against arbitrariness which is necessary for rational beings who wish to act purely autonomously; that is, by the dictates of reason rather than external force whether that be a brute fact or considerations exerted by the power of another. Thus, we have the hierarchical structure of norms: posited norms whose creation is subject to and justified by background norms which ultimately hearken back to norms which we can describe as fundamental or categorical because they must be accepted by all rational beings with the desire to act autonomously. Nevertheless, it is true to this account that the categorical imperative requires the actual and contingent willing of maxims to flesh out its content: hence it gives a place to both historical moral judgements and decisions and to principles necessary to the concept of morality in the working out of a full morality.

Kant's second formulation of the categorical imperative states: 'So act that you use humanity, whether in your own person or in the person of any other, always at the same time as an end, never merely as a means.'[71] R.M. Hare understands this as being satisfied by a utilitarian maximization of total preferences in the mode of critical moral thinking because, he claims, that principle treats each person as an end by looking to his or her preference as the yardstick of value and gives each person's preferences equal weight. Much depends on how the humanity in a person is to be regarded. Hare's treatment of it is such that not only may one ignore personal identity in the process of universalization, the very fact of discrete individuality is abstracted away so that one may fuse and sum up everyone's preferences. Taken in isolation, this formulation of Kant's categorical imperative can be understood in Hare's way. However, the character of prescriptivism resting on *individual* willing of maxims

---

[69] Kant (1996), p. 73 [4:421].
[70] For various senses of universalization, see Narveson (1985), pp. 3–44.
[71] Kant (1996), p. 80 [4:429].

into universal law and on the fundamental prescriptions as directed at the reason of individuals, leads to a more traditional understanding of the Kantian categorical imperative. As it is individuals, ultimately, as a matter of brute fact, who exercise intentionality, or will maxims, and not a collective will, the fundamental prescription must satisfy the reason of an individual that recognizes his or her individuality and separateness from others. In such a situation, it is reasonable to legislate maxims that maximize liberty to fulfil individual preferences (rather than maximization of preferences directly) and maxims that advance the realized enjoyment of that liberty, and to do so in a way that respects each individual as an equal. Personhood is a jural concept, referring to the source and bearers of rights in these fundamental prescriptions: it is as sources and bearers of such rights that such individuals are constituted as persons within such a normative system. In turn, the meaning of equal personhood is fleshed out by principles/maxims that are justified by and subject to these fundamental prescriptions. For these reasons, the Kantian categorical imperative is better implemented by a fundamental principle that respects and advances the freedom and well-being of individual human beings as equal persons.

Kant's third formulation of the categorical imperative applies these to regulating maxims in his idea of a 'kingdom of ends': '[a]ll maxims from one's own lawgiving are to harmonize with a possible kingdom of ends as with a kingdom of nature.'[72] By 'kingdom' Kant means 'a systematic union of various rational beings through common laws'.[73] This third formulation shifts the focus from single person moral rationalization to multi-person collective moral rationalization. The categorical imperative itself requires a seeking of a 'systematic union of various rational beings through common laws'.[74] The necessity of common (moral) laws follows from the fact that the categorical imperative is itself abstract and under-determinative; yet, to have any force even for rational persons it must be made concrete with more definite maxims. The under-determinativeness of the categorical imperative gives rise to the possibility of differences even amongst rational autonomous beings. This aspect of it is captured by the Principle of Cooperation postulated above (§2.4.6). And it was argued that this means that one ought to aim at realizing the best understanding of the norm concerned and the fundamental prescriptions.

---

[72]   *Ibid*, p. 86 [4:436].
[73]   *Ibid*, p. 83 [4:433].
[74]   *Ibid*, p. 83 [4:433].

Whilst Kant's project in his *Groundwork* (1996) was to describe what moral laws would be like for purely autonomous rational beings, the point of the fundamental prescriptions is to stress their conditionality for human beings who are only imperfectly autonomous. It has been pointed out that real world institutions, like IPRs, are underpinned by prescriptions. To the extent that we want these prescriptions to have a truly moral character, we have to acknowledge the fundamental prescriptions, including the obligation to seek the best understanding of the norms that knit the past, present and future of these institutions together. This means that for individual institutions at least, the persons operating and using them must act cooperatively under the Principle of Cooperation to the extent that they do want to rely on morality as a resource for making moral claims upon one another. Different institutions have different sets of officials and users, and to the extent that they can be separated from one another, they can ignore the judgements of those others. In a Kantian world of purely autonomous rational beings, these might be knitted in a single 'kingdom'. In the real world, where we act from mixed moral and non-moral motives, and where the presence of non-moral causes for action are likely to mean that institutions diverge in their justifications, the best that can be hoped for are harmonizations of understandings about moral principles in relation to individual institutions: that is, there will be multiple moral 'kingdoms' with different (and shifting) sets of persons constituting them. This is where an exploration of the way different institutions – moral, legal and other social institutions – interlock with one another, and tend to share some underpinning moral norms, is interesting. For it suggests how our fractured moral universe might aim at, and tend to progress towards (even if it does not quite achieve) the moral harmony of Kant's kingdom of ends.

2.5.3   Fundamental Prescriptivism and Human Rights

The fundamental principles generate a '*right*' in the Hohfeldian[75] sense of a claim-right (with a corresponding duty) that everyone else may assert against everyone else when, at the critical level of moral thinking, we weigh how to frame our universalized moral rules. They do not necessarily result in an obligation to act in a certain way because they do not have a direct bearing on action. But they do have an indirect bearing on action through a duty to take that claim into account in making moral determinations. This is the duty to apply the principles to the making and

---

75   Hohfeld (1923).

universalization of more direct moral rules that have their force for us as a result of our having a desire to make claims that depend on there being grounds which have objective rational force. The fundamental principles provide the grounds for our claims about human rights and may thus lay claim to be fundamental human rights principles, much for the same reasons that Gewirth argues that human rights derives from his Principles of Generic Consistency.[76] The equal right to freedom and well-being the fundamental prescriptions support is *the* 'fundamental' right because it lies at the base of all moral decision making regarding the institutions we want to justify. And they are fundamental principles about 'human' rights because the obligation to take these principles into account is one we owe to all other rational beings from whom we want to be able to claim an obligation to cooperate in building our social world.

This is the core idea in the principles of human rights in the Universal Declaration of Human Rights (the 'UDHR'): the civil and political rights to life, liberty, security of person and freedom of expression (Articles 3–21); the social, cultural and economic rights (Articles 22–28); the equality of human persons at the level of determining the fundamental framework for having such rights (Articles 1 and 2); and the recognition of duties of cooperation amongst individuals in a community that are the basis and necessary correlatives of these rights (Article 29). These individual articles are in obvious tension with one another unless they are resolved as limiting one another in the context of supporting a higher overall principle such as this general fundamental right. It is in this context that Article 27 – for both the right to participate in cultural life and share in scientific advances and their benefits, and the right to the protection of the moral and material interests of the authors of scientific, literary and artistic productions – should be interpreted and understood (cf. §4.1.1). Thus, the fundamental principles lead to an embrace of the idea of human rights, with the implication that, if these principles support IPRs, then the claims to IPRs are ultimately grounded in a human right. However, IPRs are in turn subject to the other human rights claims that are based on the equal right to freedom and well-being.

This is the 'general thesis' from fundamental prescriptivism. It claims that, once universal prescriptivism is critically examined, we are rationally led to identify prerequisites for making such a morality work and – if we make the fundamental assumption that we have an ultimate desire to base our moral claims on grounds that respect reason as far as reason is

---

[76] See Gewirth (1982), esp. ch. 1, pp. 41–78; and (1996), esp. ch. 1, pp. 1–30.

capable of providing guidance in such matters – acknowledging that it is rational, then, to prescribe the foregoing set of fundamental principles. Although the way we flesh out these abstract principles depends on the various commitments we have already made and still want to keep, these principles are derived *a priori*. There is a secondary line of argument that can be made, even without deducing *a priori*, from the conditions necessary for universal prescriptivism to work, a particular set of universal fundamental principles. We accept, instead, that a critique of universal prescriptivism leads us to acknowledge that it provides substantive constraint only if there are more fundamental background prescriptions. But we allow that various competing sets of principles may be supported and it is a matter of contingent history which one is embraced. The fact is that we have made in the global context particular historical commitments to the human rights enshrined in the UDHR. Although IP laws operate largely within the territorial boundaries of individual states, the global context is relevant because we are now mandating the IPR institutions on a global scale and we make claims for them in this context. It is the moral dimensions of IPRs as international institutions that we are concerned with when harmonization and reform of IPRs are under examination.

This line of argument is the 'special thesis', in that it argues that, whatever the truth about the general thesis may be, we have in our particular course of history embraced a particular set of principles for the purpose of fashioning our global community. The most fundamental of these are the human rights declared in the UDHR, the encouragement and promotion of respect for which is a purpose and duty of the UN under the United Nations Charter (Articles 1(3) and 55), and which its member countries are bound to take action to achieve (Article 56). The 'general thesis' leads us to the same set of principles that we, as a globalizing community, have in fact specially adopted as the most general common basis for building our international institutions. As this global ethic is ultimately rationalized in a fundamental equal right to freedom and well-being, this right must form the ultimate basis for justifying as well as limiting our claims to IPRs. That is why we must eventually turn our attention to the way IPRs promote and protect liberty and well-being as well as threaten them.

2.6 THE FUNCTION OF MORAL TERMS IN IP LAWS

We return finally to the questions with which we began this long chapter. Moral terminology is used in IP laws and related laws. What do they do?

How are their meanings ascertained? But now, we have answers if universal prescriptivism and the arguments made herein about the pre-requisite prescriptions are correct. Moral words and concepts are used in all general instructions (laws and agreements included) to express the intention that actions purporting to conform to them should be of the appropriate kind – that is, related to the type of activity that that type of term refers to, for example 'kindness' would be about treatment of animals and persons, and 'fair' would be about the relative treatment of persons – and according to prescriptions which can be universalized in a manner consistent with all the other commitments that have to be upheld. The framing of the prescriptions upon which we act is itself subject to an ultimate criterion: not Hare's preference maximization test, but the fundamental principles that we find we must accept if we begin by assuming we want to act according to norms that can be justified by grounds that have objective rational force.

Thus, the intention expressed by the use of these terms is that the persons addressed (and in laws and agreements, this would include the speakers) would ascertain their meaning and apply them in this way. The objection that the speakers did not realize that this was the intention they were expressing (and, indeed may be startled by the consequence) can be met as follows. They would in any case have intended that they wanted the moral terms to be understood as moral words with their implied consequences, even if they have not fully worked out what these consequences are. Thus the speakers (legislators) have to be taken to intend all the implications of universalization of the appropriate types of prescription, including the background principles that enable prescriptions to be made with objective rational force. The advantage of this account of the intention expressed by moral terms is that it enables us to treat the parts of legislations and agreements that contain moral terminology as meaningful. They are not, as logico-positivists would have us believe, meaningless because they do not refer to verifiable factual conditions.[77] It enables us to understand the legislators as expressing a meaningful intention even if we understand that they have not worked out all the implications of their instructions.

Legislators do want to express intentions in this way for various reasons. First, they may want actions to be subject to moral criteria rather than be of a specific type. For example, the 'fair use' or 'fair dealing' clauses of copyright laws express the intention that uses that are fair (and often subject to restrictions specified elsewhere) should be treated as

---

[77] E.g. Ayer (2006), ch. 6, pp. 104–26.

permitted by the law. The legislators may have no more specific conception of what should be permitted than that. Nor would they want to have more specific conceptions of the acts to be so permitted, because the idea of fairness and its implications captures all they want to say. Further, even if they may entertain expectations about how this term would be applied in certain factual conditions, their dominant intention would be to keep faith with the general idea of fairness and its implications. Thus, in a case of conflict between the idea of fairness and the outcome they expect from applying it, the latter is intended to give way. The necessity for this type of interpretation and prescriptive choice by the addressee is not the result of an 'indeterminacy of aim' in the will of the legislator (which is Hart's explanation for the indeterminacy of rules[78]) but the result of the legislator willing a certain mode of ascertaining the meaning of what is said.

A second reason why people may want to express an intention in this way is that even if they do want to be understood in a certain specific way, what they do want to so specify does not exhaust all the considerations and restrictions that they do want applied. An example is the fair use clauses in copyright laws that do have this type of exception or defence. Take section 107 of the US Copyright Act. Various factors are spelled out as having to be considered when determining if a use has been 'fair': the nature of the use, the character of the work, the amount that has been used as compared with the original work, the impact of the use on the market and value of the original work. Even though these are listed, one must still give further content to the idea of 'fairness' because these factors do not indicate how their presence in the facts of each case should affect the outcome, and what their force should be relative to one another (see Chapter 4 at §4.3.4). Another example is the *ordre public* and morality restriction in the EU Biotechnology Directive (which is discussed in a later chapter at §4.7.3). Even though certain uses are defined to be so excluded, this is not exhaustive.

Thirdly, the legislators or parties to the agreement may not agree as to what specific outcomes should pertain as a result of applying a certain rule or clause. One cynical explanation for the use of moral terminology in laws and agreements is that their role is to paper over disagreements to hide a hole where there is essentially nothing. A consequence of this type of understanding is that the addressee who has to apply the rule will have to take it as a licence to give it a meaning that he or she privately thinks is right. The account of moral terms given by Hare allows us to arrive at

---

[78] Hart (1994), p. 128, also Postscript, p. 252.

a less cynical understanding. There is disagreement, sometimes a very deep one, about the outcomes that should pertain. However, there is agreement at least as to the mode of reasoning that should apply: prescriptions should be used subject to universalization and all this implies. This is the way we can understand the moral terms and concepts explicitly and implicitly embedded in Articles 7 and 8 of TRIPS. They appeal to an understanding of equitability and justice and fairness as between producers and users of technology that can be universalized in a manner consistent with the other obligations enjoined by TRIPS.

2.7 MORAL THEORY AND THE MORAL DIMENSIONS OF IPRS

The foregoing makes a conception of justice, the equal right to freedom and well-being, the ultimate ground for justifying basic institutions like IPRs. The implication is that justifiable institutions of property come packaged with responsibilities for justice attached with the rights, and the idea that morality itself is an institution of principles which we establish by universalizing prescriptions which we apply to the various institutions which we have created and want to hold on to. This suggests something about the way that property institutions must be designed if they are to be justifiable. This aspiration towards justice must be built into the very core idea of the property that holders acquire and, thus, must be expressed by its central defining rules or, at least, the rules of ancillary institutions that provide the context for its interpretation, use and reform – that is, its other moral dimensions. This will be explored and expanded in the next chapter, on IPRs' moral dimension of justification.

3. The moral dimension of justification

3.1 JUSTIFICATORY THEORIES AND JUSTICE

3.1.1 Justification and the Equal Right to Freedom and Well-being

Given the theory developed in the last chapter about morality and the way moral concepts work, IPRs must have two features in order to be justifiable. First, IPRs cannot be absolute. The equal right to freedom and well-being that lends support to IPRs also requires that the non-IPR owning public has some form of right of access to the intellectual objects of such rights where this is necessary for the promotion or protection of the liberty and well-being of each individual human being as an equal person. This tension is captured explicitly in the UDHR: in the participation right (Article 27(1)) and the authors' (and, arguably, inventors') protection right (Article 27(2)), regarding the productions of authors and inventors (cf. §4.1.1). The design of the IPRs and their limits must reflect this tension. The second feature of a justifiable IPR regime flows from the way the tension between the protection and participation right is resolved, the way our general principles are given definition, and tends to be revised and refined with new and reformed commitments. This suggests that, given universal prescriptivism, the only way a legislator who intends to create an institution that is justifiable can go about achieving this is to express that intention and build into the rules of that institution the elements that allow such revision. It will be suggested (at §3.6.1) that, in order to do this, moral terms and concepts must be an intrinsic part of the critical rules delimiting the conditions under which the property rights are acquired and the extent of the rights so acquired.

It is not an accident of history that IP regimes like copyright, patents, trade secrets and trade marks employ concepts like fairness or reasonableness in their most critical rules – as in copyright doctrines of fair use or dealing. Such concepts are also built into key provisions of the most important document for globalizing IPRs: TRIPS. These are in the Article 7 reference to 'mutual advantage of users and producers of technological knowledge' and a 'balance of rights and obligations' as part of TRIPS' objectives, and the Article 8 reservation for measures necessary to protect public health and nutrition and to 'prevent abuse of intellectual property rights by right holders' and practices which 'unreasonably restrain trade or adversely affect the international transfer of technology' in its statement of principles. There are also the references to 'normal exploitation', 'unreasonably prejudice' and 'legitimate interests' of right holders (and, sometimes, third parties) in the 'three-stage tests' for exceptions and limitations that member states may make to the IPRs.[1] These types of terms are in the central rules to express the intention that the regimes reflect a justifiable balance between the property (Article 27(2) UDHR) and participation (Article 27(1) UDHR) interests of individuals and to enable the rules of the regime to adjust to reflect ever more refined understanding of this balance, even though authoritative judgements may be required to fix the boundaries. This chapter will develop and refine this justificatory theory.

3.1.2 Other Theories

The main theories offered to justify intellectual property include: Lockean labour theories, Hegelian protection of personhood theories, utilitarianism (and associated economic theories using welfare as the indicia of utility) and justice theories.[2] The claim herein is that the equal right to freedom and well-being, whose fundamental principles form the logical bedrock of all moral reasoning, operate at a deeper level than all these theories and must displace them to the extent that they are inconsistent. Chapter 2 made the case for the fundamentality of these principles. The object of this chapter is to examine how this moral principle throws light on the limitations and weaknesses of these other theories as well as their strengths. The argument is that the right offers a better explanation or resolution of some of the difficulties and mysteries thrown up by traditional justificatory accounts. As the equal right to freedom and well-being that the last chapter maintains is the basis of all moral justification is itself a principle of justice in general, we shall begin by exploring the relationship between the justice of IPRs and their justification.

---

[1] TRIPS, Art. 13 (for copyright), Art. 17 (for trade marks), Art. 26(2) (for industrial designs) and Art. 30 (for patents).

[2] On the theory of Merges (2011), see above Ch.1 at §1.4 (n. 37). On IP and theories of justice, see contributions in Grosseries, Marciano and Strowel (eds.) (2008).

3.2 THEORIES OF JUSTICE AND THE JUSTIFICATION OF INTELLECTUAL PROPERTY

3.2.1 Nozick's Entitlement Theory

Property rights – transferable rights to some form of exclusive control or use of a resource – stand in a peculiar relationship to theories of distributive justice, for they raise the question: Can they be treated as discrete objects of such theories, or are theories about the appropriate nature and extent of such rights crucial constituent elements of theories of justice themselves? It would help in simplifying any inquiry into the nature of justice if one is able to treat the constituents of property rights as the province of a separate inquiry from the justification of property. For, then, the question in a theory of justice would be about how such bundles of rights, taken as given, ought to be distributed. The problem with this approach is that both the rules about acquisition of property, and those about the extent of the property rights acquired, are about distribution of access to resources. The latter may be absolute, excluding everyone but the holder from all entitlements in a good, or limited – allowing that others may have some claim over some aspects of the good.

IPRs, of course, distribute access to the use of certain categories of ideas, and the rights are rarely, if ever, absolute. Copyright and patents are subject to limited terms, after which they become part of the public domain, freely available to all. During their term of protection the exclusive rights of control of the holders are subject to various exceptions. Even the paradigmatic examples of absolute property for lay persons, interests in land, are not truly absolute.[3] Leaseholds and freeholds are not absolute claims to land but, really, claims to bundles of rights in land for a term in time limited, respectively, by determinate periods or periods determinable. The interests in land are often subject to state claims in the form of taxation and to restrictions on use like the requirement to avoid causing nuisance to neighbours or the non-withdrawal of support. Property rights, thus, define the share that the owners *and others* have in a resource. Any theory about how such rights may justly be distributed must be concerned with the nature and extent of such rights, for the ultimate concern of any theory of justice is about the basis for distribution of liberties and goods, and property rights are themselves basic liberties (for they afford freedom from the interference of others in relation to a thing) as well as rules distributing access to

---

[3] Cf. Singer (2000), see esp. ch. 2, pp. 56–94.

goods. The theories of distributive justice of John Rawls[4] and Robert Nozick[5] provide contrasting approaches to the problem.

Nozick forcefully builds a theory of justice on a foundation of individual liberty. He argues that the right terms of justice are those that an association of persons under the assumptions of Locke's state of nature (originally free but without the advantages and protection that an association of persons can provide) would freely accept in exchange for the surrender of that original freedom: this would be the 'night watch-man' minimal state of libertarians, whose role is limited to protection against force on the person, fraud, theft and enforcement of voluntary bargains between members. In such a state, he argues, there is no room for principles of justice requiring any particular pattern of distribution of goods and resources – equal distribution, or Rawls' maximin second principle – because that would require the state to assume a greater role and burden in continually re-ordering society and *re*distributing resources and, hence, being given a greater power to restrict and interfere with individual freedom than the association that would have developed as a result of voluntary bargains that persons in the original state of nature would have made. As a result, he rejects patterned theories of distributive justice and argues, instead, for an entitlement theory: the distribution would be just if it derives from original appropriations under conditions of 'just acquisition' and subsequent transactions were 'just transfers'. He says:

> If the world were wholly just, the following inductive definition would effectively cover the subject of justice in holdings.
>
> 1. A person who acquires a holding in accordance with the principle of justice in acquisition is entitled to that holding.
> 2. A person who acquires a holding in accordance with the principle of justice in transfer, from someone else entitled to the holding, is entitled to the holding.
> 3. No one is entitled to a holding except by (repeated) applications of 1 and 2.
>
> The complete principle of justice would say simply that the distribution is just if everyone is entitled to the holdings they possess under the distribution.[6]

One observation: the appropriate conditions of acquisition and transfer that would make the resultant distribution of access to resources 'just' is never properly defined or investigated. This is significant because it is

---

[4] Rawls (1999).
[5] Nozick (1974).
[6] *Ibid* at p. 151.

extremely difficult (actually, §2.6 heretofore argues that it is impossible) to make fair rules about distribution of resources and freedoms, without actually using evaluative terms and concepts in those rules. The relevant historical conditions of the entitlement theory are '*just* acquisition' and '*just* transfers'. We should ask, 'When are they "just"?' Libertarian theorists may argue that the *transfers* would be just if voluntary – that is, not made under conditions of coercion, mistake or fraud. Even if that is granted, however, there remains the question of when the *acquisition* is 'just' and *what* may be justly acquired. Normative principles are required to identify such conditions.

Nozick begins with the assumptions of a Lockean (not a Hobbesian[7]) state of nature: one in which the law of nature commands that 'no one ought to harm another in his life, health, liberty, or possessions'.[8] He assumes a 'situation in which people generally satisfy moral constraints and generally act as they ought'.[9] Criticism that this is unrealistic will have missed the point of his thought experiment: which is to identify just institutions consistent with the idea of individual liberty by reasoning from what persons rationally pursuing their own ends but generally *ethically observant* would arrive at if free to make arrangements with one another. His point is that the outcome should be instructive about just institutions because this process would conserve the original values. The contrary supposition, that persons are generally weak in their observance of moral strictures and sometimes evil, would not suffice, for we would gain no insights about *just* institutions from the arrangements that such persons would make. Hence, Nozick admits, 'Our starting point then, though nonpolitical, is by intention far from non-moral.'[10] It is instructive to accept his method of reasoning, then, but it ought to be noted that his (and Locke's) initial premises rig the experiment in favour of a libertarian outcome, for they take for granted that natural moral rights are limited to respecting a narrow set of negative liberties only: that one should *not harm* the life, liberty, health and possessions of others. That proposition presupposes that we have a common and binding understanding of what constitutes 'harm', and what the proper bounds of each person's right to life, liberty, health and possessions are. What if these persons in the state of nature are perfectly willing to obey the constraints of morality but are uncertain, or disagree, about what those constraints are? What if both property rights (and rules about their acquisition,

---

7   Hobbes (1996).
8   Nozick (1974), p. 10, citing Locke (1986 at p. 9, section 6).
9   Nozick (1974), at p. 5.
10 *Ibid* at p. 6.

transfer and extent) and the moral grounds for justifying them and their features are themselves not givens but institutions that have to be made in the course of forming these associations?

As regards moral grounds, that is the logical position we are in once we recognize that moral values and principles are neither natural facts nor other cognitive phenomena but are prescriptions which we *make* supervenient upon certain categories of facts and circumstances. What prevents morality from being entirely subjective is the common acceptance that these principles and values must be universalizable and are meant to guide us through both familiar situations and in reasoning through new situations and disputes with one another. The only way these purposes and this criterion can be met is if there is an assumed fundamental set of principles such as those set out in Chapter 2. The result is a more full blooded set of principles and obligations than that assumed by Locke and Nozick. These would extend beyond negative liberties to positive claims upon one another because an understanding that they would not harm each other in their life, health and liberty would not be worth much without the basis for enjoying them. This basis, and any understanding that they would have possessions, depends on cooperation in an association which presupposes that moral claims can be made upon one another for such cooperation. The fundamental principles it would consequently be rational to accept for such cooperation would provide content for the conditions of 'just acquisition' and 'just transfers'.

3.2.2 Nozick and Locke's Proviso

Also illuminating in this regard is Nozick's exploration of a partial answer using Locke's reservation, that there should be 'enough, and as good left in common for others' after the appropriation.[11] Nozick reformulates this as a requirement that, at least, the situation of others should not be worsened by the appropriation.[12] What, though, would constitute making others worse or better off, or (in Locke's terms) would be leaving them with less than 'enough, and as good'? This too requires evaluation of the result, and therefore requires use of more principles than are generated or explicitly assumed by Nozick's account of the derivation of the minimalist state. What is 'as good' or 'enough'? By what criteria are we to assess if an action leaves others worse (or better)

---

[11]   Locke (1986), ch. V, section 26, p. 20.
[12]   Nozick (1974), pp. 174–82.

off? The proviso implicitly assumes a set of values and principles in operation, without which it would be incoherent. If, as argued above, these values and principles are not prior to the association but are themselves the product of the association, we have to ask: What principles and values would persons in this hypothetical state of nature have chosen to adopt as the basis of the association? The answer, it is suggested, would be the fundamental prescriptions, which, though under-determinative in abstract, co-evolve with the institutions and practices freely adopted by these rational individuals to secure their own interests, becoming more detailed as the justification of each institution actually (and contingently) adopted rules out alternative ways of universalizing the fundamental principles. Hence, an appropriation of a resource would leave 'as good' available in the commons only if the others are left as free to realize their own purposes and plans as they were before the appropriation. There would be 'enough' left, if this would enable the others to make and realize their own life plans and purposes to the fullest extent compatible with equality amongst all individuals. Unlike the 'as good' term of the proviso, the 'enough' requirement is not comparative as between the others and the appropriator's position, enjoining equality of opportunity. Instead it acknowledges the independent entitlement of others to opportunity for self-realization.

The 'as good' term leaves open the possibility of the others being left without enough for self-realization. Amongst the freedom to make plans and have purposes that that appropriator would enjoy, is the possibility of becoming an owner of property and thus having some rights over that object for the realization of his other plans. This means that the 'others' must not be worse off in the sense of being less free to become appropriators of similar resources. Nozick acknowledges that, after each appropriation of finite resources such as land, there would be a diminishing range of unclaimed resources to appropriate, which will ultimately result in someone being absolutely deprived. The nth appropriator would be barred from the appropriation by operation of the proviso. But so would the nth − 1 appropriator because his appropriation would make the nth person worse off, and so on in regress until we conclude that even the initial appropriator is unable to obtain property without making others worse off in this way. Nozick suggests that an alternative interpretation of the proviso would permit that others could be left in a position where no further appropriation is possible, as long as these 'others' were not made worse off in terms of resources available for their use. Therefore, one would not be forced to regress from the final appropriation to the conclusion that even the initial appropriation would make others worse off. However, some appropriation, at least in a limited and temporary form, is necessary for the use of a resource and, in the cases where consumption requires that others are absolutely excluded from it (such as when a fruit is eaten), the appropriation has to be absolute though such a right may be restricted to a limited portion of the available resource and conditional on some return to the commons. Hence, this alternative interpretation is simplistic unless we assume that the uses still available to others allow this type of appropriation, though more limited than the appropriation exercisable by the earlier labourers.

This suggests that the Lockean proviso can be met only if, as a condition of appropriation, the activity that results in appropriation (say, combination of labour with resources) must generate something new that adds to the total resources available to all. The acquisition of the property would be just only on the condition that the acquirer makes some return to others that is at least equal in value to that which is taken, either by a restriction on the property over the product that leaves some aspect of it in the commons, or by an assumption of a responsibility to make restitution in some other form. It is possible (as argued below at §§3.2.4 and 3.6.4) that the others-not-worse-off proviso can be met, at least in the case of IPRs, only if the property acquired is not absolute but is limited to give the non-holding public some continuing share in the new resource. Hence, regardless of how individuals decide to transfer what they have acquired, for there can be no just transfer that confers on the transferee more than what may be justly acquired, the public still retains some *rights* (morally if not legally) regarding the object of private holdings.

3.2.3 Rawls' Theory of Justice and the Equal Right to Freedom and Well-being

John Rawls' idea of a 'basic structure' of society provides arguments for making both property and the rules defining the grounds and extent of property, direct subjects of the principles of justice: whether his two principles or any other principle of justice, including the equal right to freedom and well-being. The 'basic structure' of society, according to Rawls, is 'the primary subject of justice'.[13] It comprises 'the way in which major social institutions distribute fundamental rights and duties and determine the division of advantages from social cooperation'.[14]

Rawls' 'basic structure' has two parts: spheres of government corresponding roughly with his first and second principles of justice. First, the

---

[13] Rawls (1999), ch. 2, §10, p. 47.
[14] *Ibid*, ch. 2, §10, p. 50.

constitutional convention and political process which is the subject of the first principle of equal basic liberty. And secondly, 'the distinctions and hierarchies of political, economic and social forms which are necessary for efficient and mutually beneficial social cooperation',[15] which are the subject of the difference principle for social and economic arrangements. He identifies different functions of government (which he refers to as 'branches of government') which are required to discharge the obligation of the difference principle.[16] These include: an 'allocation branch', charged with identifying and correcting departures from efficiency by means of taxation and (more to our present interest) 'changes in the definition of property rights';[17] and a 'transfer branch', which has the responsibility of ensuring the social minimum according to the difference principle. Significantly, the allocation branch may in pursuing efficiency use taxes or subsidies or 'the scope and definition of property rights may be revised'.[18] Finally, there is the 'distribution branch', whose 'task is to preserve an approximate justice in distributive shares by means of taxation and the necessary *adjustments* in the rights of *property*'.[19] Thus, it is not just the allocation of property that is the subject of the principles of justice; those principles also govern the allocation of rights made by the definition and scope of the property institution itself. And these are subject to revision. The principles of justice Rawls espouses are:[20]

> *The First Principle* (the equal basic liberties principle): 'Each person is to have an equal right to the most extensive total system of equal basic liberties compatible with a similar system of liberty for all.' *The Second Principle* (the difference principle): 'Social and economic inequalities are to be arranged so that they are both: (a) to the greatest benefit of the least advantaged, consistent with the just savings principle, and (b) attached to offices and positions open to all under conditions of fair equality of opportunity.'

He argues that these will be chosen by persons under appropriate conditions that we will intuitively accept as fair, for identifying principles to govern their choice and design of institutions in the basic structure of society: the 'original position'.[21] This 'original position' would comprise rational self-interested persons collectively choosing principles of justice

---

15   *Ibid*, ch. 4, §31, p. 175.
16   *Ibid*, ch. 5, §43, pp. 242–51.
17   *Ibid*, p. 244.
18   *Ibid*, p. 244.
19   *Ibid*, p. 245, emphasis added.
20   *Ibid*, ch. 5, §46, p. 266.
21   *Ibid*, ch.1, §4, pp. 15–19.

under certain conditions and restrictions. They are assumed to deliberate from positions of equal ability and possess general knowledge about the world and the way it would work under various possible institutions but must be ignorant of their own particular tastes and the positions they would have. This last assumption is the 'veil of ignorance'.[22] Such persons, he says, would choose his equal basic liberties and difference principles and would give the former lexical priority over the latter – that is, the former would prevail in instances of conflict with the latter. They would also give the difference principle priority over considerations of efficiency and welfare.

An important difficulty with Rawls' theory is the relationship between the first and second principles. Access to the social and economic benefits regulated by the second principle is necessary to practical enjoyment of the liberties governed by the first. It is not rational for persons in the original position to always rank the first before the second when situations raise a conflict between the two. Liberty as something valued is not separable from the economic and social resources that enable one to use it to achieve one's plans and purposes. Freedom of speech and liberty of action, though valuable in the abstract, are of no use to one who faces imminent death because he cannot afford critical life saving medicines or would be valueless to one who, despite expenditure of all his labour and time, can only obtain employment for returns at the barest subsistence level. If one already enjoys some political and civil freedoms, it is rational to give priority to obtaining just economic and social arrangements, even though the former freedoms have not been perfectly attained. This is not to deny Isaiah Berlin's observation that negative liberty (freedom from interference by other human beings) is conceptually distinct from positive liberty (freedom to realize oneself), or that the latter can be abused to justify various forms of tyranny, against which our best protection is a healthy respect for the former.[23] But the fact that an idea can be abused only argues for its employment with due care and regard for safeguards; it does not (and Berlin does not) argue for its rejection. The point, though, is that it is the freedom to have and realize one's own purposes that is the rationally primary value, and *both* positive and negative liberties are means towards ensuring that condition for everyone as equal persons.

---

[22]   *Ibid*, pp. 16–17.
[23]   Berlin (2002), pp. 166–217; see also the 'Introduction' where he clarifies misconceptions and answers critics of his distinction, pp. 30–54.

Others, amongst them Amartya Sen,[24] have noted that the two are inter-related elements of the overall idea of freedom. Our assessment of the relative priority of the matters governed by the two principles changes as each is increasingly realized. The equal right to freedom and well-being encapsulates more accurately than Rawls' two principles the fundamental idea that would rationally be adopted in the original position. It allows us to acknowledge that some well-being concerns – life, health and security – are as pressing as any of the formal political and civil liberties, and may even over-ride some of these as basic rights when urgent, yet give increasing priority to liberty as the level of development of the society or the type of institution whose design is being considered takes us to the point where this right to basic well-being has been satisfied. This is because we can use Gewirth's criterion of degree of needfulness for action to trade off the claims to additive well-being against liberty.[25]

Rawls treats the right to hold personal property as a basic right guaranteed by the first principle.[26] But the nature and design of property as an institution (being about distribution of income and wealth) are the domain of the second principle, and the right to property over means of production does not enjoy the lexical priority of the first over the second of the principles.[27] Yet the two questions are intimately linked. How secure one's property right is depends on the conditions of acquisition and holding and the strength and extent of the exclusivity of control. One example of the way in which IPRs throw up issues illustrating the conflict between these two principles is the moral problem raised when the right to life and access to medical means to health of the very poor confront the claims of patent holders of essential medicines and medical machines.[28] Another is the situation where copyright in a work potentially prevents use which may require extensive verbatim reproduction for the purpose of further speech by others, in commentary, criticism or parody.[29] These laws can, and often do, accommodate these other

---

[24]   Sen (1999). He argues that this idea of freedom is served by promoting capabilities.

[25]   Gewirth (1996), pp. 44–54. Cf. herein at §§2.5.1 and 3.6.3.

[26]   Rawls (1999), ch. 2, §11, p. 53.

[27]   *Ibid*, ch. 1, §11, p. 54: '[L]iberties not on the list, the right to own certain kinds of property (e.g. means of production) ... are not basic; and so they are not protected by the priority of the first principle.'

[28]   Cf. below ch. 8, at §8.4.

[29]   E.g. see *Ashdown v. Telegraph Group plc* [2001] EWCA Civ 1142, discussed in ch. 8 at §8.2.2.

interests. In any case, it is not always necessary that their moral claims must find a solution in the IP laws themselves – one may argue that the moral claim of poor patients should be met by improvement in health supports. However, the point here is that a rational person in the original position anticipating such situations would give these claims a force that would over-ride the IP interests if there are no other means of accommodating them. For, they are as likely to be in the position of the claimant as that of the IP holder and rationally should trade the marginal diminution of the IP right to preserve the pressing interest of the patient and, arguably, the commentator, critic and parodist, because (applying the criterion of degree of needfulness for action), in general, the portion of IP protection forgone would be less necessary to each person's ability to make and realize his or her plans than the need for access to the medical technology or to aspects of the copyright work in these types of instance.

The priority Rawls gives to the equal basic liberties principle is defended on the ground that he intends them to apply only at a stage of development when it is possible to achieve a well ordered society – stable institutions subject to principles of justice.[30] This suggests that Rawls' principles of justice are intermediate (rather than the most fundamental) statements of the requirements of justice. This would be consistent with the observation that Rawls' 'original position' already builds a bias towards egalitarianism in its specification of the veil of ignorance and his assumption that rational persons would be averse to the risk that they may turn out to occupy the position of one of the peoples disadvantaged by the system they have chosen. His 'original position' is a device justified by the idea of reflective equilibrium (see above at §1.5.1) as a method of clarifying intuitive judgements and subjecting them to rational inquiry. His argument is that the restrictions of this position reflect deeper intuitions about fairness that we all find acceptable. However, these conditions of judgement appear fair because they accord with still more basic values in the form of the fundamental prescriptions and the equal right to freedom and well-being. Therefore it is this right which should form the ultimate test for principles justifying and restricting institutions like IPRs and other property rights.

3.2.4 Justice Theory and the Design of Property Rights

The foregoing discussion shows that distributive justice is concerned not just with the assignment of property rights (who owns what resource as

---

[30]   Rawls (1999) at §1, pp. 3–8 and §69, pp. 397–405.

property) but also the way the property institution itself assigns rights over that resource. Nozick is right to point out that ensuring social and economic equality, or any other preferred pattern of distribution, would require state interference with, and restriction of, individual freedom of choice. For, otherwise, free choices by individuals regarding the destruction or disposal of their property will lead to unpatterned distributions. One of Rawls' suggested options for keeping faith with his difference principle is the use of taxation and subsidies to redistribute wealth. The other option allows, at least in part, for an accommodation of Nozick's concerns: design the property that can be justly appropriated in such a way as to give others some continuing rights in aspects of the resource.

In a moral though not necessarily the legal sense, then, both owners and non-owners will have certain *rights* in the resource. This is because the justification of the right to private property, that it is a basic liberty governed by Rawls' first principle, is conditional on a proviso that the extent of the right respects his second principle (fair distribution of resources according to the difference principle), and the latter can be satisfied only if the owner of the property is under an obligation to respect the just claims of others to fair participation in the total resource available to all. This obligation can be accommodated by limitations and provisos in the rules prescribing the extent of the property right but, if this is not (or not adequately) so accommodated, the obligation may continue to require an acknowledgement of the justness of reforms to make such accommodations or obligations to render an adequate return in some other form, one of which would be the support of taxation to enable the required redistribution. The original owner and transferees cannot, then, object that the state sanctioned use by others of those aspects, or limitations on their control and disposition of the resource, constitute unjustified interference in their property rights. This is because their original property acquisition was conditional on a moral obligation to acknowledge the entitlement of others to those aspects in the first place. Of course, then, their liberty with respect to the use or disposal of the resource would not be absolute. Persons devising rules as the fundamental basis for social cooperation with each other would have rational grounds for securing their effective freedom to make and realize personal plans (liberty and well-being) rather than formal liberty in the form of non-interference by others, and hence will favour creating limited rather than absolute private property rights.

Nozick comes closer to this solution, when grappling with the problems raised by the proviso that others should not be made worse off. He speculates that: 'Someone whose appropriation otherwise would violate the proviso still may acquire property *provided he compensates the others* so that their position is not thereby worsened; unless he does compensate these others, his appropriation will violate the principle of justice in acquisition and will be an illegitimate one.'[31] He also adds that such a theory of acquisition would require 'a more complex principle of justice in transfer'[32] in that what may not be done by acts of acquisition should not be achievable by way of transfers. He says:

> Each owner's title to his holding includes the historical shadow of the Lockean proviso on appropriation. This excludes his transferring it to an agglomeration and excludes his using it in a way, in coordination with others or independently of them, so as to violate the Lockean proviso by making the situation of others worse than their baseline situation.[33]

This is tantamount to admitting that the property right (if it is to be justifiable) comes bundled with an assumption by the owner (whether initial acquirer or subsequent transferee) of a responsibility to respect the initial conditions of justice. This is the Trojan horse in the libertarian schema which allows redistributive and other continuing considerations to operate. The property that may be justly acquired always comes with strings attached to provisos that require that persons who would defend or justify their holdings under that institution would also have to admit the responsibility to cooperate to ensure that the institution should remain legitimate, whatever our understanding of the grounds of that legitimacy would be. Nozick tries to reconcile this limited form of property right with his entitlement account of just holdings by arguing that, given these restrictions on the property rights, the rights are not 'over-ridden' externally because '[c]onsiderations internal to the theory of property itself, to its theory of acquisition and appropriation, provide the means for handling such cases'.[34] But these considerations may – depending on the theory of justice that prevails – require an obligation to respect the claim of others to some share in some aspect of that object of property, to allow restrictions to ensure competitive conditions, to admit the legitimacy of claims to redistribution in the form of taxation or some other means of returning benefits to the association. Nozick seems to assume that the Lockean proviso and the considerations regarding the terms of acquisition will be minor, but it will be argued later (at §3.6) that, especially with regards to IPRs, they play a very large role.

---

[31] Nozick (1974) at p. 178, emphasis added.
[32] *Ibid*, p. 179.
[33] *Ibid*, p. 180.
[34] *Ibid*, pp. 180–81.

Some conclusions can be drawn from the foregoing discussion of justice theory and the justification of property about the implications for the design of IP institutions. As with all property, IPRs are part of the Rawlsian 'basic structure of society' because they distribute rights of access to, and use of, critical resources for liberty and well-being. They are thus subject to the principles of justice that rational persons would choose for the design of institutions in that 'basic structure'. The key idea though, is the equal right to freedom and well-being and its fundamental principles because these are prior to Rawls' two principles. Nevertheless, both these sets of ideas require that the interests that can be appropriated must be shared. But, as this condition of sharing is a moral idea (justice) that is always being refined and developed, the institution is subject always to the possibility of reform. The way to allow this and express the idea is to build into the key terms of the institution's rules and ancillary laws moral terms because such terms, by requiring the search of appropriate universalizable principles, ultimately rest on the equal right to freedom and well-being. Such terms are potential resources for transformation of the institution, to reflect the aim of promoting and protecting the liberty and well-being of all individuals as equal persons. Before turning to the question of how IPRs promote and protect that right, we should consider the main moral theory Rawls rejected in favour of his own two principles of justice and which forms one of the most common justifications offered for intellectual property: utilitarianism.

3.3 CONSEQUENTIALIST ARGUMENTS FOR IPRS AND FREEDOM AND WELL-BEING

3.3.1 Consequentialism and IP Laws

'Consequentialism' and 'utilitarianism' are sometimes treated as interchangeable, though the former is broader, embracing ethical theories that make some preferred result of actions, practices or institutions the key criterion of approbation, whilst the latter is a family of theories that provide a prime example of consequentialism, adopting as their main criterion the maximization of an aggregate (total or average amount) of the preferred desiderata – pleasure, happiness, satisfaction, wealth, and so on. The consequentialist strain in the justification of IPRs is often explicit in the laws – the US Congress' constitutional powers to enact federal copyright and patent laws are given 'to promote the Progress of Science and useful Arts'.[35] TRIPS declares that its objectives are that IPRs 'should contribute to the promotion of technological innovation and to the transfer and dissemination of technology'.[36] The preambles to the various EU IPR related directives are replete with such references. The Information Society Directive[37] declares that harmonization of copyright to facilitate the needs of the information society must 'take as a basis a high level of protection, since such rights are crucial to intellectual creation'[38] and '[T]he protection of copyright and related rights is one of the main ways of ensuring European cultural creativity and production receives the necessary resources and of safeguarding the independence and dignity of artistic creators and performers.'[39]

Utilitarian and economic wealth maximization justifications must discharge the burden of explaining how, in the case of IPRs, these goals are compatible with the restriction of competition and consumption that these exclusive property rights impose. Some argue that 'intellectual and industrial property may be viewed as a specific competitive restriction on the production level for the benefit of competition on the innovative level'[40] and they are, 'as a rule, only temporary or specific competitive restrictions which in the long run serve to improve the wealth of a competitive society'.[41] This may be because, provided the property rights are suitably designed and limited, they can be made to 'internalize externalities when the gains of internalization become larger than the costs of internalization'.[42] Such justification is contingent on net welfare gains from the institution, a matter for empirical inquiry which is not easily resolved (cf. §3.3.3 below). The objection to consequentialism as a justificatory theory for IPRs, though, is just that the equal right to freedom and well-being explains why there is a strong consequentialist strain in IP laws whilst supplying the deficiencies of utilitarianism.

---

[35]   Constitution (US), Art. 1, s 8(8).
[36]   TRIPS, Art. 7.
[37]   Directive 2001/29/EC of 22 May 2001. See also: Directive 91/250/EEC of 14 May 1991, 6th recital; Directive 96/9/EC of 11 March 1996, recitals 7–12; Directive 98/44/EC of 6 July 1998, recitals 1 & 2.
[38]   Directive 2001/29/EC of 22 May 2001, recital 9.
[39]   *Ibid*, recital 11.
[40]   Lehmann (1985), pp. 525–40, at p. 538.
[41]   *Ibid* at p. 540.
[42]   Demsetz (1967), cited by Spector (1989) at 271.

3.3.2   Consequentialism versus the Equal Right to Freedom and Well-being

No reasonable ethical theory may disregard the consequences of its maxims or strictures. However, if the equal right to freedom and well-being and its fundamental principles are truly at the bedrock of morality as an institution, the desiderata that should be promoted are our freedom (understood as the liberty to make and pursue our own plans, projects and purposes) and our well-being (at least in as far as this is necessary for the real capacity to enjoy that liberty) rather than pleasure, or happiness, or any other utilitarian candidate. This is because, unless their use in such a criterion is treated as axiomatic, we may well ask: Why ought we accept these as ultimate guides for action, or grounds for claiming an entitlement to the cooperation of others? Many of us pursue pleasure but the requirement that we *ought* to pursue it is not part of the nature of the thing: if there is a requirement, it is a supervenient rule we have grafted upon nature by accepting a social function to that effect. The sceptic's open question challenge remains: Why should we treat its pursuit as obligatory? Some of these putative units of value appear plausible only because further moral valuation is implicitly built into the ideas. 'Happiness' as the criterion in eudaimonistic utilitarianism is an example. If 'happiness' is not treated as the same thing as pleasure or some sensible condition, and if, with Aristotle, we regard it as meaning some condition of life or being that rationally deserves approbation,[43] that form of utilitarianism turns out to be question begging. It is the grounds for such approbation that is critical to its meaning. This sceptical challenge forces one to go deeper in moral reasoning to the point where we have to admit that there is no basis for moral strictures without our first prescribing a principle. If we want the principles so prescribed to do the job of providing objective guidance with force for us as rational persons when determining what to do and settling disputes between persons, we reach that fundamental point in moral reasoning where, as argued in Chapter 2, we must rationally prescribe and commit to the fundamental principles for cooperative action with others. Hence, these principles and their objects are more fundamental in moral reasoning than the usual utilitarian candidates.

The other reason why utilitarianism ought to be rejected as a candidate for the ultimate criterion is given by Rawls: it disregards the separateness of persons by aggregating the preferred desideratum and making the

---

[43]   Aristotle (1976), Bk I, pp. 75–6 (1097b22–1098a27).

evaluation depend on the sum, total or average.[44] We have seen that the claims for cooperation in morality as an institutional project are made ultimately and irreducibly to individual persons (§2.4.3) and this gives everyone a rational reason to prescribe for the respect of each human individual as an equal person and of equal fundamental value (§2.4.4). The respect for that individuality, captured by the idea of equal personhood as regards the development of a moral framework for cooperation, is destroyed by utilitarianism's aggregative method of assessing consequences. In *A Philosophy of Intellectual Property*, Peter Drahos argues that we should reject a proprietarian approach to IPRs – one that treats them as sources of entitlement in themselves; rather, he says, they are pragmatic means to serve larger ends and they should be regarded instrumentally.[45] Instrumentalism may be strictly utilitarian. This, he appears to reject: 'But the instrumentalism we have in mind amounts to more than just a cost–benefit analysis, or asking the economic efficiency question or a simple means-to-ends approach ... They should also be driven by moral feeling rather than driving out moral values.'[46] Drahos has described his instrumentalism as having a deeply humanistic basis.[47] The equal right to freedom and well-being is just such a humanistically instrumental theory that supplies the justificatory rationale for and purpose of IPRs. It explains why we need IPRs as well as why we ought to restrict the entitlement to IPRs.

3.3.3   Economics and the Equal Right to Freedom and Well-being

The argument made here, that the equal right to freedom and well-being provides the proper ultimate criterion for the justification of IPRs, is not intended to deny the value of economic analysis or the necessity of empirical work on the economic impact of IPRs. Indeed, it explains why so much of IPR policy is driven by consequentialist reasoning – net economic benefits matter because these would constitute an expansion of the practical liberty that every individual may enjoy because they would have more options. It cannot be assumed, however, that stronger IPRs will always lead to net social gain. The results of empirical investigations as to the consequences of IP laws seem to be equivocal.[48] Besides, other economic analysts have noted that in the case of IPRs transaction costs

---

[44]   Rawls (1999) at §5, pp. 19–24 and §30, pp. 163–5.
[45]   Drahos (1996), ch. 9.
[46]   *Ibid*, p. 214.
[47]   *Ibid* at ch. 9; see esp. pp. 214–15.
[48]   See e.g. Machlup (1999); Penrose (1951).

may lead to less than optimal levels of creativity. Landes and Posner (2003) note:

> The more costly property rights are to transact over – and we have seen that intellectual property rights are likely to be highly costly to transact over – the greater the danger that allowing goods that are in the public domain to be privatized will have inefficient results. In the extreme case, if transaction costs were prohibitive, allowing the public domain to be privatized would eliminate it as a source of inputs into future intellectual property created by anyone other than the owner of the particular bit of formerly public, now privatized intellectual property.[49]

Analysis and empirical investigation of these correlations and tradeoffs are very much required and have much to contribute to our understanding of when an IPR is justifiable and how they should be structured even if we do assume this moral basis for IPRs. By their nature, they must always be tentative, subject to new tests and results, and new investigations when the laws have been modified. The nature of empirical inquiry offers a further reason why IPRs should be framed with moral terms and concepts in their key rules. Empirical conclusions are always provisional – always subject to new and better evidence. Therefore, one must make institutions in the light of the best evidence available but always before firm conclusions can be drawn. How is one to do this though? The answer suggested by the investigation into ethics is that, for basic institutions like property in ideas, the aspiration towards justice and legitimacy must be built into and expressed in the design of the institutions – in other words, moral terms and concepts must form key parts of the conditions for acquisition of rights in ideas and in the rules qualifying and limiting those rights.

3.4 LOCKEAN THEORIES AND THE EQUAL RIGHT TO FREEDOM AND WELL-BEING

3.4.1 Desert, Entitlement and Lockean Justification

The theories of Locke and Hegel have been fertile grounds for theories of justification for intellectual property rights.[50] Some amalgamate two or more of these theories. Horacio Spector attempts to resolve the apparent incompatibility of consequentialist and deontological theories of IPRs by

---

49   Landes and Posner (2003) at pp. 31–2.
50   E.g. Hughes (1988–89); Shifrin (2001).

distinguishing between 'structural' and 'positional' rules of property.[51] 'Structural rules' define the bundles of rights and obligations to be distributed amongst different individuals: answering questions about the extent of and exceptions to the property right. These, he says, should be governed with reference to economic theory and the goal of efficiency. 'Positional rules' define how such bundles of rights and obligations ought to be distributed, answering the question: 'Who owns the right?' These, he says, should be governed by the Lockean theory of property. These theories are incomplete because they typically ask us to take for granted certain value propositions – certain grounds for desert, entitlement, goals – as axiomatic or self-evident. If the bases for these norms are questioned we ultimately reach the fundamental point for prescription where the fundamental principles leading to the equal right to freedom and well-being will be preferred as the basis for moral rule making.

3.4.2   Critique of Locke's Theory of Property

Locke proposes that we acquire property over previously unowned resource by labouring on it. As we own our own labour, the mixing of that labour with the resource to produce something new results in the labourer's ownership of self extending to ownership in the product.[52] Once we strip Locke's account of its theistic metaphysical assumptions, the problems become obvious. In what way does one own even one's body and its labour? Certainly, we are mostly in effective control of our bodies and their actions. However, how do we, in the state of nature (i.e. in the absence of human associations and human rules for such associations), acquire rights against other people interfering with our bodies and our control of them? Why does the process of combining that labour with a resource lead to ownership of the product? As Robert Nozick asks: Why does the labourer not lose the labour instead of gaining the product instead?[53] These questions expose the need for a background theory about desert or entitlement which assumes ethical principles for identifying desert or entitlement. The need for a cooperative association and the set of principles that define the purpose and justification of such an association and its institutions must form the foundational premises for answering these questions.

Locke begins his argument with the premiss that the world was originally given by God to mankind in common. This bequest is

---

[51]   Spector (1989).
[52]   Locke (1986), ch. V, pp. 19–31.
[53]   Nozick (1974), pp. 174–8.

purposeful for, in conjunction, God 'hath also given them reason to make use of it to the best advantage of life and convenience'.[54] This purposive background is critical for it provides the major premiss for the argument that as appropriation is necessary for use by, and benefit of, any particular person, there must be property rights and some way of acquiring them. He uses the example of gathering fruits from un-owned land, and argues that the labour that distinguishes the gathered fruit from those on the trees must entitle the labourer to them, for, if the consent of others is a necessary incident of appropriation, 'man had starved, notwithstanding the plenty God had given him'.[55] This is an entitlement argument in that it stipulates circumstances for acquisition not as reward for merit but because this serves some given purpose which is normative. We can also identify another strain of argument in Locke's account, based on desert. The property acquisition is reward for merit; because man, in obedience to the command of God and his reason to improve the earth for the benefit of life, laboured on it, he 'thereby annexed to it something that was his property, which another had no title to, nor could without injury take from him'.[56] The obligation to labour to improve on nature and the incident of approbation and reward for that activity all require the presence of someone's intentionality to assign these functions to the set of conditions. For Locke, this intentionality is supplied by an assumption of a purposeful Creator, ascribing deontic purpose to nature.

However, these initial deontic obligations are explained rather than assumed in the derivation of the equal right to freedom and well-being and its fundamental principles. The fundamental point for moral reasoning takes the place of the state of nature, but it is not a point in history, not even a hypothetical one, but a real original point in practical reasoning reached every time we inquire into the basis of morality after the sceptical challenge has disposed of all naturalistic grounds for norms. Here one realizes the necessity of principles for guiding us in our cooperative association with others, and the necessity of willing prescriptions for these principles. The resultant equal right to freedom and well-being supplies the background justification and purpose of property institutions: the promotion and protection of the liberty, and well-being necessary to enjoy that liberty, of each human individual as an equal person. These background principles explain why we should accept the rightness of some degree of exclusive control and disposal of a resource

---

[54]   Locke (1986), ch. V, para. 25, p. 19.

[55]   *Ibid*, ch. V, para. 27, p. 20.

[56]   *Ibid*, ch. V, para. 31, p. 22. The entitlement and desert–labour strains of argument in Locke's account are identified by Becker (1977) at ch. 4, pp. 32–56.

where this is necessary for the sustenance of life and liberty, for this type of appropriation suitably restricted promotes liberty and well-being for all as equals. The restrictions necessary to promote and protect that liberty and well-being also explain Locke's proviso.

3.4.3 The Lockean Proviso

As noted above (at §3.2.2), satisfaction of the Lockean proviso (that there be 'enough, and as good' remaining after appropriation) on its own does not supply sufficient justification for a proprietary claim. For, if one cannot control or retain exclusive holding of a thing in the absence of cooperation of others in an institution conferring private rights of control, the questions remain, even if no prejudice is caused to others by the acquisition of the right: Why should others cooperate in this way? Why shouldn't the creator or labourer lose the product of his or her efforts instead? Some positive justification for the institution is required, and we have been exploring the equal right to freedom and well-being as such a basis for private property rights in ideas. The proviso remains significant, though, for the existence of prejudice or harm to others adds to the justificatory burden. It is not enough, then, to show that some general gain to all individuals may be obtained in terms of added liberty and well-being from such an institution. There is the further burden to show that such gains may be obtained without prejudice to the liberty and well-being of others, or may be obtained in a way which justly compensates those individuals prejudiced.

It would appear that the proviso cannot be satisfied by simple appropriation of the thing laboured upon. Locke argues that in the state of nature which is the condition for first appropriation, there could be 'still enough, and as good left' for others because there would be more than those others could use, 'For he that leaves as much as another can make use of does as good as take nothing at all.'[57] As noted above (at §3.2.2), the only way that this no-prejudice proviso can be met with regards to physical objects is if the property acquirer returns something to the others either by way of rights to enjoy a certain part or aspect of what has been produced or by an obligation to make returns to the commons by other means. This obligation to make commensurate returns can be facilitated by the property institution itself, through limitations on the exclusive rights giving rights to use of or the benefit of it in some way, or by an assumption by the property owner of obligations in some

---

[57] Locke (1986), ch. V, para. 31, p. 22.

other dimension to pay tax or use the property or the benefit he derives from the appropriation in some way for the common good. Keeping faith with the Lockean proviso, when physical objects are concerned, thus requires that the appropriator assumes moral obligations which are discharged through one or other of the moral dimensions of the property institution. At first sight it would appear that, where ideas are concerned, IP institutions may be designed in such a way as to avoid such prejudice to others, as ideas do not exhaust with use and are non-exclusive in employment. Despite appropriation of concepts with new elements, the appropriation rules may be designed to leave others with continued access to what was publicly available before the property right was acquired. (Patents are granted only for inventions which are novel and non-obvious and are infringed only if the claimed items which meet these criteria are made or used.) This may be thought to support strong, perhaps absolute, property claims for items suitably identified and isolated. Adam Moore[58] argues for a copyright type causal borrowing infringement rule which leaves room for new rights to be acquired by subsequent creators who arrive at the same result using pre-existing material and their own independent efforts of creation. But, under the Lockean theory he develops, the acquisition and exclusion of the IP object are justified if the situation of others would not be worse off compared with the situation before the acquisition, and, in the case of rights over creations which are strictly limited to what was contributed, the others would not be worse off (according to Moore) because they would not have had the benefit of the contribution before anyway. He then abandons traditional defences based on trading off the incentive (favouring stronger proprietary control) and dissemination (favouring public access) goals of IPRs, such as the idea/expression distinction and fair use exception for copyright and the first sale defence for patents, and, instead, would confer perpetual rights in the created elements.[59] This argument is unsatisfactory because the Lockean proviso on its own cannot provide a sufficient justification for IPRs because taking an IP object is not a simple matter of taking possession of a physical object and then demanding, of others who would have a share in it, that they justify their claims. Instead, in order for the control to be even feasible, the putative owner would have to demand the *cooperation of those others* in a system of restraint (a *prima facie* prejudice of liberty and well-being) and, therefore, it is the putative owner who would have to justify his

---

[58]   Moore (2001) at ch. 5, pp. 103–19.
[59]   *Ibid* at ch. 7, pp. 147–79.

claims to such cooperation. The right to equal liberty and well-being, it will be asserted below at §3.6, justifies this by requiring a tradeoff of protection for access.

3.5 HEGELIAN JUSTIFICATIONS OF PROPERTY

Hegel's insight is that institutions and their justifying principles evolve within history and that property rights serve personal realization.[60] Our concern for the liberty and well-being of each person may give us reason to differentiate types of property right according to how they relate to our autonomy and the level of protection we afford to them. Margaret J. Radin,[61] suggests that there are grounds for added protection to be given for property rights in things we have that are essential to realizing our personhood: '[T]he personhood perspective generates a hierarchy of entitlements: the more closely connected with personhood, the stronger the entitlement.'[62] Jeremy Waldron argues that the Hegelian justification of property rooted in the realization of personhood through the need for people to have property for the development and exercise of their liberty also supports a moral general right that all human beings have, by virtue of their being human persons, including the unpropertied, to have property.[63] The focus on the way social recognition of the nature and boundaries of the self and its realization leads to a right to property that is necessary for personhood is a contribution made by Hegelian theories of property. The equal right to freedom and well-being leads to the same conclusions whilst remaining Kantian in character because it asserts central core imperatives identifiable by reason. Kant allows for willed moral rules (his 'maxims') if they are consistent with his categorical imperative;[64] subject to this universal consistency, though, it seems plausible that a number of sets of more definite institutions and hence more refined interpretations of these moral rules can be made to realize his kingdom (total system of moral rules) of persons regarded as ends rather than purely as means.

One need not assume that these social functions for personhood and property began with persons actually being in Rawls' original position

---

[60] Hegel (1967).

[61] Radin (1993), ch.1, pp. 35–71, a reprint of Radin, 'Property and Personhood' 34 *Stanford Law Review* 957–1015 (1982).

[62] *Ibid* at p. 53.

[63] Waldron (1988) at ch. 9, pp. 323–42.

[64] Kant, *Groundwork* (1996), pp. 42–108, see discussion above at §2.5.2.

and asking: What are the ideal principles of justice for such cooperation and what are the best institutions for realizing these principles? Things happen, evolve or develop, and only later when our social structures have reached a sufficiently sophisticated degree of development do we actually ask such questions. But the continued existence of these institutions of personhood and property and their boundaries is the product of continuing cooperation in such collective intentionalities. The exact boundaries of these concepts are often in contention, and the implicit functions on which they are premissed have to be reconstructed out of the dispositions and regular set of expectations which Searle has called 'the Background'.[65] It may be added, though, that in deciding how these basic structures are to be constructed, or reconstructed, and when asking if we ought to continue to maintain some of these as they are, we ask ourselves normative questions about the ideal principles for such cooperation. It is the fact that we have to continue to cooperate that forces us to review the principles of that cooperation and, in the light of those principles, review the things we cooperate about. If they are made by human persons, they can be re-made, and that is why we do ask if they can be justified and are consistent with the principles of justice.

3.6   FREEDOM AND WELL-BEING AS THE FOUNDATION FOR IPRS

3.6.1   Moral Terms and the Justification of IPRs

It was suggested in the last chapter (at §2.6) that, because morality itself is a continuously developing project that requires that we review and reformulate and refine the grounds of our actions and cooperation, any aspiration towards justice must be built into the very core of our basic institutions, like the property that holders may acquire and, thus, must be expressed by its central defining rules or, at least, the rules of ancillary institutions that provide the context for its interpretation, use and reform – that is, its other moral dimensions. This can be done only if moral concepts and terms are used in these rules. Descriptive terms alone will not be sufficient to perform this function because, even if it is possible to perfectly work out a particular conception of the good and the right and then use descriptive words to put that conception into effect, this will fail to take into account the implication of universal prescriptivism – if it

---

[65]   Searle (1995), ch. 6, pp. 127–47; see discussion herein, ch. 2 at §2.4.8.

provides the right meta-ethical account of morality – that our moral conceptions are always being refined and revised as we adopt new institutions and reform current ones. Although universalization is a constraint on the principles we can uphold, those principles are always provisional on our being willing to prescribe them as the basis for the various institutions we continue to maintain. Knowing this, we can cast these rules in purely descriptive terms to favour one specific conception of the good and right, only if we intend consistency with that conception to take priority over consistency with legitimacy in general. It is, however, because the primary intention is that the institution should aspire to justice and fairness, that we use ineluctably moral words to express that idea, so that the addressees of the rules (judges and subjects) should understand that the institution should be interpreted and applied consistently with this aspiration even if that means that the particular ideas that the legislators had of what such institutions should do in order to be just may have to be ignored if there is an inconsistency.

Moral words and concepts serve this function because we understand them to direct us to act according to prescriptions which we can universalize by applying them consistently with the features of that institution and those of others that we intend to continue to uphold. This has the effect of making us continually make accommodations between these institutions by reforming them and by revising our understanding of what justice requires. This does not deny that legislators may, *as a matter of law*, validly make property institutions whose rules have purely descriptive and technical meanings; it only suggests what *ought* to be done if the institution is to be legitimate. The strings attached to the property we want to justify are moral strings, not legal ones. But, as they are attached to the institution, if their requirements are not expressed by the institution itself, the responsibility to aspire to justice then falls on the duty bearers to discharge that responsibility through the other moral dimensions related to that institution: acceptance of interpretative avenues of reforms where the law allows judicial discretion to reform the institution, exercise of rights in a manner consistent with the underlying justificatory principles and, ultimately, pursuit of reform through new legislation. It is to facilitate the discharge of this responsibility that the legal rules of the other dimensions of the institution – that of interpretation, exercise and reform – are also designed with crucial moral terms and concepts in their most critical rules. It should be noted that this feature of the theory is independent of acceptance of the equal right to freedom and well-being or any of its underlying fundamental principles as a particular account of the essential content of morality. It assumes only that morality is prescriptivist and that we are committed to universalizing our prescriptions by rendering our institutions consistent with our core principles, whatever they happen to be. Thus, the use of moral terms in the core IPR rules and the other moral dimensions of the institution would be necessary features of universal prescriptivism, even if we hold that the principles we actually embrace are contingent and ultimately arbitrary.

However, the additional and separable argument that is being made here is that the equal right to freedom and well-being lies at the most fundamental basis for justifying IPRs, either because its fundamental principles are rationally necessary for the scheme of morality as a social institution to do its work of guiding us in moral deliberations and in resolving fundamental disputes about the basis for cooperation and association with objective rational force, or (if this is rejected, and we hold that ultimate principles are necessarily contingent) because it lies at the root of the scheme of human rights principles that we have in fact embraced as the basis for cooperation in establishing global order (cf. §2.5.3). If correct, then, justification of IPRs imports an aspiration towards justice, requires that such institutions should promote and protect our right as equal persons to fundamental liberty, and such access to resources for well-being as are necessary for the realization of that liberty. The implications of this idea, for the types of IPR we may have and their structure, are explored in this section.

3.6.2   The Nature of Intellectual Property

The justification of a type of institution should plainly begin with its identification. It is a start that we can say that IPRs confer private individual rights of control over certain types of information or ideas. Patents grant inventors' rights to their inventions. Copyright gives authors and their assignees exclusive rights in literary, musical, dramatic and artistic, and other related works and productions. Trade marks and unfair competition or passing off laws protect commercial entities' right to certain uses of commercial indicia. However, not all information or ideas are subject to IPRs. In fact, most information and ideas are not: languages as a whole and their elements, scientific theories and laws and mathematical methods and theorems in their abstract form, news and history, conventions, customs, religious beliefs, most social institutions like family, state, and law and money. However, the list of types of IPR being created is getting longer. In TRIPS, which is responsible for much of the global dispersal and enlargement of IPRs beyond the Western nations that is the original home of these IPRs, there are – in addition to requiring protection of the four exemplar IPRs of trade secrets,[66] trade marks,[67] patents[68] and copyright and related rights[69] which will be dealt with in the next chapter – the mandatory extension of copyright protection to computer programs[70] and compilations of data,[71] and requirements for protection of semi-conductor chip layout designs,[72] design rights, plant variety rights (if plants are not protected under patents or an effective *sui generis* system or any combination thereof),[73] and geographical indications.[74] There are non-TRIPS items which have their proponents for global protection: utility models, protection regimes for traditional knowledge and folklore.

This enlargement and encroachment of the realm of IPRs onto abstract objects not previously subject to them raises more than a definitional problem. The fact is: any idea that makes or can contribute to the making of our social reality is potentially susceptible of this type of appropriation. Although, historically, only certain types of idea have been subject to this type of appropriation thus far, the fact that the realm of such forms of appropriation has been expanding makes it exigent that we have a justificatory account that explains why certain types of information and ideas should be subject to the control and disposition of private individuals and others not. Thus, one writer posits that the subject matter with which intellectual property law is concerned is the entire realm of 'human knowledge'.[75] It seems, then, that, from the perspective of one attempting to frame a justificatory account of the institution, the private rights of exclusion that typify what we think of when we speak of IPRs are only the tip of the ice-berg. The institution, by non-coverage of certain matter, by limitations on the duration and extent of such protection of exclusive private control, also determines which types of information and ideas remain in the public domain, accessible to all. Hence, *IPRs confer public rights or privileges of access* as well as private rights of exclusion. Seen in this way, the IPR institutions are about *all* ideas and information, though they only make some of them capable of private

---

[66]   Art. 39 TRIPS.
[67]   Art. 15–21 TRIPS.
[68]   Art. 27–34 TRIPS.
[69]   Art. 9–14 TRIPS.
[70]   Art. 10(1) TRIPS.
[71]   Art. 10(2) TRIPS.
[72]   Art. 35–38 TRIPS.
[73]   Art. 27(3)(b) TRIPS.
[74]   Art. 22–24 TRIPS.
[75]   Caenegem (2002) at p. 326.

appropriation. This has several implications for the way we approach the question of their justification. First, if the institution of property rights in tangible objects has a place in Rawls' idea of the basic structure of society that is to be governed by principles of justice, IPRs have at least an equal claim to similar treatment. For, the institution by positive protection and by omission distributes access, and control of access, to the use and development of every idea that makes up our social reality. The technology we have, our social institutions, how we see ourselves, the language and conceptual resources that enable us to review these things, and so on, have a social basis: and the creation and control of some of the ideas that make up the basis of this reality are the subject of IPRs. These must belong to the 'basic structure' of society.

Secondly, the way we think of the realm of IPRs, the public domain, and the commons has to be reformulated. The public domain and the commons are often used interchangeably with one another. But, under this conception, the institution of IPRs is a means of distributing the resources of ideas and information in society, comprising both the allocation of private rights of exclusion and public enjoyment of common access. The commons, then, is the entirety of all ideas and information: comprising the public domain *and* aspects of objects subject to private rights. The inclusion of objects of private exclusion in the idea of a commons is paradoxical only at first sight. The availability of a commons for public use actually implies that, at least temporarily, individuals in the public may use it in ways that exclude others from some aspect of it: pastures as commons work only if one's animals may graze, public parks can be enjoyed if one may walk over, rest or picnic on them. Does the argument for protection of the person and private property rights in tangible things extend, though, to property in ideas and allocation of resources in the intellectual domain? We must consider the characteristics of ideas and the implications of property on them for the promotion and protection of liberty and well-being.

3.6.3   The Relationship between IPRs and Freedom and Well-being

One obvious way by which property in ideas may expand the liberty of at least the owners is the control and manipulation they extend to owners over part of the world around them. Equally obviously, though, this freedom and power are obtained at the expense of restriction of others: for the rights of owners is constituted by correlated duties of restraint on non-owners.[76] This tension poses the central dilemma for any institution that allocates ideas as a resource if, as this work argues, the right of human individuals as equal persons to liberty, and the well-being necessary to enjoy that liberty, is the true principle of justice and moral justification.

This tension and these questions are not unique to justification of property in ideas. The extension of liberty of individuals by rights of protection with a correlated duty of restraint on the part of others is also characteristic of legal protection of the person and property over tangible things. Ideas, though, have three characteristics which differentiate them from land and movable property, that have a bearing on the answers we give to these questions. First, they are intangible, which makes them non-susceptible to physical control after their release to the public. Secondly, they are not exhausted by use, with the result that exclusion of others is not a naturally necessary incident of their use. And, thirdly, they play a constitutive role in our social world – they are made up of and are building blocks of our social reality. Each of these characteristics has its bearing on freedom and well-being. Like the person in Nozick's example[77] who pours tomato juice into the ocean, the contribution of authors (and other creators) who have introduced their creations to the intellectual domain share the feature that the product ceases to be susceptible of practical physical control. Of both, the question may be asked: Why shouldn't one lose the product of that labour, instead of have one's rights extended into it? Rights are creatures of normative systems: existing when participants accept or are bound by their tenets to recognize the entitlement with corresponding duty bearers.[78] Legal systems generate legal rights, moral rights are derived within moral systems. Hence, social institutions may enable control where brute force is powerless. Would such institutions be consistent with, or even be required by, the goal of promoting liberty and well-being?

In Nozick's tomato juice example, the liberty of the putative owner would be increased by such appropriation of the ocean but an institution with a rule of appropriation so generous to the appropriator would vastly diminish the liberty and well-being of individuals in general because it would inspire a land grab with little return to the public, with the

---

[76] Waldron (1993) discusses copyright in terms of the individual liberty of both owners and users. Thus Trerise (2008) argues that those concerned with liberty should reject what he calls 'strong type' IPRs (protecting *types*) for 'weak-type protection' (protecting only claims to *tokens*).

[77] Nozick (1974), pp. 174–8.

[78] Hohfeld (1923).

consequential exclusion of others from a resource which would otherwise have been enjoyed in common. This does not mean that a claim to a more discrete product that can be excluded from common availability may not tend to the general increase of liberty and well-being of all individuals who can enjoy this right of appropriation without this gain being drastically offset by the loss to the commons. As long as some discrete and limited aspect of the nature that is transformed is identifiable in a way that is meaningful or useful, it is possible for social rules (pre-eminently laws) to confer rights to it in a way that meets the requirements of justice. This enables us to distinguish the tomato juice imbued ocean from the public intellectual space in which the ideas of an author or inventor are released: unlike the case with the juice tainted ocean, it is often (though not always) possible to delimit some aspect of this space and treat them as if they were discrete. Susceptibility to useful and meaningful demarcation as a discrete object is a minimum necessary requirement, though, and not a sufficient one: for the justification of the institution still requires an account of how such institutions promote or protect liberty and well-being, and this may require that the right be subject to the appropriate limitations and conditions consistent with this principle.

There is one form of exercise of liberty that is made possible by institutions conferring such powers of control on individuals. This follows from the other characteristic of ideas and information mentioned: physical control of them is extremely limited, and becomes impossible once they have been made public. It is only through social institutions extending recognition of individual control to products of the mind that one is able to extend assertion of the self into the whole domain of ideas and information that together help us to make up our social reality. Otherwise one's participation in this space is limited to the decision to publish a creation or information of one's own, where these were not previously public. Thereafter, the idea or information is necessarily alienated from the self because of the impossibility of physical control.[79] IPRs postpone this alienation and allow the self to be asserted in the intellectual domain in the only way it is possible to do so: by conferring rights which may be asserted against others as regards the use that may be made of such objects. Thus the very intractability of ideas as objects of physical action makes the social control of persons in respect of them more important as a means of extending individual liberty. However,

---

[79]   See Chapter 7 herein at §7.4 for the possibilities and limits of technological controls.

IPRs make such liberty of individual owners possible only by depriving others of a freedom they may otherwise exercise. The very moral basis that supports private rights of control of ideas also seems to provide grounds for not having such institutions.

The second characteristic of ideas noted above was that, unlike physical objects, ideas may be used by one person without exhaustion or diminishment of its availability for others.[80] At least in this regard, the facilitation of freedom and well-being is not increased by enabling such exclusive control. In fact, all things being equal, freedom and well-being would be less extensive than they otherwise could have been because owners can then deny to others the use of the ideas for their own purposes. This has been the basis of much critique of intellectual property.[81] What can be used by many without diminishment of the resource would, as a result of IPRs, be available only to the few who are owners.[82] However, it is not quite true that all purposes may be realized without property rights in ideas. One type of project may be frustrated by the non-availability of property rights: the extension of the person and participation in the realm of the ideas by means of controlling the use of those ideas. IPRs make possible control over certain aspects of social reality that is beyond physical manipulation. Although this liberty is purchased at the cost of denying others free use of the idea, there is one way in which our liberty and well-being are increased, because different people will then have the opportunity, as potential creators, of exercising control over different ideas which would not have become part of the social reality but for the creator's contribution. Thus, although use of intellectual objects is non-exclusive, the ground of liberty and well-being offers equivocal support for property in ideas, as it generates a tension between favouring property over such objects and limiting that property in favour of public access. If every gain to liberty under any right is negated by any kind of resulting restriction of others, then there cannot be any justification for a right because every right entails a correlative restriction of others.

This apparent dilemma begins to dissolve with the appreciation that the significance of the gain to the right holder and the restriction to the others

---

[80] Stiglitz (2006), citing at p. 108, n. 10 Samuelson, Paul A., 1954, 'The Pure Theory of Public Expenditures', *Review of Economics and Statistics*, Vol. 36, No. 4 (November 1954), pp. 387–9.

[81] Amongst others Lessig (1999 and 2001).

[82] See Stiglitz (2006), p. 109, citing at n. 14 David, Paul A., 2000, 'A Tragedy of the "Public Knowledge Commons"?', available, as at 12 December 2011, at http://ideas.repec.org/p/wpa/wuwpdc/0502010.html;); Boyle (2003).

are not symmetrical. The analogy with the prescription of a right to the integrity of our bodily persons is useful here. Acknowledging such a right involves accepting restrictions as to what we may do to the bodies of others. The gain in terms of the right is the correlative result of the limitation of the natural liberty of others: the universalization of a rule providing security to our own bodies requires a tradeoff of our freedom to use the bodies of others. But the freedoms traded off are not symmetrical in their importance to the individuals: having life and control of our own physical selves is essential to our having and realizing any purposes at all, whilst having freedom to interfere with the bodily integrity of others is of less vital and general importance, though some types of purpose (the ability to have slaves, for instance) would be thwarted. We would have an objective reason to prefer a rule that gives all individuals protection of their own bodily integrity, to one that forgoes that security in return for freedom to interfere with the bodies of others. The same argument applies as well to the creation of property rights. Having some ability to exclude others in respect of some things may be vital to livelihood and the ability to realize purposes and plans. As Locke points out, we need to be able to appropriate even bounty gathered from the land if we are to consume it.[83] Property rights are different from the right to personal integrity, though. The degree of needfulness for action (or freedom) for the right holder diminishes with the amount and range of property that one has and, hence, so does the strength of the justification as compared with the countervailing concern about the concomitant restriction of the liberty for others. Although having some property is essential to realizing any purposes, the property rights over some things are more vital than others to realizing personhood. We have seen already that Radin places objects of property right on a spectrum, from personal property essential to personhood to pure commodities, arguing that we have different and stronger moral reasons for protecting the former than the latter.[84]

Gewirth's Principle of Generic Consistency also provides a basis for differential treatment of property rights. His idea of the PGC recommends that we should: act in accord with the generic rights (to freedom and well-being) of your recipients as well as of yourself.[85] To resolve conflict between rights that might otherwise arise from his principle he employs what he calls the 'criterion of degrees of needfulness for action':

---

[83]   Locke (1986), para. 25, p. 19.

[84]   Radin (1993), ch.1, pp. 35–71 (cf. herein §3.5).

[85]   Gewirth (1978); and a later summation of the derivation of this principle in (1996), pp. 16–19.

'When two rights are in conflict with one another, that right takes precedence whose object is more needed for action.'[86] In this regard, his hierarchy of categories of well-being is important and helpful because what he calls 'basic well being' generally 'takes precedence over the rights to other levels of well being'.[87] Some forms of property holdings are critical for basic survival (going to basic well-being), others for security (non-subtractive well-being). Whilst these two categories relate to purposes which all hold in common, still others are for realizing higher, and more diverse, purposes (Gewirth's additive well-being). Rights to exclusive control over intellectual objects would appear to go to additive rather than basic or non-subtractive well-being. They add to one's capabilities in the sphere of ideas. However, the control of specific ideas is a form of action, but not one that is necessary for basic survival or functioning in society. On the other hand, the *use* of ideas that are current in the makeup of the social world we inhabit may be essential to our ability to function as a full participant in it. The use of cultural ideas embodied in literary and artistic works protected by copyright may well be essential to our ability to express ourselves in the current cultural idiom and to respond to the contribution of others. A cartoon showing Mickey and Minnie Mouse in a foul-mouthed domestic dispute offers a commentary and reaction to Disney's more idyllic portrayals of family life,[88] or a parody using identifiable characters, plot elements and settings from *Gone with the Wind* to provide, in a novel form, an African American counter-commentary on Margaret Mitchell's romantically nostalgic portrayal of the Civil War American South.[89] Or, access to critical life saving medicines protected by patents may well present a situation where the patient's basic well-being needs outweigh the inventor's (or his assignees') additive well-being interest in being able to exploit the invention for profit, if the conflict cannot be resolved by other solutions.[90]

These examples suggest that the underlying principles justifying IPRs support such rights being over-ridden when in conflict with some rights to freedom and well-being of non-holders. But they do not negate altogether a justification for IPRs for, in many cases, the interest that

---

[86] Gewirth (1996) at p. 45.

[87] *Ibid*, p. 46.

[88] Waldron (1993) has a frontispiece cartoon of Minnie yelling at Mickey, 'You stupid son of a bitch! What have you got me into NOW!!?' Cf. *Walt Disney Productions v. The Air Pirates* 581 F 2d 751 (9th Cir., 1978).

[89] *Suntrust Bank v. Houghton Mifflin Co.* 268 F 3d 1257. See §4.3.4.

[90] Cf. Chapter 8 at §8.4.

others have in the created things reaches the level of basic well-being only in certain types of access or use. The ability to express oneself in and respond to the current culture that should be part of one's right of liberty rarely requires wholesale reproduction but only certain aspects for referential purposes: the interest, after all, is in expressing oneself and not repeating the expression of others.[91] Where the competing rights is not another's interest in basic well-being but in additive well-being, this competition is better resolved not by negating one or the other but by seeking a fair tradeoff. Thus, appropriate limitations and exceptions can be made to the property holdings to accommodate these competing or conflicting rights. Only the claim to absolute property over the created things would be inconsistent with the idea of there being mutual rights.

Intellectual property regimes (in particular copyright and patents systems) serve to expand liberty as well by being incentives for the creation of new ideas. New ideas add to the stock of ways of being, of doing things or looking at things and by thus increasing the options and possibilities open to us increase, at least in one sense, our liberty. This is a rather grand sounding claim to make for creations that most intellectual property tends to consist of – which may be little more than an improved paper clip or another pot boiler novel. However, even these simple contributions to our intellectual domain add to our stock of options. At the other end of the spectrum are the types of discoveries and creations that profoundly change human living conditions. One may list amongst these the discovery of penicillin and other antibiotics, pasteurization, the birth control pill, electro-magnetism, transistors, micro-chip technologies. In the field of literature and the arts, the impact on the livelihood of peoples appears less tangible and yet, when one considers *The Grapes of Wrath*, Michelangelo's *David*, Picasso's *Les Demoiselles d'Avignon*, Wren's St. Paul's Cathedral, we see the power of aesthetic works to offer new ways of conceiving the world and human relationships.

However, the equal right to freedom and well-being principle may require access to even the new elements that are the creators' contribution. Absolute appropriation of new elements by creators, even if the regimes were designed so as to leave original materials in the public domain, will deny others a participation in this addition to liberty. It is because the new ideas may powerfully transform our world that the equality term of the right would require at least partial access to the new creations, for, if these are locked up by the owners' IPRs, non-owners

---

[91]   See e.g. *Ashdown v. Telegraph Group* [2001] EWCA Civ 1142 discussed at §8.2.2 below.

will be increasingly estranged from, and excluded from participation in, the social world they inhabit. They would not be in 'as good' a position under the Lockean proviso as they would have been before the appropriation. It has already been observed that satisfaction of the Lockean proviso (that there be 'enough, and as good' remaining after appropriation) on its own does not supply sufficient justification for a proprietary claim (§3.4.3). This is because, in order for the control to be even feasible, the putative owner would have a right to the *cooperation of those others* in systems of restraint and, therefore, it is the putative owner who would have to justify his claims to such cooperation. The equal right to freedom and well-being raises considerations about both the liberty of the putative owner and that of non-holders that does require one to trade off protection and access.

Thus far in this discussion of the indirect impact of IPRs on freedom and well-being through the creation and release to the public of IP objects, it has been assumed that IPRs do generally cause a net increase in the availability of IP objects to the public. In form, the argument based on the indirect impact of IPRs on liberty and well-being is a consequentialist one: they encourage the creation and release to the public of ideas which increases the range of choice available to everyone. Earlier in this chapter (§3.3) utilitarian aggregate maximizing theories were rejected as ultimate criteria of justification because they do not take seriously the separateness of individuals and as a result do not give due weight to claims that individuals would want to be able to maintain against all others. But consequentialist reasoning can play a secondary role even when the fundamental principle is the equal right to freedom and well-being. Here the key desiderata are the promotion and protection of the freedom and well-being of human individuals as equal persons. Given this, the actual impact of IPRs on the generation and release of new ideas, and whether they promote a net increase in liberty and well-being, is relevant. Whether any particular IPR system does foster a net social utility has been questioned and is a matter for empirical inquiry. (See the brief reference to economic theories of IPRs at §3.3.3 above.) As the present thesis is an inquiry into the ethical foundations and implications of IPRs, an elaboration of those empirical questions and their possible answers is beyond the scope of this work. But nothing here suggests that economic analysis of the justification of IPRs should be ignored; indeed, the implication is that such work is highly relevant and is urgently needed for the reform of IPRs and when considering whether we should have additional or expanded IPRs and what form they should take.[92] The ethical inquiry, though, sets the context that explains why certain desiderata and goals ought to be the measures for this empirical research.

The ethical investigation identifies which empirical parameters are relevant and the way they are relevant. It is here argued that the ultimate criterion is the promotion and protection of the freedom and well-being of each human individual as an equal person. This means that the maximization of total and average wealth is a consideration because wealth (in terms of products and services that may be enjoyed) consti- tutes opportunities for achieving and enjoying liberty and well-being. But the equal right to freedom and well-being requires us to have a concern for the distribution of that wealth because it is the liberty and well-being of each human individual that is to be promoted and not liberty and well-being in aggregate. The latter is relevant only as part of the means of achieving the former. And the former is to be pursued in a way that treats each individual as an equal person – this may not mean equal achievement of wealth (for we may, as free persons, choose to pursue different objects or employ our abilities in ways which produce different consequences) but should require that each person should have equal substantive opportunities to realize their freedom and well-being. The existing elements of our social reality are not just resources for building newer ones, though they are surely that as well. In addition, however, our very participation in our own intellectual and social world is predicated on our being able to creatively use those very existing elements as part of our response to it, and in the process we may enrich their value and significance for everyone else. This way of looking at the creative process enables one to escape from the false dichotomy between embrac- ing romantic authorship[93] and proclaiming '[t]he death of the Author'.[94] Authors and inventors surely have a significant role in introducing new works and inventions even if they build on the contributions of those that came before them. However, the social value and significance of their contributions are not the results of their labour alone but depend as well on the cooperative efforts of earlier and later creators and innovators. Wendy Gordon offers an apposite critique of this Lockean line of reasoning when she observes:

> One might ask why there is a need to trace the restitutionary principle back to any other source, as there is an obvious moral attractiveness to the idea that it

---

[92] E.g. see Landes and Posner (2003).
[93] Critiqued in Boyle (1996), Lemley (1997).
[94] Barthes (1977).

is unjust for an entity to reap where it has not sown. The simplest answer is that when taken literally, as a stand-alone prohibition on free-riding, the restitutionary claim is drastically overbroad. A culture could not exist at all if all free riding were prohibited ... Culture *is* interdependence, and, requiring each act of dependency to render an accounting would destroy the synergy on which cultural life rests.[95]

Zemer builds on a similar reasoning to argue, in respect of copyright, that the public is a co-author with the individual author of every work and, hence, should have rights in the public domain balanced against authors' rights, proposing 'an indefinitely renewable copyright term in exchange for an open-ended list of fair dealing exceptions'.[96] In this present work, the argument for a public share through rights through the public domain does not have to depend on arguing that the public contribution amounts to co-authorship and on the nature of this concept: it proceeds rather on the basis that there is a public contribution and, because of this contribution and the other circumstances of what amounts to just acquisition, the public has a moral right in such a share. And the proposal is for reform and adjustments through IPRs' moral dimensions to be spelled out in the following chapters.

Thus, giving authors and inventors absolute rights to their works and inventions will make succeeding authors and inventors worse off, even if the proprietary rights are designed to leave the initial, generic stock ideas freely available. The Lockean proviso that there should be enough and as good remaining for others will be violated because succeeding authors and inventors will become less and less able to respond to their own context because they can only use the cultural resources that are available from an earlier world now made more distant by the very contributions of authors and inventors. Besides this, even if these others are not interested in being creators, they are prejudiced as purely consumers. Where, previously, they would have had, *ex hypothesi*, free use of all the world's intellectual resources, an increasing proportion of these resources would now only be available on conditions set by private individuals. They may have gained in terms of the increased pool of ideas available to them (on the assumption that IPRs do induce a net increase in ideas) if they can meet the IP owners' prices, but there is now increased inequality of enjoyment because such access is dependent on earning capacity. Thus, both the liberty and equality terms of the equal right to freedom and well-being would require IPRs designed for just apportionment of control

---

[95] Gordon (1992) at p. 168.
[96] Zemer (2007), quote at p. 223.

of owners and access by the public through limitations on protection and exceptions to the rights.

3.6.4   Freedom and Well-being and the Structure of IP Rights

The equal right to freedom and well-being requires a concern for the liberty and well-being of *each* human individual and not liberty and well-being in aggregate. Hence, each person should have equal substantive opportunities to realize their freedom and well-being.

This distributional concern may be met in various ways. Taxation and state redistribution is a possibility. A better way, though, is to build into the design of the way the wealth is acquired and held – that is, into the property rights – entitlements given to the non-holders to enjoy aspects of the thing comprising that wealth. The way this distributional concern is discharged is a matter of law making by democratically established and elected legislatures. The foregoing ethical inquiry reveals that the underlying justification for such property does not allow the property claimants to have absolute entitlements but only rights that are qualified by an understanding that others have interests in the objects which must be respected as well. This explains why the legislative questions about the design of the property rights and redistribution by state means are not merely questions of power but moral issues, and it explains why it may be argued that owners have a moral obligation to promote the making of laws, relating to intellectual property and related institutions, which give effect to these interests of others.

Thus, alongside proprietary rights, the law also defines (using Hohfeld's jural concepts[97]) aspects over which there are no property rights, where the public then consequently enjoys a privilege of access. Sometimes the conditions of access may be reviewed and re-determined as a consequence of re-interpreting the moral terms in the rules. The idea of incorporating the aspiration to a just distribution into the property rights is also a better one (than the device of taxation) for achieving respect for the equality of all individuals because any access provided in the definition of the property automatically results in the resource being provided to all on an equal basis without the need for further governmental intervention to ensure its distribution.

This is unlike taxation and redistribution, for which centralized decision making is required, with all the dangers of inefficiency, rent seeking and corruption. In contrast, access through limitations and exemptions is

---

[97]   Hohfeld (1923).

free, automatic and a privilege for all individuals. Of course, sharing of benefits occurs through market availability as well, which respects both the proprietary right (which gives owners the right to withhold access) and the public interest in access (through the opportunity to participate at the right price). It will later (at §7.3) be suggested that the justificatory basis may also affect the way property and markets interact. However, free modes of access are necessary as the guarantee of a minimum respect for equality. With physical objects, it is not feasible to build public access entitlements into the property right to any substantial extent because the physical control and consumption of such things are exclusive. This is not so with property in ideas because, being non-rivalrous, the use may be non-exclusive. Therefore the use of the design of the property right to reflect this distributional concern is a real option. The public may be given a privilege of access (using Hohfeld's jural concepts,[98] where correlatively there are no-rights) by building into the property right conditions of acquisition and rules of limitation and exemptions which reflect this distributional concern. Many of the moral terms and concepts actually found in our current IPR regimes serve, or can be made to serve, such a purpose. This will be shown in the next chapter. A complementary way of accommodating this distributional concern is through laws setting limits on how these rights may be exercised. Some of these are explored in Chapter 7, which considers the examples, in this regard, of the role played by the common law (§7.3.2), competition and antitrust laws (§7.3.3), rules on remedies and enforcement (§7.3.4) and compulsory licensing (§7.3.5).

The consequentialist case for IPRs – relying on their impact as incentives for contribution of new ideas expanding our world of options – also generates a tension between creators' entitlement to control their creations, and public access. To a point, it favours stronger IPRs, for the stronger the right granted, the stronger the incentive and, hence, the greater the production of such ideas. But this case also entails that these ideas should be available to the public – for it is premissed on there being a net gain in liberty and well-being to all individuals as a result of such institutions. This means that the benefits should be shared either as of right or on conditions required by the owner (usually a price for licence or acquisition), or a combination of both methods of distribution. The latter, though, requires that the creator's rights of control should be alienable. Alienability would weaken the link between such right of control and the personhood of the owner. Alienability of these rights is

---

[98]   *Ibid.*

supported by the direct personal liberty and well-being argument as well as the consequentialist argument that liberty and well-being are increased by its effects on overall contributions of new ideas. Alienability adds to individual freedom by affording owners one more option: the power to exchange the rights for something else that is valued by the owner. But this would mean that we would treat the having of such rights as less integral to our personhood than some other right of personhood – say, our right to basic physical liberty or the right to our physical integrity which we may waive to some extent but normally may not bind ourselves to waive.

A logical consequence of this is that the proper point of balance in the tension between the liberty claims of owners to control and that of non-owners to access as a necessary part of their self-realization, would shift quite considerably in favour of the latter, and thus support strong limitations on the owner's exclusivity in favour of public access. This is supported by the consequentialist considerations. The argument based on the institutions' effects as incentives to contribution also requires that there be various ways that non-owners may come to share in the benefits of these contributions. The nature of empirical inquiry also offers a further reason why IPRs should be framed with moral terms and concepts in their key rules. Empirical conclusions are always provisional – always subject to new and better evidence. Therefore, one must make institutions in the light of the best evidence available but always before certain conclusions can be drawn. How is one to do this? The answer suggested here is that, for basic institutions like property in ideas, the aspiration towards justice and legitimacy must be built into and expressed in the design of the institutions – in other words, moral terms and concepts must form key parts of the conditions for acquisition of rights in ideas and in the rules qualifying and limiting those rights.

3.6.5   Protection of Freedom and Well-being and the Public Domain

Lockean arguments for property thus provide two strong reasons against absolute proprietary rights over ideas. First, even if the ideas do originate from the author or inventor, their value is the result of a matrix of interlocking ideas and institutions. Hence, if the property right is a reward for the new value added in terms of increased resources for liberty and well-being for all, the entitlements to use the ideas must be distributed in a way to reflect this shared contribution to the value of the intellectual object. Secondly, the Lockean proviso can be honoured only if the creator offers something in return to the others: either directly via property institutions designed to ensure partial sharing of the created ideas, or indirectly through obligations reflected in the other moral dimensions of IPRs (particularly as regards exploitation and enforcement in the dimension of exercise) to share the benefits of the ideas. Non-right holders will be worse off as consumers and creators in an absolute IPR scenario because they would not enjoy the same equal liberty to fully participate in the world of ideas they inhabit that their predecessors, before any one began to acquire IPRs, did, but would, instead, be limited to a different and older world of ideas. They would become less than full participants in a world changed by ideas that belong to others and have become, as a result, less equal and less free.

3.7 CONCLUSIONS ON JUSTIFYING IPRS

The paradoxical result is that the equal right to freedom and well-being argument for property rights in IP also provides arguments for participation rights of non-owners in some preservation of the public domain. Although, to qualify as valid laws, the property institutions need not incorporate the moral terms and concepts that express an aspiration towards their legitimating rationale, the persons who create and continue to maintain these institutions have a moral reason to do so, and this explains why IP laws often do include such provisions. The ways these latter moral claim-rights are legally recognized and entrenched will be dealt with in the next chapter.

4. The dimension of design: National systems

4.1 JUSTIFYING IPRS AND THE JUSTICE OF IPRS

4.1.1 The Rhetoric of 'Balance' and its Point

The language of 'balance' is often employed in discourse regarding IPRs: balance between private right and public interest, between incentivizing artistic and technological innovation and the public domain. This is captured in the UDHR reference to rights in intellectual property, Article 27, in its juxtaposition of a participatory right (in paragraph 1) with the proprietary right (paragraph 2) protecting the moral and material interests of creators:

> Article 27
>
> 1. Everyone has the right to freely participate in the cultural life of the community, to enjoy the arts, and to share in scientific advancement and its benefits.
> 2. Everyone has the right to protection of the moral and material interests resulting from any scientific, literary, or artistic production of which he is the author.

Examples of this idea in IP legal instruments include: the provision of the TRIPS Agreement on objectives (Article 7) referring to 'a balance of rights and obligations'; and the preamble of the WIPO Copyright Treaty 1996 ('WCT') which recites, 'Recognising the need to maintain a balance between the rights of authors and the large public interest, particularly education, research and access to information, as reflected in the Berne Convention'. Part of its attractiveness must lie in the image of the balancing scales of justice: a metaphor that suggests that in distributing rights and obligations, rewards and burdens, we are guided by criteria that are carefully calculable. It is not a suggestion that withstands examination well, for even a cursory scrutiny yields more disturbing questions than clarity. What are we weighing? Even if we are agreed that the tradeoff is between private incentives and public advantage, there is the problem of the rate of exchange between one consideration and another: How far should public access be curtailed for the provision of private incentives? And, if the answer is, only in so far as the public benefit from the private gain is not offset by the resulting disadvantages to the public, we are still left with the question: How are we to understand the public interest? These questions identify a need for a common value that is basic, whatever other purposes and objects we may have, as the measure of the tradeoffs to be made when we seek to strike a 'balance' between the various interests and claims. The two previous chapters have sought to identify this basic value: freedom, in the sense of our liberty to have and carry out our life's purposes and plans, and the sources of well-being necessary for the exercise of that liberty. It is because, objectively, we rationally ought to share this fundamental value that our institutions in the basic structure of society, which includes IPRs, ought to be designed to maximize this value. And it is because this value is basic that, generally, we ought to promote free markets, as these generally promote freedom – of choices, of individual planning – through their power to match demand with supply.

However, as the claim to this freedom is a right that belongs to each individual human being as an equal person, the pursuit of maximization of this freedom is constrained by the requirement that each person's right as an equal to that freedom and well-being should be respected. Not all freedoms are equal. Some are more necessary to enabling action than others; hence, when the tradeoff is between a general claim to fostering creativity and the need of an individual that goes to basic well-being (essential to survival or being able to act at all), the latter ought to carry greater weight. This weighted tradeoff between types of freedom favours IPRs generally, because creators (and persons who are the object of private confidences) have interests in some measure of control over ideas and information that they have created (or, in relation to confidences, in information which relates to them) that is more vital to each creator than the more diffuse interest of the general public, the members of which may find that their freedom of action would be only mildly constrained by the restriction necessary to protect the IP interests of the former. But there is a point at which the marginal yield from the extension of the private individual right in intellectual property is so attenuated an increase in the owners' freedom that the balance of tradeoffs with the public interest freedom to use the ideas and information does weigh in the latter's favour. And there are occasions when the creators' interest in control of their ideas and information conflict directly with some individual's claim to basic well-being, such as when a key interest in freedom of speech (cf. §8.2.2) and medicines and medical technology vital to saving lives (cf. §8.4) are involved. In each of these cases the moral rights of each member of the public are in potential conflict with the owners' right to control of such ideas and information and must, at some point, prevail over the latter. What this theory offers is an explanation of why it is right, why we employ the language of 'balance' when we speak of IPRs and, although it does not provide calibrated measures of adjudicating the tradeoffs mentioned, identifies freedom as the fulcrum of that balance. This explains why IPRs ought to reflect both private owners' property and public members' participation rights embraced by Article 27(1) of the UDHR, and why the former should not be absolute. It supports a moral framework for approaching the design of IPRs as institutions which suggests that the justification of IPRs is inextricably bound up with the justice of IPRs.

4.1.2   The Function of Moral Terms

Now we are in possession of the inklings to the solution of the riddle of the rules in Chapter 1: a theory about why moral terms and concepts abound in the central rules of IPRs and an explanation of what they do. If there is agreement on a specific conception of the demands of justice, then the object of the design of IPRs (or any other part of the basic structure of society) is in principle plain, even if the detailed working out of the structures may be elaborate. The idea would be to simply embody the entitlements suggested by that theory in rules of descriptive words as clearly and plainly as possible. It would be desirable to avoid moral terms. When used, they should be interpreted as shorthand for that background understanding. But we do not have such an agreed, uncontroversial conception of justice and its requirements. Although it is here submitted that the equal right to freedom and well-being is the core idea that provides the foundation for all moral reasoning and morality, this theory also suggests that the detailed scheme of morality is a matter that we refine and redefine as we develop our institutions. The equal right to freedom and well-being ought to inform our moral choices. But its under-determinativeness (cf. §2.4.6) allows, even requires us, to make commitments that feed back into a greater definition of that right. (Although this means there may be local variations consistent with that right, our commitment to the globalization of IPRs with increasing global reach means that we are also committing to globalizing a single international fundamental morality for such institutions.) One result of this under-determinativeness is that it is impossible to achieve justice by casting the rules of IPRs in purely descriptive terms. Moral terms must be employed in the design of such institutions or in some of its other related dimensions. These moral terms and concepts serve three inter-connected purposes. First, they express the intention that the institution be justifiable. A distinction should be observed between *giving effect* to a moral concern and *expressing* that concern in legislation. The creators of an institution may have the intention to legislate according to a certain moral idea, and carry out that intention, by employing rules which are devoid of moral terms. For example, if legislators are concerned that punishment for crimes should not be cruel and unjust, but have deter-mined that only capital punishment by lethal injection for murder would not, under any circumstances, be cruel or unjust, they could frame the rule in terms that the offender shall be put to death by lethal injection. They would have moral concerns and, according to their understanding of what those concerns dictate, have enacted a form of punishment that effectively satisfied their concerns. What they would not have done, is to *express* the intention that the punishment should not be cruel or unjust. To do the latter, moral language or rules implicitly requiring the employment of those moral concepts must be used. Although there may not be agreement about the exact design of the institution that would be justifiable, there would be agreement that it should be legitimate.

The use of moral terms, and only the use of moral terms, can adequately express this idea. Secondly, the moral terms in the rules enjoin the officials of the system to search for appropriate universalizable prescriptions. This is where the observation that moral principles are characteristically universalizable prescriptions is significant in the theory of IP rights. If morality is itself a social institution whose maintenance under Searle's constitutive rules[1] is a continuing project of rational universalization of prescriptions (§1.2.3), it is impossible at the time the IPR laws are made to frame in non-moral terms rules reflecting the full content of the justificatory norms of those institutions because they are being fleshed out as we go along. Thirdly, the moral terms enable change, even transformative adaptation, of the institution towards legitim-ate forms. They give the rules some interpretative flexibility: by inviting the search for appropriate prescriptions, they enable officials entrusted with the task of interpreting the rules to adapt the institution to meet this aspiration. Such terms reflect directly some of the fundamental moral prescriptions justifying IPRs as social institutions. The way they are interpreted, and hence universalized, become then part of the process of *clarification and affirmation* of these fundamental principles. Because they are built into the core of the IPRs themselves and the rules in related

---

[1]   Searle (1995), cf. §1.2.2.

dimensions, they ensure that the IPRs tend towards compliance with the scheme of justice they enjoin, at least as far as the language used and rules of precedent and adjudication applicable by that legal system will allow. These moral dimensions are seeds charged with dormant potential for development of the institutions, to be awakened on the rare cases when concerns about their extent, power and reach are implicated. When such cases arise, these dimensions become transformational opportunities to re-examine the balance between property and public domains and the role that particular rule in the institution plays in maintaining that balance. This re-examination and re-appraisal of the institution also become opportunities for re-invention[2] of the institution to the extent that the structure of the relevant rule and the rule as to precedents and interpretation of that legal system will allow. Such re-invention could, of course, result in the subversion of the expectations that legislatures, or parties to the international convention, had of the institution when making the law. This raises issues of legal theory about whether such expectations should in themselves count against such interpretative latitude, and whether they argue against use of moral terms and concepts in legal rules and against recognition of any moral element as an aspect of the basic idea of law.

These are issues which will be reserved for exploration in Chapter 6 on the dimension of interpretation and legal theory. It may be said, in anticipation, that the use of moral terms in legal rules and, perhaps, the very idea of law itself, if we can accept that that idea incorporates a moral aim (itself admittedly highly contentious), expresses an intention that the legal institution and system should be open to such re-examination and re-invention. It is, then, possible for startling new interpretative developments to be true to such intentions whilst at the same time confounding legislative expectations. Such an approach would mean that the institutions and legal systems are not closed systems of rules entirely separate or separable from the rest of the social world, including its moral aspects, but an integral part of it, dynamically interacting with the rest of it. This is the aspect that makes the moral content of IPR rules potentially so profoundly and radically transformative. They are also transformational opportunities because choices in such cases are also choices about the moral justifications of the institution and, ultimately, choices about the morality that make up part of our social reality. Not only are such opportunities occasions which can transform

---

²   See Sherman and Bently (1999) for a history of the re-invention and reshaping of British IPRs.

the institutions, decisions about such matters also transform the underlying moral reality. The previous chapter identified a specific conception of the justification of IPRs – one aiming at a balance between property protection and participation rights in a public domain that aims at protecting and promoting the liberty and well-being of all human individuals as equal persons; and Chapter 2 put forward a specific conception of morality – one ultimately expressed in the idea of an equal right to freedom and well-being. However, the transformational potential of these moral dimensions is independent of the correctness of these conceptions, because all that is required for this is that the question presents us (and the officials who have to make the interpretative decision) with an ineluctable moral aspect. When confronted with such a question, it is the simple idea of universal prescriptivism which, if we wish to answer it honestly, draws us into an investigation of the justification of the institution and the moral underpinnings of that justification. This does not presuppose any particular justification or conception of morality because different people may begin with different conceptions and may wish to prescribe different principles upon which to operate. It is precisely because these possibilities are open that these opportunities are potentially so radically transformative: because we are asked why we should choose one option over another, and when we propose one principle over another, we ask ourselves again, why we should make that choice over another and why others should acknowledge the value or rightness of that decision and, therefore, seek ever more fundamental reasons for our decisions. Chapter 2 argues that rational investigation will lead to the fundamental principles outlined therein that comprise the equal right to freedom and well-being, which then goes on to recommend a specific justificatory conception. Such cases are moments when we clarify our options and, if those previous chapters are right, are led to affirm specific answers. Even if those conclusions are wrong, though, it will remain true that a genuine attempt at addressing the moral questions will involve such a search for moral foundations, and, hence, transformative decisions have to be made.

4.1.3 The Object and Structure of this Chapter

The purpose of this chapter is to identify the main moral terms and concepts embedded in the central rules of the exemplar IPRs and establish three things about them. First, that they *can* be understood as serving the function ascribed above, even if they are not always understood as doing so. Secondly, that such an understanding will clarify some of the mysteries concerning their interpretation. Thirdly, the fact that we *do* use moral terms in the rules regarding the conditions of existence and extent of the IP rights means that we must *want* morality to have objective rational force in this dimension. The legislators or parties that have framed the rules with such terms have opted for language which works to yield an objective meaning only if they share this desire, if nothing else. Legislators and parties are not neutral amoralists in this project of morality; rather they, and the IP institutions with these rules, are part of a world committed (at least in part) to a moral world, so that both types of institution (the legal and the ethical) draw on and reinforce one another. The exemplar IPRs explored for these purposes are: trade secrets and related protection (§4.2), copyright (§4.3), patents (§4.4) and trade marks law (§4.5). It will also link promotion of liberty and well-being with the personhood of creators through the moral rights provisions (§4.6) and the morality and *ordre public* restrictions on IP rights (§4.7). It will end by identifying the role of these moral terms and concepts as a resource for the protection of the public domain (§4.8).

4.2 MORAL TERMS IN THE LAW OF UNDISCLOSED INFORMATION

4.2.1 Undisclosed Information Protection and Freedom and Well-being

'Undisclosed information' is the title TRIPS (Article 39(1)) gives to the category of matter that is protected in various legal systems under a variety of regimes: in common law systems by the breach of confidence action, in civil law systems by laws on protection against unfair competition and, often, under trade secrets legislation. These regimes share the common characteristic of being concerned with information that has not been made public and relate to the right to prevent such information being used or disclosed without authorization. They stand, as such, in contrast with the other main IPRs which are essentially about either private control of information and ideas that have been made public or have their value in the potential for public exploitation. The latter are about private rights in matters which are (or potentially will be) in the intellectual commons – that collection of ideas and information to which the public has access. The collection of regimes concerned with protection of undisclosed information is about information and ideas which are not, and are not to be, part of the intellectual commons. This makes these laws anomalous as an IPR, but their inclusion in the same grouping for practical and theoretical purposes is justified because they are about control of the boundary into that realm, marking that point of transition between controls of ideas which are mainly personal and physical to forms of use where the main controls have to be legal. The other IPRs are related to basic rights of controls over certain information that are closely related to the author or inventor who obtains the rights, and respect that right at the same time in that they are designed to induce the voluntary disclosure of the information to the public by providing other rights and benefits. Hence, trade secrets laws themselves assure some continued measure of control for the purpose of inducing activities that ensure that the benefits of using the information at least may be available to others.

Copyright generally protects unpublished works and includes the right of withholding publication, but it also assures the right holder of control over certain aspects of the relevant types of information (original literary and artistic works) of a certain measure of continued control even after publication – the right of reproduction, public performance, adaptation, and so on. Patents are the quintessential *quid pro quo* offer in exchange for disclosure of inventive ideas to the public.[3] Thus, the conditions for existence of the right in Article 39(2) of TRIPS reflect this boundary role: the information must be 'secret', have 'commercial value because it is secret', and the person lawfully in control of the information must have taken 'reasonable steps under the circumstances … to keep it secret'. Steps to assert and maintain control negate intent to abandon it. This is only a partial answer because, even if one has not abandoned the control, the questions that remain are: Why, if that control fails for whatever reason, should the law come to that person's aid? And when should that aid be given? The law's explanation as to 'why' may be reconstructed, after we have identified its answer as to 'when' the law does aid the person who makes a disclosure. Article 39(2) of TRIPS stipulates that persons 'shall have the possibility of preventing information lawfully within their control from being disclosed to, acquired by, or used by others without their consent'. The critical phrase that requires us to seek a justificatory theory (the 'why' question) when determining the extent and exception to the right (the 'when' issue) is what follows: 'in a manner contrary to honest commercial practice'. This is plainly a moral concept. The law provides some guidance on its interpretation, for a footnote to the treaty text explains that the phrase 'shall mean at least practices such as breach of contract, breach of confidence and induce-ment to breach, and includes acquisition of undisclosed information by third parties who knew, or were grossly negligent in failing to know, that

---

[3] See *Kewanee Oil Co. v. Bicron Corp* 416 U.S. 479 (1974).

such practices were involved in the acquisition'. A rationale for trade secrets protection and the common law breach of confidence action may be found when we explore how they promote and protect liberty and well-being. This affords further justification for grouping undisclosed information protection with the other IPRs. Even though it is about non-public information and keeping them non-public, the protection is really about affording the public the benefit of the disclosure of such information, albeit of a limited kind. There are some ways in which such protection does facilitate contribution to the public. It is often not feasible to work commercially valuable ideas (e.g. industrial processes, valuable food and drink recipes) on one's own, without employees or partners. Protecting disclosures with a view to commercially working the idea expands this liberty – if the idea is worked – by expanding the possibilities that are available to others in commerce through enjoyment of the benefits of others with access (under these obligations of non-disclosure) working these ideas. There is, of course, the tradeoff in liberty in that others are excluded from direct access to the ideas and, hence, from working the ideas themselves. This can be considerable, for, if there is no legal restraint on disclosees, the ideas may be disseminated to everyone to work the ideas themselves or enjoy the benefits of many others working the ideas. Both utilitarianism and the principle of an equal right to freedom and well-being point in the same broad direction: towards rules for limited rights of restriction in respect of undisclosed information over which the 'owner' has some form of special access or control because of the benefits of such a system to everyone in general.

To that extent they reinforce one another. But utilitarian theories may justify greater protection if the gain in welfare were positive. It may even justify extending protection to situations where the secret may be reverse engineered or where the holder works the secret in the open. The fact is, that in the common law of breach of confidence actions and in major trade secrets protection systems, the reverse engineer and persons who obtain legitimate public access to the secret are under no obligation to exercise restraint.[4] A theory of justification based on promoting the liberty and well-being of individuals provides a better fit for this feature of the law than a utilitarianism based on maximizing welfare. The reality

---

[4] E.g. the National Conference of Commissioners on Uniform State Laws (1985) *Comment* to US Uniform Trade Secrets Act (1979, amended) on 'improper means', observes that 'Proper means include ... 2. Discovery by "reverse engineering"'; cf. §4.2.3 below. For English common law, see Cornish and Llewelyn (2003), p. 313, and *Mars UK Ltd v. Teknowledge Ltd* [2000] FSR 138.

is that the potential welfare benefits of the various permutations of restrictive rules we may adopt are practically incalculable. There are the familiar problems for all consequentialist theories, of defining benefit and settling on a means of measuring it. And, it has been argued earlier (in Chapter 2) that at the most fundamental level of moral reasoning, it is more rational to prescribe the fundamental principles than embrace utilitarianism as a basic criterion for all moral rules. There is, however, a further reason for rejecting utilitarianism for a deontological approach to undisclosed information protection and other IPRs. Not only are the consequences of such systems practically unpredictable, it is the peculiar point and purpose of such institutions to generate new possibilities and conditions which make the future even more unpredictable. The question we may pose here is: If we do not know how things will turn out, and we are encouraging developments that make this even more unforeseeable, how should we plot a direction for progress? It would seem that the only answer we can really give is that, however things do turn out, we should put ourselves in a position to say that it is a result of adhering to principles that were fair.[5] Where consequences are practically incalculable – as when we ask if a rule as to permissibility of reverse engineering should be embraced – we should forswear the impossible attempt to calculate the consequence and simply embrace the principle promoting individual right to freedom and well-being.

Thus, under the idea of the principle of maximizing the freedom and well-being of individuals as equal persons, it is reasonable to prescribe more specific principles which protect some types of information disclosed or withheld under certain types of conditions. It requires positive rules of law to fix these conditions and boundaries. But the moral justification and the legal rules have a reflexive relationship with one another – the justification influencing and underpinning the form of the rules. The rules will incorporate terms and concepts which allow adjustments and revision of our understanding of their intended effect as we continually revise our understanding of how far our powers to restrict information's availability to others *ought* to be balanced against the liberty of others to act in their own interest when using the information. The precise balance of these 'ought' considerations is, in turn, a matter of universalizing the justifications we give for these and other legal institutions relating to information – in particular other IPR regimes. The critical fulcrum of this reflexive balancing between institutional rules and moral justification, as already mentioned, is the moral terms and concepts

---

[5] This applies Rawls' pure procedural justice (1999) at §14, pp. 73–8.

within the rules forming the institution itself. The TRIPS Agreement assumes an existing collection of legal regimes which already attempt to embody this idea, and it is to these we must now turn.

4.2.2   Unfair Competition

Moral terms and concepts are ubiquitous in IP rules. Trade secrets protection is sanctioned internationally by Article 10*bis* of the Paris Convention, which requires member states to assure nationals of the Paris Union countries of effective protection against unfair competition (cl. 1) and (in cl. 2) provides this definition: 'Any act of competition contrary to honest practices in industrial or commercial matters constitutes an act of unfair competition.' This concept is patently an evaluative one; a moral idea as we herein understand the idea for it requires that we treat it as having a content that provides guidance with objective rational force. Yet, the tendency towards ambivalence amongst lawyers – treating moral terms like these as empty of a core meaning and yet somehow constraining – is exemplified by a 1994 WIPO study: the Article 10*bis*(2) definition of unfair competition 'leaves the determination of the notion of "commercial honesty" to the national courts and administrative authorities'.[6] It goes on to note: 'Any attempt to encompass all existing and future acts of competition in one sweeping definition – which at the same time defines all prohibited behaviour *and* is flexible enough to adapt to new market practices – has so far failed.'[7]

Some source of prescription is necessary to give the concept content. But this is not entirely arbitrary. The same paper notes that one can draw from the particular acts enumerated in Article 10*bis*(3) as unfair competitive practices a 'common aspect' of unfair market behaviour in 'the attempt (by an entrepreneur) to succeed in competition without relying on his own achievements in terms of quality and price of his products and services, but rather by taking undue advantage of the work of another or by influencing customer demand with false or misleading statements'. And it acknowledges that the intention is that the guidance provided by this content should be objective (i.e. binding irrespective of one's particular preferences): '[a]t first sight, the notion of "honesty" seems to refer to a moral standard, and some sort of *legal/ethical standard* is indeed involved'; '[t]he most important factor for determining "unfairness" ... is derived from the *purpose* of unfair competition law ... the

---

6   WIPO, 'Protection Against Unfair Competition' (1994), p. 18, para. 20.
7   *Ibid*, p. 23, para. 29.

protection of competitors, the protection of consumers and the safe-guarding of competition in the interest of the public at large'.[8] But this standard is not fixed by conventional practice or subjective fiat; rather, it is subject to rational clarification, refinement and even reform. For the report observes:

> [A] *businessman's standard of behaviour* logically serves as a starting point. A practice that is condemned as improper by all businessmen can hardly qualify as a 'fair' act of competition.
>
> On the other hand, certain practices may be generally accepted within a branch of business but nevertheless considered 'improper' by other market participants. In such cases, there has to be some *ethical correction* of the actual standards of behaviour … Ethical standards dictate in particular that the interests of consumers must not be unnecessarily impaired …
>
> When determining 'honesty' in business dealings, all these factors have to be taken into account. In practice, the concept of unfair competition has increasingly become *a balancing of interest*.[9]

This 'balancing of interests' is, of course, an idea that really requires us to develop a conception of justice, wherein the claims of the participants in a social system are identified and given their due weight. It calls on a deeper layer of moral thinking wherein we regard morality itself as a social enterprise that we call on, as a basis for framing rules for social cooperation. The notion of 'honest practices in industrial or commercial matters' in Article 10*bis*(2) of the Paris Convention begins with our conventional notions but also requires us to review and reformulate those notions with those broader concepts of justice in mind.

4.2.3 Trade Secrets Protection

In systems with statutory trade secrets protection, this notion of fairness as between information holders and the public is built into the concept of 'misappropriation' which is the essential condition for incurring an obligation or liability. For example, under the US Uniform Trade Secrets Act (1979),[10] injunctive relief (§2) is available for '[a]ctual or threatened misappropriation' and damages (§3) 'for actual loss caused by misappropriation'. 'Misappropriation' is defined (§1(2)) to mean acquisition under

---

8   *Ibid*, pp. 24–5, para. 31–3.
9   *Ibid*, p. 25 (footnotes omitted).
10   The Uniform Trade Secrets Act (1979, amended 1985), *supra* n. 4 above, has been adopted in 46 states of the United States, save for the District of Columbia, US Virgin Islands, Massachusetts, New York, New Jersey and Texas.

conditions of knowledge or constructive knowledge that 'the trade secret was acquired by improper means', or unauthorized disclosure by a person who 'used improper means to acquire knowledge of the trade secret' or when he disclosed or used it knew or ought to have known that that knowledge derived from someone who had used improper means to acquire it or who owed a duty to the claimant to maintain its secrecy or restrict its use, or derived from someone who acquired it under circumstances giving rise to such a duty. The notions of 'improper means' and 'circumstances giving rise to ... a duty [to maintain secrecy]' are, hence, critical in the concept of misappropriation.[11] Neither is defined, though a partial list of 'proper means' is provided in the Commissioners' comment to that model law which includes discovery by independent invention or under licence from the owner of the trade secret, or by reverse engineering of a product obtained by fair and honest means such as purchase on the open market, or by observation of the item in public use or display, and the obtaining of the trade secret from published literature. The Commissioners' comments note that:

> Improper means could include otherwise lawful conduct which is improper under the circumstances; *e.g.*, an airplane overflight used as aerial reconnaissance to determine the competitor's plant layout during construction of the plant. *E.I. du Pont de Nemours & Co., Inc. v. Christopher.*[12]

At the bedrock of these key terms is a matrix of moral notions of what parties ought to be able to expect from one another as a matter for fair play in competitive economic and social interaction. Moral concepts mandate and facilitate this reflexive review and reform process at the heart of this law. This can be seen in the example of the common law action for breach of confidence.

4.2.4   The Common Law Breach of Confidence Action

The elements of the common law action for breach of confidence in the UK and other common law jurisdictions are encapsulated in that often cited formulation of Megarry J in *Coco v. AN Clark (Engineers) Ltd*:[13]

> [T]hree elements are normally required if, apart from contract, an action for breach of confidence is to succeed. First, the information itself, in the words

---

[11]   *Ibid*, s 1(1).
[12]   *Ibid*, National Conference of Commissioners on Uniform State Laws (1985) *Comments* on s 1.
[13]   [1968] F.S.R. 415.

of Lord Greene MR in the *Saltman* case … must 'have the necessary quality of confidence about it'. Secondly, that information must have been imparted in circumstances importing an obligation of confidence. Thirdly, there must be an unauthorized use of that information to the detriment of the party communicating it.[14]

Each of these elements uses terms or refers to concepts that are evaluative in nature. The first – 'necessary quality of confidence' – requires that the information must not be in the public domain: it should not be substantially known or accessible to the relevant part of the public and the claimant should enjoy value or protection from detriment in that inaccessibility.[15] However, the degree and type of accessibility that would negate the necessary quality of confidence are related to the criteria by which the information's secrecy is valued. There must be something that the *public* ought to recognize as worth protecting; as being above the minimum threshold of being not mere trivial tittle-tattle.[16] The courts find this easily satisfied when the information has commercial value from being saleable or from giving a competitive advantage to others or threatening commercial damage to the 'owner'. This would account for the recognition of the value of the information. It does not follow simply from this that, therefore, the control of the information by the person in possession of it, or of whom it is about, should be promoted and protected. Indeed, the object of promoting freedom and well-being might suggest otherwise, since non-protection would enable others to get what is worth pursuing. This first element merely identifies something that is worth being concerned about and, hence, that should be the subject of a law dealing with protection of and access to information. There is some doubt as to whether the third element, unauthorized use or disclosure, includes a requirement that there be detriment to the plaintiff. Though it is in Megarry J's formulation in *Coco v. Clark*, he also expressed some uncertainty over it.[17] If it is required, this means that the impact of a disclosure has to be evaluated for some recognized harm: the nature of the impact is a factual descriptive matter, but the assessment of the effect as positive or negative requires some prescriptions. Due attention to the prescriptive aspect of identifying a detriment may suggest reasons for the hesitancy about its inclusion as a criterion for a maintainable action.

---

[14] *Ibid* at 419.
[15] Gurry (1984).
[16] *Coco v. Clark*, cit. above n. 13 at 421.
[17] *Ibid.*

Requiring detriment may exclude some cases where there are no further purely factual consequences beyond the disclosure to the public; yet one may want to recognize that the disclosure *per se* (i.e. over and beyond any commercial loss or emotional distress that may or may not be caused) is an injury. But the suggestion that the subject's commercial or privacy interest may have been violated is not a further factual finding, it is an evaluative judgement that certain types of information about persons, not already known to others, ought to be within the privileged control of that person. The necessity of this element may be in doubt, as the work it would have been intended to do is already borne by the other elements;[18] and by the public interest consideration which operates both as a ground for the existence of protection as regards government information,[19] and as an excuse for disclosure. This suggests recognition of underlying moral prescriptions to the effect that there are rights of personhood that extend beyond our bodily integrity: to information about ourselves and our relations, to our reputation in public, and so on. Norms, legal and cultural, are required for this extension of control. Though we have more effective physical control over our bodies, it remains insecure to the extent that others may use force to violate it. And, though much weaker, we have some physical control over the access that others have to information about ourselves – by the use of walls and screens and the seclusion of our private areas and, nowadays, by encryption of our files and data. But physical control is of limited efficacy on its own and the measures necessary to exert it involve limitations on our freedom – one may purchase privacy at the cost of living like an eremite; hence, certain *social* extensions of control over personal information are an element of individual freedom. The choices about how far these controls may extend and who may enjoy them and under what conditions are thus choices about the distribution of freedom and, hence, are moral questions involving principles of justice. It is the second element in Megarry J's formulation, though, that most clearly and directly refers to a background morality. He says that the circumstances of disclosure must import an obligation of confidence

> [I]f the circumstances are such that any *reasonable man* standing in the shoes of the recipient of the information would have realized that *upon reasonable*

---

[18]   See Cornish and Llewelyn (2003) at para. 8–39.

[19]   *Attorney General v. Guardian Newspapers (No 2)* cit. below n. 21, per Lord Keith at 639; *Commonwealth of Australia v. Fairfax* (1980) 147 CLR 38 per Mason J at 51–2; see Cornish and Llewelyn (2003) at para. 8–39.

grounds the information was being given to him in confidence, then this should suffice to impose upon him the equitable obligation of confidence.[20]

The requirement that information have been *imparted* is limiting, but broader is *Attorney-General v. Guardian Newspapers (No 2)* (per Lord Goff):

> I start with the broad principle (which I do not intend in any way to be definitive) that a duty of confidence arises when confidential information comes to the knowledge of a person (the defendant) in circumstances where he has notice, or *is held to have agreed*, that the information is confidential, with the effect that it would be *just in all the circumstances* that he should be precluded from disclosing the information to others.[21]

It becomes clearer that the point of the requirement is not really how the information was obtained but what this *ought to have* signified to the acquirer/recipient about the basis on which he or she holds the information. This requires that we apply ideas about justice. Not justice as the strict application of law, for it is what should be the applicable legal rule that is in question. Rather, it is the background moral theory about the appropriate basic distribution of rights and obligations we ought to be able to expect from one another that is to be applied in determining when the information ought to be taken as being held in confidence. Both Megarry J's reference to the 'reasonable man' and Lord Goff's reference to situations where the recipient is 'held to have agreed' that the information is confidential, treat the test as an objective one – independent of the subjective perceptions of either plaintiff or defendant. They leave open the question of whether it is objective because the standards concerned are taken to be social facts, verifiable by anthropological inquiries as to what people hold to be just (whether this is a convention or common intuition), or that the principles of justice can be worked out by reasoned normative inquiry. Even if we begin with a conventional or intuitive understanding of the principles of justice (or any other type of moral criteria), it is part of our conventional understanding of moral norms that they are to apply with objective rational force. The argument made in Chapter 2 is that, in seeking to make sense of this, we are led to revise our moral conventions and our intuitive understanding as we seek ever more fundamental grounds for our moral practices until we reach the necessity of affirming fundamental principles which lead us to embrace the equal right to freedom and well-being as that basis for justice. Lord

---

[20] Emphasis added. *Coco v. Clark* cit. above n. 13 at 420–21.
[21] Emphasis added. [1988] 3 All ER 545 at 657.

Goff subjects his broad principle of confidentiality to three limiting principles:[22] (i) it applies to information only to the extent that it is confidential (in particular it cannot be regarded as confidential once it enters the public domain, that is, when it is generally accessible); (ii) the duty of confidence applies neither to useless information, nor to trivia; (iii) the public interest in confidential information being preserved and protected may be outweighed by some other countervailing public interest in disclosure.[23]

Thus, a closer examination of the central test for the obligation in the law on action for breach of confidence yields the somewhat paradoxical result that it has, as a justifying rationale, not just the principle of protecting the confider's ability to control information but also the principle of promoting the freedom and well-being of individuals, which also justifies promoting access to that information. This favours a rule that treats information disclosed to anyone as *prima facie* free for use, for the person making the disclosure will have had the option of not making that disclosure if he had so chosen. But one may uphold a restriction against use or disclosure if the disclosee has surrendered that *prima facie* freedom by a voluntary undertaking to assume that burden of that restriction. By extension, that burden may be assumed in circumstances where one may be understood to accept such an obligation and one is free to refuse the disclosure and does not object to receiving the information. This respects the freedom of both parties who enter into the bargain for that restriction, as well as explaining why the reverse engineer and the incidental public recipient are usually under no similar obligation. Those creatures beloved of law teachers and judicial dicta, the accidental over-hearer or lip reader of conversations on a public bus[24] and the finder of confidential documents wafted by a breeze onto the street,[25] have not assumed such obligations. In the case of reverse engineering, the 'owner' would have chosen to release a product embodying the information (or from which it may be discerned) to reap the benefits of that form of exploitation knowing that the possibility of third parties

---

[22]   *Ibid* at p. 658.

[23]   E.g. see *Re Smith Kline and French Laboratories Ltd* [1990] 1 A.C. 64 (UK HL): use, by health and licensing authorities, of confidential information submitted for obtaining approvals, to assess rival equivalent generic drugs for marketing approvals.

[24]   *Malone v. Metropolitan Police Commissioner (No. 2)* [1979] 1 Ch. 344, per Megarry V.C. at 376.

[25]   In *Attorney General v. Guardian Newspapers (No. 2)* cit. above n. 21, per Lord Goff at pp. 658–9.

acquiring unfettered access is a possibility. Yet, the general rule that there is usually no obligation of restraint in the absence of voluntary assumption of that responsibility is but a feature of the deeper principle that individual freedom is to be promoted. Sometimes, the promotion of individual freedom requires restraint without such explicit or even implicit undertaking, where such restraint should be expected because such rules enable one to act and form associations more freely: for example in family and personal relations. Thus, with disclosures in matrimonial[26] and family settings,[27] the imposition of the obligation of confidentiality is independent of contract and is best explained as intended to promote conditions within such relationships where one may speak and behave freely without fear of public intrusion. This applies as well to communications made in the context of close friendship.[28]

However, this freedom from restraint in certain relationships and contexts is purchased at the price of restraint as to disclosures by the parties. Freedoms conflict and priority must be given to one or another. But they are not equal because the freedom from restraint in family, matrimonial and other close relations is in general more vital to enabling action for all individuals than the freedom to tattle. On the other hand, the English courts at least have found that the situation is different for relationships of casual sex where, one supposes, expectations of loyalty are lower, and the balance tips in favour of the freedom to kiss and tell (or freedom of speech).[29] This is the converse of the situation where one may infer an implicit bargain of confidentiality, where, instead, the understanding is that parties place a premium on retaining their independence and freedom, and the participants engage in relations in face of the risk (though they may have hoped otherwise) of indiscretion. It is because the basic principle is the idea of freedom as substantive liberty – that is, the promotion and protection of our capacity to carry out plans, preferences and purposes rather than the negative concept, absence of restraint save those we undertake to assume – that the idea of reasonableness that is the source of the obligation of confidentiality in the common law action contains the seeds, until recently latent, of protection even in cases of surreptitious taking and invasion of privacy, where the offending party never accepted any understanding of such an obligation.

---

[26] *Argyll v. Argyll* [1967] Ch. 302.

[27] *Albert v. Strange* cit. below n. 32.

[28] *McKennitt v. Ash* [2006] EWCA Civ 1714.

[29] *A v. B & C* [2002] EWCA Civ 337; note also the Court of Appeal's observations on which this case was distinguished in *McKennitt v. Ash*, *ibid* at para. 30.

For promotion of freedom and well-being may require that a person should be able to act without undue constraint from intrusion and public scrutiny where the public interest in such information is low, and private loss of freedom of others through the corresponding restriction is insignificant in terms of their freedom to achieve their own plans, preferences and purposes. The underlying principle may call for extension of the law to afford such protection where it is otherwise unavailable; the remarkable turnabout of the common law action in the sphere of privacy protection in the UK is just such a case.

4.2.5   Protecting Privacy under the Action for Breach of Confidence

The development of the breach of confidence action as a means of protection of privacy traverses an arc from non-protection in *Kaye v. Robertson*[30] in 1990 to *Campbell v. Mirror Group Newspapers*[31] before the House of Lords in 2004, where the protection extended to a street photograph of a supermodel leaving the premises of a Narcotics Anonymous meeting. The trajectory of this arc reflects the force of the equal right to freedom and well-being. Although *Albert v. Strange*,[32] the seminal case for the breach of confidence action, dates back to Victorian times and concerns the protection of the Queen's domestic privacy, the conventional wisdom as recently as 1990 was that that action did not afford protection of privacy. The understanding in *Kaye* was that the limitations of the action for breach of confidence prevented its use to protect against the type of invasion of privacy where information was obtained by *unauthorized intrusion* rather than abuse of confidential *disclosure*. In *Kaye*, counsel conceded and the Court of Appeal assumed it was correct that a TV star claimant – whose distressed image whilst recovering in a hospital room following a motor accident was published in a tabloid – did not have an action for breach of privacy, and that a breach of confidence action would fail. Though the photograph's subject was confidential information and its use was unauthorized, the absence of a purposeful communication or grant of access by the then disoriented claimant meant that a key element of the action was missing – *disclosure* upon an understanding, whether explicit or tacit, of confidentiality which the recipient must be taken to have accepted. Central to this classic (narrow) conception of the action for breach of confidence is the *relationship* of trust or confidence that a reasonable man would recognize

---

[30]   [1991] F.S.R. 62.
[31]   Cit. below n. 48.
[32]   *Albert v. Strange* (1849) 18 L. J. Ch. 120.

as arising in certain settings of communication. The requirement that there be some kind of relationship of trust and confidence is not, in principle, an insurmountable objection against protection of privacy, though. One can conceive of *everyone* in a community as being in a relationship, by virtue of being community members, where it is understood that there should be a just balance between the individual's autonomy as regards control of information about himself or herself, and others' freedom to realize themselves and their own projects through use of information (even of others') to which they have access. Where the line is drawn, when identifying the relevant types of information and in what circumstances they are (and when they are not) subject to such private control, requires a determination of this 'just balance' in each instance of decision about various situations of protection and access. But there can be just expectations that there will be restrictions on the uses of certain types of information even without the specific imposition of confidentiality upon the disclosee because both parties ought reasonably to accept that their general interest in liberty would be better ensured if even some acts accessible to others can be performed with the assurance that there will not be unreasonable intrusion into their privacy.

These may include cases where the circumstances of the activities were such that the restriction on others against access or use of the information would be of slight consequence in terms of degree of needfulness for action, as compared with the increase in freedom for individuals generally if they did have that assurance of privacy. These would cover activities at home or other private settings, and can even stretch to certain acts in a publicly accessible setting.[33] But this would require a more liberal conception of the relationship of confidence, which regards this relationship as *always existing* by virtue of one being mutually in the community of common humanity, and would transform the right from a 'special right', that is, one that arises because of specific choices or transactions, to a 'general right' accruing because of one's membership in the human race.[34] There have been significant milestones in this development, including *Hellewell v. Chief Constable of Derbyshire*,[35] in which it was held that the police, who had taken photographs of a suspect who was later convicted of theft, did owe a duty of

---

[33]   See the *Campbell case*, cit. below n. 48.

[34]   The distinction between general rights and special rights is one that H.L.A. Hart (1984) makes, and which is used by Waldron (1988) to develop a distinction between Special-Right based justifications and General-Right based justifications for property; see esp. ch. 4, pp. 106–24, and ch. 5, pp. 128–36.

[35]   [1995] 4 All ER 473.

confidence to the subject not to use the photograph for unauthorized purposes but, in that case, they had not violated that duty by distributing it to a traders' group operating a shop watch scheme. It was not a special compact between discloser and disclosee that created the confidential relationship, because the subject was not in a position to refuse photography, but the more general compact of society that sets out the terms of access. This general compact theory explains developments in the law relating to surreptitious taking (where there is, by the nature of the case, no intention to disclose the information let alone impose any conditions for its receipt) and public interest defences which over-ride the special intention of the parties, where a theory of the obligation based on the will and intention of the communicating party cannot. It is the balance of principles justifying control (to advance their autonomy) by individuals over information that they generate against principles justifying access to use of information by others (also necessary to advance their own autonomy). It is a short step from this to a holding that one may be justly understood to accept, even in respect to strangers, certain limits against intrusion and use of information thus obtained binding on our conscience by the mere fact of our mutual membership in society. The authority for this has always been there at the heart of the law of confidentiality, in the idea of unconscionability and the possibility of a direct appeal to morality which must logically rest on the basic prescriptions. And this step reflects an acknowledgement that the real justification of the breach of confidence action is a General-Right based argument (founded on obligations we owe one another merely by our being human) rather than a Special-Right based argument (arising from specific transactions),[36] since it does not rest on any compact between suspect and the police. It is significant that this justification is a General-Right based argument as it requires one to derive the obligation from a general feature of the human condition and, hence, to call on or construct a moral foundation such as the equal right to freedom and well-being argued for in Chapter 2. The real argument against this approach was not anything intrinsic to the juristic basis of the law of confidentiality but other principles in political morality that argue for restraint on the part of courts and a general deference to the lead given by the legislature. This is reflected in the various appellate opinions delivered in *Kaye*.[37] For example, Glidewell LJ:

---

[36]   Cf. n. 34 above.

[37]   *Kaye v. Robertson*, cit. above n. 30.

It is well-known that in English law there is no right to privacy, and accordingly there is no right of action for breach of a person's privacy. The facts of the present case are a graphic illustration of the desirability of Parliament considering whether and in what circumstances statutory provision can be made to protect the privacy of individuals.[38]

This does not mean that the right of privacy was not part of institutional morality of English law at that time. On the contrary, the judges would not have been expressing their opinion that there was a need for rules protecting privacy if they had not deemed it their duty to speak out against its absence. This is where the Human Rights Act 1998 ('the HRA') marks a watershed in this area of the law in the UK. It gives the human rights provisions of the ECHR some application in UK law. Though the HRA does not invalidate a clear and unambiguous law passed by Parliament,[39] it casts a duty on Parliament to take into account the ECHR rights.[40] Most significantly, it makes it unlawful for a 'public authority' (which includes a UK court or tribunal) to 'act in a way which is incompatible with a Convention right', except where the courts are strictly bound to give effect to or enforce the legislation and the primary legislation 'cannot be read or given effect in a way which is compatible with the Convention rights'.[41] This means that the courts, in interpreting and applying statutes and the common law, must do so, in as far as the common law tenets of interpretation and principles precedent allow, in a manner consistent with respect for those rights. The key ECHR rights relevant to development of the law of the tort of breach of confidence are Articles 8 ('Everyone has the right to respect for his private and family life, his home and his correspondence') and 10 (right to freedom of expression). The impact of this on the development of the law of the breach of confidence action to protect aspects of privacy was almost immediate. The critical breakthrough was made in *Douglas v. Hello! Ltd (No. 1)*,[42] when a celebrity couple sought an interlocutory injunction until trial, in an action for permanent injunction and damages, against a weekly newspaper in respect of the pending publication of unauthorized photographs which had been taken at the couple's wedding celebrations.

---

[38] *Ibid* at 66.

[39] Section 3(2) Human Rights Act 1998.

[40] The courts may make a declaration of incompatibility between primary legislation and ECHR rights, though this will not affect the operation or enforcement of the incompatible primary legislation: s 4 Human Rights Act 1998.

[41] Section 6 Human Rights Act 1998.

[42] *Douglas and others v. Hello! Ltd (No. 1)* [2001] F.S.R. 40.

The couple had authorized another weekly newspaper to take and (subject to their vetting and right to veto publication of any particular photo) publish photographs of the event. The couple and the latter newspaper were the claimants in the action. The couple had made it known to persons entering that part of the hotel that no unauthorized photographing or video taping of the event was to be made and that the event was to be regarded as a private occasion. However, the court could not rule out the possibility that the trial may establish (as indeed it later did[43]) that the photographs had been taken by an intruder with whom no specific relationship of trust or confidence had been established.[44] All the judges found for different reasons that the balance of convenience test for interlocutory injunctions favoured the defendant as any potential damage could be compensated in damages.

The judgments of Sedley and Keene LJJ grappled directly with the invasion of privacy point and extended the law of breach of confidence to protect privacy. Of these, Sedley LJ gave the boldest statement of the basis of this extension: 'The law no longer needs to construct an artificial relationship of confidentiality between intruder and victim: it can recognize privacy itself as a legal principle drawn from the fundamental value of personal autonomy.'[45] He observed that, if the step from confidentiality to privacy protection involved an innovation, 'this is precisely the kind of incremental change for which the [Human Rights Act] is designed'.[46] Section 12 of the Act requires the courts, when they are considering any relief which might affect the exercise of the ECHR right of freedom of expression, to have particular regard of the importance of that right in the case of journalistic, literary and artistic material, and to be satisfied that the applicant is likely to establish that publication should not be allowed. He found that this did not mean that Article 10 had presumptive priority over the other rights, including the right of privacy under Article 8, and that, in any case, the fact that they (as a 'public authority') were required by section 6 to act consistently with all the rights meant that the competing strictures of all the rights meant that they had to be qualified by one another with the outcome to be 'determined principally by considerations of proportionality'.[47] Proportionality is meaningful only if there is a common value or desideratum which all the rights protect or promote, so that the competing claims may be given due balance in that

---

[43]   *Douglas v. Hello! Ltd (No 3)* [2003] EWHC 786 (Ch).
[44]   *Douglas v. Hello! Ltd (No 1)* cit. above n. 42, see Brooke LJ, at para. 59.
[45]   *Ibid* Sedley LJ at para. 126.
[46]   *Ibid* at para. 129.
[47]   *Ibid* at para. 137.

the restriction of one right may be justified by an equal or greater advancement of that value by virtue of another right. This is where Sedley LJ's identification of the 'fundamental value of personal autonomy' as the basis of privacy provides common ground for the ECHR rights and the basis for the legal principles of the breach of confidentiality action. Personal autonomy requires the liberty and capacity to plan and carry out actions: this identifies the equal right to freedom and well-being at the heart of contemporary breach of confidentiality action. This extension and re-conceptualization of the basis of the law of breach of confidence was confirmed by the House of Lords in *Campbell v. Mirror Group Newspapers Ltd*,[48] so much so that one of the Law Lords opined that 'The essence of the tort is better encapsulated now as misuse of private information.'[49] That case was brought by a famous model against a British newspaper which had published a photograph of her at the doorstep of a building embracing two persons, captioned: 'Therapy: Naomi outside meeting'.

This accompanied a news story revealing that the supermodel had been attending Narcotics Anonymous meetings to overcome addiction to drugs. Her claim was based on, amongst other grounds, breach of confidence. As the claimant had previously protested that she had not engaged in substance abuse, rebuttal of this specific claim was considered fair game for the press. Hence, it was conceded that she was not protected against the publication of the fact itself that she was an addict and was undergoing therapy. Her claim was that she retained rights which were infringed when the defendant proposed to go beyond this and made public the following additional details: the fact that the therapy was with Narcotics Anonymous, the details of the therapy and the photograph. The last mentioned feature in the case was the one that truly tested the boundaries of the expanded tort, as the photograph portion of the claim did not fit the old conception of the tort. This is far removed from the disclosures made in confidential occasions and breach of trust situations that typify the classic version of the tort. Even if the photographer had received a tip-off that was made as result of a breach of confidence,[50] the photograph by itself was of a subject matter that occurred in a place that

---

[48]   [2004] UKHL 22.

[49]   *Ibid*, per Lord Nicholls at para. 14.

[50]   Lord Hoffmann found that the 'cause of action fits squarely within both the old and the new law' (*ibid*, para. 53) because the newspaper must have known that the information about her attending Narcotics Anonymous was confidential and, by implication, could only have reached them via breach of confidence.

was both in public and open to public view. This could be a circumstance in which it would be just to impose an obligation of confidence only if one has rights even against strangers as regards information that may be accessible to them in places they were perfectly entitled to go. The UK's highest court found this right in the idea of reasonable expectation of privacy, the violation of which is a threshold requirement for a claim for breach of privacy action (though they divided 3–2 on the application to the facts as regards proportionality); where this threshold requirement has been satisfied, its ruling is that the courts have also to consider, under the heading of 'proportionality', whether the publication should be actionable having regard to other rights and matters of public interest. This would include the public interest in the freedom of the press. Like Sedley LJ in the *Douglas case*, Lord Hoffmann (though he was in the minority on the outcome) was able to locate the ultimate basis of the legal principle in the idea of human autonomy: 'What human rights law has done is to identify private information as something worth protecting as an aspect of human autonomy and dignity.'[51]

The principle of a fundamental equal right to freedom and well-being that this work argues undergirds the main justificatory principles of the law of breach of confidence, explains two features of this re-conceptualized tort: first, why one may owe obligations of confidentiality or respect to privacy to persons with whom one has not developed a relationship or trust or any prior understanding; secondly, how proportionality works. To take the points in order: a possible conception of liberty consisting of freedom in the absence of duties would not support any right of privacy, for this depends on there being duties of restraint. But, then, neither would it support even the negative liberties of Isaiah Berlin,[52] for respect for liberty, freedom of expression and conscience requires an acceptance of duties of restraint from coercion in such matters. This requires all relevant persons should cooperate to uphold a scheme of principles that requires such restraint, which then begs the question of the basis for calling for and expecting such cooperation from one another. This is where recognition that freedom to form and realize purposes and plans is (as Gewirth rightly argues[53]) a fundamental good and that, so far as is necessary to secure this, we have a fundamental obligation to cooperate to promote and protect, for each of us as equal persons, a right to a scheme of liberty and such degree of well-being as

---

[51]   Lord Hoffmann, *ibid*, para. 50.

[52]   Berlin (2002).

[53]   Gewirth (1978 and 1996), cf. discussion of Gewirth's PGC herein at §2.5.1.

to realize that liberty (cf. §2.4.7). This right is the basis of the autonomy and human dignity on which Lord Hoffmann and Sedley LJ construct the legal principle for the protection of privacy. A pre-existing relationship or understanding of trust between defendant and victim is unnecessary because the very basis which even strangers in society are rationally impelled to accept as morally binding upon each other, for the purpose of securing their liberty from illegitimate coercion upon their person and interference with their plans, provides the grounds for reasonably expecting that they should be free from exceptional scrutiny and publicity. Autonomy also requires respect for freedom of speech and expression. This is where the matter of proportionality must be considered. Having freedom and well-being as the basis for a scheme of moral rights for equals provides us with a criterion for deciding when our interest to freedom of expression (to give as well as receive information and other forms of communication) should give way to our interest in privacy. This is basically at the point where the resulting scheme of freedoms for all persons as equals is greater if we tilt in one way rather than the other. This, as suggested earlier (cf. §2.5.1), is best resolved by Gewirth's criterion of degree of needfulness for action: which gives priority to promoting or protecting the more urgent and important conditions and capacities for action for individuals before satisfying other types of claim.[54] This best explains why the victim's privacy interest trumps the press' freedom of expression argument in the *Campbell case*: promoting an individual's efforts at recovery from addiction is more important than the satisfaction of the curiosity of others in the details of that struggle.

4.2.6   Undisclosed Information Protection as an IPR

Promotion of freedom and well-being explains the place of protection of undisclosed information in the spectrum of IPRs. Its place in the spectrum of IPRs is curious because it lacks the full indicia of property rights as the right is not fully alienable except, perhaps, where the right is grounded in contract. It may be waived, but that is not equivalent to the ability to transfer the right to others.[55] This may be an academic problem rather than a practical one as what matters is what one may do with the rights rather than the label we should apply, but it does raise the question

---

[54]   Gewirth (1996), p. 45 (cf. §2.5.1).

[55]   Though confidential disclosees of commercially valuable information may acquire their own interest in the information enforceable against third parties with notice, *OBG Ltd v. Allan* sub. nom. *Douglas v. Hello! Ltd (No. 3)* [2007] UKHL 21.

of why, in traditional academic practice, this regime should be treated in the same group as copyright and patents. As a form of personal liberty though, it takes its place at the beginning of that spectrum: with control of information and ideas that relate to one especially and which are within one's practical power of denying to others – because one can sometimes decide whether to reveal information or not, whether to work the matter in public or not. The institution gives especial control over aspects that are particularly important to personhood – by the protection it gives to disclosures in private relations – but is designed to encourage use of commercially valuable information and ideas in a way that enables the public to enjoy some of the fruits of their use, that would otherwise be unavailable to it, by encouraging limited disclosures that are essential to commercial exploitation. Copyright and patents are on the same spectrum but further along because, whilst respecting that right of personal control, they are designed to induce publication of the ideas for the promotion and protection of freedom and well-being of all human persons. As with privacy protection under the breach of confidence action, copyright and patent in respect of the moral rights of authors and inventors, give special protection of certain aspects critical to maintaining personhood by rendering some limited rights inalienable (see below at §4.6). The apparent conflict of principles, in embracing elements that at the same time promote publication and sharing on the one hand, and control and inalienability on the other, is dispelled once one realizes that the true underlying principle is the protection and promotion of the freedom and well-being of individuals, which supports both the exercise of control where this enables personhood and the limitation of it where the equal liberty of others is concerned.

4.3   MORAL TERMS IN COPYRIGHT LAWS

4.3.1   The Moral Ideas in the Central Rules of Copyright

The balance between protection for the personhood of authors and their interests over their creations, and the claims of users and the public to access for the promotion of their personhood, is a tension that plays itself out in much of the structure of copyright law. In the common law breach of confidence action, this adjustment is made through judge made concepts which are inherently moral and malleable. In copyright, and patent laws to be considered later, which are mainly creatures of statute, these features have to be built in through the key ideas in the statutory words. Among the critical concepts expressing this tension is the originality requirement that is a threshold quality for existence of the right, and the requirement that borrowing from the work should be of at least a substantial part to constitute infringement, which defines the extent of the right over the creation. The originality rule requires that the work should owe something of its form, structure or content to the independent creativity or effort of the author before he or she obtains copyright protection, reflecting his or her personhood. But the promotion and protection of freedom and well-being also supports access of others to copyright matter. Much of this access is facilitated by the market through exploitation of the works through making copies available for purchase and through licensing of the exercise of rights. However, the protection and promotion of the freedom and well-being of persons also requires that others should have a degree of free access to those works where such access is vital to freedom and well-being. Leaving the distribution of such access to the market may violate the requirement of equality of persons (§3.6.3). Adjustments for equality are facilitated by exceptions, sometimes couched in moral terms. This includes fair dealing exceptions, the most general being the American style general fair use exception. An important international provision which captures this idea is the 'three-step test' examined in the next chapter (§5.3.2). Even ostensibly descriptive or technical terms import the idea of the proper balance between the property and participatory rights of individuals.

These twin principles may be found in the idea–expression dichotomy which is central to copyright, and in the criterion of substantiality of use, for the amount of borrowing from the copyright work which would constitute an infringing use. At the international level, this theme is reflected in the balance struck in the UDHR (cf. §4.1.1 above) between the right of authors to protection of their 'moral and material interests' in their productions (what we may call the 'property right'), and the right of everyone to 'freely participate in the cultural life of the community, to enjoy the arts and to share in scientific advancement and its benefits' (the 'participation right').[56] This 'balance', it is here argued, ultimately grounds in the idea that the equal right to freedom and well-being is fundamental. It is not argued that these terms encapsulate such an idea; rather, these rules enable such a conception of justice to be expressed in the institutions, even if the makers of the laws or conventions had other conceptions in mind and had given no thought to such a justification. This claim sounds perverse but is not really so because the use of such words signifies an intention that the right moral result should be

---

[56] Art. 27 UDHR.

achieved, whatever conception the framers of the rules may have had of such words (be they 'fair', 'reasonable', 'just', 'legitimate', etc.), by applying the concept of universalization and prescriptiveness in a search of principles which have objective rational force, and which provide the moral ground and purpose of the idea of a system of law. It is not surprising, then, that some of these themes appeared in the first major cases to interpret the first true copyright statute. *Donaldson v. Beckett*[57] laid to rest over half a century of contention and uncertainty over the questions of whether there was a common law copyright, its nature and whether it survived the English Statute of Anne (1710),[58] the first real modern copyright law, which replaced the prior system – when the Stationers' Company's (comprising printers, publishers and booksellers but, notably, not authors) monopoly on licensing printing came to an end with the expiry of the Licensing Act in 1694.[59] The Statute of Anne gave authors and their assigns protection for 14 years, which would be renewed if the author was living at the end of that period, for a further 14 years. At same time it left a public domain comprising works which had fallen out of copyright or were partially accessible to the public for free. It was this public domain, and the attempted balance between property and participation rights, which was threatened by the argument, mounted almost at once by publishers, that there persisted a perpetual common law copyright that survived the Statute of Anne and continued after the rights under that Act had expired. There was a saving provision (section 9) which provided that the Act did not extend 'either to prejudice or confirm any right' of any person to printing books. The tide for the proposition that there was a perpetual and surviving common law copyright reached its highest point with the victory of the publishers in *Millar v. Taylor* in 1769 in the Court of King's Bench.[60]

Five years later, in 1774, the House of Lords in *Donaldson v. Beckett* over-ruled *Millar v. Taylor* on the critical point, holding that: there was a common law perpetual copyright to first print and publish unpublished works; that the common law did not take away from the author the right to reprint the book after publication; *but* (on the narrowest 6–5 majority) the effect of the Statute of Anne was that, if there was such a common law right of action after publication, it was 'taken away by the statute 8th Anne' and the author 'was precluded from every remedy except on the

[57]　(1774) 2 Bro. P. C. 129; (1774) 4 Burr. 2408.
[58]　8 Anne, c. 19 (1710).
[59]　Sources for the history of this episode: Ricketson (1984), pp. 58–70; Laddie, Prescote and Vitoria (1995), ch. 2, pp. 18–22.
[60]　(1769) 4 Burr. 2303.

foundation of the said statute, and on the terms and conditions prescribed thereby'.[61] The outcome really turned on considerations of the policy and morality of the common law, for the arguments based on precedent, history and statutory interpretation were at best equivocal. The remaining arguments relied on the purpose and policy of the law, and ultimately brought into play justificatory questions about the role of the common law courts.[62] These questions were: whether there ought to be copyright protection as a matter of right and policy; and the ancillary but distinct question of institutional morality, about whether the courts ought to be the chief instrument for fashioning this right. The arguments for the common law copyright were based both on grounds of entitlement ('It is certainly not agreeable to natural justice, that a stranger should reap the beneficial pecuniary produce of another man's work'),[63] and consequentialist incentive ('It is wise in any state to encourage letters, and the painful researches of learned men ... by securing to them the property of their own works').[64] Thus there was, almost at the very inception of copyright, a grappling with the most fundamental questions relating to the justification of intellectual property rights dealt with in the last chapter.

There were concerns about the delimitations of the subject matter of the right: doubts about the propriety and practicality of property in ideas because of their vagueness and intangibility.[65] And there were arguments about the justice of the institutions, wherein entitlement and consequentialist grounds for the property right were met with concerns about the natural and social rights of 'all the rest of mankind'; a tension which argues against an absolutist conception of the property right in favour of one that balances the property interest against the claims of the commons. The upshot of the debates in *Millar v. Taylor* and *Donaldson v.*

---

[61]   The critical third question before the court at (1774) 2 Bro. P. C. 129 at 145; (1774) 4 Burr. 2408.

[62]   'It could be done only on principles of private justice, moral fitness, and public convenience; which, when applied to a new subject, make common law without a precedent; much more when received and approved by usage': per Willes J, *Millar v. Taylor,* cit. above n. 60 at 2312.

[63]   *Ibid*, per Willes J at 2334/5; see also Aston J at 2340, 'For this is originally the author's: and, therefore, unless clearly rendered common by his own act and full consent, it ought still to remain his.'

[64]   *Ibid*, per Willes J at 2334/5.

[65]   *Ibid*, see Yates J at 2357–65. In *Donaldson v. Beckett*, see Baron Eyre. References to the judicial grounds in *Donaldson v. Beckett* are as reported in Cobbett's "Parliamentary History of England", London, 1806–1820, vol. XVII, reproduced in Tallmo, *The History of Copyright.*

Beckett, as finally settled by the House of Lords in the latter, is that this justificatory tension applies to the institution but was best determined by positive law making by the legislature.[66] It demanded that there be a balance between public interests in the intellectual commons and property protection of ownership. This demand for balance requires that boundaries be drawn but provides uncertain and controversial guidance as to where exactly these boundaries should be drawn, making this an inappropriate area for wholesale judicial innovation. This, more than any of the judicial grounds given in *Donaldson v. Beckett*, explains the eventual outcome in favour of a legislative regime pre-empting a common law one, and why it was allowed to remain. Copyright has been mainly a creature of statute since.[67] However, the underlying justificatory tension remains; hence, judicial resources for shaping law continued to, and still remain, an active means of expressing it, exploiting the interstices of statutes and the moral concepts in the statutory rules which reflect them. The following subsections explore how this justificatory tension runs through such central rules of copyright.

4.3.2   The Idea–Expression Dichotomy

The idea–expression relationship was a theme emerging with the difficulties with, and objections to, property rights in ideas that the early cases of *Millar v. Taylor*[68] and *Donaldson v. Beckett*[69] grappled with when considering the justification of copyright in the context of a putative common law protection co-existing with the statutory regime. The principle implicit in the institution[70] appeared as a statutory rule in section 102(b) of the US Copyright Act of 1976:

> In no case does copyright protection for an original work of authorship extend to any idea, procedure, process, system, method of operation, concept, principle, or discovery, regardless of the form in which it is described, explained, illustrated, or embodied in such a work.

---

[66]   In *Donaldson v. Beckett* (Tallmo text see prev. note), see De Grey LCJ, Lord Camden.

[67]   The ghost of the common law copyright in unpublished works was finally laid to rest by the abrogation of the common law rights by s 31 of the Imperial Copyright Act 1911 for the UK and such of His Majesty's dominions to which that Act extended (s 1(1)).

[68]   Cit. at n. 60.

[69]   Cit. at n. 61.

[70]   For judicial expressions of this doctrine in other countries see Sterling (2003) at §6.03, pp. 221–2.

This is the culmination of a line of American common law jurisprudence which can be traced from *Baker v. Selden*[71] in 1879, where the copyright in a work describing a method of book keeping was held not to be infringed by the reproduction of the column entries illustrating this method which was necessary to effecting the idea in the system. It includes the case of *Nichols v. Universal Pictures*[72] in which Learned Hand J observed that the difference between an idea and its expression in a work was in the degree of abstraction, where the bare idea of a plot (e.g. star crossed lovers frustrated by family objections) would be unprotectable whilst the detailed plot, elements of characterization and dramatic incidents may be protectable expression. This distinction allows for protection against literal copying and a good degree of non-textual tracking of the original work, but leaves a portion of the abstract conception of the work in the public domain for reworking by other creators. The embodiment of the doctrine in statute in the US has meant that US courts have legislative sanction to develop the principle as a limitation on the property. This has led to the principle, in cases of non-literal reproduction, that where an idea can practically be effected only in a very limited number of ways, that idea is said to 'merge' with those non-literal aspects of the expression, with the result that copying of those structural elements of the work will not be infringing. Important use of this merger principle has been made as regards protection of computer programs against non-literal (or non-textual) infringement in the widely influential *Computer Associates v. Altai*[73] 'abstraction–filtration–comparison' test of the Second Circuit Court of Appeals. This test conceptualizes a computer program at several levels of abstraction beyond the literal coding: into systems and sub-systems and structures, each having its function which is deemed to be an unprotectable idea. Also unprotectable were so much of the systems and structures (and sub-parts thereof) that, because of considerations of necessity or efficiency, could only be designed in the way embodied in the protected program. These unprotected features of the structure, system or organization of the program have to be filtered out and it is the remaining elements that will be used for comparison with the defendant's work for an assessment as to whether the borrowing has been substantial enough to constitute infringement. This test is a rejection of (and reaction to) an earlier test propounded by the Third Circuit Court of Appeals in *Whelan*

---

71   101 U.S. 99 (1879).
72   45 F. 2d 119 (1930).
73   982 F. 2d 693 (2nd Cir., 1992).

v. Jaslow[74] which treated the structure, system and organization of a program as protected expression and left only the ultimate purpose of the program as the unprotectable idea.

The *Altai* test places a greater premium on giving to non-right holders in programs access to structural elements of the work for the purpose of learning and incorporation into new, and possibly competing, programs. The concept of unprotectable 'ideas' in such cases is not a purely technical one but involves choices about the proper balance between protection of property and public participation in the work. The first express embodiment of this concept in a general international convention[75] is Article 9(2) of TRIPS adopted in 1994: 'Copyright protection shall extend to expressions and not ideas, procedures, methods of operation or mathematical concepts as such.' Although the idea–expression dichotomy is not explicitly stated in the Berne Convention, the WCT declares (at Article 2) that 'Copyright extends to expressions and not to ideas, procedures, methods of operation or mathematical concepts as such.' The wording is almost identical to the provision in TRIPS except that instead of saying that 'Copyright *shall* extend to expressions …', creating a rule, it says '*Copyright extends* …', suggesting acknowledgement of an existing rule.[76] For parties to the WCT at any rate, copyright cannot extend to ideas. As for WTO member states, it is notable that the non-protection of ideas in copyright is an explicit mandatory *ceiling* on IP protection in TRIPS. TRIPS mainly sets minima protection obligations on member states and usually does not restrict higher or more extensive protection. The basis of this is Article 1(1), which provides that 'Members may, but shall not be obliged to, implement in their law more extensive protection than is required by this Agreement.' However, this is followed by the qualification 'provided that such protection does not contravene the provisions of this Agreement'. Extending copyright protection to ideas and so on does contravene the

---

[74]　*Whelan Associates Inc. v. Jaslow Dental Laboratories Inc.* 797 F. 2d 1222 (3rd Cir., 1986).

[75]　The EU 'Software Directive' (Council Directive 91/250/EEC of May 1991) did at Art.1(2) provide that the protection under that Directive applied to the 'expression in any form of a computer program' but '[i]deas and principles which underlie any element of a computer program … are not protected by copyright under this Directive' – now Art. 1(2) Directive 2009/24/EC. And the regional North American Free Trade Agreement signed by Canada, the US and Mexico in 1992 did provide at Art. 1705(1) for parties affording protection for works (in addition to those covered by Art. 1705 (2) thereof) that 'embody original expression within the meaning of [the Berne] Convention'.

[76]　Invoking Vienna Convention on the Law of Treaties, 1969, Art. 31(3)(a) & (b).

prohibition in the second half of Article 9(2). Article 9(2) requires the legal systems of member states to grapple with this distinction as a substantive concept and, if as maintained here, this requires a conscientious drawing of the line between what belongs to the copyright holder and what belongs in the public domain for the rest of the community based on the justification of copyright as an institution, then it places the question of the moral basis of copyright at the centre of one of the key rules that define the scope of the regime. Although the distinction is not overtly moral in character, its application – as may be observed from the foregoing references to the US implementation of this principle – quickly forces the judges and legal systems to choose between giving some content to the notion of ideas being unprotectable, and hence make evaluative decisions about the limits of the realm of copyright, or hollowing out the concept until it becomes an empty mantra, dutifully noted and then passed over for some more substantive principle. One finds the former approach in the US because of section 102(b) of its Copyright Act.

A contrast is provided by the dominant trend in other common law systems where there is no similar statutory enshrinement of the dichotomy. This is exemplified by UK law. Although the idea–expression dichotomy and what it means has been a repeated theme in judicial exposition of copyright theory in common law systems, its general application has never been statutorily encoded in UK copyright law (though there is a reference in relation to computer programs)[77] and one can even doubt its existence as a discrete rule. Lord Hoffmann in *Designers Guild Ltd v. Russell Williams Textiles Ltd*[78] observed as regards the principle: 'What does it mean? ... "it all depends on what you mean by 'ideas'".'[79] He identified several versions of this conception.[80] One strand of this theme is that it is simply impossible to have property in an idea whilst it is still purely in the mind: '[T]here can be no copyright in an idea which is merely in the head, which has not been

---

[77] Copyright, Designs and Patents Act 1988 (UK), s 50A(1): 'It is not an infringement of copyright for a lawful user of a copy of a computer program to observe, study or test the functioning of the program in order to determine the ideas and principles which underlie any element of the program if he does so while performing any of the acts of loading, displaying, running, transmitting or storing the program which he is entitled to do.'

[78] [2001] F.S.R. 11, at para. 23.

[79] *Ibid* at para. 23, citing Lord Hailsham in *L.B. (Plastics) Ltd v. Swish Products Ltd* [1979] R.P.C. 551 at 629.

[80] Ang (1994), pp. 111–53, gives a similar treatment of the dichotomy.

expressed in copyrightable form.'[81] This is a trivial platitude, but the inaccessibility of such ideas is an important point of departure. In such a state, the creators' control of the ideas is absolute but of little practical utility to him or her. It is a benefit both to the creators and to the community that they put their creations in some communicable form, at which point they become vulnerable, as they have become accessible, to being taken by others. It is at this point that everyone's general interest in their own expression of personhood as well as ability to use creations by others that have been made accessible should rationally lead one to cooperate in a scheme which gives one a limited control over certain types of idea thus rendered accessible, to provide security with personhood which at the same time allows enough right of access to equally protect the interests in personhood of others. Thus, this version of the idea–expression dichotomy forms the basis of the idea of sharing which informs the other strands of this principle. The other distinct versions of the idea–expression dichotomy that Lord Hoffmann identifies are as follows. The second comprises instances of non-coverage under a separate rule identifying categories of things subject to copyright – because there is 'no connection with the literary, dramatic, musical or artistic nature of the work'. The third consists of non-substantiality: when the feature is not original or is commonplace, the use of that feature in itself would not be infringing. Both these concepts apportion property control and participation access between owners and public as an expression of the central theme of sharing. The non-protectability of ideas is, then, not a distinct rule with the UK copyright system or those systems following it. Instead, it exists as a thematic concept informing the way other rules in the UK copyright law are understood and interpreted. As a principle for interpreting and applying those other key rules of the regime, it works to require the law to give expression to the fundamental tension between property and participation claims that reflect the principle of promotion and protection of liberty and well-being. How the courts interpret and apply these other key rules can either fulfil that implicit bargain, or dilute and nullify its promises.

4.3.3   Originality and Substantiality

The words 'original' and 'originality' are not explicitly used in the Berne Convention for the Protection of Literary and Artistic Works[82] (henceforth 'the Berne Convention' or simply 'Berne'), except in relation

---

[81]   *Designers Guild* cit. above n. 78, per Lord Hoffmann at para. 24.

[82]   Adopted in 1886; references herein are to the 1971 Paris Revision unless otherwise indicated.

to protection of translations, but the criterion is derived from the essential idea of authorship that runs through its text.[83] The TRIPS Agreement, which imports[84] the main substantive provisions of the Berne Convention (except for the moral rights clause at Article 6*bis*), also seems to treat the point as being too obvious to require mention, except as regards 'compilations' (Article 10(2)), where there is an express requirement that those compilations 'which by reason of the selection and arrangement of their contents constitute intellectual creations shall be protected as such'. In civil law systems, this originality criterion requires some element of creativity bearing the mark of the author's personality, though there may be some relaxation of this standard in relation to utilitarian works, such as in French *'petite monnaie'* and the German *'kleine Münze'* ('small change') doctrines.[85] To some extent this ensures that non-creative works belong in the public domain unless this threshold is met. In the US, the originality criterion was held in the Supreme Court decision of *Feist v. Rural Telephone*[86] to require a 'modicum of creativity' in the authorial determination of the final form of the work: this meant that there had to have been some scope for choice about it; in the case of compilations, some scope for the author's individual decision making about the selection or arrangement of the facts or other material included in the compilation. The 'sweat of the brow' interpretation of originality, that would have treated the effort in gathering and verifying the data as sufficient, was rejected. This is a major departure from the trend in the UK and other common law copyright systems, and it is illuminating to note the influence of the background moral reasons that came into play in the formulation of this relatively new doctrine by way of the constitutional basis for the US law. The *Feist* court in O'Connor J's judgment observed:[87]

> It may seem unfair that much of the fruit of the compiler's labor may be used by others without compensation. As justice Brennan has correctly observed, however, this is not 'some unforeseen byproduct of a statutory scheme'[88] ... It

---

[83] The assumption that originality is essential for all protected works is implicit in the provision requiring that translations be protected as 'original works' – Art. 6 of the 1886 text, Art. 2(3) of the 1971 Paris Revision. See also Sterling (2003), p. 292, para. 7.06.

[84] Art. 9(1) of the TRIPS Agreement requires members to comply with Art. 1 to 21 inclusive of Berne save for Art. 6*bis*.

[85] See Sterling (2003), pp. 292–302, para. 7.06–7.11.

[86] *Feist Publications, Inc. v. Rural Telephone Service Co.* 499 U.S. 340.

[87] *Ibid* at 349–50.

[88] Citing *Harper & Row v. Nation Enterprises* cit. below n. 109 at 589.

is, rather, the 'essence of copyright,'[89] ... and a constitutional requirement. The primary objective of copyright is not to reward the labor of authors, but '[t]o promote the Progress of Science and useful Arts.' Art. I. § 8, cl. 8. [US Constitution] ... To this end, copyright assures authors the right to their original expression but encourages others to build freely upon ideas and information conveyed by a work.

The court found the mandate for this solution in the constitutional basis of the legislation that enjoins the advancement of science and arts. As a consequence the originality criterion then plays a role (albeit a modest one) in parcelling out the property interest of authors in the control of their expression whilst preserving for the public domain, in favour of the participation interest of the public, some element in the intellectual object in a manner consistent with Article 27 UDHR and, one might add, the equal right to freedom and well-being. By contrast, in the UK the originality requirement is very minimal: it is satisfied if the author's skill, judgement and labour are spent to create the final work even if not all the elements of it are new and even if it is not creative. Even mere lists of data or other items may be protected under 'compilations' as a literary work if skill, judgement and labour are expended in making the list,[90] though (as a result of the EU 'Database Directive'[91]) a 'database' would have to meet the higher, more stringent criteria of constituting the author's own intellectual creation by reason of the selection and arrangement of the contents of the database.[92] Generally, though, protected works do not have to possess any literary or aesthetic merit.[93] Hence, the contribution level required is low: they must comprise elements that are the result of the creator's skill, judgement and labour and are not merely copied. The 'originality' criterion, thus, sets a fairly low threshold for the existence of copyright in the UK. As a device for achieving a fair balance

---

[89]   *Ibid.*

[90]   Copyright, Designs and Patents Act 1988 (UK), s 3(1)(a), see *Ladbroke v. William Hill* cit. below n. 94.

[91]   96/9/EC of 11 March 1996. A 'database' is defined (at Art. 1(2)) to 'mean a collection of independent works, data or material arranged in a systematic or methodical way and individually accessible by electronic or other means'.

[92]   Copyright, Designs and Patents Act 1988 (UK), s 3(A)(2); cf. 96/9/EC 'Database Directive' *ibid*, Art. 3(1). This effectively makes the requirement for 'databases' equivalent to the US *Feist* standard.

[93]   A possible exception in the UK copyright statute is the problematic case of works of 'artistic craftsmanship' which is one of several types of item defined to constitute an 'artistic work': Copyright, Designs and Patents Act 1988, s 4(1). See *George Hensher Ltd v. Restawile Upholstery (Lancs) Ltd* [1976] A.C. 64, HL.

between protection and the public domain, its direct role is minimal. Like the idea–expression dichotomy, its real role in this regard is an indirect one as a factor in the assessment of the extent of protection to be afforded under the test of 'substantiality' for infringement, where the taking from the work is a partial one. Through this test, these concepts regulate the aspects of the work which are protected. In all copyright systems, once there is copyright over a work, the reproduction or other use of it falling within one of the exclusive rights over the whole of that work would, in the absence of a defence under a limitation or exception to the right, be an infringement. There would be infringement as well if this were done in respect of an aspect or part of the work that would constitute a 'substantial part' of it. In the UK system, substantiality of taking would involve an inquiry as to the quality as well as the quantity of what was taken, but 'the question of whether he has copied a substantial part depends more on the quality than on the quantity of what he has taken'.[94] It is this qualitative element that imports evaluative criteria, potentially including the moral considerations regarding the fairness of the reach of the property right that go towards its justification, into the judicial determination of the extent of the protection afforded by copyright. This is where exploration of the moral dimensions of IPRs illuminates the subject, for it predicts and justifies this type of outcome.

It claims that moral terms and concepts are a requisite part of the structure of such a property right because they are there to express the aspiration towards justification as well as to enable development towards that object, and that where possibilities for these are restricted in one area, that same function would have to be served by some other aspect of the system. In this regard, the contrast between the US and the UK systems illustrates these points in various ways. The US has a slightly broader and richer concept of originality after *Feist*, and in the non-protection of ideas principle embodied as an explicit rule in the system under section 102(b) of its Copyright Act. With these concepts, its system manages to directly address the question of the just apportionment between an author's property interest and the public's participation rights. The UK system gives a much more technical and reduced scope to both these concepts. The result is that much of the justificatory burden that is borne in the US by these concepts falls, in the UK, on the requirement of substantiality for infringement by partial taking, with this function being

---

[94] *Ladbroke (Football) Ltd v. William Hill (Football) Ltd* [1964] 1 W.L.R. 273 HL, per Lord Reid at 276; see also Lord Evershed at 283, Lord Hodson at 288.

facilitated by the idea that 'substantiality' is primarily a qualitative matter. (Though the functions are argued to be equivalent, it is not here contended that the results will be identical.) It is, thus, able to treat commonplace selections and arrangement of materials, such as the tables of weights and measures and other almanac data often found in diaries, as so lacking in originality that the copying of only these elements would not be infringement.[95] The role of the idea–expression dichotomy as a moral principle within the UK copyright law is also strikingly illustrated by a comparison of the treatment of non-literal takings from computer programs in the US and the UK. It has already been observed (above at §4.3.2) that a consequence of the principle of non-protection of ideas (as opposed to expression) in copyright of a work being statutorily enshrined, as in section 102(b) of the 1976 Copyright Act of the US, is that it can be directly applied as a substantive rule on its own. In the absence of a similar statutory embodiment of the idea–expression dichotomy, the UK copyright law pursues the same objective through quite a different rule and in a somewhat different way, though allowing non-literal borrowing to a much lesser extent. Again, the recourse has been to use the flexibility that may be found in the qualitative aspect of substantiality in the infringement criterion. An early first instance decision in the UK held that there could be non-literal infringement of computer programs and suggested that when assessing the substantiality of copying to determine if infringement had occurred, the US *Altai* 'abstraction–filtration–comparison' test[96] could be applied.[97]

Although agreeing that there could be non-literal infringement of programs, this approach was rejected in the later case of *IBCOS Computers Ltd v. Barclays Mercantile Highland Finance Ltd*,[98] also a first instance decision, where the judge preferred merely to ask if the non-literal aspects copied were a substantial part of the whole of the copyright protected program and that the subsistence or extent of the copyright was not affected by the fact that a function could be achieved by one or a limited number of ways. The precedents point in different directions but the latter would appear to give a more limited role to the principle that copyright protection is not to extend to ideas. However, in a third High Court review of the issue of non-literal infringement of copyright in programs, *Cantor Fitzgerald International v. Tradition*

---

[95]   *G.A. Cramp & Sons, Ltd v. Frank Smythson, Ltd* [1944] A.C. 329 HL.
[96]   See §4.3.2, *Computer Associates v Altai* cit. above n. 73.
[97]   *John Richardson Computers Ltd v. Flanders* [1993] F.S.R. 497 at 527.
[98]   [1994] F.S.R. 275.

(U.K.) Ltd,[99] the judge (Pumfrey J) held that substantiality was to be judged, not in the light of how much use a system made of that part of the code or whether it would work without it, but the amount of skill and labour and judgement in design and coding that went into that part as compared with the collection of modules viewed as a whole.[100] This is a perspective that would allow some non-literally similar aspects of the coding to be treated as too general or insubstantial to be substantial even though a vital part of the architecture. In a later High Court decision[101] the same judge held that (where the defendant had not had access to the source code of the protected program) similarity in the way the program functioned as experienced by the user was an instance where the claim for non-textual copying of the *literary* copyright should fail. For, though the 'business logic' of the program as experienced by the user was one that those devising the claimant's program had intended, 'that is not relevant skill and labour' – the reasoning being that the literary copyright protected the coding and structure of the program but, as there was no access to these, the claimant could not rely on the overall function or functions of the program as these were not matters to which the concept of a literary work (or any of the other categories of protected works) extended. As the judge explained:

> I do not come to this conclusion with any regret ... As a matter of policy also, it seems to me that to permit the 'business logic' of a program to attract protection through the literary copyright afforded to the program itself is an unjustifiable extension of the copyright protection into a field where I am far from satisfied that it is appropriate.[102]

It can be seen that, though the statutory schema is different, the principle behind the idea–expression dichotomy that underlies even the UK copyright law (and which it must observe as a consequence of Article 9(2) TRIPS and the 'Software Directive'[103]), that there be an apportionment between the extent of the copyright ownership and the public's claim to participation through some reservation for the public domain, still manages to find expression in the positive law. The flexibility within the idea of substantiality and the relevance, in this regard, of the quality as well as the quantity of what is taken, allow for adjustments to be made

---

99   [2000] R.P.C. 95.
100 *Ibid*, 131–5.
101 *Navitaire Inc. v. Easyjet Airline Co. Ltd (No. 3)* [2004] EWHC 1725 (Ch).
102 *Ibid* at para. 130.
103 EU Directive 91/250/EEC of 14 May 1991, Art. 1(2). Now Art. 1(2) Directive 2009/24/EC.

with reference to the ultimate justification of IP rights. This last is either wholly subjective or it is objective, as Chapter 6 will argue, in the only way it can be: it is objective in that the moral requirement of universal-ization requires that the theory of justification must be consistent with the other aspects of the institution – that is, with the idea of it being law and with the main features of copyright. The idea of substantiality alone, however, cannot accommodate all our concerns for a just sharing of resources as between creators and the consuming public. It cannot accommodate the situations where just sharing may require free public access to much, or all, of the work. Nor is it suggested that it will be desirable that the idea of 'substantiality' should be treated as being so malleable, for it would then fail in its primary purpose of marking out the boundary of the property. There are instances when the qualitative considerations as they bear on substantiality will require practically total identical borrowing before an infringement can be made out: an example would be the very simple and rudimentary drawing of a hand marking out an 'X' in literature teaching one how to fill in a ballot sheet in *Kenrick v. Lawrence.*[104] The low level of originality in the author's contribution and the general interest in basic ideas being available for the use of others amply support these results and these do exemplify how the value considerations in the fundamental justificatory theory of the institution work upon so apparently technical a concept as 'substantiality' through the idea of measuring this by the 'quality' of what is taken. But there are limits to the flexibility of the concept. Very properly, substanti-ality of use cannot be denied where there is a high degree of creativity involved in an aspect of the work that is taken, yet one might want to excuse the taking in the interest of just sharing. Then, the job of facilitating that justificatory background purpose cannot be done by the idea of substantiality in infringements. One must then turn to the limitations and exceptions.

4.3.4   Moral Terms in Copyright Exceptions and Limitations

Exceptions and limitations to copyright protection form the most import-ant ways that the value of the creations are shared between creators and the public. It should be no surprise that these are hedged around with moral terms and concepts. Broadly viewed, the national approaches to exceptions and limitations take two generic forms. By far the most represented is a closed list system that is typical of the civil law *droit*

---

[104]   *Kenrick & Co v. Lawrence & Co* (1890) L.R. 25 Q.B.D. 99.

auteur system. Perhaps a modification of this, which incorporates in some degree the other approach, is found in the UK system and other common law systems following its lead, where the defences are specific but couched in terms that allow for limited flexibility and are embedded within common law doctrines which allow for some judicial discretion. The other generic approach, which truly forms a diametrically different alternative, is an 'open' system. The leading example is the fair use defence in section 107 of the US Copyright Act, though recently Singapore and Israel have amended their respective copyright legislation to adopt similar open defences clearly modelled on the US section 107.[105] In neither type of system are the moral dimensions irrelevant but they allow, in varying degrees rather than in categorical contrasts, different ways of expressing these dimensions. The open system gives a greater role to the judiciary and scope for development of the law towards legitimacy through the moral dimension of interpretation. The closed system places a premium on the other moral dimensions, of exercise and reform, and places the onus on legislatures to ensure that the institutions are legitimate. Before it was statutorily encapsulated in the 1976 Copyright Act[106] the US fair use defence was a common law defence whose roots date to the 1841 case of *Folsom v. Marsh*.[107] By 1968 a US District Court was able, as a result of this rule, to treat as non-infringing the making of charcoal-drawn faithful copies of critical stills from frames of an amateur movie, which captured the assassination of President Kennedy in Dallas, to illustrate and support the defendant author's theory in a book about that tragic event. The court observed, 'The doctrine is entirely equitable and is so flexible as to virtually defy definition.'[108]

By that time, a Bill for a major revision of the Copyright law containing a statutory encoding of the fair use defence and its criteria was before Congress, and the District Court was able to refer to it for guidance. Later enacted in the 1976 Copyright Act, section 107 provides: '[T]he fair use of a copyrighted work ... for purposes such as criticism, comment, news reporting, teaching (including multiple copies for class-room use), scholarship, or research, is not an infringement of copyright.' It goes on to add that in determining whether a use has been fair, the

---

[105] See Singapore's Copyright Act (Chapter 63) ss 35–7, and Israel's Copyright Law 2007, s 19.

[106] Title 17 USC.

[107] 9 F. Cas.342.

[108] *Time Inc. v. Bernard Geis Associates* (D.C.NY. 1968) 293 F. Supp. 130 at 144.

factors to be considered include: '(1) the purpose and character of the use, including whether such use is of a commercial nature or is for nonprofit educational purposes; (2) the nature of the copyrighted work; (3) the amount and substantiality of the portion used in relation to the copyrighted work as a whole; and (4) the effect of the use upon the potential market for or value of the copyrighted work'. It is fair to say that when any use encompassed by an exclusive right would cause substantial prejudice to the owner of the copyright work by directly competing with or superseding an economic exploitation of the original, the person seeking to claim fair use exception for it has a heavy burden to discharge. For example, even though that section expressly states that the fact that a work is unpublished shall not be a bar to a finding of fair use, if that is justified by all the above factors, the scooping of ex-President Ford's memoirs, which were soon to be published, by an article containing quotes which, though short (approximately 300 words), described in his own words critical episodes in his presidency (relating to his pardon of Nixon), was held not to be fair use, despite the historical and newsworthy importance of the quotes, because it jeopardized the work's market for pre-publication serialization.[109] It may be that, with publication of the full memoirs imminent in any case, the public's (as opposed to the newspapers') liberty and well-being did not require fair use to be upheld.

There are situations where the making of unauthorized copies of the whole copyright works can be fair use. These are explicable in terms of the net increase to individual welfare and liberty that results from a finding of non-infringement, despite consequent curtailment of the owner's right of control. An instance is the holding that time shifting of broadcast programme items by home viewers may be fair use.[110] This extends the liberty of home viewers, giving them a choice as to time of access, without affecting the copyright owners' income stream – as long as the time shifting practice is restricted to single instances of private non-commercial re-use. Another employment of the fair use principle explicable in terms of the resulting expansion of freedom and well-being is the doctrine of transformative use. The Supreme Court in *Campbell v. Acuff-Rose Music, Inc.*[111] held that the more 'transformative' a use – that is, the more it alters the original work with a 'new expression, meaning or message' by adding something new, with a different purpose or character – the greater the likelihood of it being fair use and the greater

---

[109] *Harper & Row Publishers, Inc. v. Nation Enterprises* 471 U.S. 539.
[110] *Sony Corporation of America v. Universal City Studios* 464 U.S. 417.
[111] 510 U.S. 569.

the burden for a showing against fair use based on the other factors to be considered. In the words of Souter J:

> Although such transformative use is not absolutely necessary for a finding of fair use, the goal of copyright, to promote science and the arts, is generally furthered by the creation of transformative works. Such works thus lie at the heart of the fair use doctrine's *guarantee of breathing space within the confines of copyright*, and the more transformative the new work, the less will be the significance of other factors, like commercialism, that may weigh against a finding of fair use.[112]

Thus, a parody of a popular song ('Pretty Woman' by Roy Orbison) remained fair use despite the commercial character of the use, the creative nature of the original work, the use of a highly distinctive line of the work ('Pretty woman, walking down the street') and bass riff at the heart of that work. The transformative use doctrine has been applied for a finding of a sufficient possibility of a fair use defence (for a reversal of a preliminary injunction) in a case where the defendant parodied a novel, *Gone With the Wind*, in a new work, *The Wind Done Gone*, which borrowed from the former's characters, locales, setting and plot, to parody its depictment of slavery and race relationships in the American antebellum South.[113] It has also been applied to allow use of thumbnail copies (reduced versions of the original of limited visual value) as links in a search engine for locating the original images on the World Wide Web, because these thumbnails did not displace the market for the original and contributed something different (search capability).[114] The transformative use doctrine serves to promote and protect the freedom and well-being of individuals because the individual's freedom to express himself or herself by using part of existing culture is enhanced. It trades off part of the owner's degree of control but the exchange is not of interests of equal priority. In the doctrine properly applied, the loss to the owner would be marginal, but a transformative use involves, to a greater degree, the expression of the user. For example, in the *Wind Done Gone case*, the erosion of Margaret Mitchell's estate's ability to economically exploit the copyright in *Gone With the Wind* is slight, if any. But the positive application of the doctrine allows the transformative user to play with and comment on an important cultural phenomenon with a bearing

---

[112] *Ibid* at 579. Italics added.

[113] *Sun Trust Bank v. Houghton Mifflin Co.* 268 F 3d 1257 (11th Cir., 2001).

[114] *Kelly v. Arriba Soft Corp* 336 F. 3d 811 (9th Cir. CA, 2003), and *Perfect 10 Inc. v. Amazon Inc.* 508 F. 3d 1146 (9th Cir., CA, 2007) reversing doubts on the point expressed in *Perfect 10 v. Google Inc.* 416 F. Supp. 2d 828.

on race history in America without having to have the by or leave of the owner of the copyright in the latter book. The author could have made the same broad political point in some other way perhaps, but the point is that, should one want to, one should be able to add one's highly distinctive colour to the cultural icon as a possible way of viewing that part of the culture. And to achieve that, there is no other way but to use some of the work's most distinctive characteristics. Here the principle of degree of necessity for action (which includes speech) is pertinent: for, the more transformative a work is, the more self-expression (rather than the mere borrowing of another's speech, which is the result of slavish copying) is involved and, hence, the greater the degree of necessity of action implicated in such freedom, as contrasted with the much lesser necessity for action associated with the ability of the owner to prevent such speech by others.

Another way in which freedom and well-being are increased is that the transformative work adds to the wealth of culture available for enjoyment and consumption since it does not simply supersede the copyright work. The Supreme Court in *Campbell* cast its rationale for the doctrine in consequentialist terms: the promotion of science and the arts that underpins the Constitutional mandate for Congress' legislative power for copyright. However, that is not an obstacle to locating the ultimate basis of fair use in a right of individuals to freedom and well-being, for that right may also be said to justify the promotion of science and the arts as a goal (cf. §3.3.2). Wendy Gordon gives another powerful explanation and justification of the fair use exception, suggesting that 'fair use is ordinarily granted when the market cannot be relied upon to allow socially desirable access to, and use of, copyrighted works'.[115] This would embrace the circumstances where transfer of control to the defendant would be socially desirable but the defendant is not able to purchase the right to use in the market, and the creators' incentives would not be substantially impaired by allowing the exception. This is insightful because it reconciles both protection and exception in terms of maximizing the social benefits of the copyright institution. But the idea that there are forms of access and use by others that may be deemed 'socially desirable', even though they would be denied by the normal operation of the market, rests on the assumption that there are goals and values that are independent and external to market that are relevant to this assessment. Indeed, these are presupposed when fashioning the basic institutions which shape the market. The idea that individual liberty and

---

[115]   Gordon (1982), 1657.

well-being are independent and fundamental criteria explains why copyright should exist to promote creativity and yet allow uses which foster and permit more creativity and expression when the tradeoff in terms of incentives to creativity is marginal and insubstantial. Whether one agrees or disagrees with the foregoing theory about the justification of copyright and the fair use exception, it remains true that it is the moral character of the terms in which that defence is cast that calls for this plumbing into the background justification of the institution. And it is the characteristic feature of moral terms, that they require the formulation of suitable prescriptions, that facilitates the expression of this aspiration to legitimacy by allowing the institution to adapt to reflect these concerns. The words 'fair use' refer in the broadest terms to the idea of justice as between the interests of owners and that of the general public.

They allow judicial decisions to develop the specific rules for particular types of situation in a manner that is reflective of and, at the same time, refines this background idea of justice as it relates to copyright. The American fair use doctrine forms a critical contrast to the dominant European approach which employs a closed list of limitations and exceptions. The latter is encapsulated by Article 5 of the EU's Information Society Directive,[116] which identifies one mandatory exception to the reproduction right (transient or incidental copying for transmission or lawful use[117]), five or so permissible exceptions to the reproduction right,[118] and another 15 or so exceptions to that right and the right of communication to the public.[119] For added measure, these are further subject to the restrictions of the 'three-step test',[120] so that this formulation becomes, not a matrix for generating appropriate exceptions and limitations, but an additional circumscription of the possible list of defences. The contrast should not be exaggerated because even the US copyright statute is replete with more specific and tightly drawn exception provisions, and the fair use defence is a necessary recourse only when the situation is one that has not been provided for. That exception, though, is an important acknowledgement that the public has a generalized claim on the copyright material that cannot be fully expressed by the more specific defences. A middle ground is the UK approach, where the fair dealing defences are far more restricted than the American fair use

---

[116]   Directive 2001/29/EC of 22 May 2001.
[117]   *Ibid*, Art. 5(1).
[118]   *Ibid*, Art. 5(2)(a)(e).
[119]   *Ibid*, Art. 5(3)(a)–(o).
[120]   *Ibid*, Art. 5(5). For the 'three-step test' see next chapter at §5.3.3.

exception.[121] These are limited to fair dealing for specified types of purpose: the fair dealing exceptions for research or private study, criticism or review, and for the reporting of current events.[122] It will be seen in Chapters 7 and 8 that where the American copyright law makes use of the fair use doctrine to allow certain significant exceptions, the same underlying imperatives being denied similar expression by the more restrictive rules of other systems result in a shifting of this search for legitimacy to one or other of the other dimensions. These include the ancillary legal rules relating to exercise, say, under the common law rule of public policy or competition law principles in the dimensions of exercise, or the dimension of reform which is reflected by the intervention of constitutional and human rights laws or by legislative activity. Even when deeply buried, the ghosts of the underlying moral conception of copyright haunt its rules.

4.4   MORAL TERMS IN PATENT LAWS

4.4.1   Patents and Freedom and Well-being

The subject matter of patents, inventions, are unlike copyright works in that their point and value lie less in their capacity to express the personhood of the creator than in the utility of their functions for promoting the personhood of all users. There are types of copyright works that are exceptional in that they are chiefly utilitarian; for example compilations and databases, and computer programs. However, in many ways their exceptional character is acknowledged in the law in that their inclusion in the scheme of copyright protection has to be specially provided for or specially reiterated to obviate doubt about their place in the institution.[123] Whereas copyright protection applies where there is a choice about the form of the work that is said to be the author's expression of the idea, rather than to the idea itself, patent laws concern themselves with the essential elements of the functional creation that is

---

[121]   See summary of the 'fair use' doctrine in Laddie, Prescote and Vitoria (1995), Vol. 1, para. 2.104–2.105.

[122]   Sections 29 and 30, Copyright, Designs and Patents Act 1988.

[123]   In TRIPS by Art. 10(1) and (2); in the Berne Convention scheme by declaration in the WCT at Art. 4 and 5; in the EU system by the 'Software' (Directive 91/250/EEC of 14 May 1991 now superseded by Directive 2009/24/EC of 23 April 2009) and the 'Database' (Directive 96/9/EC of 11 March 1996) Directives.

the invention itself rather than functionally immaterial variations of that idea; use is inessential for expression, but they promote well-being by being useful. Whereas the expression of the users' personality is at best only reflected weakly by the choice to slavishly adopt the expression of a copyright work and such copying is generally not required to enable respect for the free speech and expression of others, patent restrictions are intended to significantly reduce the users' capacity of action in respect of making or using the essential ideas of the invention. Short of the moral right to be identified as the inventor,[124] rights in the invention are not necessary for expressing the creator's personhood. This is not a complete argument against patent protection. The institution also promotes overall freedom and well-being by inducing invention and disclosure that may not otherwise occur: by encouraging their inventors to make the use of their ideas available, initially at a price acceptable to the owner during the patent term and, later, after the patent expires, freely. Patents generally promote freedom and well-being indirectly, by inducing the innovations which expand our possibilities and choices.

A positive tradeoff of liberty, from the incentive for creation bought by some restriction of access, is plausible because the furthering of the general good by patents does not usually require denial of basic well-being. For example, restricting access, during the patent's term, to a new, more efficient motor, does not usually put the life and other aspects of basic well-being of others (who will be able to make and use other motors on which patents have expired) at risk. Of course, this already assumes that the right is not absolute and eternal but one that is shared with the public through a limited term. (If patent rights had been absolutely acquired from the distant past, the curtailment of liberty and well-being this would have entailed would be unimaginable.) But, even so limited, the criterion of degree of necessity for action may very strongly favour access in some critical cases: for example, when life saving medicines and medical technology are involved. This poses a problem for the design of the institution. If exceptions are made for the matters critical for basic well-being, the exceptions would work to retard promotion of new inventions that are most needed for well-being. As a result, the solution should mainly lie outside the patent institution. In the case of medicines and medical technology, for example, this may mean reforms should address the health system as a whole rather than the patent system. (This discussion is pursued further later, cf. §8.4.) But the imperative to find such a solution is rooted in the concern for the

---

[124] Cf. §4.3.2.

promotion of freedom and well-being that is the basis of the justification for patents. The patent owners would have a special responsibility, because of this linkage, to seek and support a solution because they benefit from the cooperation of others in this system of restraint. The effect of the foregoing observed features is that the patent rules are likely to be more descriptive, technical and non-evaluative than for copyright. An exception is the *ordre public* and morality objections to patents, but this is ill suited to solving the justificatory dilemma because it results in blanket non-protection (and non-promotion) of the subject matter, and is based on objection to the thing itself rather than the justice of ownership of it. (See next subsection and §4.7.) There remains the purely utilitarian calculus, as to which arrangement of ownership control and users' access best promotes the overall utility. It is possible to frame such rules with evaluative terms, with the result that the interpreters of the rules (ultimately the courts) would be left with the task of striking that appropriate balance, just as they bear part of that burden with the copyright laws – especially in systems with the open standard 'fair use' defences. But this is inappropriate.

An instance by instance incremental rule development process may be more suited to clarifying conflicts of principle than situations where the principle is clear but the choice may depend on decisions made in respect of other aspects of the system at the same time. In cases where cool reflection about the moral entailments of other aspects of the system as a whole is required, legislatures may intend for courts to work out these implications without them (the members of the legislatures) being agreed or clear about the way this should be done: they only need be agreed as to the nature and type of process of reasoning to be applied, which would be reflected in their choice of the words 'fair' or 'reasonable' and the like. In cases where the consequence of one rule may be counter-balanced or aggravated by decisions about other rules in the system, it will be much better that the various rules of the system be assessed together and framed at the same time as a whole. This is a mode of action that is unavailable to judges who sit and decide cases and rules one by one, at the mercy of the caprice of litigation. On the other hand, the construction of schemes incorporating considerations and counter-balancing items and the making of compromises is precisely the mode of operation that a democratic rule making forum is best equipped to undertake.[125] This is why copyright is largely a matter of statute, and

---

[125]   Waldron (1999). See also *Diamond v. Chakrabarty*, cit. at n. 142, for judicial observations at n. 146 and accompanying text below.

patents, where the former types of issues of principle are minimal, should be regulated by laws that incorporate minimal moral content. This does not mean that moral issues of justification are unimportant to the structures of the regime: it is just that these considerations should have been borne in mind when these structures were framed, and premium is placed on the clarity and certainty of the rules rather than their adaptability in the hands of the courts. Even so, there are, albeit in exceptional types of cases, residual issues of principle, with the result that these descriptive, technical terms are not totally devoid of moral content.

4.4.2 Moral Concepts in Patent Laws

Patents are an inducement, in the form of a grant of monopoly on making and using and other commercial exploitation of the invention for a limited time (under TRIPS, this would be at least 20 years after the filing of the application for a patent[126]), for contribution to the total pool of ideas and knowledge by their disclosure and eventual free release to the public. To ensure that this reward is not too cheaply earned, the invention claimed must meet certain standards that are, for the most part, descriptive:[127] the invention must be new, that is, not have been available to the public before through use or description; involve an inventive step, that is, not have been obvious to a person with ordinary skill in the art; and be capable of industrial application or, in some systems, be useful. Given the technical nature of these ideas, it is perhaps surprising that they afford any room for moral considerations. One aspect of the patent regime where moral considerations and controversy have played a part is the very identification of the types of thing for which patents may be granted. In TRIPS, this would be 'inventions in all fields of technology'.[128] In the first statute governing patents in the UK, section 6 of the Statute of Monopolies of 1623,[129] the patentable subject matter was 'any manner of new manufacture'. The description was intended to be limiting. In a statute which codified the common law hostility to other forms of monopolies,[130] section 6 identifies an exception, when a

---

[126]   Art. 33 TRIPS Agreement.

[127]   Art. 27(1) TRIPS Agreement.

[128]   *Ibid*, which also provides that (subject to some transitional provisions) 'patents shall be available and patent rights enjoyed without discrimination as to ... the field of technology'.

[129]   21 Jac. I c.3.

[130]   *Darcy v. Allin* (1602) Noy 173; The *Case of the 'Clothworkers of Ipswich'* (1615) Godbolt 252.

legitimate monopoly by patents may be granted for inventions. Advances in the possibilities of technology push the boundaries and reveal assumptions that belie the apparent moral neutrality of the phrase. This is especially true of biotechnological innovations whose challenges (cf. §4.4.3) illustrate the feedback loop between IPR laws and their effects, which forces a re-evaluation of our moral assumptions. In the UK the 'manner of new manufacture' description for patentable subject matter remained until the Patent Act of 1977 introduced a new approach in line with the EPC.

The EPC leaves 'invention' undefined except for a specific list of excluded matter.[131] This acknowledges the protean nature of the notion 'invention'. A mixture of policy and principle concerns about appropriation of ideas animates the express exclusions: '[d]iscoveries, scientific theories and mathematical methods'[132] as such are excluded because these, in their pure forms, would not be of direct application in any art. They are regarded as not being so much human creations as human discoveries of pre-existing truths: '[a]esthetic creations'[133] as such are already dealt with by other IPR regimes, mainly copyright and designs protection, and it would seem are excluded as a matter of policy, as are 'programs for computers'[134] and 'presentations of information' as such.[135] The exclusion of 'schemes, rules and methods of performing mental acts, playing games or doing business'[136] as such, though, expresses an intention that certain categories of human creations should be preserved from private appropriation. Australia's Patents Act 1990, on the other hand, still uses the 17th Century description, defining a 'patentable invention' as 'any manner of manufacture within the meaning of section 6 of the Statute of Monopolies'.[137] The decision of Australian High Court *National Research Development Corporation v. Commissioner of Patents*[138] reveals the policy and evaluative concerns that inform our understanding of this apparently technical concept and give it the flexibility to adapt in an ever more technologically complex world:

> The inquiry which the definition demands is an inquiry into the scope of the permissible subject matter of letters patent and grants of privilege protected

---

[131]   Art. 52 EPC. The 2000 Revision of the EPC adds the TRIPS formula that the inventions covered include those 'in all fields of technology' in Art. 52(1).

[132]   Art. 52(2)(a) EPC.

[133]   Art. 52(2)(b) EPC.

[134]   Art. 52(2)(c) EPC.

[135]   Art. 52(2)(d) EPC.

[136]   Art. 52(2)(c) EPC.

[137]   Patents Act 1990 (Australia), s 18(1)(a).

[138]   (1959) 102 CLR 252.

by the section. It is an inquiry not into the meaning of a word so much as to the breadth of the concept which the law has developed by its consideration of the text and purpose of the *Statute of the Monopolies* ... The right question is: 'Is this a proper subject of letters patent according to the principles which have been developed for the application of s. 6 of the *Statute of the Monopolies?*'[139]

4.4.3   The 'Oncomouse' in the US and Canada

The underlying moral assumptions are illustrated by the contrasting treatment of patent protection of 'higher life forms' in the US and Canada which use virtually identical formulae for describing the subject matter that can be patented. Section 101 of the US Patents Act[140] makes patents available for 'any new and useful process, machine, manufacture, or composition of matter, or any new and useful improvement thereof'.[141] The US Patent and Trademark Office (PTO) has accepted since 1987 – after the US Supreme Court in *Diamond v. Chakrabarty*[142] had declared in 1980 that the statute could 'include anything under the sun that is made by man',[143] including man-made microorganisms – that patentable subject matter could include 'non-naturally occurring, non-human multicellular living organisms'.[144] The Supreme Court observed

---

[139]   *Ibid* at 269.

[140]   Title 35 USC.

[141]   This is virtually unchanged from that in the Patent Act of 1793 authored by Thomas Jefferson except that the 1793 Act spoke of 'new and useful *art*' (s 1, emphasis added) instead of the 'new and useful process' in the 1952 Act.

[142]   447 U.S. 303 (1980); by 5–4, majority judgment by Burger CJ.

[143]   *Ibid* per Burger CJ at 308–9, 'The Act embodied Jefferson's philosophy that "ingenuity should receive a liberal encouragement." ... The Committee Reports accompanying the 1952 Act inform us that Congress intended statutory subject matter to "include anything under the sun that is made by man."' Citing: S. Rep. No. 1979, 82d Cong., 2s Sess., 5 (1952); H.R. No. 1923, 82d Cong., 2d Sess. 6 (1952). But laws of nature, natural phenomena, and abstract ideas, are not manmade and are, hence, not patentable. Hence, in *Association for Molecular Pathology v. Myriad Genetics, Inc.* 133 S. Ct. 2107, the Supreme Court held that a naturally occurring DNA segment (unlike cDNA which has been modified by human intervention) such as the precise sequence of the BRCA1 and BRCA2 genes, which can be used to determine nucleotide sequences relevant to breast cancer, are not themselves patentable notwithstanding that extensive effort and expense had to be expended to arrive at their discovery. This ruling does not exclude the patentability of method claims using the knowledge of BRCA1 and BRCA2 sequences in new applications.

[144]   1077 O.G. 24, 21 April 1987, see US PTO Guideline 2105 Patentable Subject Matter – Living Matter [R1].

that a statute is not to be confined to the applications contemplated by the
legislators and that this was especially true in the field of patent law,
where '[a] rule that unanticipated inventions are without protection would
conflict with the core concept of the patent law that anticipation
undermines patentability'.[145] Although it noted *amici* arguments citing
the risks that such research poses in terms of pollution, disease, loss of
genetic diversity and depreciation of human dignity, the court held itself
'without competence to entertain these arguments' because, it observed,
'The choice we are urged to make is a matter of high policy for
resolution within the legislative process after the kind of investigation,
examination and study that legislative bodies can provide and courts
cannot.'[146] Patents subsequently granted in the US have included Harvard's patent for 'Oncomouse', a mouse genetically modified for susceptibility to tumours, useful for cancer research, a patent for which was
disallowed in Canada. The Canadian Patent Act defines an 'invention'[147]
as 'any new and useful art, process, machine, manufacture, or composition of matter, or any new and useful improvement in any art, process,
machine, manufacture or composition of matter'. Despite this near pitch
perfect echoing of the Jeffersonian formula in the American counterpart,
the Canadian Supreme Court in *Harvard College v. Canada*[148] came to
the opposite conclusion: that it was not intended to embrace the patenting
of higher life forms, like mammals, and that the decision to widen the
scope of the Patent Act to cover such matters involved value choices that
in a democracy should properly be the domain of the legislature. In
Bastarache J's leading judgment, the 'phrases "manufacture" and "composition of matter" do not correspond to common understandings of
animal and plant life'.[149]

And, even if the definition is capable of supporting a broad interpretation,
'Given the unique concerns associated with the grant of a monopoly right
over higher life forms ... Parliament would not likely choose the Patent Act
as it currently exists as the appropriate vehicle to protect the rights of
inventors of this type of subject matter.'[150] The conundrum posed by
diametrically contrasting interpretations of virtually identical provisions is

---

[145]   *Diamond v. Chakrabarty*, cit. above at n. 142, per Burger CJ at 316.
[146]   *Ibid* per Burger CJ at 317.
[147]   Patent Act, R.S.C. 1985, c. P-4, s 2.
[148]   *Harvard College v. Canada (Commissioner of Patents)* [2002] S.C.C.D.
480.6065.00–01; 5–4 majority judgment by Bastarache J (at 117), dissent by
Binnie J (at 1).
[149]   *Ibid* at 79.
[150]   *Ibid* at 80; see also 107–8, 110–15 and 119.

the result of a problem inherent in the very nature of the patent institution itself: How does one define the scope of an institution whose very purpose is to contribute to change through innovation which may potentially introduce conditions which will expose and challenge the very assumptions, technological and moral, which are the basis of our initial understanding of what that institution would produce? Of course, the purpose of patents is to encourage invention of the unexpected, but some inventions may be more unexpected than others. The machine centric model that was the paradigm for inventions in the age of the Jacobean and Jeffersonian statutes allowed some of the moral issues related to owning ideas to be dormant until the accretion of new ideas generated a technological climate which rendered that model obsolete. Once this restrictive boundary is breached, the question of how a new one may be reconstructed comes alive, with the potential that every aspect of human activity may come within its scope. Every action has an object and may be improved upon and made more efficient, with the result that the idea of 'inventions' may apply to these improvements. The requirement that the invention should be useful in some industrial or commercial pursuit appears to set some practical limitation except that more and more aspects of our lives appear to be capable of an industrial application. Does it apply to games, ways of thinking, and so on? Can one own the idea of some types of living thing? What if that living thing is a human being, or shares some human element? From defining the scope of permissible monopolies in rather mundane things like playing cards and watermills for the promotion of human convenience, the delimiting of patents has arrived at defining the boundaries of the human.[151]

Given that commercial and technological innovation will always be testing the boundaries of the field that patenting covers, no interpretation of the definition of its subject matter may be morally tone deaf if the institution is to continue to make a positive contribution. Even if the judicial approach is to give deference to legislative intention, the question will remain: At what point in the transformation and expansion of technological possibilities do we reach the type of innovation and claim to patent monopoly that goes beyond the premises that the legislature could have been expected to assume for its embrace of the unexpected? And, when this happens – as it did with different responses in the *Diamond v. Chakrabarty*[152] and *Harvard College v. Canada*[153] cases – should the correct judicial response be to continue allowing the patents until there is legislative intervention, or to

---

[151] Cf. *LELAND STANFORD/Modified animal* cit. below n. 253 and *HOWARD FLOREY/Relaxin* cit. below n. 252 discussed at §4.7.2.

[152] Cit. above n. 142.

[153] Cit. above n. 148.

preclude such patents unless there is such intervention? Neither approach avoids decisions with value laden implications. The way that technological breakthroughs, such as those in genetics resulting in the potential for creating new types of living thing, promote new possibilities and pose new kinds of questions, is well encapsulated in the main judgment in the Canadian 'Oncomouse' case, which referred to matters considered by the Canadian Biotechnology Advisory Committee ('CBAC') in its recommen- dation[154] that the matter be resolved by legislation rather than be left to the courts. Amongst these is the capacity of higher life forms to self-replicate, with the result, in the case of a patent over a type of living thing, that the owner's monopoly is more extensive, with far more reaching implications for the restriction of others, than ordinary inanimate invention. This is because patents would cover not only the organism produced by the inventor but its progeny. For example, they will circumscribe farmers' ability to replant second generation crops from patented seeds or other propagation material gleaned from legitimately sown plants, and expose to liability 'bystanders' who inadvertently cultivate, or rear new stock, of the patented plant or animal.[155] These concerns were canvassed before the Canadian Supreme Court soon after *Harvard College*, in *Monsanto Canada Inc. v. Schmeiser.*[156]

This case was an appeal by a farmer who had been found to have infringed a patent for the gene which had the effect of enabling the soy plant to withstand a certain pesticide. His field was found to have been sown mostly with plants with this gene. The Supreme Court held that, as the patent claims were limited to the gene, the process and the resulting cells, but did not include the plant, they did not violate the holding in *Harvard v. Canada* that higher life forms (which includes plants) are not patentable. However, despite these restricted claims, the inevitable presence of the gene and resulting cells as embodied in the full grown plant was held to be the infringing *use*[157] of the patented subject matter. The claim was not (and, the majority held, should not be read as) limited to the gene and cells *in vitro*. The possession of these through their presence in the plants raised a presumption of possession with a view to use (which would be infringing); a presumption which the farmer was held to have failed to rebut despite the fact that he had not applied the pesticide to the crop. This was because there was use in the sense that the crop was ready, should that have proven necessary, for pesticide application. This meant that, through patent rights

---

154   Canadian Biotechnology Advisory Committee (June 2002).
155   *Harvard College v. Canada*, cit. above at n. 148 at para. 123–4.
156   (2004) SCC 34.
157   Section 42 of the Patents Act (Canada).

in genes and cells, there could effectively be patent power over the resultant life form, despite the majority holding *Harvard College v. Canada*. Another ground cited by the CBAC, and taken up by the majority judgment in *Harvard College* for treating higher life forms as a fundamentally new category of invention, which requires legislative intervention before it can be brought within the patent regime, is the potential that the patents over such technological innovations will eventually extend to human life. This potential exists because no essentially technical distinction can be drawn between such technology as applied to animals and human life once we except patents over higher life forms. As Bastarache J notes: 'There is no defensible basis within the definition of invention itself to conclude that a chimpanzee is a "composition of matter" while a human being is not.'[158] Certainly no such distinction can be found if we attempt to treat the words delimiting the field of potentially patentable types of subject matter – whether these be 'manner of new manufacture', 'new and useful … machine, manufacture, or composition of matter' or simply 'invention' – as having a purely descriptive, technical meaning. They certainly are words with such primary significations. But they are also ones chosen by the legislature to delimit the boundary of a monopoly institution with a view to establishing a just balance between property and participation of the public over created ideas.

The latter view introduces an interpretative flexibility where the decision, whether to exercise that flexibility, will be informed by the courts' judgment of their competence in rule making vis-à-vis the legislature (essentially whether the legislature would have expected they would exercise such discretion), and whether the proper balance can be struck by case by case judicial rule making at least as well as by legislative action. The latter, more flexible reading, allows the courts to employ a moral distinction. This is vital because, once the threshold of microorganisms to multi-cellular creatures is crossed, it is difficult to find a plausible scientific or technical ground for drawing a boundary line on the basis of our ability to manipulate or control the result that does not also include human beings. This argument does not rest on the assumption that the moral distinction between human beings and animals is universally accepted and uncontroverted. In fact serious philosophical positions have been taken, notably by Peter Singer,[159] against the special moral status most of us give to human beings as a form of specieism. His position is sound if it is pain and suffering in the abstract that we want to

---

[158] *Harvard College v. Canada* cit. above at n. 148 at para. 130.
[159] Singer (1986).

minimize and pleasure or happiness (again in the abstract) that we want to maximize. However, it is *human* pain and suffering that moves us with the concern to reduce these matters and *human* pleasure and happiness that constitutes objects of pursuit for us. The question, why this ought to be so may be asked, and the inescapable truth is that we must make a moral choice when we answer that question when we make rules such as the one about whether patent rights ought to extend to human persons and human matter. Such choices (whether by the legislature or the courts) not only make law but also make or refashion the morality of that legal institution as well because the choices will reflect the moral grounds we adopt as its justification or defence. The account of moral prescriptivism given in Chapter 2 provides the case for a special regard for human liberty and well-being: because, if morality is a created institution of prescriptions intended to appeal to addressees with objective rational force, these must be aimed at securing and promoting the objective and most general interests (liberty and well-being for the exercise of that liberty) of those addressees: the human beings which these prescriptions are meant to motivate and guide. However, the present contention that this boundary determination inevitably involves choices reflecting moral views does not rest on this claim – that human persons do have a favoured position in moral reasoning – being correct.

It will remain correct even if we adopt the view that special protection against instrumental use ought to extend to, say, all sentient creatures capable of suffering, and draw the line at patentability there: we would still be making not a purely technical determination but drawing a distinction with a moral purpose in mind; one that will also condition other choices about the extent, exemption to and permissible exercise of the monopoly right. This decision reveals the pregnant moral issues that lie beneath the technical appearance of the question of whether patent protection should extend over living (or higher living) things. The real difference between the majorities in the *Harvard College* and the *Schmeiser* decisions was not about which interpretation was more faithful to the intention of the legislature or whether determination of moral issues lay within the competence of the judiciary. The intention, given the nature of patents, is that the courts will have to rule about subjects whose nature may be unexpected, and there would be moral implications about the reach of ownership of ideas however the courts rule. The difference, really, was whether such questions and the solutions to them are better left to the legislature to frame (the *Harvard College* majority) or treated as open, at least initially, to the courts to resolve (the *Schmeiser* majority). In both cases, the moral dimension is implicit, but present, and the difference lies in that the former seeks a resolution in the dimension of reform (in the hands of legislature, which is addressed later in Chapter 8) and the latter in the dimension of interpretation (addressed in Chapter 6). As a result, there is an underlying moral dimension to such decisions. This ought to be openly acknowledged so that the nature of the moral choices and implications for the institution may be addressed. Yet, the moral considerations in the interpretative dimension are not wholly inert. When the US PTO set its guidelines on the basis of *Chakrabarty*, it understood this to render all living things patentable, but with a notable exception for human beings. Its guidelines noted: 'If the broadest reasonable interpretation of the claimed invention as a whole encompasses a human being, then a rejection under 35 U.S.C. s 101 must be made indicating that the claimed invention is directed to nonstatutory subject matter.'[160] Hence, the US PTO has rejected an application for an invention combining a human embryo with that of an animal.[161] Presumably, 'anything under the sun that is made by man' (*Chakrabarty*) does not quite mean everything that may be man-made. Again, one encounters officials reading into apparently neutral descriptive words possible limitations, founded on their being understood as written on the basis of implicit but fundamental, morally pregnant, assumptions about the reach and purpose of the institutions.

4.4.4 Patentable Subject Matter under the EPC and in the EU

Other systems have sought to pre-empt interpretative approaches by legislative action. The EPC uses the open, undefined description 'invention' – since 13 December 2007, clarified as including inventions 'in all fields of technology'.[162] It also commits its European member states to understand that this excludes a list of matters where the application relates to 'such subject matter or activities as such'.[163] In the EU, the 'Biotech Directive'[164] attempts to confront the policy conundrums raised by such technology and provide the kind of framework that the American and Canadian Supreme Courts have suggested is better established by legislative bodies. Consideration of this Directive shows that legislative measures cannot completely obviate the making of moral decisions in the dimension of interpretation. It requires (Article 3(1)) that inventions

---

[160] US PTO Guideline 2105 Patentable Subject Matter – Living Matter [R1] cit. above n. 144.
[161] Weis (2005).
[162] Art. 52(1) EPC under the 2000 revision; see above n. 131.
[163] *Ibid*, Art. 52(3).
[164] EU Directive 98/44/EC of 6 July 1998.

which meet the main criteria of novelty, inventive step and susceptibility to industrial application, be patentable even if they contain or consist of biological material or a process for the production, processing or use of biological material. This essentially opens or confirms the applicability of patents to the field of biotechnology. However, it also excludes 'the human body, at the various stages of its formation and development, and the simple discovery of one of its elements, including the sequence or partial sequence of a gene' from constituting patentable inventions (Article 5(1)), though it distinguishes, and renders patentable, '[a]n element isolated from the human body or otherwise produced by means of a technical process' (Article 5(2)). These provisions attempt to obviate moral considerations in the interpretation of the rules, and to take this decision out of the hands of patent offices and, ultimately, the judiciary, by using clear and technical expressions to draw the line between patentable and unpatentable features; in the process it cannot avoid confronting where (unpatentable) humanity ends and non-human objects begin. It is not entirely successful because issues of interpretation remain about when an element is 'isolated' from a human body, and the degree of human intervention which will render a process which uses a biological process into a 'technical process'.

An example of how interpretation of a technical expression may import underlying moral assumptions about the proper balance between property and participation is provided by the European Patent Office's (EPO's) *NOVARTIS II*[165] decision on Article 53(b) of the EPC. This provision makes an exception to patentability for 'plant or animal varieties'. The EPO's Enlarged Board of Appeal held that that exclusion did not apply to an invention comprising a genetic modification to plants even if the breadth of the claim may include one or more plant varieties, if the subject matter claimed does not identify a specific plant variety or several specified plant varieties.[166] It explained that the exclusion is intended to prevent dual protection of the same subject matter under the EPC and the plant varieties protection scheme under the UPOV Convention[167] but does not prevent protection which overlaps regarding the same field.[168]

---

[165] *NOVARTIS/Transgenic plant G1/98* [2000] E.P.O.R. 303, on referral from *NOVARTIS/Transgenic plant* T1054/96 (OJ EPO 1998 pp. 509–63).

[166] *Ibid* at para. 3.10; applied in *NOVARTIS/Anti-pathogenic compositions* T 1054/96 (*Novartis III*).

[167] International Convention for the Protection of New Varieties of Plants 1961 (as revised in 1972, 1978 and 1991).

[168] *NOVARTIS/Transgenic plant G1/98*, cit. above n. 165, Reasons para. 3.7 & 3.8.

The difference is that whereas the patent would cover any plant or grouping of plants with a certain (genetic) structure or trait, plant variety protection is concerned with groupings defined by their whole genome. Hence, although the patented invention could be embodied in a single plant with the necessary gene and could be used to develop a plant variety or several different plant varieties, the claim would not – on this argument – be to those varieties. The inventor may develop a plant variety with the patentable genetic characteristic as a practical step towards marketing the product, but such a development is not formally a necessary step to realizing the invention – which is just the insertion of the gene into the plant – even though that would be a necessary step in its commercial exploitation. The EPO's Enlarged Board of Appeal was able to avoid a finding of dual protection under the patent and plant variety protection regimes by focusing on the way the two systems define their respective subject matter, and treating as irrelevant the practical overlap between the fields that are protected. Whether this should be the correct approach depends on the reason for concern about avoiding dual protection under different regimes.

If the concern is with avoiding unnecessary duplication of incentives spurring innovation, the EPO's approach would appear to have a point. It treats the inventor and the plant breeder as two separate individuals – as they could, but need not necessarily, be. Thus, the availability of patent protection is not redundant even though, with further steps, the plant varieties protection may also be obtained. If, however, the concern is with the balance to be struck between the property rights of owners and the participation rights of the (non-right holding) public, then the focus will be on whether a balance that is sought to be achieved by one regime may be upset by the intrusion of the rules of appropriation of another regime. For those concerned about the latter, it is a question of whether the extension of protection over matters in the same field would practically interfere with the balance of rights that would be of paramount relevance, rather than concern about whether the subject matter of the rights may be formally distinguished. The opinion proffered by the referring Technical Board of Appeal, which was ultimately rejected by the Enlarged Board of Appeal, appeared motivated by this concern with the balance of rights. The referring Board opinion rejected the 'literal approach', concerned with whether there was a claim directed at plant varieties, for a 'substantive' approach which asked if the claimed invention included embodiments (even if not identified in the claim) that were plant varieties.[169] It observed that the adoption of the literal

---

[169]   *NOVARTIS/Transgenic plant* T 1054/96 cit. above at n. 165, para. 9–22.

approach would, 'in effect, be, to abdicate any responsibility for examining the substance of the claim, and the outcome of an application would depend on the verbal skill of the patent attorney concerned'.[170] The mysteries of the interpretation of this exclusion would be dispelled if it is, instead, accepted that the intention expressed in rather plain words is to exclude patent claims under the EPC over groups of plants or animals because property over these types of idea require special rules, such as those that may be afforded under the UPOV Convention for plant varieties. A 'variety' is the lowest taxonomic grouping for plants. Under this interpretation, the specification of such a grouping is not meant to distinguish higher categories of groupings (like species or genus) but to ensure that no category (since higher orders like 'genus' and 'species' would include 'varieties' as well) of such matter would be included. And the idea, it could have been argued, is that an equivalent approach would be taken to animal groups as well. The term 'animal varieties' does not have an equivalent technical connotation to 'plant varieties'. Its use suggests anticipation that a similar *sui generis* regime may be developed in this area. However, this line of argument had been rejected already as regards claims for animal inventions in the *HARVARD/Oncomouse* EPO Technical Board of Appeal decision.[171]

The outcome is that concerns relating to the morality of the patenting of life forms as such, as opposed to the morality of their exploitation and publication, are rendered irrelevant when the EPO applies and interprets the EPC. The key ground for this outcome, though, is a reliance on a rule of interpretation adopted by the EPO in *LUBRIZOL/Hybrid plants*[172] which requires that any exception in the EPC to patentability of an invention susceptible of industrial application 'must ... be narrowly construed'.[173] This interpretative rule forsakes a search for the right balance, for an outright presumption in favour of IP protection. It should be noted that the inventor will not be left without protection for his contribution even if his claim cannot extend to a description that would embrace varieties. He, or she, would have protection for the microbiological process of applying the gene to an individual plant or seed. But, qua inventor, he or she would not get protection for the plants themselves. However, protection under the plant varieties protection scheme may be

---

[170] *Ibid* para. 20.

[171] *HARVARD/Oncomouse* (T19/90), cit. below n. 294, para. 4.1–4.8; see also *HARVARD/Transgenic animal (T315/03)* cit. below at n. 300 at 324–7 (para. 11.1–11.8).

[172] T 320/87, [1990] E.P.O.R. 1731.

[173] *HARVARD/Oncomouse* (T19/90) cit. below n. 294, para. 4.5; see also *HARVARD/Transgenic animal (T315/03)* cit. below at n. 300 at 310 (para. 4.3).

obtained if the inventor were to use that innovation (perhaps in association with a plant breeder) to develop a new plant variety. The claimant would then have to satisfy the requirements and abide by the exemptions of the special regimes developed for these types of innovation. It is pertinent in this regard that plant varieties protection exemptions to the right holder's rights are not co-extensive with those of the patent owner under the EPC: notably, UPOV permits an optional exception for the so-called 'farmers' privilege' of re-using for propagation on their own farms the product of harvests from their own holdings,[174] which has no equivalent in the patent regime. The effect of overlapping protection with the patent regime[175] is that a farmer may be restrained from such practices under patent law (albeit this may be by a different person from the holder of the plant variety right), even where the national legislature may have enacted the exemption for the farmer's privilege under the plant varieties protection regime.

The effect is to circumscribe and exclude the already limited access for participation by farmers that may be created under a plant variety regime. It also undermines efforts to obtain recognition of 'farmers' rights' or privileges to equitably participate in sharing of benefits from the use of plant genetic resources, which are grounded in the contribution indigenous farmers all over the world have made, and continue to make, by traditional farming practices that conserve a healthy diversity of genetic material with potentially useful traits, which may be vital to food security,[176] and incidentally provide the resources on which IP innovators build. Such encroachment, on the participatory access allowed by the law, occurs whenever IPR protection regimes overlap unless the exemptions are carefully reserved or crafted to be co-extensive because the exclusions under the property rights are cumulative whilst the exemptions are

---

[174]   UPOV Convention, Art. 15(2), which provides: 'Notwithstanding Article 14 [acts requiring the plant variety right owner's authorization], each Contracting Party may, within reasonable limits and subject to the safeguarding of the legitimate interests of the breeder, restrict the breeder's right in relation to any variety in order to permit farmers to use for propagating purposes, on their own holdings, the product of the harvest which they have obtained by planting, on their own holdings the protected variety'.

[175]   See Blakeney (2005) on the overlapping of the UPOV and patent regimes for plant innovations.

[176]   See discussion and legal options in Blakeney (2002a), and the article on 'Farmers' Rights' which the FAO adopted as Art. 10 in its International Undertaking on Plant Genetic Resources, cited in Blakeney, *ibid*, p. 10, ref. FAO (2001); see now International Treaty on Plant Genetic Resources for Food and Agriculture.

non-mandatory. It is more than merely plausible that the concern to avoid dual protection with existing and potential regimes for protection in these fields is grounded in a desire to avoid such inconsistencies in policies. The interpretation that was, instead, adopted by the Enlarged Board of Appeal has then emasculated the no-plant-or-animal-varieties exclusion by making the result turn on the drafting dexterity of the prosecuting patent attorney. This reflects a shift, since the adoption of the EPC in 1973, towards expansion of patent appropriation. This would, in fact, be a value laden decision – reflected in the *LUBRIZOL* interpretative presumption in favour of a narrow reading of exceptions to patentability in the EPC – readjusting the balance between the property and participation rights. The point is not that one outcome is clearly right or wrong (though the argument herein does favour wider exceptions) but that the *moral* choices are an unavoidable part of the dimension of interpretation when the expanding scope of patentable subject matter encounters a distinctly new field. Notably, the related exclusion in the 'Biotech Directive'[177] adopted by the EU in 1998 provides at Article 4(1) that 'Inventions which concern plants and animals shall be patentable if the technical feasibility of the invention is not confined to a particular plant or animal variety.' This much more clearly expresses an intention that patent protection can overlap with plant varieties protection.

It is a product of political processes where making of moral choices is not an embarrassment but, often, a necessity. The moral commitments being unavoidable one way or another in such cases, these questions are better addressed head on by recognition of the moral dimension of interpretation when the tension between the claims to property and participation can be expressly articulated. It is not suggested that a 'moral answer' can be read off some community moral code or system of philosophy, without the real exercise of moral choice by the judge; however, neither is it the case that the choice is in the nature of an entirely free and arbitrary decision by the judge. It may be observed that the advantage of an explicit recognition of such a moral dimension is to focus attention on the nature of the choice, on how morality works and how it at once constrains one to a mode of decision making in the search for universalizable principles, and yet give the person entrusted with the decision the power to make choices with implications for the rest of the system. It highlights how (as Hare notes in *Freedom and Reason* (1963)) it simultaneously presents us with the phenomenon of moral choice and

---

[177]   EU Directive 98/44/EC of 6 July 1998.

the constraint of reason. Both modes of legal adaptation – rule interpretation and legislation – incorporate a moral dimension. In the legislative forum, politics reign and, in a democracy, is intended to produce a compromise of interests, principles and parties. This is not a criticism of the process, for it is a function of political processes in democracies to produce solutions about social, political and economic cooperation and terms of competition where there are disagreements, even fundamental disagreements.[178] But it will be argued (in Chapter 8) that even here, where moral considerations may be admitted to be weak in the face of political power relations, moral arguments have a role.

4.4.5 The Role of the Other Dimensions of Patent Systems

As the central rules of patent systems are generally descriptive and expansive, occasions (such as described in the preceding subsections) when the boundaries of the field of patentable subjects are tested, are quite rare. It should be no surprise, then, that the expression of the participation right is redirected to the periphery of the institution. This is seen in attempts to exploit the morality and public policy restrictions on patent protection (cf. §4.7 below), and the judicially created rules for controlling exercise of patent rights (cf. Chapter 7 at §7.3.2). In addition there are specific defences which national systems do enact to preserve participatory interests in some areas, though, for WTO countries, these are now subject to the three-step test in TRIPS.[179] There are many specific provisions for exceptions subject to detailed conditions in national patent laws but nothing with the width and amorphous adaptability of the US fair use exception for copyright. By far the most significant rule that ensures a sharing of the idea with the public is the term limitation, which is fairly short relative to the duration of protection under copyright. TRIPS requires that the protection must be provided for at least 20 years from the filing of the application for a patent,[180] and that is the general rule prevailing worldwide with some extensions offered in some jurisdictions in the case of medicines.[181] The result is a tradeoff of strong protection for a limited and short period for totally free access by

---

178 Waldron (1999).
179 Art. 30 TRIPS. Cf. Chapter 5 below at §5.3.
180 Art. 33 TRIPS.
181 To correct for curtailment of exploitation because of regulatory restrictions on marketing until approval for public use has been given. E.g.: in the US, Title II of the Drug Price Competition and Patent Term Restoration Act of 1984 adding s 156 to Patents Act (US) 35 USC (the 'Hatch–Waxman Act' 1984); in

the public thereafter. Hence, the case for a strong general exception that applies in the case of copyright does not prevail for patent systems. Yet, there may be cases when such strong rights can be abused or run counter to vital interests safeguarded by the participatory right. The primary avenues for addressing such concerns would seem to lie in the dimension of exercise (cf. Chapter 7).

4.5 MORAL TERMS IN TRADE MARK LAWS

4.5.1 Trade Marks and Freedom and Well-being

Trade mark law presents a different kind of problem from copyright and patents in that the contribution of trade marks to freedom and well-being is indirect, and legal protection for them is not, in the main, given over them as matters that we consume. But that is changing and, it will be seen, it is this change that raises the most problematic issues for justification for trade mark protection. Significantly, it is at this point of change where the moral dimension finds its most explicit expression in the rules. The traditional forms of trade mark protection aim at preserving control over the aspects of their use which tell us about the goods or services with which they are used. Owners of trade marks have exclusive rights to use them in relation to goods and services with which they are associated. The justifications most often given are twofold. First, they save consumers time and effort in search by enabling them to be confident that they signify that the goods or services have sources which are familiar to them (either from previous experience of use or as a result of marketing efforts) so as to have an expected quality or character. They save on testing, sampling and other means of investigating such quality and character. But, it may be noted, they do not in themselves ensure quality, character or even consistency, for that is not a requirement for protection, and the trade mark user may fail to ensure that the goods produced or services rendered meet expectations. But experience should teach the addressees what to expect – or even not to expect anything where the trade mark user has failed to be consistent. Hence, the second part of the justification. If the trade mark owner can be assured of exclusive use of the trade mark for the purpose of indicating trade source, he or she has an incentive to supply goods and services with these marks

---

the EU, the Supplementary Protection Certificates scheme introduced by Regulation 1768/92/EEC; in Australia under the Intellectual Property Laws Amendment Act 1998, s 70 Patents Act 1990; in Singapore, s 36A(1)(c) Patents Act.

in such a way as to build an expectation that the marks can be trusted to indicate a consistent quality and character, assured that others cannot ride on this reputation, and, thus, is enabled to reap the rewards of this effort. The second justification is that trade mark rights protection thus encourages producers to produce goods and services of quality. These two interlinked functions of trade marks indirectly promote the liberty and well-being of all. By enabling people to rely on them when making consumption decisions, they enable planning and save everyone time and expense. By encouraging producers to invest in quality, they increase the range of consumption options available to all. Conversely, the exclusive rights traditional trade mark protection gives the owner are powers over certain elements of speech and expression which are secured by restricting the liberty of others to use certain signs, symbols, words, and so on.

This is the tradeoff that requires examination. It will help to consider the functions of trade marks as types of speech and expression: just what trade mark users say and how they say it. Trade marks *denote* a trade source connection between goods and services with which they are used. When so used, they may also have further *connotations*: indications raising expectations as to certain qualities or character associated with the connection thus denoted. These connotations are part of the meaning of the mark, which people learn through experience of use, or association as a result of marketing, and are the result of expenditure and effort by the trade marks owners. In effect, owners are encouraged to act so as to cause people to assign certain connotations to the marks, and to do this they are given exclusive rights over certain uses of them. They have control, therefore, over uses of certain elements of speech (words and other signs), so that they can control the meaning of those elements. Although giving them this control results in a corresponding restriction on the liberty of others, the essence of the traditional form of this institution is that the potential value of this exclusive speech, the ancillary connotation as to quality and character, can be gained only by certain conduct: acts to maintain the quality of the associated goods and services. (The expansion of trade mark owners' interest in control over these connotations and the consequent impact on trade mark law and its rationale have been intricately mapped by Rosemary J. Coombe in *The Cultural Life of Intellectual Properties* (1998) and this phenomenon and analysis of it by Coombe and other critics will be dealt with shortly at §4.5.3.) Even though advertising can also be used to build associations in the minds of consumers, it is investment in quality of production and delivery that is the primary mode of building such connotative meaning because expectations built by advertisements can be ruined by experience of a disappointing product or service. Thus, the trade marks users' ability to exercise this form of expression – that is, the ability to signify a certain connotation that accompanies the denotation of an association with a source – ultimately rests not on what they say but what they do as they use these marks. This is to the mutual benefit of owners and others as the increased liberty of the owner (in the form of the ability to assign certain types of meaning to their marks) also results in gains to consumers in reliability. If the protection the law offers trade mark owners is strictly confined to this form of speech, the corresponding restriction on the liberty of speech of others will be of slight significance.

Whereas owners have high interest in the specific marks which they use (at least where they already use or are prepared to use them as trade marks) and exclusive use by them is necessary for them to make certain articulations which the general public also supports, members of the general public do not have the same stake in their own ability to make *those* uses of specific marks. There is an asymmetry in the degree of necessity for action[182] that favours ownership of trade marks by those who employ them with their goods and services. The central rules of acquisition and infringement in traditional trade mark protection appear to be aimed at encouraging this form of speech and ensuring that the property is narrowly restricted to this form of speech alone. Thus, trade mark protection is acquired by the registration of signs which distinguish the users' goods and services from those of others, or are capable of acquiring such distinctive capacity. The right is infringed when an identical mark is used with goods and services identical to that for which it has been registered, or when a mark so similar to the owner's as to raise a likelihood of confusing a substantial portion of the addressees, is used with goods and services either identical or similar to those for which the mark has been registered.[183] This ensures that the right extends only in so far as it protects that particular form of speech, and that others remain free to use the sign for other forms of speech and expression. So confined, there is hardly any need for elements in the rules of this type of property to encapsulate and express the moral dimension of its justification, because the justifying balance is already built into the technical and descriptive aspects of its rules. One would expect few moral terms and concepts in the central rules of the institution, and this is true of the traditional trade mark protection. It would have been true of the institution as a whole were it not for extensions of trade mark protection beyond this basic form.

---

[182]   Cf. Gewirth's criterion of degree of necessity for action at §§2.5.1 & 3.6.3.
[183]   TRIPS Agreement, Art. 16(1).

4.5.2 Moral Terms and Concepts in Trade Mark Laws

The international requirements for national provisions for registration and protection of trade marks are to be found in the TRIPS Agreement (Articles 15–21) and the Paris Convention[184] (Articles 6–10). Although the Paris Convention uses moral terms to define unfair competition,[185] the provisions dealing with registered trade mark protection manage without explicit use of moral terms. This is explicable in terms of the limited conflict between property and participation interests in the account of traditional trade mark protection given above. However, this simple description is rendered problematic by more recent developments in trade mark use and protection. This difference points to the relationship between the use of moral terms and concepts in legal rules, and concerns about the proper balance to be struck to reflect the bounds between the property and participatory interest. The more problematic the latter concern, the more likely that one should find the use or introduction of such moral terms and concepts. There are several features of traditional trade mark use as well as developments of more recent vintage that tend to make this balance problematic. First, trade marks are not confined to names (like 'John Deere' and 'Marks & Spencer') and invented words (like 'Kodak' and 'Häagen-Dazs'), which are of very limited general use, but also words of common speech (like 'dry' and 'baby' in 'Baby-Dry'[186]) and words that were originally trade names that have come to acquire an ordinary signification (like 'Xerox', which is used as 'xerox' for photocopy). This is the result of the way we use signs to signify many different things, sometimes using the different associations in expressive play, puns and allusions. This does not seriously undermine the distinction between the owner's and general public's speech interests, as we can generally distinguish between trade mark use and other uses, and marks which have become essentially generic usually lose their protection under the law. But trade mark protection has been encroaching onto what was previously free participatory space and the resultant shift has created tensions along a subjacent fault line in the boundary between trade mark and other forms of speech.

This tension along the fault line is exemplified by the question that arose in the UK as to whether a non-owner's use of a trade mark in the

---

[184] Paris Convention for the Protection of Industrial Property, 1883 (as revised amended, latest 1979).

[185] *Ibid*, Art. 10*bis*(2): 'Any act of competition contrary to honest practices in industrial or commercial matters constitutes an act of unfair competition.'

[186] *Procter & Gamble Company v. OHIM*, Case C-383/99 P [2002] ETMR 3.

course of trade must be a trade mark use before it is infringing. Before 1994, the law on trade marks required that the use of a registered trade mark had to (amongst other things) constitute 'use as a trade mark' before it would be infringing.[187] The Trade Marks Act 1994 introduced a different formulation: 'use in the course of trade'. Section 10(1), which identifies one form of infringement, provides: 'A person infringes a registered trade mark if he uses in the course of trade a sign which is identical with the trade mark in relation to goods or services which are identical to those for which it is registered.' There is no reference to trade mark use. The question raised is: Has the protection broadened beyond trade mark use? Early dicta suggest that it has.[188] In 2001 this question came squarely before the High Court in *Arsenal v. Reed*.[189] The trade mark owner was a football club which had registered a badge, names and a device which it used. The defendant ran a merchandise business which included the sale to fans of the club's team, memorabilia bearing these signs. The acts came within the literal terms of section 10(1) but the defendant asserted that there could be no infringement without trade mark use and that (as the judge also found) he had not made such use but, rather, used the marks 'as badges of allegiance'. The judge, Hugh Laddie J, referred two questions of construction of the 'Trade Marks Directive'[190] (which the UK Act was intended to implement) to the European Court of Justice (ECJ). First: In such circumstances and where the specifically listed defences of the Directive are absent, is it a defence if a use 'does not indicate a trade origin (i.e. a connection in the course of trade between the goods and the trade mark proprietor)'? Secondly: If so, would the fact that the signs 'would be perceived as a badge of support, loyalty or affiliation to the trade mark proprietor be a sufficient connection'? Rather than answering directly whether non-trade mark use would be a defence, the ECJ ruled[191] that, in these circumstances[192] 'the proprietor is entitled … to rely on Article 5(1)(a) to prevent its use' and

---

[187]   Trade Marks Act 1938, s 68(1). Cf. Cornish (1989), para. 17-064.

[188]   Jacob J in *British Sugar Plc v. James Robertson & Sons* [1996] RPC 281 suggested that trade mark use is not required for infringement, and the Court of Appeal in *Philips Electronics v. Remington Consumer Products* [1998] RPC 283 left the point open for further consideration.

[189]   *Arsenal Football Club Plc v. Reed* (No.1) [2001] R.P.C. 46.

[190]   EU Directive 89/104/EEC of 21 December 1988. Article 5 made the use of an identical trade mark with identical goods for which it had been registered infringing if this is done 'in the course of trade'.

[191]   *Arsenal Football Club Plc v. Matthew Reed*, Case C-206/01 [2003] Ch. 454.

that '[i]t is immaterial that, in the context of that use, the sign is perceived as a badge of support for or loyalty to the trade mark proprietor'.[193]

This represents a significant shift of trade mark protection from securing exclusive rights to trade mark use to exclusivity in trade use, from protection of goodwill, to property in signs. It may be obvious that the Trade Marks Directive and the 1994 UK Act are intended to shuck aside the restriction of trade mark use, but that begs the question of where the line marking off the right of others to use these signs for other purposes is to be redrawn. The required context, 'use in the course of trade', is fairly broad. The problem is that members of the public may want to purchase items bearing signs that are identical or similar to trade marks for the purpose of expressing something about themselves rather than for what they say about the goods or services. It is in their interest in freedom of speech that producers are free to supply articles with such signs in the course of trade. This is mitigated somewhat by the central requirement for infringement that the use by others must be such as to raise a likelihood of confusion.[194] However, in the EU[195] (and under TRIPS[196]), this does not apply where the infringement takes the form of the use of identical signs with the same types of good for which they are registered; rather, it applies only where the marks are only similar to that registered or the goods they are applied to are only similar to that for which the marks are registered, or both. Another concession to the free speech interests of non-owners is exceptions to the property right in the

---

[192]   Absence of the Directive's specifically identified defences and where identical signs are used in relation to identical goods for which they have been registered.

[193]   *Arsenal Football Club Plc v. Matthew Reed*, Case C-206/01 cit. above at n. 191, at para. 62 (at 486).

[194]   TRIPS Art. 16(1).

[195]   Directive 89/104/EEC, Art. 5(1)(b). Though the EU law appears to broaden this concept under the Directive by adding that this 'likelihood of confusion' 'includes the likelihood of association' between the sign and the mark, the jurisprudence of the ECJ suggests that this does not obviate the requirement that the claimant prove a likelihood of confusion: see *Sabèl v. Puma AG, Rudolf Dassler Sport*, Case C-251/95 [1998] ETMR 1; *Marca Mode CV, Adidas AG and Adidas Benelux BV*, Case C-425/98 [2000] ETMR 723. Cf. Phillips (2003), para. 10.143–10.155 for criticisms of this interpretation.

[196]   TRIPS Agreement, Art. 16(1) provides that: 'In the case of the use of an identical sign for identical goods or services, a likelihood of confusion shall be presumed.'

EU.[197] However, these are not aimed at enabling users to give indications about themselves (save the very limited right of traders to use their own names or addresses), but are intended mainly to preserve trade interests in giving indications about their goods[198] provided such uses are in accordance with honest practices in industrial or commercial matters. The result is that, at least where identical signs are being used with identical goods, the property right in the signs will trump free speech interest in using the signs for self expression unless the courts are able to find a resource for fashioning a *modus vivendi*. This background concern and its roots in the justification for the property right explain the agitation in the UK courts which subsequently materialized. When the parties in the *Arsenal case* returned to the UK High Court,[199] Laddie J took the ECJ's point, that the property of the registered owner had to be protected against the prejudice to essential function of a trade mark, but understood this to imply that trade mark use was required for infringement. On the trade mark owner's appeal, the Court of Appeal held[200] that the point to be considered was not the purpose of the use but the impact of the use.

The use of the marks, even as badges of allegiance, would have prejudiced the owner's property interest in the essential function of the trade marks. This, according to the ECJ, is 'to guarantee the identity of the origin of the marked goods or services to the consumer or end user by enabling him, without any possibility of confusion, to distinguish the goods or services from others which have another origin'.[201] This function, the Court of Appeal observed, would be vitiated even when the signs are used as badges of allegiance and even if there were no confusion as to origin because, especially if such use is widespread, their ability to serve as guarantees of origin would be impaired,[202] must be noted that both the UK Court of Appeal and the ECJ were at pains to explain that the circumstances of Article 5(1)(a) of the Directive (use of identical signs with identical goods or services) should not in all cases

---

[197]   Directive 89/104/EEC, Art. 6(1).
[198]   Their character, quality, purpose and so on, or to indicate the purpose of a product or service, especially accessory or spare parts function.
[199]   *Arsenal Football Club Plc v. Reed (No. 2)* [2003] 1 C.M.L.R. 13, [2002] EWHC 2695 (Ch).
[200]   *Arsenal Football Club Plc v. Reed (No. 2)* [2003] EWCA Civ. 696; [2003] R.P.C. 39.
[201]   *Arsenal Football Club Plc v. Matthew Reed*, Case C-206/01, cit. above at n. 191, at para. 48.
[202]   *Arsenal Football Club Plc v. Matthew Reed (No. 2)* cit. n. 200 above, at para. 48.

lead to a finding of infringement. The ECJ, after alluding to that provision, observed: 'The exercise of that right must be *reserved* to cases in which a third party's use of the sign affects or is liable to affect the functions of the trade mark, in particular its essential function of guaranteeing to consumers the origin of the goods.'[203] The UK Court of Appeal understood from this that it 'could not be the law' that the Article 5(1)(a) circumstances are conclusive as to infringement.[204] Although the ECJ seeks to locate a basis for limiting the rights in Article 5 in the proviso in Article 5(5),[205] the court appears to have read restrictions into that proviso. Instead of providing a further limit on Article 5(1)(a), that proviso aims at preserving any national law protecting the owners' interest in the marks' other functions from being reduced by or taken as excluded by the earlier provisions enjoining protection of the guarantee of origin function. The laws protecting these other functions should remain unaffected 'where use of that sign without due cause takes unfair advantage of, or is detrimental to, the distinctive character or the repute of the mark'.[206] It does not, however, support the ECJ's assertion that:

> The proprietor may not prohibit the use of a sign identical to the trade mark for goods identical to those for which the mark is registered if that use cannot affect its own interests as the proprietor of the mark, having regard to its functions.[207]

---

[203]   Emphasis added. *Arsenal Football Club Plc v. Matthew Reed* Case C-206/01, cit. above at n. 191, at para. 51.

[204]   *Arsenal Football Club Plc v. Reed (No. 2)*, cit. above n. 200 para. 39.

[205]   *Arsenal Football Club Plc v. Matthew Reed*, Case C-206/01, cit. above n. 191, at para.53.

[206]   Directive 89/104/EEC, Art.5(5): 'Paragraphs 1 to 5 shall not affect provisions in any Member State relating to the protection against the use of the sign other than for the purposes of distinguishing goods or services, where use of that sign without due cause takes unfair advantage of, or is detrimental to, the distinctive character or the repute of the mark.'

[207]   *Arsenal Football Club Plc v. Matthew Reed*, Case C-206/01, cit. above n. 191, at para. 54. More recently, the ECJ has made clear that 'these functions of the trade mark' to be preserved from impairment include that of 'communication, investment or advertising' (though not purely descriptive purposes), such that a comparative listing in an advertisement by a competitor using the trade mark to truthfully identify the mark's *proprietor's products* as ones which the competitor's are lawfully made in imitation of (as in smell-alike perfumes) could be 'use' falling foul of Art. 5(1)(a) of Directive 89/104/EEC and be infringing (unless within the defence for comparative advertising where all the conditions of Art. 3a(1) of Directive 84/450/EEC are satisfied): *L'Oréal SA v. Bellure NV*, Case C-487/07 [2010] *Bus. L.R.* 303. This considerably reduces the scope of legitimate

This would appear to be a proposition drawn from the underlying justificatory theory of the institution mandated by the Directive and the implicit assumptions of Article 5(5), whose key words 'without due cause' suggest a recognition of rights of non-owners with counter-balancing claims, and 'unfair advantage' which implies that there may be circumstances where advantage may be fairly taken of the distinctive character or repute of the mark. Perhaps it is better to say that the above proposition seeks rather than draws upon a justification. The reference to the proprietor's 'own interests ... having regard to [the mark's] functions' requires one to answer a question: Just what are those interests? To equate these with all uses which the proprietors are interested – or may have an interest – in prohibiting, would be too wide, for this presumes that we should all promote whatever interests they have. Why? Others have interests in the uses of the mark as well. The question is ultimately one of distributive justice as between trade mark owners and public users. The participatory interest of non-owners continues to exert an influence on the rule defining the extent of the property right, showing how the moral dimension of the IPR can glimmer through the cracks opened as the realm of property intrudes upon the public domain.

4.5.3   Trademarks as Objects

The problem of non-owners' interest in the use of words which also have a trade mark function is compounded by the way owners of marks now also use them as items of consumption in themselves, inviting end users to employ them as means of self-expression. The commingling of a mark's functions to denote source as well as to express allegiance in the 'Arsenal' type marks, and the problems raised in that case are, thus, not restricted to emblems of sports clubs. Owners of marks in the context of trade and trade literature use their control over them to expand the ideas that people may associate with the marks, from the quality and character that may derive from a source connected with a familiar mark, to other ideas associated with the sources which they invite the consumer to share

---

uses left to non-owners and was only very reluctantly applied (as it was bound to do) on resumption of the case by the referring UK Court of Appeal in *L'Oréal SA v. Bellure NV (No. 2)* [2010] EWCA 535. The Court of Appeal's expressed reservations include concerns that this rule restrains honest competition (para. 16–19) and restricts the right to freedom of expression (both the right of the trader to tell, and of consumers to hear, the truth) (para. 8–15). It observed: 'Moreover there is no harm to the trade mark owner' other than the harm of 'letting the truth out' – para. 15, per Jacob LJ.

and express. Owners of trade marks use advertising, promotional campaigns and a consistent business strategy to build a 'brand'. The definition of 'brand' is illusive but the following two elements have been suggested as characteristic: '[T]he maintenance of name recognition through advertising, and, as a corollary, the affirmation of a certain commitment made to the consumer, which makes use of that same name recognition.'[208]

The trade user's interest in the marks has expanded into creations which form a significant part of modern culture and hence our shared intellectual commons. Amongst others, Rosemary Coombe[209] observes the expansion of the American trade marks protection to accommodate this expanding interest of their owners:

> The transition to seeing the connotative value (public associations or cultural meanings) as the property of those who 'own' the denotative signifier (the mark) as a marketing proxy is accomplished by expansion of the theory of 'misappropriation' to deal with intangibles, and the idea of trademark 'dilution' now accepted by many courts.[210]

She cites Keith Aoki on the transformation of trade mark law in the 20th Century:

> [T]he old rationale of preventing consumer confusion over competing market goods has yielded to the current rationale of protecting from 'dilution' or 'misappropriation' the integrity of a set of positive meanings which have been 'created' by the trademark owner's investment. This recent conception of a trademark as property imports 'author reasoning' into trademark law. The trademark owner is viewed as a 'quasi-author' who 'creates' a particular set of meanings attached to a mark by investing time, labor, and money, thereby justifying expansive rights in a mark.[211]

It seems, then, that the various moral terms and the references to the trade marks proprietors' 'interests' in the various judicial observations and provisions in statutes, directives and treaties do not so much point to a justificatory rationale as require the reconstruction of one as we consider the relevant interests at stake. It has already been observed that the traditional core of trade mark protection promotes liberty by giving the owners a privileged form of speech by preventing use by others of identical or similar marks which result in a likelihood of confusion as to

---

[208]   Chevalier and Mazzalovo (2004), p. 11.
[209]   Coombe (1998).
[210]   *Ibid* at 68.
[211]   *Ibid* at 61 where Coombe quotes Aoki (1993) at 4; ref. also Aoki (1994).

the origin of the goods and services with which they are used. Though such speech by others is restricted, the tradeoff generates an increase in liberty because the interests of others in such speech is slight whilst there are gains, in search savings and ability to plan, to be made through the incentive it provides to producers to live up to the expectations generated by past productions by securing to them the benefits of such consumer recognition. Such protection over the denotive function of trade marks allows owners to add to, and essentially control, the connotative meaning of a mark by their actions (efforts at ensuring consistent quality and character). The extensions stretch this argument but not necessarily to breaking point. As the sports team allegiance cases like *Arsenal* show, the protection now extends to the owners' ability to be the source of signs which consumers use to express their association, affiliation or allegiance to the owner of the signs. The traditional employment of trade marks makes use of their ability to connote a certain quality or character of the product or services. In this extended employment, the focus is their ability to connote the character of the *consumer*. This is a matter of the free speech interests of the consumer. At first sight, it would appear that the trade mark owners do not have a similar free speech stake in the matter that would justify their having rights to control supply of the signs for such use. But the meanings which the consumers project by the use of the signs – whether as fans of Arsenal Football Club, supporters of Benetton outfits or bearers of Louis Vuitton handbags – are dependent on the owners' control of the mark to successfully project the connotations with which they associate. Central to this is the denotative function of the marks – their ability to point to the owner as the source (or party associated with the source). The consumers use this to signify their association, affiliation or allegiance to that owner and hence project the same images and values which these signs connote, whether these be a football club and its team, or a commitment to a certain vision of exclusive good taste of a luxury mark, or a dedication to environmentally sound or equitable labour practices of a producer.

Consumers are able to do this only because the trade mark owners have built such reputations through promotional activities and, ultimately, through adherence to the relevant modes and principles of production. Hence, the consumers' capacity for such expression depends on the owners' conduct and their control of the supply of the mark for purpose of signalling consumer association, affiliation or allegiance. Legal means affording such control is justified in terms of promotion of liberty because that control enables consumer expression and the consumer choice of such expression encourages and rewards the associated conduct by the owner because they would have to buy the products with which the signs are used. This latter feedback loop gives the consumers a twofold expressive power: for, by their choice of favoured signs, they not only project to others certain images and values, but they also provide economic support for their cause. Trade marks are not only a way for producers to influence consumers; the former's concern to preserve the images and values of the marks transforms them into a means by which consumers, voting with their wallets, influence producers. The ability to prevent uses which result in a likelihood of confusion about the source (the traditional core of trade marks protection) is not sufficient to protect this consumer signalling function because that function can be impaired by acts which do not result in confusion. For example, the supply of Arsenal jerseys and scarves and other articles with badges of support by persons other than the club severs the link between moral and economic support. The use by others of a mark which is similar enough to that of a trade mark owner's to evoke association with the mark but not confuse the public as to the source will weaken the tendency of people to associate certain values and images with that mark, or introduce other images and values which confuse the message the sign conveys. However, others may have alternative and counter messages: the variety of which, and the tensions with which they co-exist and conflict with IPRs, are wonderfully explored in Coombe's *The Cultural Life of Intellectual Properties* (1998). Consider the posters and T-shirts that proclaim: 'Enjoy Cocaine'[212] in the script and colours of COCA COLA, which makes one pause to consider both the puerility and perniciousness of a slick promotional slogan; or '*MECCA COLA*' for the alternative cola drink with Islamic affiliations which, because of the use of the 'cola' and the familiar red and white colours of the more familiar soft drink of Western origin, invites consumers to reconsider how consumer choices reflect our (perhaps subconscious) affiliations. This is where the expanded protection which the law offers owners problematically encounters serious conflict with the participatory interests of the non-owners. Just as our concern for freedom of expression would justify privileging the trade mark owners' invitation to consumers to join symbolically with them in their cause or principles or ideals, it would also recognize the claims of a right to contest the validity of those images or the claim to represent those values, or to critique them because the equal right to freedom and well-being that must ultimately underpin the former also lends support to the latter.

---

[212] Injuncted in *Coca-cola Co. v. Gemini Rising Inc.* 346 F. Supp. 1183 (E.D.N.Y. 1972). See Coombe (1998) at p. 72 for critique.

Indeed, the very basis suggested above for supporting protection for this extended employment (the encouragement of affiliative use by consumers) by trade mark owners demands that non-owners have rights to fairly subject this encouragement to examination and critique. When the denotation of a producer engenders connotations as to the nature, character or quality of the goods or services, the feedback loop between the consumers and producers is fairly direct. That is because these aspects of the goods or services immediately are accessible to the consumers through their direct experiences. A bad one will lead to a decision to seek goods and services sold under a different mark. Where the consumers' interest is affiliative – based on the producer's character, adherence to a tradition, code of practice, and so on – their ability to assess this through experience of the goods or service is at best indirect and, often, this may not be possible at all. They must rely on secondary sources of information and insight as to whether a trade mark owner that claims to be 'green' is truly environmentally conscientious; whether a sporting goods producer that espouses athletic virtues and vigour is also exploiting young labour, either directly or through its suppliers; whether a fast food chain pitching to kids really caters for a healthy diet. Even in respect of affiliative notions based on the lifestyle preferences and aspirations of consumers – say, a certain image of luxury or appeal to national spirit – which are matters which the consumers will have to judge for themselves, they have an interest in others being able to challenge and suggest a reassessment of these preferences and aspirations. Often, these challenges will not take the form of a trade mark infringement. But the trade mark law itself has been expanding the scope of protection offered under the idea of protection against trade mark dilution.

4.5.4   Moral Terms and the Protection Against Trade Mark Dilution

This expansion of protection is marked by the progression from protection against confusing use to protection against diluting use which has its roots in a seminal 1927 article by F.I. Schechter,[213] who argues that the rationale of modern trade mark law should lie in the protection of the 'selling power' of a trade mark which depends upon its uniqueness and singularity which can be 'vitiated or impaired upon [use with] ... non-related goods':

---

[213]   Schechter (1927) at p. 825; though Phillips (2003 at p. 366, n. 14) traces the idea 'watered down' (*verwässert*) to a German origin dating from 1925.

The real injury in all such cases ... is the gradual whittling away or dispersion of the identity and hold upon the public mind of the mark or name by its use upon non-competing goods. The more distinctive or unique the mark, the deeper its impress upon the public consciousness, and the greater its need for protection against vitiation or disassociation from the particular product in connection with which it has been used.[214]

The concept has since evolved. It now embraces, as regards marks which have become famous, protection against extended forms of vitiation, beginning with the adoption of the doctrine in US state legislation and reaching an initial culmination in the Federal Trademark Dilution Act of 1995. An equivocal mandate for similar expansion of the traditional extent of trade mark protection lies in a TRIPS Agreement provision which seeks to expand the protection required for 'well known' marks in Article 6*bis* of the Paris Convention for the Protection of Industrial Property. The Paris Convention provision requires member countries to give the owner of a mark (even if unregistered), that is a well known mark in that country, a right to prevent or cancel the registration of, or prohibit the use of a trade mark which is liable to create confusion. The TRIPS Agreement augments this protection for well known marks in several ways: it is to apply to service marks as well;[215] more significantly for the present point, it applies to goods and services which are not similar to that for which the trade mark is registered if 'use of that trade mark in relation to those goods and services would indicate a connection between those goods or services and the owner of the registered trademark and provided that *the interests of the owner* of the registered trademark *are likely to be damaged* by such use'.[216] Much would depend on how this 'interest' is conceived but, as the interest in protection against confusing use is already addressed by other provisions, some wider conception of such interests must have been intended. In the US this was quickly followed by the Federal Trade Mark Dilution Act of 1995, which protected famous marks against dilution, where 'dilution' was defined as the 'lessening of the capacity of a famous mark to identify and distinguish goods and services' regardless that there is no competition with the owner of the mark or the absence of a likelihood of confusion, deception or mistake. Cases suggest that this would embrace acts that tend to cause 'blurring' or 'tarnishment' of the mark, now statutorily confirmed by the Trademark Dilution Revision Act of 2006

---

[214] Schechter (1927) at p. 825.
[215] TRIPS Agreement, Art. 16(2).
[216] Emphasis added. TRIPS Agreement, Art. 16(3).

which largely supersedes the above Act and amends the Trademark Act of 1946 by providing that the owner of a mark that has become famous may, subject to equitable principles, obtain an injunction against any person who 'commences use of a mark or trade name in commerce that is likely to cause dilution by blurring or dilution by tarnishment of the famous mark, regardless of the presence or absence of actual or likely confusion, competition, or of actual economic injury'.[217] Further remedies are also available if the person against whom the injunction is sought in a claim for dilution by reason of the blurring wilfully intended to trade on the recognition of the famous mark, or in a claim for dilution by reason of tarnishing wilfully intended to harm the reputation of the famous mark.[218] 'Dilution by blurring' is defined as 'association arising from the similarity between a mark or trade name and a famous mark that impairs the distinctiveness of the famous mark'.[219] 'Dilution by tarnishment' is defined as 'association arising from the similarity between a mark or trade name and a famous mark that harms the reputation of the famous mark'.[220] Free speech interest can be curbed by such rights if these are not, in turn, restricted. Marking the appropriate border can be controversial and place undue burden on legislative foresight if the provisions are set out in purely descriptive and technical terms.

The exclusions on actionable dilution include: '[a]ny fair use',[221] '[a]ll forms of news reporting and news commentary'[222] and '[a]ny noncommercial use of a mark'.[223] The fair use exclusion is the most general. To ensure that the free speech interests are protected, the provision goes on to elaborate that this includes 'a nominative or descriptive fair use, or facilitation of such fair use, of a famous mark by another person other than as designation of source for the person's own goods or services'. And this includes 'use in connection with – (i) advertising or promotion that permits consumers to compare goods or services; or (ii) identifying

---

[217]   15 U.S.C. s 1125(c)(1).

[218]   15 U.S.C. s 1125 (c)(5).

[219]   15 U.S.C. s 1125 (c)(2)(B). All relevant factors may be considered, including the degree of similarity with the famous mark, the degree of inherent or acquired distinctiveness of the famous mark, the extent to which the owner of the famous mark is engaging in substantially exclusive use of the mark, the degree of recognition of the famous mark, whether the user intended to create an association with the famous mark, and any actual association with the famous mark.

[220]   15 U.S.C. s 1125(c)(2)(C).

[221]   15 U.S.C. s 1125 (c)(3)(A).

[222]   15 U.S.C. s 1125 (c)(3)(B).

[223]   15 U.S.C. s 1125 (c)(3)(C).

and parodying, criticizing, or commenting upon the famous mark owner'.[224] In the EU, a comparable form of protection is afforded for 'marks with a reputation'. However, there are no explicit provisions for freedom of speech. Instead, there is a greater use of moral terms. Thus, the burden of striking the right balance between private property and public participation falls on the interpretation of these. Article 5(2) of the Trade Mark Directive permits the EU's constituent states to give a trade mark owner whose registered mark 'has a reputation' in the state the right to prevent use of an identical or similar sign with goods or services that are dissimilar to those for which the mark has been registered 'where the use of that sign without due cause takes undue advantage of, or is detrimental to, the distinctive character or repute of the trade mark'. One finds herein a few crucial terms whose meanings require an exploration of, and affirmation of, the basis of this balance. It has been suggested that 'detriment' can take the form of 'blurring' or 'tarnishing',[225] though others have warned that these metaphors should only be used with the greatest caution outside the context of US law.[226] The words 'without due cause' suggest that there are uses that take advantage of, or that are detrimental to, the distinctive character or repute of a mark that are nevertheless justifiable. The specification that the 'advantage' taken that may be prevented should be 'undue', indicates that some use of the reputation or distinctive character of the mark should be permissible if proportionate to whatever constitutes 'due cause'. The EU provision does not have the US law's direct reference to protection against dilution by 'blurring' or 'tarnishing', nor the express exemptions of the latter for fair use. Its comparatively more open textured and vague terms can be thought to raise the question of whether the same ideas are intended. This question would overlook a prior and more fundamental intention, though. The fact is that more explicit and direct statements about what is to be protected and exempted have been avoided. Arguments that these terms must be code for some more direct intention miss the possibility that the basic intention is to direct a search for more explicit ideas that can fill out these terms. The search must be a principled one governed by the rules for interpreting and using moral terminology, namely prescription of the types of rule suitable for the terms and universalization of them in a manner consistent with all the key structures of the institution that one also intends to affirm. As such, they are capable of development in a

---

[224]   15 U.S.C. s 1125 (c)(3)(A).
[225]   *Premier Brands v. Typhoon Europe* [2000] F.S.R. 767, see Cornish and Llewelyn (2003), para. 17-100.
[226]   Phillips (2003), para.11.15.

direction parallel to the US law but they are also an invitation to the courts and other official interpreters to participate in this development in a cautious, perhaps piecemeal, but principled fashion. A key idea in this search for a justifiable division between property and participatory spheres is the 'interests of the owner' which is referred to in the TRIPS provision.[227] This requires an inquiry as to what those interests are and why they, or some of those interests, ought to be protected. Where the foundational principle is the equal right to freedom and well-being of each person, as this work contends, then it also argues for the exceptions to protection as part of the general public's right to use and participate in the intellectual commons. The more the protection of a trade mark owner's interests extends beyond its guarantee of origin function to other expressive interests in the signs, however much value it adds to it, the more the freedom of expression of non-owners is engaged. This moral dimension of trade marks is a resource that the law makers rely on when framing the rules in this way – whether they thought of it at the time in these terms or not. An investigation of its nature will reveal that, as much as it requires protection of ownership, it also calls for a defence of the right of participation.

4.6 PERSONHOOD AND ALIENABILITY AND MORAL RIGHTS

4.6.1 Alienability and Liberty

Liberty is increased if the property rights acquirable are alienable, indeed they become property as distinguished from personhood rights when they become so alienable. Alienability promotes liberty because the possibility of transferring the right gives the author an extra, and valuable, mode of exploiting the right, though it means losing the right to another. But this weakens the bond between individual personhood and the right to control such ideas, because a decision by the community to treat such rights as alienable reflects a determination that these are less integral to personhood than other rights that are non-alienable. This distinction is reflected in many IP laws by the different treatment given to most IPRs as contrasted with the few, and highly limited, moral rights given to authors and inventors. The vast bulk of IPRs are assignable (and, indeed, intellectual *property* rights are often distinguished from moral rights) and

---

[227]   Art.16(3).

are meant to be commercially exploitable, with the result that the valuable ones are generally held by investors rather than creators. Assignability enables creators to sell those rights for market value but can also work to their disadvantage qua creators because, once assigned, those rights may be used to exclude even the creators from making use of the material covered by those rights in their further creations. Therefore, if the principle of freedom and well-being of potential creators forms the basis for justifying these rights, it also requires that these be limited in favour of access by non-right holders, especially creators who have transferred their rights. This non-alienable element featured more strongly in some of the earliest copyright laws than it does in modern legislation. The initial UK copyright law, the Statute of Anne,[228] and the later US Copyright Act of 1790[229] provided that the right reverted to the author at the end of the first 14 year term, if then living, to be renewed for a further 14 years. This seems to recognize the link of personhood to this type of property right and that complete alienation may work against personhood. It went some way towards protection of the author's economic interest and interest in continuing control of his work despite an initial transfer of his rights which was likely to have occurred when he was at some disadvantage. The abandonment of this reversion feature in copyright is an attenuation of this link between IPRs and protection of the person.

4.6.2 Moral Rights

However, we may find the rump of the law's concern for the promotion and protection of freedom and well-being as a necessary right, which enables each human individual to express his or her personhood, in the category of IP related rights which we call 'moral rights'. These remain with the creators of copyright works and inventors and are typically inalienable. This is particularly well exemplified in the author's right system in the French copyright law. This includes the author's right 'to respect for his name, authorship and his work' which is 'perpetual, inalienable and imprescriptible'.[230] The French Intellectual Property Code also protects the author's right of divulgation (to determine the method and conditions of disclosure),[231] and '[n]otwithstanding assignment of his right of exploitation … a right to reconsider or of withdrawal,

---

[228] 8 Anne, c. 19 (1710), s 11.
[229] 1 *Stat. 124*; 1st Congress, 2d Sess., c. 15, s 1.
[230] Intellectual Property Code, Art. L121-1.
[231] *Ibid*, Art. L121-2.

even after publication'.[232] Some of these moral rights are in the Berne Convention under Article 6*bis*:

> Independently of the author's economic rights, and even after the transfer of the said rights, the author shall have the right to claim authorship of the work and to object to any distortion, mutilation or other derogatory action in relation to, the said work, which would be prejudicial to his honour or reputation.

But such protection is omitted in the TRIPS Agreement.[233] Although explicable in that that agreement is essentially concerned with economic rights of exploitation as a trade related issue, a consequence – given the importance of TRIPS in extending IPRs throughout the world – is a trend towards de-linking of IPRs and personhood. The moral right of inventors under the Paris Convention takes the very limited form of a legal right to be mentioned in the patent.[234] This reflects the highly utilitarian and essentially non-expressive function of inventions in modern society. Although attenuated and restricted, and often treated as quite different from the rights of exploitation, moral rights grow from a common stem with the latter in that they too are justified by their role in extending the freedom and well-being of authors.

4.7 PUBLIC POLICY AND MORALITY AND THE *ORDRE PUBLIC* RESTRICTIONS

4.7.1 Public Policy and the Equal Right to Freedom and Well-being

The exemptions or limitations of protection out of consideration of, variously, public interest[235] or morality[236] or *ordre public*[237] are the IPR

---

[232]   *Ibid*, Art. L121-4, subject to indemnification of the assignee for any prejudice caused.

[233]   Art. 9(1) of the TRIPS Agreement requires compliance of Art. 1 to 21 of the Berne Convention (1971) and its Appendix save that it excepts from this compliance Art. 6*bis* and the rights derived therefrom. The attenuation of moral rights as a result of developments in international conventions and the requirements for protection of economic interests in creations in digital media are noted by Dufay and Pican (2004).

[234]   Paris Convention for the Protection of Industrial Property, Art. 4*ter*.

[235]   E.g. for UK: *Lion Laboratories v. Evans* [1984] 2 All E.R. 417, *Hyde Park Residence Ltd v. Yelland* cit. below n. 238, *Ashdown v. Telegraph Group* [2001] EWCA Civ 1142.

rules which tend to be those which contain the most direct and explicit discussion in judicial opinions about the nature of morality, though they are, perhaps surprisingly, not the best modes by which the equal right to freedom and well-being is expressed. Public policy objections to IPR protection operate in UK law as an exception to copyright and negate confidentiality protection,[238] and the morality and *ordre public* restrictions (examined below at §4.7.2) bar patents in certain cases. However, if the equal right to freedom and well-being is the bedrock for morality as well as the basis for promoting and protecting IPRs on the grounds that they conduce to extending liberty by giving individuals more options and extending the control of owners over otherwise uncontrollable ideas, then moral objections should be treated conservatively. They should not be grounds for objecting to IPRs, or restricting the protection given them, unless they seriously threaten that foundation itself. The mere fact that the morality of a work, or its immorality, is contrary to that foundation or other moral precepts drawn from it will not in itself amount to such a threat because one of the logical grounds of that equal right is the principle of transparency (§2.4.5), which argues for freedom of expression and openness in matters relating to the institution of morality: the very desire to ground morality on reason requires for its fulfilment that this institution be open to challenge. Speech, even when in direct contradiction to the idea of that fundamental right or when flouting its principles is not incompatible with that principle, indeed will be protected by that principle, unless it threatens the conditions under which reasoned moral discourse is possible. The development of the public policy exclusion in the UK copyright and breach confidence law from the no-protection-for-iniquity rule to the public interest defence reflects this transformative process by which a moral concept in a rule is re-interpreted and revised to reflect the fundamental principles which logically underpin the institutions themselves. In the early action for breach of confidence case of *Gartside v. Outram*,[239] Page Wood VC in

---

[236] E.g. for UK, *Glyn v. Weston Feature Film Co* [1916] 2 Ch 261, *Hubbard v. Vosper* cit. below n. 242, *Gartside v. Outram* cit. below n. 239, *Initial Services v. Puterill* cit. below n. 241.

[237] E.g. Art. 53(a) EPC, Art. 6 EU Directive 98/4/EC dated 6 July 1998, and the ECJ judgment in *Netherlands v. The European Parliament* (Case 377/98) cit. below n. 270.

[238] For the different way public policy operates against copyright and confidentiality protection see *Hyde Park Residence Ltd v. Yelland* [2001] ch. 143, esp. per Aldous J at para. 64–7, pp. 167–8.

[239] (1856) 26 L.J Ch. 113.

rejecting the claims against disclosure of accounting fraud held that 'there is no confidence as to the disclosure of iniquity'.[240] A few subsequent cases are explicable on this narrow ground, including disclosures as to criminal conduct,[241] or religious ethical codes which may prescribe dangerous medical treatment to be practised behind closed doors.[242] Ungoed Thomas J in *Beloff v. Presdram*[243] advanced *obiter* a narrow rule for the exception:

> The defence of public interest clearly covers and, in the authorities does not extend beyond, disclosure, which as Lord Denning M.R. emphasized must be disclosure justified in the public interest, of matters carried out or contemplated, in breach of the country's security, or in breach of law, including statutory duty, fraud, or otherwise destructive of the country or its people, including matters medically dangerous to the public; and doubtless other misdeeds of similar gravity.[244]

For Lord Denning, however, iniquity was 'merely an instance of just cause or excuse for breaking confidence. There are some things which may be required to be disclosed in the public interest, in which event no confidence can be prayed in aid to keep them secret.'[245] There can be occasions when the claimant has done no wrong but would be seeking to restrain disclosure of information, which would otherwise be protected as confidential, which the public has an interest in receiving, such as the report at the centre of *Lion Laboratories v. Evans*[246] that a test device used by the UK Home Office to establish that drivers were driving under the influence of alcohol may have serious flaws. This same progression can be found in the public interest defence in relation to copyright. In the 1915 case of *Glyn v. Weston Feature Film Co.*[247] Younger J, who had already held that there was no infringing use because there was no substantial copying on the facts, went on to observe *obiter* that the episode in the plaintiff's sensual novel (of a young man's three week adulterous liaison) which she alleged had been copied, would not have

---

[240]   *Ibid* at 113.
[241]   Violation of the Restrictive Trade Practices Act, *Initial Services Ltd v. Puterill* [1968] 1 Q.B. 396.
[242]   *Hubbard v. Vosper* [1972] 2 Q.B. 84, CA UK.
[243]   [1973] F.S.R. 33.
[244]   *Ibid* at 57. The observation was dicta because the plaintiff had not established the basis of her claim to ownership of the copyright in the memorandum.
[245]   *Fraser v. Evans* [1969] Q.B. 349 at 362.
[246]   Cit. above n. 235.
[247]   Cit. above n. 236.

been afforded relief, at least in a court of Chancery, even if there had been copying because of the immoral nature of the material: 'Now it is clear law that copyright cannot exist in a work of a tendency so grossly immoral as this'.[248] By the case of *Hubbard v. Vosper*[249] in 1972, where the plaintiff's case for protection of scientology's secret ethical code was based on copyright in the founder's text as well as the obligation of confidence, the objection to protection was already being framed mainly in terms of the nature of the public interest defence rather than the immorality of the work. Given that later jurisprudence has emphasized that, whereas with breach of confidence the public interest may erode the entire basis of protection, with copyright, where the protection remains grounded in statute, the public interest exception must operate as a distinct exception,[250] one may expect that the right of free speech and expression will be raised in support in such cases for upholding the copyright protection (cf. §8.2.2).

4.7.2 The EPC's *Ordre Public* and Morality Restriction

Moral concepts facilitate a transformative re-conceptualization of the morality restrictions in IP laws, requiring one to refer to and reformulate the most basic principles underpinning the institutions. The development of the *ordre public* and morality restrictions in the EPC in the hands of the EPO tribunals and the courts illustrates this well. Article 53 of the EPC provides that 'European patents shall not be granted in respect of (a) inventions the publication or exploitation of which would be contrary to "ordre public" or morality'. The EPO Technical Board of Appeal has interpreted '*ordre public*' as a concept that 'covers protection of public security and the physical integrity of individuals as part of society', and 'morality' as a concept related to the 'belief that some behaviour is right and acceptable whereas other behaviour is wrong ... being founded on the totality of norms which are deeply rooted in a particular culture'.[251] The Board's definition of morality suggests an adoption of a meta-ethic of subjective conventionalism – treating norms as identified by the cognitions or usage of a referent group of people. One may find scattered

---

[248]   *Ibid*, p. 269.
[249]   Cit. above at n. 242.
[250]   *Hyde Park Residence Ltd v. Yelland* cit. above n. 238, esp. per Aldous J at para. 64–7, pp. 167–8.
[251]   *PLANT GENETIC SYSTEMS/glutamine synthetase inhibitors (T356/93)* [1995] EPOR 357 (EPO Tech Bd of Appeal) at 322 (Reasons para. 5); applied *HARVARD/Transgenic animal (T315/03)* cit. below at n. 300 at 322 (para. 10.2).

through the EPO tribunals' grounds of decisions remarks that suggest that such a conventionalism prevails. For example: the rejection of the opposition's assertion that a patent violates Article 53(a) EPC with the view that it falsely assumes 'that there is an overwhelming consensus among the Contracting States that the patenting of human genes is abhorrent';[252] and discussion as to whether patenting of animals is unethical in *Western* society, and the holding, regarding the patentability of animal–human chimeras, that as:

> [T]here is at present no consensus in Europe[an] society about the desirability or otherwise of this technology, and public opinion is still being formed on this and related matters. It would be presumptuous for the EPO to interfere in this public debate.[253]

In *LELAND STANFORD*, the EPO Opposition Division held that:

> The provisions of Article 53(a) EPC are intended to exclude from patentability not subject-matter that is controversial, but rather that kind of extreme subject-matter (e.g. letter bombs and anti-personnel mines) which would be regarded by the public as so abhorrent that the grant of a patent would be inconceivable (see Guidelines, CIV, 3.1).[254]

However, on occasions this conventionalism is belied by interpretative choices that limit the relevance of the actual views of society or any particular segment of it. In *PLANT GENETIC SYSTEMS*,[255] the EPO limited the probative value of surveys of public opinion on the grounds that they do not necessarily reflect *ordre public* concerns or moral norms that are deeply rooted in European culture, because surveys of particular groups tend to reflect their specific interests and bias. This dismissal of public polling was repeated in *HARVARD/Transgenic animal*.[256] Nevertheless, the resort to a meta-ethical assumption of conventionalism is overwhelming, in the EPO decisions and commentary on them,[257] and is

---

[252]   *HOWARD FLOREY/Relaxin* [1995] E.P.O.R. 541 (EPO Opp. Div.) at 552 (para. 6.4.3); see also 550 (para. 6.2.1).
[253]   *LELAND STANFORD/Modified animal* [2002] EPOR 2 (EPO Opp. Div.) at 16, at para. 51, p. 23.
[254]   *Ibid* at 23 (para. 51).
[255]   Cit. above n. 251 at 369 (para. 15).
[256]   *HARVARD/Transgenic animal (T315/03)* cit. below n. 300 at 323 (para. 10.4) and 336–8 (para. 3.2.19–3.2.21).
[257]   See e.g. Warren (1998), Warren-Jones (2006), offering qualified support for the use of empirical research to identify this European moral consensus, and

especially plain in *HARVARD/Transgenic animal* where the EPO Technical Board of Appeal, on hearing appeals against the Opposition Division's refusal to invalidate the *Oncomouse* patent (for a transgenic rodent modified to be prone to cancer for cancer research) rejected one of the appellants' arguments, that the Opposition Division had not established that its members' views were representative of European society, with the explanation that its members' views were quite irrelevant. It observed:

> Quite the contrary, the task of the Opposition Division was to assess whether or not the exploitation of the invention conformed with the *conventionally-accepted* standards of conduct in European society [citing *PLANT GENETICS*]. The Opposition Division had to make that decision, as with all decisions between opposing parties, only on the basis of *evidence* placed before it by the parties in support of their arguments and with no consideration for personal opinions.[258]

A better understanding, though, of the EPO's approach is afforded by universal prescriptivism, in particular the version defended here in Chapter 2 which embraces the equal right to freedom and well-being as foundational, because it provides a better justification for the outcomes the EPO has embraced. Though the EPO relies on moral conventions, it has not confronted the question that is posed once it is recognized that our conventions about morality include the understanding that its rules, principles and values are to be treated as having objective rational force. If it does so, it would have to undertake a reflection about the nature and underpinnings of the moral assumptions it finds conventionally prevailing, to arrive at that equal right to freedom and well-being (cf. Chapter 2 at §§2.3 and 2.4). This would explain the result and how it may hold that its own decision makers' private views on the moral issues are not relevant and yet find itself making prescriptions of its own. These are not its officials' personal morality but prescriptions they have to adopt in making sense of the rule subject to universalization that takes into consideration the moral basis of IPRs that is implicit in all the other rules and judgments within the EPC patent system. In other words, the morality and *ordre public* exclusions are not understood on their own but against the background of the general moral commitments already implicit in the rest of the IPR law and its justification. However, once we

---

arguing for a minimalist approach; and Thomas and Richards (2004), suggesting that a more sophisticated understanding of prevailing norms should be applied.

[258] Emphasis added. *HARVARD/Transgenic animal (T315/03)* cit. below n. 300 at 311 (para. 4.6).

cast off conventional tests based on practices of society, the process of moral reasoning becomes unmoored unless the ultimate basis of the morality can be rationally grounded, as Chapter 2 suggests, in some set of fundamental prescriptions. Beyleveld and Brownsword have suggested in a study based on the *Oncomouse* series of EPO decisions up to the grant that, in the European Community at least, this test should be human rights as embraced by the ECHR and UDHR, as these contain 'the substantive moral requirements that the Examining Division must employ because they are part of the constitutional arrangements that institute the Contracting States [of the EC] as a single legal community'.[259] The same terminus has been reached in Chapter 2 of this work by the rational exploration suggested by our understanding of the character of morality as universal prescriptivism. Chapter 2 suggests (at §2.4) that this leads to an embrace of the equal right to freedom and well-being for each individual human being as a person as the foundational moral principle. It has been acknowledged that this draws very much upon and is akin to Gewirth's PGC (cf. §2.5.1) which Beyleveld and Brownsword hold 'is implicit in the framework of European critical cultural morality',[260] and it has been argued herein that this principle underpins and explains the UDHR human rights which reflect our international commitments (at §2.5.3). In this light one can see how it is possible to maintain the morality of the IPR system and yet require a restrictive interpretation of the exclusions on moral and *ordre public* grounds. The EPO Opposition Division decision in *HOWARD FLOREY/Relaxin*[261] is a case in point: the objections included the argument that the patent application for a DNA fragment encoding for H2-relaxin should be rejected because the publication or exploitation of such an invention would be contrary to '*ordre public*' or morality (Article 53(a) of the EPC). The opponents' submissions included the following arguments:[262]

1.   that the carrying out of the invention would require the isolation of the DNA sequence from tissue extracted from a pregnant woman

---

[259]   Beyleveld and Brownsword (1993, quote at 68) considered the decisions on examination (*HARVARD/Oncomouse (V4/89)*, cit. below n. 291), on appeal (*HARVARD/Oncomouse (T19/90)*, cit. below n. 294), and re-examination, cit. below n. 296, discussed below at §4.7.4.
[260]   Beyleveld and Brownsword (1993) at 31.
[261]   Cit. above n. 252.
[262]   *Ibid* at 549 (para. 6.1).

and that, as this would involve making use of pregnancy for a technical process for profit, it would be an offence against human dignity;

2. that the patenting of human genes involving dismemberment of women and their piecemeal sale, being tantamount to a modern form of slavery, would be an infringement of the human right to self-determination; and

3. that the patenting of human genes, as the patenting of human life, is intrinsically immoral.

The Opposition Division rejected these arguments. In relation to point (1), it answered that the women from whom the DNA fragments were taken had consented to this as part of necessary gynaecological operations, that many life saving substances were isolated from human volunteers in a like manner; hence, there was no reason to perceive the use of human tissue so taken as immoral.[263] It reasoned that the slavery and dismemberment argument in point (2) was misconceived as patents covering DNA encoding human H2-relaxin or any other human gene did not 'confer on their proprietors any rights whatever to individual human beings'.[264] The only stage at which a woman was involved in making the invention was as the voluntary source of the mRNA (from which the cDNA for the relaxin would be derived). The Opposition Division's findings of fact here appear unassailable but are somewhat disingenuous because the crux of the dispute as to whether these acts infringe against human dignity or the right to self-determination turns not on the facts but on the moral significance that we attach to the use of a fragment of an individual human person's genome. If a person's identity and essential individuality are held to be expressed in his or her genome to the extent that our respect for the human individual extends to our treatment of the structure of the genome or parts of it, then we have strong moral reasons to object to proprietorship over it and commercial use or dismemberment over it. The Opposition Division's findings are a rejection of such a view of the matter. But it does not quite articulate the reasoning behind this rejection. Its findings and reasoning offer the beginning of an argument, though, that does suggest why the invention and use of it under conditions of voluntary donorship and beneficient purpose and effects is compatible with human dignity and the right to self-determination. This is bound up with the moral significance we attach to individual

---

[263] *Ibid*, 550 (para. 6.3.1–6.3.2).
[264] *Ibid*, at 550–51 (para. 6.3.3), quote at 550.

autonomy. However, this reasoning requires an explicit discussion of the moral significance which we attach to the facts of the invention. It is the Opposition Division's answer to argument (3) that is the most interesting from the view of the mode of reasoning employed. It held that the argument that human life was being patented was unfounded as DNA is:

> Not 'life' but a chemical substance which carries genetic information and can be used as an intermediate in the production of proteins which may be medically useful. The patenting of a single human gene has nothing to do with the patenting of human life.[265]

The fact that the DNA sequence is a chemical substance is an undeniable one; however, the question of whether it should be accorded the respect we give to human life and whether it is thus morally distinguishable from other human proteins requires an evaluative decision as to how to treat the facts and the artefact. The Opposition Division does go on to offer reasons which illustrate how the ways our legal determinations delimit the extent of our person and our control over its products are ultimately reflections of underlying ethical choices about the relative rights the individual has against the public and the claims the latter has against the former. The opponents' arguments would appear extreme to many because most of us would share the Opposition Division's assumptions – that once non-vital human tissue is removed from one's body with one's consent, it ceases to be an integral part of our bodily self, and is an artefact on its own. At issue in the differing views of the opponents and the Opposition Division is the way an individual human person is identified: whether this should extend to DNA sequences extracted or derived from her body. In the same way, the observation that a living human body is an integrated collection of organs and tissue – though that is true as a matter of physical description – does not carry the implication that there should be no special treatment of it. Within the scheme of the equal right to freedom and well-being that is proposed herein, it may be argued that the law's treatment of the human individual's physical boundaries in *HOWARD FLOREY* may be justified on the basis that the promotion and protection of human liberty are better advanced by regarding such extracted tissue and DNA as extraneous to the person, because such extension may be generally less necessary to facilitating the actions of individuals than the advancement of science and medicine that is promoted by limiting the extent of the human person at this point. That the tissue and DNA are physically separated from the original body is not

---

[265]   *Ibid* at 551 (para. 6.3.4).

as telling as might at first sight appear because we may treat separable products of ourselves as remaining integral to our personhood: an example of this is the moral right of an author to claim authorship and to prevent derogatory treatment of the author's works that are protected under many copyright authors' right laws as inalienable rights of the author.[266] In our IPR systems, this is reflected in the varying ways in which national systems have acknowledged and rendered inalienable the moral rights of authors and inventors (cf. §4.6.2 above) respectively in their works and inventions. These extend personhood beyond the purely physical. On the other hand, rules and decisions such as the *HOWARD FLOREY/Relaxin* EPO determination, fix the physical boundaries of the protected person.[267]

4.7.3 The EU 'Biotech Directive'[268]

This demarcation of the human body is one that, after serious opposition to earlier drafts on ethical grounds,[269] is mapped out by the EU Biotech Directive in a manner to distinguish the elements that may be appropriated through patents from unpatentable aspects of the human body and its products. Though the demarcation hinges on certain physical features – isolation from the human body or production by a 'technical process' (Article 5(2)) – the relevance of these features depends ultimately on ethical evaluations and the effects and implications of such choices. These ethical choices are apparent in the grounds that the ECJ considered in its decision to reject the application to have that Directive annulled in *Netherlands v. European Parliament*.[270] The Kingdom of the Netherlands had submitted that the Directive breached the fundamental right to respect for human dignity in the law of the European Community in requiring that isolated elements of the human body be open to patenting, as human matter is thus reduced to being means to the ends of others. The ECJ decision essentially affirms the European Parliament's demarcation of the human body and its natural elements *in situ* from elements

---

[266]   Art. 6*bis* Berne Convention.
[267]   See *Moore v. Regents of University of California* 51 Cal. 3d 120, for another such determination of the boundaries of the protected physical person, this time by the Supreme Court of California.
[268]   EU Directive 98/44/EC of 6 July 1998.
[269]   The history of its passage includes an earlier European Parliament rejection of a joint text (of the European Parliament and the Council) by the Conciliation Committee: referred to at Recital 4 (*ibid*).
[270]   [2002] F.S.R. 36 (Case C-377/98).

that are either by technical means isolated from that body *or* produced for industrial application. The recitals of the Directive identify the ethical tension between the benefits of promoting technological innovations in this field by encouraging investment in it generally,[271] the fundamental principles 'safeguarding the dignity and integrity of the person',[272] and attempts to resolve it by the demarcation just mentioned.[273] It is submitted that this is explicable by reference to the more fundamental right which must be rationally found to underpin the principles of respect for human dignity and freedoms in the ECHR and UDHR: the equal right to freedom and well-being (cf. §2.5.3). That right would support both promotion of technological innovation through patents and protection of the integrity of the person. However, as it also recognizes that the boundary of the 'person' to be protected is also an institution to be constructed by rules subject to the fundamental principles themselves, it allows that the tension between these two competing claims to liberty may be resolved by Gewirth's criterion of degree of needfulness for action (cf. §2.5.1), which says that: 'When two rights are in conflict with one another, that right takes precedence whose object is more needed for action.'[274] Respect for and protection of personal integrity are necessary for individual action and are a right that rational agents would accept: and the rational agent would accept that this should extend beyond that mere point of will that identifies the Kantian agent, to at least all aspects of the human body that are necessary to sustain that will. As seen above (§4.6.2), this extends to interest in aspects of intellectual products of the person. But at some point, elements of the physical body (e.g. extracted non-essential tissue and DNA) are in fact less essential for that will to be sustained by that body. At this point, the claim of others to liberty and well-being through promotion of technology becomes more important because such technologies also promote their ability to act. This right, though it identifies the primary consideration, does not settle exactly where that demarcation should be made. This is where a political decision by the relevant legislature is necessary. Hence, such decisions should (under the Principle of Cooperation cf. §2.4.6) be accepted so long as they are in good faith and not unreasonable attempts to respect that right.

Thus, one may find justification for the ECJ's acceptance that human dignity is safeguarded by the guarantee in Article 5(1) of the Biotech

---

[271]   EU Directive 98/44/EC of 6 July 1998, recitals 1–3, 10.
[272]   *Ibid* at recitals 16 and 43.
[273]   *Ibid* at recitals 16, 20 and 21.
[274]   Gewirth (1996), p. 45.

Directive that the human body in the various stages of its formation and development and the simple discovery of its elements cannot constitute patentable inventions; whilst, under Article 5(2), '[a]n element isolated from the human body or otherwise produced by means of a technical process, including the sequence or partial sequence of a gene, may constitute a patentable invention, even if the structure of that element is identical to that of a natural element'.[275] The equal right to freedom and well-being provides the key which unlocks the puzzle of demarcation between the human person and those of its productions that are capable of appropriation. It also explains the link between patents and concerns about the context in which the subject matter (the inventions protected) are discovered or used. These were reflected in the ancillary grounds raised by the applicant in relation to the breach of the right to respect of human dignity and the objections in respect of the *ordre public* and morality exclusions. In respect of the former, the ECJ quite rightly observed that concerns about assurances that the rights of the donor of the human elements and the recipient of the benefits of the resulting invention to give (or withhold) free and informed consent were ethical matters to be addressed by separate laws and institutional frameworks regarding research and medicine rather than the patent law itself. But this simple disposal of the question out of hand as one that was 'clearly misplaced'[276] did not adequately acknowledge the connection that does exist with the patent system. Those that support and uphold the patent system ultimately rely, for its moral grounding, on the same principle that animates this concern about respect for human autonomy in research and the practice of medicine. Moreover, the patent system is designed to make a critical contribution in both these fields, as an inducement to research efforts and as a source of new medicines and medical technologies. The fields of activity are distinct but hardly unrelated. The practical concern that may have been behind the concern of the applicant is that whereas patent interests may generate the political will supporting legislation extending the patent system, a similar conviction may be lacking for the complementary expression of the same principle in these other fields. Once the patent rights are secured, the danger is that those other concerns would be regarded as other problems for other people. Though the claims of moral principles are universal, crossing boundaries of activities, the interests of individuals in them are variable – sometimes

---

[275] *Netherlands v. European Parliament*, cit. above n. 270 at 586–7 (para. 71–5).
[276] *Ibid* at 587 (para. 79).

the principles are in their favour and others against, or irrelevant to their immediate concerns. Yet, the patent system is part of a larger system of laws and institutions. In this case, its value as a contributor to the general liberty and well-being of persons assumes a context in which the activities that lead to inventions or which make use of them are subject to institutions that generally provide substantial assurance that liberty and well-being are promoted and protected. The disposal of the questions on the basis that these matters are to be addressed by laws and institutions is a pragmatically correct one on the assumption – which the ECJ was entitled to make – that the European Community, being a well ordered polity, would address these potential problems with the appropriate separate laws. This reasoning explains the relationship between the patent system and its rules for exclusion of certain inventions on the grounds of *ordre public* and morality that were addressed by the ECJ in *Netherlands v. European Parliament* and other decisions before EPO tribunals.

The ECJ rejected the objection of the applicant in the *Netherlands* case, that the exclusion (under Article 6 of the Directive), where the commercial exploitation of the inventions would be contrary to *ordre public* and morality, breached the principle of legal certainty in that it gave 'national authorities a discretion in applying concepts expressed in general and ambiguous terms'.[277] The ECJ reasoned that some 'scope for manoeuvre'[278] was necessary to take into account the use of the patents in local circumstances; and that the concept was a well known one used in international legal instruments such as the EPC, and that Article 6(2), in fact, went further in defining the concept as it identified four applications that were specifically considered unpatentable. These four applications are: (a) processes for cloning human beings; (b) processes for modifying the germ line genetic identity of human beings; (c) uses of human embryos for industrial or commercial purposes; and (d) processes for genetically modifying the genetic identity of animals which are likely to cause them suffering without substantial medical benefit to man or animal, and also animals resulting from such processes. The understanding that the four stipulated instances of subject matter that would be unpatentable on this ground refer to some shared, more fundamental, norms of the civilization, may be given a descriptive conventional meaning. But, as we have seen above (§4.7.2) with the developing EPO jurisprudence in cases like *PLANT GENETICS*[279] and *HOWARD*

---

[277] *Ibid* at 582 (para. 35).
[278] *Ibid* at 582 (para. 38).
[279] Cit. above n.251.

FLOREY/Relaxin,[280] a better explanation is a prescriptive approach that seeks universalizable fundamental principles, on the basis that this method is required by the conventional assumption we make that moral rules have the characteristic of objective rational force. In *WARF/Stem Cells* the EPO's Enlarged Board of Appeal, applying a regulation encapsulating the 'Biotechnology Directive's' Article 6(2)(c) prohibition against use of the human embryo for industrial and commercial purposes, discerned from this provision the legislators' concern with preventing misuse of technology through commodification of human embryos and with the protection of human dignity.[281]

The ECJ recently relied on that Directive's recital 16 declaration that 'patent law must be applied so as to respect the fundamental principles safeguarding the dignity and integrity of the person' to make far reaching holdings in *Brustle v. Greenpeace E.V.*[282] that Article 6(2) 'must be understood in a wide sense',[283] 'so that … any human ovum must be regarded as a "human embryo" within that provision as soon as fertilized';[284] that this includes a 'non-fertilized human ovum into which the cell nucleus from a human mature cell has been transplanted and a non-fertilized ovum whose division and further development has been stimulated by parthogenesis', because they are 'capable of commencing the process of development of a human being';[285] that a stem cell taken from a human embryo at the blastocyst stage may also constitute a 'human embryo' within that provision if it is found by the referring German court to 'be capable of commencing the process of development of a human being';[286] that there is such use of the human embryo rendering the invention unpatentable where the implementation of the invention requires a destruction of a human embryo at an earlier stage (as

---

[280] Cit. above n. 252.

[281] *WARF/Stem Cells* G2/06 [2009] E.P.O.R. 15, at 140 (Reasons para.18). Harmon (2006) sees from the progression of EPO Art. 53(a) decisions, including the Examination Division decision in *WARF*, a shift towards re-engagement with the public discourse exploring the moral questions in the context of certain inventions, and argues for the principle of solidarity as a central unifying value to the patent system which supports adaptations more favourable to an expanded public domain. The present work suggests that the principle of an equal right to freedom and well-being embraces and explicates this idea of solidarity.

[282] *Brustle v. Greenpeace E.V.* (ECJ, 18 October 2011, Case C-34/10), see para. 32.

[283] *Ibid*, para. 34.

[284] *Ibid*, para. 35.

[285] *Ibid*, para. 36.

[286] *Ibid*, para. 37.

in the production of embryonic stem cells from a cell line production of which requires destruction of a human embryo), even if the claims of the patent itself do not concern the use of a human embryo;[287] that use of 'human embryos' so understood for scientific purposes falls within the concept of 'uses of human embryos for industrial and commercial purposes' in that provision rendering the invention unpatentable.[288] The argument that has been made here is that this ultimately grounds in the equal right to freedom and well-being. As patents, by encouraging the introduction of new technological options, expand our possibilities for realizing liberty and well-being, this would ordinarily support a restrictive reading of the *ordre public* and morality exclusion.[289]

This goal would only be undermined by technologies that are harmful or dangerous and have no positive uses or would be released under conditions where there are no real prospects that there can or will be effective institutional measures to prevent those harmful or dangerous abuses. But as *Brustle v. Greenpeace E.V.* shows, this consequentialist promotion of liberty and well-being cannot be at the expense of the individual human person whose liberty and well-being is the justifying ground of that pursuit. There is a connection between the patent system and other institutions (like those maintaining law and order in general, food safety, environmental protection, or ethical research, etc.) wherein the assumption of the overall beneficial character (or, at least, harmlessness) of the former is partially dependent on the same underlying moral rationale being respected and operative in those other institutions. Potentially though, this exclusionary bar may also be invoked where the derivation of the invention or its use involves a violation of the equal right to freedom and well-being, and the other relevant rules of the law do not adequately address that violation, because the morality of an invention's exploitation must also be assessed with the context of the law constraining derivation and use in mind. The wider use of the *ordre public* and morality exclusion is not an appropriate instrument for correcting deficiencies elsewhere in the regulatory system,[290] but may have to be pressed into service if all else fails. The wider significance of this – beyond the EU and EPC countries – is that Article 27(2) of the

---

[287]   *Ibid*, para. 49.

[288]   *Ibid*, para. 46.

[289]   A similar conclusion is reached by Moufang (1994), grounding his argument on the value of freedom he found permeating the patent system, whose call for legislative action to clarify the borderline in relation to patenting human cell lines and genes anticipated the EU 'Biotech Directive'.

[290]   As argued in Laurie (2004).

TRIPS Agreement permits WTO members to exclude from patentability inventions 'the prevention ... of the commercial exploitation of which is necessary to protect *ordre public* or morality, including to protect human, animal or plant life or health or to avoid serious prejudice to the environment'. Hence, other countries may adopt similar laws and use the same potential for adaptation in such provisions. Thus, the moral dimension of IPR depends on and creates moral duties and rights in other legal institutions, and vice versa.

4.7.4   Freedom and Well-being and *Ordre Public* and Morality

On a first encounter, an initial EPO explication of the similar exclusionary rule, the *HARVARD/Oncomouse* decisions, would appear to be an obstacle to this interpretation, as it appears to adopt a utilitarian approach to the issue. The *HARVARD/Oncomouse* series of decisions have become a minor epic of the EPO jurisprudence on Article 53(a) of the EPC, which renders unpatentable inventions whose 'publication or exploitation would be contrary to "ordre public" or morality'. It concerned an application claiming a method for making a non-human mammalian animal with a gene expressing a proclivity towards cancerous growth. These included claims for such animals, more specifically, mice, bearing this gene. The Examining Division of the EPO initially rejected those claims on other grounds,[291] though it went on to opine that the patent law was not the right legislative tool to address the concerns – about interference with the course of evolution, cruelty and ill-treatment of animals, and threats to the environment – posed by such an invention.[292] Its reason for this conclusion was that the intention behind Article 53(a) was to exclude innovations that would lead to threats to public order or criminal or generally offensive behaviour; and that, as the 'invention might have a beneficial effect on mankind',[293] it did not fall in this category. The Technical Board of Appeal in *T19/90*,[294] however, disagreed and remitted the case to the Examination Division with the direction that

---

[291]   *HARVARD/Oncomouse (V4/89)* [1990] E.P.O.R. 4: sufficiency of disclosure under Art. 83 EPC, and for being a claim to an animal variety under Art. 53(b) EPC, on which points the Examining Division's decision was reversed by the Technical Board of Appeal *(T19/90)*, cit. below n. 294.

[292]   *Ibid* at 10–11 (para.10).

[293]   *Ibid* at 11 (para. 10.3).

[294]   *HARVARD/Oncomouse (T19/90)* [1990] E.P.O.R. 501.

> The decision ... [as to whether the *ordre public* and morality ground of exclusion] is a bar to patenting the present invention would seem to depend mainly on a careful weighing up of the suffering of animals and possible risks to the environment on the one hand, and the invention's usefulness to mankind on the other.[295]

It is the phrase in this test (to be referred to, for brevity's sake, as the '*T19/90* test'), 'careful weighing up', that appears to suggest a utilitarian calculus. The Examination Division (which on remittal held that the claims cleared the exclusionary bar[296]) on re-examination held that the great benefit to mankind of advances against cancer outweighed the suffering to animals (which would be reduced by confining the research testing to a more promising, and hence more limited, population of potential subjects) and the risk to the environment and ecology given that one may assume that there would be careful safeguards imposed on the research practices. After a hiatus during which the Biotech Directive had been adopted and refinements to the EPC rules introduced, opposition proceedings that had begun in 1993 resulted in a narrowing of the admissible claims in 2003.[297] Amongst the changes that had been introduced was new EPC Rule 23d(d) which specifies that under Article 53(a) patents shall not be granted for 'processes for modifying the genetic identity of animals which are likely to cause them suffering without any substantial medical benefit to man or animal, and also animals resulting from such processes'. The Opposition Division held that the balancing test of *T19/90* was superseded by this more specific one,[298] hence the claim had to be limited to test animals since those which extended to others would be likely to suffer without any corresponding substantial medical benefit to man or animal. Thus, those pertaining to genetically modified rodents were allowed, whilst the claims directed broadly to non-human mammalian animals as such were disallowed.[299] The *Oncomouse* patent survived appeal though it may be said to have squeaked through. The Technical Board of Appeal[300] held that conflict with Rule 23d(d) would be a conclusive objection to the patent under Article 53(a),[301] but clearing its restrictions did not mean it

---

[295]   *Ibid* at 513 (para. 5).
[296]   [1991] E.P.O.R. 525.
[297]   *HARVARD/Oncomouse* (Decision of the Opposition Division) (2001) O. J. of the EPO 473.
[298]   *Ibid* at Reasons para. 9.3.
[299]   *Ibid* at Reasons para. 10 and 12.
[300]   *HARVARD/Trangenic animal (T315/03)* [2005] E.P.O.R. 31.
[301]   *Ibid* at 317 (para.7.4).

necessarily satisfied that article because there were cases that will not come within the rule's ambit, and other considerations had to be borne in mind.[302] In relation to modified animals, the test in *T19/90* had also to be applied and satisfied. Like the *T19/90* test, Rule 23d(d) is a balancing test but is more specific in that it is 'triggered' only when there is 'a likelihood – but no more than a likelihood – of [animal] suffering', no matter how minor,[303] resulting from the exploitation or publication of the patent.[304] Then, when so 'triggered', if the claimed invention's exploitation or publication is without a likely corresponding substantial medical benefit (i.e. where 'the suffering and medical benefit both exist in relation to the use of the same animal') to man or animal, the claim is not allowable under Article 53(a).[305] This test is narrower than the whole ambit of Article 53(a) because it identifies one of the circumstances where a case may definitely be said to violate that provision. But this leaves room then for some additional considerations to be raised as grounds upon which the patent would be disallowable under what the Board calls a '"real" Article 53(a) assessment'.[306] The *T19/90* test is broader than Rule 23d(d) in several significant ways. First, whereas that latter considers only *medical* benefit to man or animal, the former allows consideration of all benefits to mankind.[307] Secondly, the former additionally weighs risk to the environment against such benefits.[308] Thirdly, whereas the latter looks for trigger points – a likelihood of animal suffering to invoke it, and an absence of likelihood of medical benefit to man or animal that is substantial is sufficient to conclusively rule out the patent – the former requires 'a careful "weighing up" of the matters to be balanced' and, thus, a consideration of the *extent* and *degree* by which the animal suffering or risk to environment is outweighed by the invention's usefulness to mankind.[309] This allows a consideration of the possible use of non-animal alternatives to the invention.[310] Fourthly, as the Board noted, the *T19/90* test qualifies itself in that it states that the decision under Article 53(a) EPC would depend '"*mainly*" on' this careful

---

[302] *Ibid* at 316 (para. 6.2) and 317 (para.7.4).
[303] *Ibid* at 320 (para. 9.4).
[304] *Ibid* at 316 (para. 6.2).
[305] *Ibid* at 319–20 (para. 9.1–9.3), 321 (para. 9.7), 328–9 (para. 12.2.1–12.2.4) and 330–31 (para. 13.2.1–13.2.4).
[306] *Ibid* at 323 (para. 105); see also 322 (para.10.1).
[307] *Ibid* at 323 (para. 10.5).
[308] *Ibid*.
[309] *Ibid* at 323 (para. 10.6) and 329 (para. 12.2.5).
[310] *Ibid*.

weighing of identified considerations, thus allowing 'for other considerations to be taken into account, either by way of adapting the test ... or
by way of considering other matters outside the framework of the test'.[311]

The Board found that the claim directed at genetically manipulated
rodents (embracing all animals within the taxonomic order *Rodentia*) did
not satisfy Rule 23d(d) because it included classes of animals that were
not established to be test subjects for human cancer research and, hence,
there was an absence of correspondence between the medical benefit
sought and the animal suffering anticipated.[312] And, for good measure
though this finding is dispositive against the patent, at the second stage of
the test (or second test), 'on a "real" Article 53(a) EPC assessment', the
Board found that this claim would have failed under the *T19/90* test as
well, as the same considerations applied because the usefulness to
mankind of the invention was essentially restricted to the medical
benefits and the other considerations of degree of animal suffering and
availability of non-animal alternatives for testing, if established, would
have worked even more against the patent.[313] However, the Board
allowed an amendment which restricted the claim to genetically modified
mice for which there was this required correspondence between animal
suffering caused and likelihood of substantial medical benefit to humans
gained, which was held to clear the restrictions of Rule 23d(d).[314] (It may
be observed that at this stage, since relative degrees of suffering and
benefit are not investigated, logically, any medical benefit to human
beings or animals irrespective of its extent would enable the invention to
pass this test, so long as the benefit is 'substantial'. It seems here that
'substantial' would mean real and not vanishingly insignificant or specu-
lative.) The amended claim restricted to genetically modified mice would
also satisfy the *T19/90* test on the second stage, 'real Article 53(a)
assessment', for the same reasons which operated in relation to Rule
23d(d) and the additional considerations did not operate to negate
them.[315] The possibility of non-animal alternatives was not borne out by
evidence,[316] nor was that based on environmental risk, when one considers that the risk of escaping test subjects is minimal given the conditions

---

[311]   *Ibid* at 323 (para. 10.7).
[312]   *Ibid* at 328–9 (para. 12.2.1–12.2.4).
[313]   *Ibid* at 329 (para. 12.2.5).
[314]   *Ibid* at 330–31 (para. 13.2.1–13.2.4).
[315]   *Ibid* at 331 (para. 13.2.5).
[316]   *Ibid* at 332 (para. 13.2.7).

and regulations under which laboratory mice are kept.[317] But the reasoning of the Board becomes rather awkward when it comes to balancing of the *degree* of animal suffering against the extent of human benefit. It held that any degree of animal suffering would invoke the balancing test as it was 'not only distasteful but *effectively impossible* for the Board (or any other decision making instance) to make findings as to degrees of suffering'.[318] However, after noting that 'any animal suffering is sufficient to bring Article 53(a) EPC into play and requires a balancing benefit', it went on to conclude that 'the degree of animal suffering is of no assistance in making the T19/90 test'.[319] This appears to be a refusal to *weigh* the suffering to animals against gains to humans. Are we, then, to assume that any substantial gain to man will be sufficient for the invention to pass the Article 53(a) test? This would convert what on its face would seem to be a utilitarian calculus into a test that has the hallmarks of a deontological duty or right. The use of a utilitarian calculus is not the only way to read the direction to make a 'careful weighing up'. For one thing, as the Board found when it realized that it was 'effectively impossible ... to make findings as to degrees of suffering',[320] there is no metric available for correlation of human benefits to animal suffering or risk to the environment, or for trading off losses in any of these for gains in the first.

The *T19/90* test does not explain how the various considerations are to be weighted. The direction, if it is to be followed faithfully, requires that one inquires into the relationships and the method for making such a correlation; requires, in logic, that one should explore the very foundations of one's ethical reasoning and apply the resultant methodology. It is highly unlikely that the Technical Board of Appeal in *T19/90* had anything like the fundamental prescriptions and the equal right to freedom and well-being explicated in Chapter 2 in mind, but that is the rational outcome of the task it set. That equal right to freedom and well-being gives a primacy to human freedom and well-being, but does provide a way of relating animal welfare and environmental risks to this consideration, because these other considerations provide the context in which human liberty and welfare are enjoyed. We can apply the criterion of degree of needfulness to (human) action to the question,[321] and ask if allowing the exploitation or publication of that type of invention would

---

[317]   *Ibid* at 332–3 (para. 13.2.8–13.2.9).
[318]   *Ibid* at 332 (para.13.2.6). Emphasis added.
[319]   *Ibid.*
[320]   *Ibid.*
[321]   See Gewirth (1996), p. 45, and Ch. 2, §2.5.1.

promote or retard our general ability to make plans and have purposes, and successfully achieve them. For example, unnecessary cruelty to animals with little gain to human liberty or well-being would damage the way we value life in general; damaging the environment will reduce our potential freedom and well-being in future. On the other hand, the potential gains in our ability to make such plans and have purposes is a very strong argument for upholding patents for new ideas, especially where the harms to animals and the environment can be addressed by other laws regulating the implementation of the ideas. Hence, the principle gives a strong weighting to human benefits conferred by making the invention available. This is consistent with, and offers a more coherent justification for, the eventual outcome of the *HARVARD/ Transgenic animal (T315/03)* appeal from the Opposition Division in the Oncomouse series, even though a precise metric identifying equivalences between these considerations cannot be worked out: the gains to human freedom and well-being from the invention's exploitation and publication will trump allowing patenting unless over-riding losses in this regard can be established to flow from resulting animal suffering or risk to the environment. The equal right to freedom and well-being would reconcile the *HARVARD/Oncomouse T19/90* test with its more circumspect treatment by later EPO authorities which preferred a narrower restrictive rule. In *PLANT GENETIC SYSTEM/Glutamine Synthetase Inhibitors*,[322] the EPO's Technical Board of Appeal opined that, as regards the *ordre public* restriction, Article 53(a) constituted 'a bar to patentability for inventions the exploitation of which is likely to seriously prejudice the environment'.[323] The case dealt with claims for technology for genetically modifying a plant to resist certain herbicides, and claims for such modified plants. Mindful of the unprecedented power and control of genetic modifications which biotechnology puts into the hands of humankind and that these techniques can be used for constructive or destructive purposes, it ruled that it had to be established that it would be contrary to *ordre public* and morality if the claimed subject matter 'relates to a misuse or destructive use' of the technology.[324] The *T19/90* 'balancing exercise' was distinguished as 'perhaps useful in situations in which an actual damage and/or disadvantage (e.g. suffering of animals …) exists'.[325] As has been shown, the two approaches do not necessarily conflict. Though it more clearly embraces a narrow exclusion in favour

---

[322] Cit. above n. 251 (Opposition by Greenpeace).
[323] *Ibid* at p. 370 (Reasons para. 18).
[324] *Ibid* at p. 370 (Reasons para. 17.1).
[325] *Ibid* at p. 373 (Reasons para. 18.8).

of patenting inventions which have constructive uses, the *PLANT GENETIC SYSTEMS* test does not remove the need for moral analysis and the potential recourse to the fundamental prescriptions which must logically underpin such analysis. The notions of 'misuse' or 'destructive use' of any form of technology presuppose a moral perspective from which one may speak of proper purposes of technology. In *LELAND STANFORD/Modified animal*,[326] the EPO's Opposition Division applied an interpretation of the provision that is possibly even more narrow: holding that

> as long as a claimed invention has a legitimate use, it cannot be the role of the EPO to act as moral censor and invoke the provisions of Article 53(a) EPC to refuse on ethical grounds to grant a patent on legal research and directed to an invention indisputably associated with medical benefits.[327]

The application in that case claimed an animal–human chimera, exemplified by an immuno-suppressed mouse inserted with human blood and platelet producing tissue which is to be taken from human foetuses and babies below the age of three. There is a potential medical gain from research in that the resultant chimeric animals are a source of hematopoietic tissue, are animal models for haematopoesis, and may be used as test subjects for HIV/AIDS therapies. Although the Opposition Division acknowledged that such chimeras 'instinctively [appear] distasteful, if not immoral, to many people at first glance'[328] (and this should have ruled out the claim if the notion of *ordre public* and morality applied by the EPO were truly conventional), it found that there was 'at present no consensus in Europe society about the desirability or otherwise of this technology' and that '[i]t would be presumptuous of the EPO to interfere in this public debate'.[329] One may wonder at the abdication this involves, as Article 53(a) requires that the EPO attempts to make some sense of the notion of *ordre public* and morality when the occasion requires. Given the analysis made above with respect to the *HARVARD/Oncomouse* series of decisions and *PLANT GENETIC SYSTEMS*, one may perhaps justify the test applied in this case, though not the mode of reasoning by which the Opposition Division came to it. The basis for this is that the conventional moral notions ought to be set aside for what, on deeper reflection, is a morally justifiable project. Liberty and well-being would

---

[326] Cit. above n. 253.
[327] *Ibid* at 23.
[328] *Ibid* at 23.
[329] *Ibid*.

be advanced by medical research and no human being is harmed by the technology or the way it was derived. Some may dispute this conclusion because a human–animal chimera may constitute such harm by impairing the dignity of the human person. But this debate would be framed in terms of moral principles, such as the equal right to freedom and well-being, rather than the supposed presence or absence of consensus on the point. It is often observed, by those who favour a reduced scope for the *ordre public* and morality bar, that patents only secure the property right by providing a wholly negative right of exclusion of others from the use of the invention and that they do not confer an unconditional positive right on the owner to use them.[330] The argument is that it is a matter for other areas of law to control their use and publication. Sometimes, the suggestion is also that objections to patents for such inventions are misguided as the absence of a patent would only make them more freely available.[331] The point is a valid one for inventions already made: refusing patents for them does little to inhibit the technology and, in fact, removes at least one legal obstacle to its use by others, though it might deter investments in their development by those seeking to make a profit. But a better rationale can be given for the *ordre public* and morality ground of exclusion, if it is understood in terms of the patent institution's function as a promoter of new technologies and an inducement for research and development. The point of refusing certain applications that fail the exclusion test is not the inhibition of those particular inventions (since these would already have been invented) but the inhibition of inventions of that nature by eliminating potential patents as an induce-ment for inventive effort and investment in pursuit of them. The *ordre public* and morality bar serves to remove such incentives. Of course, this does nothing to inhibit those whose objectives do not include financial gain. However, the point of the exclusion would not be the prohibition of such inventive efforts as such, but would be, instead, the disentanglement of the patent institution from such schemes. This analysis makes the *ordre public* and morality ground of exclusion an integral part of the overall justification for the patent system. The system's purpose is to induce beneficial innovation, and the exclusion is there to ensure that the

---

[330]   E.g. see EU Directive 98/44/EC of 6 July 1998, Recital 14; *PLANT GENETIC SYSTEMS* cit. above n. 251 at 371–2 (para. 18.2–18.5).

[331]   See e.g. *HARVARD/Transgenic animal (T315/03)* cit. above n. 300 at 334 (para. 13.2.12): 'Since a patent grants a temporary monopoly, only a patentee and its licensees can work the patent during its life … such a monopoly period may actually mean that the use of modified mice is for an initial period lower than it would otherwise be.'

inducement does not extend to innovations that are likely to be wholly or overwhelmingly detrimental to the common good. This supports the line of decisions cited above that favour narrow and clear tests for exclusions. If the thesis argued for in Chapters 2 and 3 is accepted, then the common good would be conceived of in terms of promotion and protection of freedom and well-being of all human beings as equal persons. The grounds for formulating the tests would be framed in terms of whether the type of invention would promote freedom and well-being and whether it could be made available or exploited under conditions that would not be wholly or overwhelmingly destructive of liberty and well-being generally. The stress on the moral dimensions of the morality exclusions yield a conclusion that is paradoxical, in that the scope of provisions directed at negating IPRs in creations capable of immoral uses should be read restrictively to eliminate only those without redeeming potential because the abuse may be addressed by other laws. But it confirms that such exclusions have an important place in the justification of patents and other IPRs in that they are intended to ensure that these do become inducements for productions without redeeming features.

4.8 THE MORAL DIMENSIONS AND PROTECTION OF THE PUBLIC DOMAIN

4.8.1 Rights to a Public Domain

The justifying rationale for IPRs finds its bedrock in a principle which requires a legitimate balance between property and participation interests. This chapter has shown that the main features of the IPRs are explicable in terms of this rationale. Though the laws may only imperfectly accommodate this imperative, and the moral terms in the core rules are either inappropriate or are not interpreted as they might have been to make the necessary accommodations, deficiencies within the very structure of the IPRs themselves may require responses in those other areas of the system – in the moral dimensions of exercise and reform, as will be seen later. It is appropriate, then, to conclude this chapter with an assessment of how successfully these institutions manage to strike the right balance between property rights and the participation interest in the public domain. The public domain has been described by Jessica Litman as 'a device that permits the rest of the [copyright] system to work by leaving the raw materials of authorship available for authors to use',[332] without which, 'it might be impossible to tolerate copyright at all'.[333] She contrasts this way of conceptualizing the public domain with 'Commentary on the public domain [which] has tended to portray it either as the public's toll for conferring private property rights in the works of authorship[334] or as the realm of material undeserving of property rights'.[335] This latter conceptualization of the public domain essentially treats it as copyright's shadow: the negative which remains after the areas of positive appropriation under IPRs have been demarcated.[336] It is a negative, shadow area because it is always liable to be effaced when some other positive claim to an IP right falls upon it or part of it. Subject matter not covered by one form of IPR may become appropriated under another: for example, when the EU created *sui generis* database protection over databases of data and other material which would not have been protected under copyright for lack of the requisite element of originality.[337] Both these positive and negative conceptions of the public domain can be criticized: the former for being too vague and uncertain to be useful, and the latter in characterizing the unappropriated knowledge as a kind of 'scientia nullius', as 'an instrument of dispossession' working to the disadvantage of non-dominant groups, denying claims to legal control and use of knowledge which are not recognized by standard IPRs.[338] The previous chapter and the foregoing sections of the present one provide an alternative way of conceptualizing the public domain and the commons

---

[332]   Litman (1990), at 968. See also Boyle (2008) which describes several contests between IP and the public domain in the information environment.

[333]   Litman (1990), p. 977.

[334]   *Ibid* at 967 citing Gorman, 1980, 'Fact or Fancy? The Implications for Copyright', 29 *Bull. Copyright Soc. U.S.A.* 560, at 560–61; Krasilovsky, 1967, 'Observations on Public Domain', 1 *Bull. Copyright Soc. U.S.A.* 205, 210–18 at 210–18; Patterson (1987) at 7.

[335]   Litman (1990) at 967; citing Nimmer, M. and Nimmer, D., 1989, 1 Nimmer on Copyright § 2.01[B]; Denicola, R.C. 1981, 'Copyright in Collections of Facts', *Columbia L Rev.* Vol. 81, No. 3, Apr. 1981, 516–542, at 512–22; Goldstein, 1983, 'Derivative Rights and Derivative Works in Copyright', 30 *J Copyright Soc. U.S.A.* 209 at 218.

[336]   See Caenegem (2002), who describes the traditional notion of the public domain in the course of a critique re-examining the value of the concept at p. 324, as one that is 'traditionally defined in the negative, as consisting of those "intangible goods" *not* subject to intellectual property rights'.

[337]   EU Directive 96/9/EC of 11 March 1996, Ch. III, Art. 7–11.

[338]   See Caenegem (2002), quote at 330.

that meets this criticism. (See especially §§3.6.5 and 4.1.1.) As justification of ownership is accompanied by responsibility to acknowledge the due claims of non-owners in the moral, if not in the legal, sense, both owners and non-owners have rights in IP objects as a consequence of our wanting to justify IPRs as institutions. Owners have proprietary rights of exclusion but, as they also have the moral duty to acknowledge just claims to access and sharing in the benefits of the IP objects, non-owners would have corresponding moral claim-rights to access and sharing. These non-owners' (moral) rights are: rights to fair use of aspects of the creations as part of their just share of the entire intellectual domain to reflect their right to participation in this realm as equal persons; to access where necessary to reflect their right to basic freedom and well-being (in particular where a right to freedom of expression, or to basic nutrition and health is concerned), and to access to, or retention of control of, certain aspects of their works or other creations by creators – even after alienating the commercial interests in them – to reflect their continuing interest in their creations as a means of expressing their personhood.

These are moral rights, rather than legal ones, in that they give the claims of individuals to protection of some types of interest a certain prevailing weight (in Ronald Dworkin's metaphor, they operate as 'trumps'[339]) in moral reasoning against arguments based on the general welfare. This is a different defence of the public domain from that more generally advanced, that it is necessary for the common good, because the individual rights thesis argues that there should be certain forms of common access even if the common good (in the sense of general welfare) would be furthered by extensions of IPRs or stronger rights. They complement one another, however, where the 'common good' is understood as a good that people have in common: in this case, an interest in something shared and available to all, rather than some overall accumulation of benefits. The individual rights, then, are rights to a commons. They are non-proprietary, but, rather, are participatory rights. They are intellectual property rights in the sense that they are rights in intellectual property in the same way that a moral right is such a right, though not a property right. It was suggested in the previous chapter (at §3.6.2) that it is more helpful to treat the entire realm of ideas as a commons, an intellectual commons, with IPRs as private rights in certain elements of the commons rather than as protected interests in matters that are separated from and competing with the commons. Such private rights may be reconciled with the idea that their subject matter is in the

---

[339] Dworkin (1977), 'Introduction' at p. xv and ch. 12, pp. 266–78.

commons if the rights are designed in such a way that they are somehow also shared at the same time. This is possible if the rights are temporary, a loan from the commons with the understanding that they will be returned; if there are aspects of the subject matter, even as the private rights subsist, which are freely available to all, or available on market terms, where there is an understanding that such availability is a matter of right and not conditional on the IP owner's consent; and if there are some types of element of the intellectual commons which can never be appropriated. The public domain would include these aspects of elements which are so available. The foregoing sections of this chapter have been an exploration of the various ways that this idea is reflected in the core structures of some of our main IPRs. The rights in the public domain according to this account are moral ones but they are embodied, or given legal force, in varying degrees by the laws. The advantage of exploring the matrix of principles which form the justificatory basis of IPRs as *moral* rather than legal principles is that we can identify the moral commitments we rationally have to make as we maintain such institutions. This enables us to understand the moral implications of having such institutions for our choices and actions beyond such institutions and beyond purely legal questions. This is because, unless we wish to abandon that justification, we must continue to treat their rationally underpinning principles as universally binding when addressing the moral questions raised in these other dimensions as well. This relationship between justification of these institutions and commitment to their justificatory basis explains why we can argue that in these other dimensions, these moral principles have a binding force. (This effect is discussed in Chapter 7 in respect of the exercise of IPRs and in Chapter 8 in respect of their reform.) Further, the nature of the institutions to be justified (and, it may be added, the fundamental principles that are a requisite basis of morality as an institution) largely determine the content of the justificatory principles that can be accepted. That these are *moral principles* rather than legal rules enables us to separately speak of what the rules of law are (that which are authoritatively settled by legislation or judicial precedent) without abandoning the perspective that enables us at the same time to identify what they *ought to be* as a consequence of commitment to certain essential features of the institution. The role of moral terms and concepts in the IPR laws and those laws of its related exercise and reform dimensions, however, enables us to explain how the laws as they are can be made to adjust to reflect that underlying moral dimension, subject to settled legal practice relating to the limits of judicial discretion as regards case law development and legislative interpretation. (The role of the moral dimension in the interpretation of laws and legal reasoning is discussed in Chapter 6.) One may speak, then, of these moral rights of both owners and users having various degrees of legal force and recognition, because there are a variety of ways that laws reflect this moral dimension. There would then be various degrees and manner of legal expression of such non-owners' moral rights in the promotion and protection of the public domain. There could be implicit employment in the course of interpretation, or explicit recognition through use of the express terminology in the key institutional rules. There would be various forms of entrenchment of these rights in the ordinary as well as constitutional and human rights laws: from presumptions against proprietary control to absolute bars against contractual waiver[340] or legislative circumscription. Exceptionally rare and limited though these various legal avenues for defence of the public domain may be, the significant effect of justifying IPRs where the equal right to freedom and well-being forms the most basic criterion for moral justification, is that we are led from justification of these proprietary claims to concern for the justice of such institutions and, hence, to the moral right of non-owners for a fair share of these resources which mandate, in turn, legal expression of these underlying moral rights. In this way, the moral dimension is a product of the laws as well as an intrinsic part of the laws.

4.8.2 Legal Protection for the Public Domain

The law can be and often is, in various ways, structured to give expression to participation rights in the intellectual commons. This is done most directly through use of moral terms in the key structural rules determining conditions of acquisition, and the strength, limitation and duration of rights, within the IPR regimes. The participation interest is also expressed through the moral claims of non-owners, which owners who want to justify their claims are bound to acknowledge in the other moral dimensions of exercise and reform. However, the public domain appears to be susceptible to private capture by contractual waivers and technological controls. Licensors of IPRs are often able to stipulate

---

[340] For example, the EU 'Software Directive' (Directive 91/250/EEC of 14 May 1991, now repealed and replicated in Directive 2009/24/EC of 23 April 2009) entrenched the user's right to make a 'back up' copy of legitimately acquired computer programs against contractual waiver: see Art. 5(2). For the UK, see s 50A(3) Copyright, Designs and Patents Act 1988. This device has been used beyond the EU: see for example the Singapore Copyright Act (Chapter 63), s 39(4).

conditions which extend their rights vis-à-vis licensees or to obtain rights in the licensees' innovations. Copyright material can now be protected by electronic copyright management systems controlling access or use of the materials – e.g. DVDs and DVD player systems – and there are laws to protect the integrity of these technological controls.[341] One consequence of such means of protection is that the technological controls may be configured to offer more extensive protection and more restrictive access than the general copyright law. For example, it has been held by a US court that the *access* control measures protected by the Digital Millennium Copyright Act,[342] not being a form of exclusivity covered by the Copyright Act, would not be subject to the fair use doctrine (cf. §7.4).[343] Regarding the public domain as a matter in which the public has participation rights contrasts with the conception of it as the shadow that remains after IP protection has claimed its share of the total intellectual domain. Describing the public domain as IP's shadow is somewhat misleading, however, because it is not altogether without positive defence in law.

Amongst its academic defenders, David Lange[344] is one who has called for judicial activism in the recognition and use of a variety of means to protect the public domain: restraint on over-reaching theories of protection,[345] a presumption against new forms of claims,[346] appointing counsel to act as guardian *ad litem* for the public domain,[347] by explaining (where it is sensible to recognize new or doubtful IP claims) what is not covered by such claims, and, as often as possible, diversion of claims from IP theory to adjacent areas of law such as unfair competition, contracts or some specie of moral rights.[348] It has been seen, though, that opportunities for such activism have not always been exploited.[349] Judicial activism is not the only avenue by which the public domain may resist encroachment by IP proprietarianism. There are also administrative

---

[341]   WIPO Copyright Treaty 1996, Art. 11; WIPO Performances and Phonograms Treaty 1996, Art. 18; Digital Millennium Copyright Act (US) s 103 adding Chapter 12 to the Copyright Act (Title 17 USC) including s 1201; Art. 6 & 7 EU Directive 2001/29/EC of 22 May 2001.

[342]   Section 1201(a) Copyright Act, Title 17 USC (US).

[343]   *Universal City Studios v. Corley* 273 F 3d 429 (2001 2nd Cir. 2001) (US).

[344]   Lange (1981).

[345]   *Ibid* at 173.

[346]   *Ibid* at 175.

[347]   *Ibid* at 176.

[348]   *Ibid* at 303.

[349]   See e.g. *NOVARTIS/Transgenic plant G1/98* cit. above at n. 165 and following text in §4.4.4.

authorities and political fori at regional and international spheres who have certain powers to resist such encroachment. For example, some laws mandating protection for technological measures for protection of copyright works also vest in certain authorities the function of monitoring their possible use to encroach on aspects that should have been accessible to the public under exceptions to copyright protection and the power, albeit highly restricted and rather weak, to act to counter this abuse. These are discussed later at §7.4.2 and §8.3.1. Political fori at the international level are also sites where the public domain may be defended. An example is the furore over the role of IP protection under TRIPS and the WTO's response, which are detailed in Chapter 8, in respect of patents and access to medicines (at §8.4). Of course, the judicial role of refining and reformulating the rules in the course of interpreting laws is critical for maintaining a just balance between protecting private rights and preserving the public domain. The use of moral terms and concepts in the key rules for IPRs themselves discussed in this chapter not only empowers but also requires that the courts act to preserve this balance.

5. International IP laws and the moral dimension of design

5.1 INTERNATIONAL IP LAWS AND THE DESIGN OF IPRS

The international legal framework for IP laws is a critical constraint for the arguments and suggestions that have been developed heretofore. Though IP laws are made by national legislatures and operate within the territorial jurisdiction of each legal system separately, the major international IP instruments such as the Paris Convention,[1] the Berne Convention,[2] the Rome Convention[3] and, most important of all, the WTO TRIPS Agreement[4] set constraints on each country's freedom of manoeuvre. They impose restrictions, such as reciprocity or national treatment and, most crucially, provide for mandatory minimum levels of IP protection intended to hedge in the member states' options as to the design and development of their IP laws. The relevance of these arguments and suggestions, then, depends on the degree to which this international framework either reflects such a justificatory theory or, at least, allows the implications of such a theory to be worked out in the national systems. This will have to be explored.

This chapter will focus on the moral principles underpinning the TRIPS Agreement and the scope of play given to the justificatory theory by the exceptions and limitations provisions, especially the so-called 'three-step' tests. These are critical because TRIPS, as seen in the previous chapter, contains the overarching requirements of mandatory minima protection, incorporating and adding to those of prior international conventions, on conditions and in terms that are in large part

---

[1]   Paris Convention for the Protection of Industrial Property (1967 revision with 1979 amendments).

[2]   Berne Convention for the Protection of Literary and Artistic Works (1971 Paris Rev. with 1979 amendments).

[3]   International Convention for the Protection of Performers, Producers of Phonograms and Broadcasting Organisations, 1961.

[4]   Agreement on Trade Related Aspects of Intellectual Property.

couched in plain descriptive or technical terms.[5] It is the principles by which these conditions and rights, and the exceptions and limitations to them, are understood and interpreted that are mainly expressed with overtly moral terms. Hence, it will be these principles that will have to be examined for any potential for adjusting the institutions to reflect the balance of property and participation rights.

5.2 REALPOLITIK AND MORALITY IN THE MAKING OF GLOBALIZED IP LAWS

International law and relations, even that pertaining to trade and economics, is a realm that one might think is governed more by power reflecting realpolitik theory and Machiavelli[6] than moral considerations. Seen in terms of the broad arc of its trajectory,[7] economic realpolitik appears to make a good candidate for an explanatory theory for late 20th Century globalization and the development of IPRs. The active involvement of US (and European) IP producers in the initiation and execution of these trends, and the considerable role of US economic clout in providing them with impetus, cannot be denied. But such realpolitik has its limits. A more fine grained analysis reveals the roles of other actors and processes which provide hope for reasoned, ethically grounded, reform; though, perhaps, this hope persists only in the interstices of the international legal framework.

Braithwaite and Drahos, for example, observe that 'states are not unitary in the way that realist theory supposes'.[8] The interests of the various actors within the major economic powers (the US included) are not without competing tensions of their own. The result is that some of

---

[5] In addition to abiding by the national treatment principle (Art. 3) and the 'most-favoured nation treatment' principle (Art. 4), the TRIPS Agreement requires (at Art.1(1)) that 'Members shall give effect to the provisions of this Agreement', though '[m]embers may, but shall not be obliged to, implement in their laws more extensive protection than is required by this Agreement'. And Art. 1(2) provides that 'Members shall accord the treatment provided for in this Agreement to the nationals of other Members'. TRIPS, then, specifies mandatory minima either by incorporating prevailing international conventions or adopting provisions reflecting standards either prevailing in the US and EU or compatible with them.

[6] Machiavelli (1961).

[7] Ref. Ryan (1998), Drahos and Braithwaite (2002).

[8] Braithwaite and Drahos (2000), p. 483; on 'contest of actors', see ch. 20, pp. 475–506.

the principles accommodating tensions in interests between owners and users will find their way into the international regimes. International alliances being forged by these actors can provide a counter-weight to the main economic interests driving the international norm making process. Power dominates international (and national) norm making but does not dominate exclusively. Interstices and chinks open along the fault lines of power relations to open roles for weak actors with the result that all parties want in some way (and however weakly in relation to their other objectives) to appeal to a set of moral ideas that will enrol others to their projects.

Christopher May develops in *A Global Political Economy of Intellectual Property Rights* (2000) a critique of intellectual property rights (particularly as required by TRIPS) as commodification of knowledge as a key part of the knowledge structure by which power, and the interests of the powerful, are both exercised and expressed. His 'dual-dialectic' of material forces of production driving a Marxian dialectic of change and Hegelian ideational factors shaping and providing the context for material forces, gives a role for moral reflection to play an important role through justificatory critique. Hence, he also observes that the justificatory schemata used to support property (and IPRs) gives rise to an immanent critique that supports sites of resistance on behalf of the commons and for a re-balancing in favour of individual (as opposed to corporately owned) rights.[9]

Recourse to a global ethics is required because TRIPS makes reference to and calls upon a background morality that the international community is presumed to share. The 'general thesis' postulated herein (at §2.5.3) is that universalization and prescriptivism at the core of what characterizes moral reasoning will lead, as a result of a desire to ground our moral claims in reason as far as reason is capable of providing guidance in such matters, to the fundamental principles which sum up in the equal right to freedom and well-being. This is the main burden of Chapter 2. An alternate, 'special thesis' (cf. §2.5.3), is also advanced, that – whatever the cogency of the argument that such a fundamental right may be derived *a priori* – we have in fact, as an international community, embraced human rights as our fundamental norms for international cooperation. Those principles are enshrined in the UDHR and commitments to those ideas are made in the UN Charter. These too are explicable by a still more fundamental equal right to freedom and well-being.

---

9   May (2000), see esp. ch. 4, pp. 91–126, and ch. 6, pp. 162–81.

Beyleveld and Brownsword have made such a 'special thesis' argument in relation to the European patent system on the basis that Western Europe at least has adopted the European Convention for the Protection of Human Rights and Fundamental Freedoms as its most basic morality.[10] The same argument, though, can be made of the rest of the world as an international community through its adoption of the Universal Declaration of Human Rights, and its obligation to promote and protect fundamental human rights under the UN Charter.[11] This is an argument that is increasingly explored in academic writings.[12]

The status of some claims to IPRs as a human right is recognized in Article 27 of the UDHR in the 'right freely to participate in the cultural life of the community' (Article 27(1)) and 'the right to the protection of the moral and material interests' of the author (Article 27(2)). As observed in the last chapter (§4.1.1), it calls for a balance between the right to property in created ideas, and the public right to participation. The reference here is to human rights *principles* as part of the background ethic of our international relations and institutions, including international law, rather than the international *law* of human rights. Even the provisions drafted with the intention that they should have direct legal effect are couched in terms which preserve this balancing requirement and wide scope for judges and other interpreting officials to construct this borderline.

Drahos argues for an instrumental approach in which 'intellectual property rights would be pressed into service on behalf of human rights', observing that '[l]inking intellectual property to human rights discourse is a crucial step in the project of articulating theories and policies that will guide us in the adjusting of existing intellectual property rights and creation of new ones'.[13] This effort must begin with acknowledging and clarifying this moral dimension. The arguments made in Chapter 2 (especially §2.5.3) contribute by making the protection and promotion of the equal right to freedom and well-being the ultimate good and the

---

[10] Beyleveld and Brownsword (1993), discussed herein at §4.7.2, see n. 259 (Chapter 4) and accompanying text.

[11] Cf. UN Charter, Art. 1(3), 55 and 56.

[12] E.g. see articles in De Greiff and Cronin (eds.) (2002), esp.: Nussbaum (2002), ch. 4, pp. 117–50; Pogge (2002), ch. 5, pp. 151–96; and Habermas (2002), ch. 6, pp. 197–214.

[13] Drahos (1998). The interface between IPRs and human rights, and the latter as a source of grounds for limitations on the former, are explored by the contributors to the volume Grosheide (2010a); see esp. Grosheide (2010b), Dreyfuss (2010), Gordon (2010), Overwalle (2010).

criterion of needfulness for action the test for making appropriate tradeoffs when there are conflicting rights claims based on this equal right.

5.3 THE MORAL TERMS IN TRIPS

5.3.1 Moral Terminology in the TRIPS Agreement

Albeit the product of international trade realpolitik, many of the TRIPS Agreement's key provisions use ethical terminology. Articles 7 and 8 set out the 'Objectives' and 'Principles' of TRIPS' IPRs:

Article 7

Objectives

The protection and enforcement of intellectual property rights should contribute to the promotion of technological innovation and to the transfer and dissemination of technology, to the *mutual advantage* of producers and users of technological knowledge and in a *manner conducive to social and economic welfare*, and to *a balance of rights and obligations*.

Article 8

Principles

1. Members may, in formulating or amending their laws and regulations, adopt measures necessary to protect public health and nutrition, and to promote the public interest in sectors of vital importance to their socio-economic and technological development, provided that such measures are consistent with this Agreement.

2. *Appropriate measures*, provided that they are consistent with the provisions of this Agreement, may be needed to prevent the *abuse* of intellectual property rights by right holders or resort to practices which *unreasonably* restrain trade or adversely affect the international transfer of technology.

These set the context for interpreting the rest of TRIPS.[14]

At Chapter 1 (§1.1) it was observed that the words 'balance of rights and obligations', 'appropriate measures', 'abuse of intellectual property rights' and 'unreasonably' in relation to trade restraint and adverse effects

---

[14]   See Yu (2009), also for their origins and development.

on international transfer of technology, presume and entail – if they are to be given meaningful content – a background set of principles which justify IPRs. It was argued in Chapter 2 that the use of such moral terms can be understood as signifying, notwithstanding the diverse expectations of the parties as to the outcome of their use, that they should at least be used as moral words: that is, drawing their content from universalization of the appropriate types of prescription. Such a theory was advanced in Chapter 3. In the previous chapter it was shown that that theory is broadly explicatory and consistent with the main features of the institutions even if the rules do not fully accommodate the principle that there should be balance between the property and participation rights that is consistent with the equal right to freedom and well-being. This would explicate 'balance of rights and obligations': it would be the balance of the property interests of owners and participatory interests of the public, where the competing claims are resolved by Gewirth's criterion of needfulness for action (cf. §2.5.1), which says that: 'When two rights are in conflict with one another, that right takes precedence whose object is more needed for action.'[15] It would explain how the 'mutual advantage of producers and users' is to be assessed: in terms of the tendency of the rule to promote and protect the freedom and well-being of all human beings as equal persons.

That fundamental right also provides us with the context for making determinations as to what is an 'abuse' of IPRs or would be an 'unreasonable' restraint of trade. These call for extra-legal normative concepts, namely morality, to be applied. An 'abuse' of IPRs is not identical with a breach of the law in the first instance, because the idea refers to a wrongful use of a *right*. The owner is exercising, on this hypothesis, what is within his proprietary rights in law at least, though that act is somehow wrongful. However, the prevention or correction of that wrongful use may require the enactment of a law, and the point of Article 8(2) is to specify just when and how such a law may be made.

Proponents of strong IPRs may seek to limit the scope of these principles by arguing that the measures, to promote public health and nutrition and to protect the public interest member countries permitted under Article 8(1) and the appropriate measures that are acknowledged under Article 8(2) as necessary to prevent the abuse of IPRs, are both subject to provisos that these must be 'consistent with the provisions of this Agreement', and are therefore subject to the rights mandated by

---

[15]   Gewirth (1996), p. 45.

TRIPS.[16] This is question begging, because it treats the parts specifying IPR protection as privileged when the consistency that is required must be with the *whole* of TRIPS and this must include the balance of rights and obligations between producers and users of technology that Article 7 declares is the object of protection and enforcement of the TRIPs IPRs.

The generally explicit, rigid and uncompromising language of the IPR conferring provisions of TRIPS does mean, though, that the main avenues for promoting and protecting these other interests should be through exploiting the flexibilities available in the provisions regarding exceptions and limitations, and through conditions attached to measures related to enforcement and exploitation of the IPRs. As regards the latter, Article 41(1) requires that 'enforcement procedures ... are available ... so as to permit effective action against any act of infringement of intellectual property rights covered by this Agreement'. It should be noted that the 'rights' for which effective enforcement procedures must be provided are those conferred by TRIPS presumably read as a whole. The 'rights' as expressed in the rights conferring portions of that Agreement are meant to be understood as subject to and curtailed by expressly permitted exceptions and limitations[17] (otherwise it can be, rather absurdly, maintained that a refusal to grant damages where a legitimate exception applies is a violation of Article 41) and the counter-vailing measures member countries may enact or exercise under Article 8 bearing in mind the objectives of Article 7. Thus, in circumstances where the IPRs may be so curtailed, there would be no 'act of infringement' of the TRIPS rights. The possibilities opened by this approach are explored later in Chapter 7 on the dimension of exercise.

The other key provisions defining the range and limits of the IPR protection to be afforded are the exceptions and limitations allowed under TRIPS, most notably the 'three-step test', of which Article 13 for copyright is an instance.

---

[16]   Correa (2007), p. 108, citing and quoting Carvalho, N. Pires de, 2002, *The TRIPS Regime of Patent Rights*, The Hague: Kluwer Law International, p. 118: Art. 8(1) "'in no way permits exceptions to the rights conferred by TRIPS provisions'". However, Correa goes on, 2002, p. 110, to observe that 'This consistency should be assessed in the light of Articles 7 and 8 and of the Preamble; that is, taking social and economic welfare into account.'

[17]   Correa (2007), pp. 410–11.

5.3.2   The 'Three-step Test'

The 'three-step test' sets out the conditions for permissible exceptions, or limitations, to copyright exclusivity. As set out at Article 13, they must (1) be confined to 'special cases' which (2) 'do not conflict with a normal exploitation of a work' and (3) 'do not unreasonably prejudice the legitimate interests of the right holder'. This test, with slight variations in wording, is repeated for the conditions on permissible limitations on and exemptions to protection of various other IPRs. For industrial designs (Article 26(2)) and patent protection (Article 30),[18] the permissible derogations from protection are required to be 'limited exceptions' which 'do not unreasonably conflict with the normal exploitation' of the rights and 'do not unreasonably prejudice the legitimate interests' of the owner, which are qualified by words which interestingly are omitted in the case of the copyright provision – 'taking account of the legitimate interests of third parties'. In relation to trade mark protections, the conditions speak of 'limited exceptions' that take into account the 'legitimate interests of the owner of the trademark and of third parties' (Article 17). The explicit references to the legitimate interests of third parties require more explicit development of the idea of balance of rights and obligations in Article 7. The 'three-step test' is used again as the general framework for exceptions and limitations in Articles 10 and 16 respectively of the WIPO Copyright Treaty and the WIPO Performances and Phonograms Treaty of 1996. It is for this reason that the test merits much closer examination.

5.3.3   United States – Section 110(5) of the US Copyright Act

An important opportunity for such accommodation arose in the WTO Dispute Settlement Body Panel decision in the matter of *United States – Section 110(5) of the US Copyright Act*.[19] It was an opportunity missed.

The first condition – that 'Members shall confine limitations or exceptions to exclusive rights to certain special cases' – was held by the Panel to mean that limitations and exceptions in national legislation

---

[18]   The WTO Dispute Settlement Body adopted on 7 April 2000 a Panel Report, *Canada – Patent Protection of Pharmaceutical Products* (WT/DS114/R dated 17 March 2000) which held that Canada's regulatory review exception allowing use of patented inventions during term in making submissions for regulatory approvals for marketing of pharmaceuticals came within this exception.

[19]   WTO document no. WT/D160/R, 15 June 2000. For a decision relating to patents see *Canada – Patent Protection of Pharmaceutical Products, ibid.*

'should be clearly defined and should be narrow in reach and scope'.[20] But the Panel noted this 'did not imply passing a judgment on the legitimacy of the exceptions in dispute',[21] and rejected the EC submission that 'certain special case' equated with 'special purpose'.[22] Rather, drawing from a definition of 'special' as connoting 'having an individual or limited application or purpose', the conclusion was that the exception or limitation should have 'a narrow scope as well as an exceptional or distinctive objective'.[23]

It may be observed that the Panel has performed a definitional legerdemain in dissecting a single compound phrase ('certain special cases') into its components to derive a meaning quite different from what the whole would have suggested. The natural obverse of 'certain special cases' is the general case. It suggests that there would be exceptions to the general trend in some cases (the natural meaning of 'certain ... cases') where there is a reason for a different treatment. An inquiry into the reason for a different treatment in some cases would require an exploration of the rationale of the general case giving and accounting for, in terms of this rationale and its limitations, the exceptional instances. This would direct one to the claims towards legitimacy that the law makes for this institution of exclusive rights, and the role of exceptions in that claim, which lies at the very heart of the three-step test. The Panel's compartmentalized definition enabled it to sidestep the legitimacy question at this stage. The result is that the Panel's interpretation of this condition is the first step in avoiding the moral claims at the heart of the institution which the three-step test was meant to reflect and embody.

The second condition of the test, that the exception or limitation should 'not conflict with a normal exploitation of the work', calls, crucially, for an interpretation of 'normal exploitation'. 'Exploitation' was found to mean 'making use of' or 'utilising for one's own ends'. 'Normal' was held to have both an empirical and a normative connotation: the empirical meaning refers to what is 'regular, usual, typical or ordinary' and requires fact finding about current practices. The normative meaning connotes 'conforming to a type or standard', and implies a more dynamic approach. It takes into account technological and market developments, which would encompass not only current exploitation but also potential exploitation that 'with a certain degree of likelihood and plausibility,

---

[20]   *Ibid*, para. 6.112.
[21]   *Ibid*, para. 6.108.
[22]   *Ibid*, para. 6.111.
[23]   *Ibid*, para. 6.109.

could acquire considerable economic or practical importance'.[24] Thus, the Panel ruled that an exception or limitation would conflict with normal exploitation of a work 'if uses, that in principle are covered by that right but exempted under the exception or limitation, enter into economic competition with the ways that rightholders normally extract economic value from that right to the work (i.e., the copyright) and thereby deprive them of significant or tangible commercial gains'.[25]

This interpretation totally disembowels the three-stage test. Whereas 'normal' in this context might have suggested a reference to conformance with standards and principles consistent with the underlying justification for IPRs (copyright in this case), the Panel appears to have assumed a near absolute proprietarian intention. This proprietarian assumption ignores the declaration in TRIPS itself (Article 7) that those who have IP rights, have obligations to users as well.

Unsurprisingly, given this proprietarian reading of the second condition, the 'homestyle' exception satisfies it only because the exception, to authorization of playing dramatic musical works on homestyle devices in public, is of little practical and economic importance,[26] and the 'business exemption' does not satisfy it as '[r]ight holders of musical works would expect to be in a position to authorize the use of broadcasts of radio and television music by many of the establishments covered by the exemption'.[27] Of course they would, as would any self-interested party presented with the possibility of gain. The question is whether they have a *right* to such an expectation. The presumption in favour of protection of all the authors' economic interests brushes aside all the other considerations which the TRIPS Agreement itself embraces to give this expectation sole dominance. A consequence of these readings of the first and second conditions of Article 13 is that the third limb of that test (the third condition) becomes otiose, a result which the Panel had warned itself against when it began interpreting the provision.[28]

The Panel found that '"prejudice" connotes damage, harm or injury',[29] and 'reasonable' means '"proportionate", "within the limits of reason, not greatly less or more than might be thought likely or appropriate", or "of a fair, average or considerable amount or size"'.[30] These ideas of

---

[24]   *Ibid*, para. 6.166, 6.178 and 6.180.
[25]   *Ibid*, para. 6.183.
[26]   *Ibid*, para. 6.218.
[27]   *Ibid*, para. 6.210.
[28]   *Ibid*, para. 6.97.
[29]   *Ibid*, para. 6.225.
[30]   *Ibid*, para. 6.225.

proportionality and appropriateness clearly imply a perspective with a certain purpose in mind for making such assessments. It found that 'interests' encompasses a 'legal right or title to a property or use or benefit of a property (including intellectual property)',[31] but it refers as well to 'concern about a potential detriment or advantage, and more generally to something that is of some importance to a natural or legal person'.[32] It may be observed that the first part of the definition employs a tautology, for the purpose of the test is to define where the limits of those legal rights may be set. If one is left with the second part of the definition to work with, identifying what amounts to a 'potential benefit or detriment' would require one to identify some concept of the 'good' by which benefit or detriment may be assessed. One is already required to adopt an extra-legal normative standpoint by which advantage and disadvantage may be comprehended.

Reasoning from the requirements of agency ethics suggests that the most basic and universal 'good' that must be recognized by rational agents is the capacity and freedom to aim at and achieve one's purposes, whatever they be. This neutral perspective becomes a moral one when making prescriptions to support this fundamental imperative leads one to principles which drives one to conclude, if one wants to rationally universalize them, that not all purposes are equally acceptable. This is where the concept of legitimacy fits in and must be developed and applied. This is also where the Panel makes its most abject abdication of its duty. It began well enough, appearing to grasp the extra-legal issue at the heart of the use of the word 'legitimate' in the three-step test when it observed:

> [T]he term relates to lawfulness from a legal positivist perspective, but it has also the connotation of legitimacy from a more normative perspective, in the context of calling for the protection of interests that are justifiable in the light of objectives that underlie the protection of exclusive rights.[33]

However, whereas the Panel was able to identify the interests of right holders in the pursuit of economic gain as one of the objectives served by the protection of exclusive rights, it totally failed to develop an understanding of what the countervailing interests of the others may be, and how these are to be balanced against one another to arrive at a comprehensible notion of proportionate and appropriate claims to have a

---

[31]   *Ibid*, para. 6.223.
[32]   *Ibid*, para. 6.223.
[33]   *Ibid*, para. 6.224.

right of excluding others in the pursuit of profit. The legitimacy of right holders' claim to such rights is assumed right away: 'Given that the parties do not question the "legitimacy" of the interest of rightholders to exercise their rights for economic gain, the crucial question becomes which degree or level of "prejudice" may be considered as "unreasonable".'[34] In this way, the Panel could arrive at the conclusion that 'prejudice to the legitimate interests of rightholders reaches an unreasonable level if an exception or limitation causes or has the potential to cause an unreasonable loss of income to the copyright owner'.[35]

In the absence of a developed conception of the relevant countervailing interests, and an explanation of why the pursuit of the owner's economic interests is legitimate, the remainder of the application of this question became a matter of assessing the impact of the exceptions and limitations on the right holders' ability to derive economic benefit from their copyright works. Restriction of this would be unreasonable whenever the impact of the curtailment is substantial. In essence, the ideas of proportionality and appropriateness have been discarded.

5.3.4 An Alternative Reading of the 'Three-step Test'

The interpretation adopted in this decision castrates the three-step test as an avenue in the TRIPS Agreement by which the WTO and its member countries may honour its promises to non-holders of ownership rights in Articles 7 and 8. The critique made here points out an alternative vision of these tests.

The 'certain special cases' or 'certain limited cases' requirement can be understood to enable the members to make exceptions or limitations on IPRs where the general justification for protection, afforded by the idea of promoting and protecting the equal right to freedom and well-being of persons, sometimes requires that IP protection be denied in favour of participation interests, because this would advance liberty and well-being more than property restrictions.

The idea of 'normal exploitation' with which exceptions must not conflict must, as the Panel decision observes, extend beyond current normal practice to refer to some evaluative conception of what should be the norm. However, the criterion should not be merely defined by what is

---

[34] *Ibid*, para. 6.226.
[35] *Ibid*, para. 6.229.

of economic interest to owners but be a more balanced one,[36] reflecting the advancement of mutual interests of producers and users through the promotion of technological innovation and transfer and dissemination of technology which TRIPS professes to be its aim in Article 7. The idea of a balance of property and participation rights which realizes the equal right to freedom and well-being is proposed as a solution.

This balance, and this right, help us to identify what counts as the 'legitimate interests of rightholders'; these would be interests necessary for the extension and preservation of our individual freedom and well-being in a manner that is consistent with our recognition that we each have an equal right to such interests. The criterion of needfulness for action,[37] which this principle uses to adjudicate between competing claims to rights, helps us to identify when the prejudice to that right (which is at least to some degree permissible) becomes 'unreasonable'. This would be when the curtailment of the proprietary right in favour of the public interest in access and use encroaches on creators' and innovators' right of self-expression to a greater extent than any gain – from that marginal encroachment – to the freedom and well-being of the individuals in the public.

Although quantifying this tradeoff will be problematic, some aid towards making such comparisons is afforded by Gewirth's hierarchy of rights, giving priority to basic, then non-subtractive and, finally, additive well-being.[38] Basic well-being consists of essential pre-conditions necessary to survival, physical integrity and mental equilibrium; non-subtractive well-being, of abilities and conditions necessary to preserving one's general level of purpose fulfilment and abilities; and additive well-being, of conditions needed to increase such purpose fulfilment and abilities. These indicate that the authors' and inventors' interests in their own creations and inventions should trump, as going towards their additive well-being (self-realization), with the limitation that there must be some recognition of the interest of others in their additive well-being, and that the rights of the former should give way, if necessary, to further the basic well-being of others.

For patents, the stress on this counter-balancing consideration of a public participation interest is made all the more strong because of the obvious importance of the availability of technological innovations to

---

[36]   The Max Planck Institute for Intellectual Property and Competition Law has sponsored a declaration (5 January 2011) calling for an interpretation of the test embodying the idea of balanced rights.

[37]   See text with n. 15: Gewirth (1996) at p. 45. Cf. also §§2.5.1 and 3.6.3.

[38]   See Gewirth (1996), p. 14, and quote in Ch. 3 at §3.6.3 at text with n.87.

critical aspects of liberty and well-being, in the qualification in Article 30 that it is *unreasonable* conflict with normal exploitation that is to be avoided, and the express requirement that this test should be applied, 'taking into account the legitimate interests of *third parties*' (emphasis added).

5.4 TRIPS-PLUS

The TRIPS Agreement in 1994 was not the end of international expansion IPRs. It was followed by 1996 WIPO treaties on copyright (WCT) and performances and phonograms producers' rights (WPPT) in the digital realm. These clarified for parties that protection extended to digital media and introduced the right of communication (or right of making the protected matter available) to the public, and protection for technological measures used by right holders to control access or use of the works or protected subject. The US has been using bilateral Free Trade Agreements (FTAs) as a means of promoting levels of IP protection in partner countries that exceed the minima required by TRIPS. For example, the general author's life plus 50 years standard term of protection of copyright required by Berne and TRIPS was supplanted under the US–Singapore FTA and others with the US model of a life plus 70 years standard.[39] This is possible for WTO members because TRIPS permits more extensive protection than it requires but not derogations from its minima.[40] The provisions on exemptions and limitations set conditions on when such exceptions may be made rather than mandate such defences. This is a ratchet that increases protection of property to the detriment of the moral participatory right.

This is a reminder of the dominance of economic power and pure national self-interest in the shaping of the international IPR regime. All the more reason, then, that the limited avenues for expressing the moral dimension, and the balance of the moral property and participation rights, such as the various 'three-step tests' provisions, should be taken seriously and developed.

---

[39] United States–Singapore Free Trade Agreement, Art. 16.4(4).
[40] Art. 1(1) TRIPS Agreement.

6.   The moral dimensions of law: Interpretation and aims

6.1   THE MORAL DIMENSIONS OF LAW

The roles that previous chapters have ascribed to the moral dimensions of IPRs invite a series of ripostes. It has been suggested that moral terms and concepts provide, and are intended to provide, flexibility within the central rules of IPRs and that these are interpretative resources for adjusting the balance between property and participation rights in intellectual property. And it has been contended that the interpreters have to seek appropriate types of prescription for these moral terms and concepts, such as can be universalized consistently with the critical aspects of the institutions which we still want to uphold.

The critical question is: Why should we not treat legal rules, even when they incorporate moral terms, as having purely *legal* meanings? That is, why shouldn't they be given meanings by whatever method the law assigns them content? This does not mean that, if one wants to be able to refuse universalization of the norms used, one has then to abjure reliance on prescriptivity. Prescriptions may still be relied on and used in the various dimensions of the system. But they will not have the character, under Hare's theory,[1] of being *moral* prescriptions if their use is not subject to universalization. They would rather be more like imperatives – 'shall' commands rather than 'ought' prescriptions. It may be argued that this is possible because, though IPRs are creatures of a normative institution, they are the creation of *legal* rather than moral norms. This argument will successfully exclude reliance on moral norms if it is possible to conceive of the system of legal norms as purely social creations: a convention[2] or a habitual obedience to a sovereign backed by

---

[1]   Hare (1952, 1963, 1981 and 1997); see explication herein at §1.2.1, and §§2.1 and 2.2.

[2]   E.g. the convention amongst officials of a legal system accepting a rule of recognition validating other legal rules in Hart (1994), see esp. ch. V & VI and the Postscript §3(i) at pp. 254–9.

sanctions.[3] The justification of IPRs in general or of particular features of their institutional design, may then be separated entirely from questions about the validity, existence or interpretation of the laws, and exiled to a purely political realm (legislature, or courts when exercising political discretion) for generating the social facts that are the sources of law. These are questions of legal theory, about the nature of interpretation in law and, ultimately, about the interpretation of the concept of law itself and its recommendations for the design of laws. This chapter adumbrates responses to these queries for, though the moral dimensions of IPRs are also the moral dimensions of law, the latter is an entire field of inquiry unto itself and must lie beyond the space and subject limitations of this work. Nevertheless, some observations relating to the way legal theory impinges on the moral dimensions of IPRs are made in this work (cf. §2.6), and it will be necessary here to identify the main connections.

6.2   MORAL MEANINGS AND LEGAL INTERPRETATION

6.2.1   Intentions and Moral Terms

It is the observation that constructive interpretation requires grounding in objective morality that leads some legal positivists who are moral sceptics as well to prefer a speaker's intention model for identifying the meaning of legislation.[4]

The problems with treating the meaning of any legislation as something which may be settled by reference to the speakers' intentions are well known.[5] The judge, in seeking to be faithful to the speaker's intention model of interpretation, would often have to impute a view to the legislation on the counterfactual hypothesis of what that legislature would have wanted had it thought of the circumstances. These types of problem force the judge to construct a so-called 'legislative intention' and confront us with the question of how one construction is superior to another.

One common expectation that we must assume that the law makers have, is that they all want and expect that their enactment should have the force and character of law: that is, they do not merely want to make rules that will be obeyed and enforced, but they intend they have the character

---

3   Austin (1998).
4   E.g. Allan (1998), ch. 8, pp. 171–87.
5   Marmor (1992), ch. 8, pp. 155–84.

of law. We assume this because the law makers, if they are rational, must at least want the judges to treat the application of the law as obligatory. Logically therefore, it is necessary that they should also want its application to be morally binding on the judges, if no one else.

The problem of resolving multiple intentions becomes even more acute when the legislature uses moral terms. This is because, in using these terms, the speakers may have the expectation that they require a particular outcome, *A*. But, as explained in Chapter 2 (especially §2.6), they would also be expecting that this outcome is whatever applying the true nature of that concept would entail, even if they are not at all clear about this nature, and they intend also that whoever the injunction is directed at would seek to act consistently with the nature of the concept.

The argument that the obligatory character of law as seen from the internal perspective of the participants entails a purposive conception of law that aspires to fulfilling the general fundamental principle, then, is a more general instance of when a moral concept is used in law. For we have reason to treat every law maker as intending that what they enact has this purpose. In which case, fulfilling the intention of legislature would lead us, in as far as any intention can be coherently obtained, to a Dworkinian interpretivist approach: that is, one that seeks to be supported by and is consistent with a theory that offers the best justification for the institution, given the features that are to be treated as essential to that institution.[6] The suggestion herein is that, at the most general level of the idea of law as an institution, this role is best performed by a theory of it that is consistent with the principle of the equal right to freedom and well-being as the foundational criterion.

6.2.2   Legal Meanings and Morality in Legal Interpretation

Moral evaluation in the interpretation of laws is one of the moral dimensions of IPRs. This is because, at some point in the interpretation of laws, at least in some types of cases, it is necessary to make a moral determination that affects the outcome.

It is the belief in the subjectivity of morality and the desire to shield the concept of law from the controversies of morality that motivate many legal positivists. (This is, as will be observed below at §6.3.1, also reflected in the carefully explicit drafting of the EU 'Biotechnology

---

[6]   Dworkin (1986).

Directive'.[7]) H.L.A. Hart[8] regards laws in fully developed legal systems as rules which can be identified and validated by secondary rules of recognition, which are themselves ultimately established through acceptance as social facts by the officials of that system. Although, in Hart's theory, the ultimate rule of recognition's status rests on social acceptance rather than recognition under another secondary validating rule, he does make the concession that even such a rule may have its own 'penumbra of uncertainty' that is open to interpretation.[9] This carries with it the implication that the underpinning political values, that MacCormick[10] agrees are necessary commitments, become relevant principles for clarifying what the rule of recognition itself requires. These principles then become applicable to choices to be made in clarifying penumbral uncertainties in primary rules of obligation. This gives a very central role to moral evaluation in legal interpretation.

Another variant of legal positivism would allow that legal interpretation must involve moral evaluation, but would make a distinction between 'following' a rule (or applying it) and interpreting one. Joseph Raz, for example, makes a distinction between adjudication and unregulated disputes.[11] Adjudication occurs in cases which are regulated by a source that is treated as authoritative. In such cases, judges must apply the law. They exercise law making discretion only to the extent that they are able to distinguish a rule made by the authority or are in a position to over-rule it, that is, substitute their authority for the former. Law making discretion, though, is not a licence to exercise arbitrary power for, in Raz's theory, though not constrained by law, judges remain under a legal duty to 'adopt those rules which they judge best'.[12] The duty to adopt the best rule is a duty to decide according to a moral judgement. According to Raz, the judge in deciding what is the best rule is only morally constrained since the legal constraint is only to apply that rule *upon* judging it best. The law itself – by virtue of the situation being one of unregulated disputes – does not help in the making of that determination. This means that moral evaluation has a substantial role in the way laws are understood and developed in adjudication even if they are limited to

---

[7]   EU Directive 98/44/EC of 6 July 1998. Cf. discussion in Ch.4 at §§4.4.4 and 4.7.3.
[8]   Hart (1994).
[9]   *Ibid*, pp. 123, 147–54, and in the Postscript, p. 251.
[10] MacCormick (1994).
[11] Raz (1979), Ch. 10, pp. 180–209.
[12] *Ibid*, p. 197.

the judges' powers to distinguish and over-rule what at first sight would appear to be regulated disputes.

Andrei Marmor, in the course of defending the legal positivist thesis of separation between law and morality, admits:

> [I]f it is true that the law is always a result of an interpretation, and if it is also true that interpretation always involves evaluative considerations, then it follows that determining what the law is always involves considerations about what it ought to be.[13]

But he distinguishes between 'understanding' a rule and 'interpretation' of one, reserving 'interpretation' for the creative act involving 'the substitution of one expression of the rule for another'.[14] For him, then, adjudication does not always involve interpretation: often it is simply a matter of applying the rules. He makes the point to refute the argument that because legal rules appear to be always 'defeasible' – are always potentially open to revision by interpretation in the light of other rules and principles – moral evaluation is therefore *always* entailed in any attempt to understand what the law requires. He then makes a distinction between understanding what the law requires, and what ruling the judge will make, arguing that because the former is distinguishable from the latter, the conceptual separation between law and morality that is a central tenet of legal positivism is not threatened by the defeasibility of any standard understanding of the law.[15] In preserving legal positivism in this way, though, he gives a tremendous role to moral evaluation, for surely what judges and everyone who wants to, or has to, obey the law are concerned with is not the abstract understanding of the rule but how the judges go about arriving at the formulation of the rule that they will actually apply.

In Ronald Dworkin's conception of law as Law as Integrity, the interpretation of law to be adopted is that conception of it required by an account of it that fits its essential features and offers the best justification for them.[16] Determining the account that provides the best justification plainly involves moral evaluation. Moral evaluation is also required when it comes to determining the essential features that must be satisfied by the dimension of 'fit'. Dworkin's account of legal interpretation takes certain features of the law as accepted common ground to begin with –

---

[13]   Marmor (2001), p. 72.
[14]   Marmor (1992), p. 151.
[15]   *Ibid*, pp. 79–80.
[16]   Dworkin (1986).

otherwise, one would have no basis on which to start the process of interpretation, and the contending parties cannot be said to be arguing about the same thing. However, once the justifications for these accepted features are explored, it may be found that they are not all consistent with, or supported by, the same justifications. Hence, the question of which features are to be retained as essential may come under review. The necessity of moral judgement thus permeates the entirety of the approach to legal interpretation that he advocates. Whatever the differences, then, between Dworkin and these positivist critics as to whether the grounds which judges use to decide 'hard cases' may be described as 'law', they appear to agree that evaluative moral criteria must be employed.

6.2.3   Moral Theory and the Interpretation of IP Laws

As IPRs are institutions defined and constituted by laws, the moral dimension in interpretation of law plays an intimate and crucial part in the constitution and definition of their existence and extension.

In Chapter 4, the survey of the critical central rules of some of our most paradigmatic IP rights has shown how major decisions going to the core of the institutions have involved moral principles relevant to the justification of the institutions, sometimes leading to a radical revision of that branch of the law. Examples of this include the *volte face* performed by the UK courts on protection of privacy through the breach of confidence action (§4.2.5), the 'transformative use' doctrine in the fair use exception in US copyright law (§4.3.4), and the implicit moral assumptions regarding the balance between protection to promote innovation and public claims to share in ideas informing the interpretation of nearly identical provisions defining the scope of patentable subjects in the US and Canada (§4.4.3). Even when a decision was made which extended the coverage of the patent institution, as when the EPO came to narrow the scope of the exclusions against plant and animal varieties in the European Patent Convention (cf. §4.4.4), it was relying ultimately on an underlying presumption of policy and principle favouring patentability where the criteria of novelty, inventive step and susceptibility to industrial application can be met, rather than any truly technical or descriptive concept.

According to the general universal prescriptivist thesis given essentially by Hare, such moral judgements would not be subjective matters. The judges must be guided by principles they wish to adopt but these must be principles that they are willing to universalize consistently with the other institutions and practices that they are committed to upholding.

It is not suggested that judges all reason in this way when interpreting the law. The argument is that this is the constraint that logically applies once we admit that we are confronted with having to make a value decision, and that we want to make that decision on reasoned grounds as far as reason is able to provide guidance. (It can be taken that no judge will hold that his or her arbitrary whim will be sufficient.) In the case of legal interpretation, universalization would require that the principles adopted must be consistent with support for the other aspects that the judges hold are essential to the institutions that they are maintaining: that is – that type of IPR, and the institution of law that makes IPRs possible. Thus, the moral principles that justify IPRs and the institution of law in general provide the background moral content that helps to define the IPRs.

The last chapter suggested (at §5.2) that our commitments in a world of globalized IPRs arrive freighted with commitments to systems of laws that give fundamental respect to human rights and fundamental liberties. The moral principles that underpin them are always potentially a consideration in the interpretation of IPRs because they form the background fundamental principles which constrain us in the way we formulate and universalize the moral rules we use to justify IPRs, though it may be only in rare circumstances that these considerations surface and are explicitly considered in the grounds of judgement. If the more specific thesis that is here named fundamental prescriptivism is correct, then the relevance of human rights principles is not a contingent one but is a logically necessary foundation of moral reasoning and making any moral claims at all (cf. §2.5.3). This is because that reasoning leads eventually to the logical necessity of embracing the fundamental principles and the equal right to freedom and well-being, or abjuring moral arguments altogether.

6.3 THE MORAL DIMENSIONS OF LAW AND THE DESIGN OF IPRS

6.3.1 Legal Theory and the Design of IPRs

The creation of IPRs is informed by the desire that they should be justifiable for two reasons. First, they are institutions in a legal system and the character of law requires that the system as a whole should aim at justice and, as a critical resource allocating parts of that system, they must bear a large burden of that objective. Secondly, whatever their primary motives, law makers must claim the cooperation of other law makers and officials of the legal system in the enterprise of law, at least in part on moral grounds. Therefore, they must want to justify the institutions as projects. This Humean desire (cf. §2.3.2) commits them to the idea of morality and, hence, to the ultimate grounds for justifying these and all other basic institutions: promoting and protecting the liberty and well-being of all human individuals as equal persons (cf. §2.4.7). This, it has been argued, means that IPRs must strike a balance between property and participation rights and thus requires, as this balance is always being refined, the use and recognition of moral concepts and terms in their central rules (§§3.6.4, 4.1.1 and 4.1.2).

IPR and other property rules are (as maintained herein at §3.2.4 and §3.6) directly subject to the most basic principles of justice because they are part of the 'basic structure' of society in Rawls' sense of that idea.[17] This means that those principles (the equal right to freedom and well-being) become the reference points for morally evaluating the rules of such institutions and their interpretation, though not necessarily the entire test for their legal validity. It is under such conditions that positive law is required for framing the rules specifying the conditions of appropriation and the extent, duration of and exception to the property rights that may be acquired.

Ought the critical rules of IPRs, then, be framed entirely, or mainly, in terms of evaluative or moral terminology? An extreme version of this would lead us to adopt the generality of Nozick's formulation, 'just acquisition';[18] and, one might add, 'just property' (§§3.2.1 and 3.2.4). This is not vacuous because moral reasoning, as has been contended herein at Chapter 2, will lead us to the fundamental principles and the equal right to freedom and well-being. But these are under-determinative (cf. §2.4.6) in the absence of already present choices about specific institutions which aim at realizing these principles.

We can, and in a large part we do, use descriptive rather than purely evaluative language to frame these aspects of our property institutions. Principle as well as pragmatic reasons may be given for the employment of descriptive rather than purely evaluative language in rules. It enables persons to have a relatively secure expectation of how these rules will be applied. This promotes certainty and efficiency which are supported by the equal right to freedom and well-being as well, because the ability to have projects, make plans and realize purposes does depend on expectations regarding the basic institutions of cooperation being reasonably reliable.

---

[17] Rawls (1999), see: ch. 1, §2, pp. 6 & 7; ch. 2, §10, pp. 47–52; ch. 4, §31, pp. 171–6; and ch. 5, §43, pp. 242–51. The 'basic structure' is discussed above in Ch. 3 at §3.2.3.

[18] Nozick (1974), p. 151.

Such a philosophy is at least part of the explanation of the thinking behind the EU 'Biotechnology Directive's'[19] provisions which declare or clarify its other provisions. For example, after Article 3(1) made even inventions containing biological materials patentable if they are new, involve an inventive step and are susceptible of industrial application, it was felt necessary to add at Article 3(2) that biological material isolated from its natural environment or produced by means of a technical process may be a subject of an invention even if it previously occurred in nature. After Article 5(1) established that the human body and the simple discovery of one of its elements cannot constitute patentable inventions, it was considered necessary to add at Article 5(2) that 'An element isolated from the human body or otherwise produced by technical process ... may constitute a patentable invention even if the structure of that element is identical to that of a natural element'. Most obvious of all, after Article 6(1) imposed the morality and *ordre public* restriction, Article 6(2) went on to list particular types of technology that, at least, would be unpatentable on these grounds. It is in the full consciousness that these criteria raise controversial moral issues inseparable from the 'technical' legal questions, that these provisions attempt to limit the controversy and doubt by explicit statement.

This is illustrated by *WARF/Stem cells* where the EPO's Enlarged Board of Appeal, applying a regulation encapsulating the Biotechnology Directive's Article 6(2)(c) prohibition, held that the claim for an invention which used human embryonic stem cell culture for research, which at the time of the patent application could only be derived by means involving the destruction of a human embryo, violated this prohibition and was, hence, unpatentable.[20] It did not have to, and thus declined to, consider arguments based on the nature and character of the EPC Article 53(a) *ordre public* and morality prohibition because the issue was disposed of by the direct application of Article 6(2)(c) of the 'Biotechnology Directive'.[21]

The polar modes of defining property rights – in either purely descriptive or evaluative terms – should be rejected, in favour of a combination of both. Property institutions should be framed mainly in descriptive terms but subject to reservations and qualifications in moral language in the key conditions, limitations or exceptions, which express the idea that the institution is intended to be justifiable by the society's

---

[19]   EU Directive 98/44/EC of 6 July 1998.
[20]   G2/06 [2009] E.P.O.R. 15. See also *Brustle v. Greenpeace E.V.* (ECJ 18 October 2011, Case C-34/10) cf. §4.4.2 above.
[21]   *Ibid*, p. 143 (Reasons for the decision para. 31 & 32).

most basic principles of cooperation and provide the flexibility. The latter are meant to allow for appropriate adjustments subject to the constraint of the universalizability requirement and its prerequisite background principles, and ought to be interpreted to allow them to do this work. Examples of this already discussed include the use and interpretation of the word 'fair' in fair dealing or fair use copyright exceptions, especially the transformative use doctrine developed by the US Supreme Court (§4.3.4). Another illustration of this is afforded by the way the ECJ had to posit more specific rules to flesh out the notion of 'abuse' of a dominant position in respect of a refusal of copyright licences in European competition law, which is to be discussed in the next chapter (at §7.3.3). The WTO Dispute Resolution Body's Panel decision in *United States – Section 110(5) of the US Copyright Act*,[22] discussed in the last chapter at §§5.3.2–5.3.4, is an example of when this opportunity to allow moral terms and concepts to do this work has been spurned.

Even where the rules are framed almost entirely in descriptive terms, perhaps because certainty and predictability are at a premium, the moral concepts underpinning the institution remain relevant in an interpretative role – always potentially a basis for revising a rule or understanding of what it requires.

6.3.2   The Recommendations of the Moral Dimensions of IPRs

If the principle that is described here as the equal right to freedom and well-being does constitute the ultimate criterion for moral justification of IPRs, then one may expect that IPRs would have the following further characteristics.

First, some interests in information and ideas may be so essential to the expression of the personhood of the creator that the protection for these aspects of the interest would have an inalienable character; however, these inalienable rights would lie alongside other interests in information and ideas that, being less essential to the expression of personhood, would be alienable property rights where property controls would further the liberty and well-being of individuals generally (cf. §4.6.1).

Secondly, as liberty and well-being further both by the possibility of individual control of ideas as well as access to ideas we would expect that the intellectual property *rights* supported by the principle of

---

[22]   WTO document no. WT/D160/R, 15 June 2000.

autonomy would include both rights of property and *rights to the public domain* (cf. §4.8.2).

6.4   A CODA ON REALISM AND THE MORAL DIMENSIONS OF IPRS

One implication of universal prescriptivism as an account of moral terms and concepts is – as it works by requiring that we universalize the actual prescriptions we make to other relevant instances – it is able to supply us with an account of the content of the moral terms and concepts in IPR systems outlined in Chapter 4. It points us to the values and principles we already implicitly affirm, when we have such systems in the first place, and challenges us to continue universalizing them as we interpret these terms and concepts.

We can refuse to universalize those values and principles but, according to universal prescriptivism, only by: (i) adopting different principles and values in justification of the systems which we are willing and able to universalize instead; or (ii) abandoning the project of justifying and accounting for the justice of these systems; or (iii) abandoning the project of treating the provision of reasoned grounds for our actions and commitments as a commitment in itself. The last option involves a rejection of universal prescriptivism itself. Option (ii), it can be argued, cannot be taken without abandoning something we want legal systems and their institutions to have: the feature of being able to be, at least *prima facie*, reasons by virtue of their being legal, for carrying out the acts they require.

Legal positivists reject the proposition that a connection between legal character and moral obligation is a necessary part of the concept of law. The link between the two under the assumption of a universal prescriptivist account of morality is one of the issues that has been explored in this chapter. But it is not necessary here to oppose this legal positivist tenet. Even if we accept that the conception of legality *can* be based on criteria that do not have to include moral obligation, we would nevertheless want the legal systems and institutions we make and uphold to have such a character because we want judges to accept that they are obliged to apply and uphold the laws. Not merely to acknowledge that there is a practice amongst judges of treating them as valid, but to actually hold that they are bound to so treat the laws they find valid.

We want, if we want to enjoy, exploit and enforce IPR laws, to hold everyone to, at minimum, a *prima facie* obligation to respect IPRs as legal institutions because it would be very difficult to maintain an institution if the only reason for habitually obeying its rules was sanctions. If an institution is made up of social functions that can be recast in the form, 'X counts as Y in C', the law may create an IPR merely by specifying that under certain circumstances (X in C) the IP right (counts as Y) exists.[23] But if our conception of law does not also imply social obligation but only signals the factual possibility that sanctions may be applied, the strength of the social institution becomes dependent on enforcement. Judges and other officials of the legal system would have no reason to regard enforcement as obligatory merely by virtue of legal validity and existence. Hence, in practice, even if not by virtue of the concept of law, we do want the legal institution to have an obligatory character.

This is the reason why we use moral terms in IPRs: to reflect our intention that the institutions should have a character that we find justifiable and legitimate. Given this basic desire, it is necessary that moral terms and concepts are used, if universal prescriptivism is correct, because only with the use of these would we, and the judges applying them, have the ability to understand their requirements in a way that fits our moral commitments. Thus, justification and legitimacy depend on the presence of such moral terms. And, given this basic desire, we want to be able to justify reforms to the laws, whether to make IPRs stronger or more accessible to non-owners, by appeal to reasons other than pure power. These dimensions of IPRs, their exercise (the enjoyment, exploitation and enforcement of these rights) and their reform, are the subject of the next two chapters.

---

[23]   MacCormick and Weinberger (1986) propounds an institutional theory of law based on John Searle's social theory (explained above at §1.2.2).

7. The moral dimension of the exercise of IPRs

7.1 MORALITY AND THE DIMENSION OF EXERCISE

IPRs' dimension of exercise includes the enjoyment of the existence of those rights as social facts, exploitation of those rights for economic advantage and enforcement when those rights are flouted. These raise several questions regarding the theory of moral dimensions of IPRs that has thus far been developed. Why should those who enjoy, and seek to exploit and enforce IPRs, share the moral project of the law makers? The owners of IPRs do not directly make the laws. Nor are they, generally, judges or other officials of the legal system. Why should they share in this collective intentionality? Can they avoid the burden of justification with its moral commitments and merely rely on their rights in law? One response to this question might be that we have to justify our actions, even if only to ourselves. However, it is when we also want to make moral claims on others that we are led to admit the moral claims of others on the same basis (§2.3.2) and are drawn on the path of moral commitment towards the fundamental prescriptions and the equal right to freedom and well-being (§2.4). Do we have to make moral claims when it comes to the enjoyment, enforcement and exploitation of IPRs? This chapter identifies why people who seek to enjoy, enforce or exploit IPRs often make such moral claims, and how this provides the moral background for various laws related to the exercise of IPRs.

7.2 ENJOYMENT, EXPLOITATION AND ENFORCEMENT OF IPRS

7.2.1 Enjoyment of IPRs

Owners of IPRs enjoy IP rights when they have the expectation, and the entitlement to the expectation, that others should respect their IP rights. The previous chapter explained why this expectation is based on a moral claim: that everyone owes each other cooperation in a legal system that aims at promoting and protecting the freedom, and the well-being necessary to enjoy that freedom, of each human individual as an equal person. And, to be efficacious as law, this legal system must be at least minimally successful in realizing that aim. As a result of this obligation to cooperate, there is an obligation to recognize and comply with the rights and duties of institutions of that legal system, including the IPRs generated by them.

7.2.2 Exploitation of IPRs

The idea of 'exploitation' covers all economic use of IP rights. The foregoing discussion about the moral basis upon which respect for IPRs is enjoyed explains why it makes sense to speak in the language of morality, about extra-legal obligations regarding how IPRs are used. For instance, Article 8 of the TRIPS Agreement permits member countries to enact 'appropriate measures' to 'prevent the *abuse* of intellectual property rights by rightholders'. There is a temptation to dismiss such language as an empty sop to factions with fears as to the power IPR holders would wield under the TRIPS mandate. That may, as a matter of fact, have been the belief of some of the parties that adopted the Agreement. Despite this, though, there are reasons to treat such words as having their face value. For one, if the word 'abuse' does not have any meaning, then member countries would be free to take 'appropriate measures' whenever they deem fit – surely a result that was never intended by the drafters of that phrase. For another, since it is up to member countries to decide on the measures they would take under this Article, there is no reason why they should allow themselves to be held captive by the cynical interpretations that others may have. One of the themes of this work is the transformative potential of moral words in legal instruments, in that they provide the basis for a re-invention of the institution from within the rules towards a more just and legitimate balance between the property and participation rights in IPRs. The way the word 'abuse' in Article 8 may be interpreted is one such opportunity. The notion of 'abuse' of IP assumes that there are proper purposes for the IPRs that TRIPS mandates, that govern how we critique their use. This requires that we work out a theory of their justification. The contention here is that, when one does attempt to work out such a theory, one should arrive at an implicit subscription to the principle of an equal right to freedom and well-being. Though the notion of freedom generally supports a free market and, hence, freedom in how one uses one's IPRs, there are occasions when such a use would conflict with the right of others to freedom and well-being. Such conflicts are to be resolved by the criterion of needful-ness for action.[1] This would often favour free use of one's property rights because such freedom affects the owner's capacity to act more urgently than the corresponding curtailment affects the liberty of others. But there are occasions when the basic well-being of others is affected, and there would be a moral, if not legal, obligation to recognize the claims based on respect for that basic well-being.

Some examples of such occasions have become international *causes célèbres*. When Microsoft came to dominate the market for the supply of operating systems for PCs, it sought to use its copyright in Windows as leverage in a number of ways: by bundling its browser program (Internet Explorer), which faced stiff competition with that provided by another software supplier, with Windows; and by negotiating for advantageous terms and positioning for its programs with PC suppliers in return for licensing use of Windows. This eventually embroiled it in competition law litigation in, amongst others, the US and the EU, which will be discussed in the following section. For the present, the interest is in the fact that there is even serious debate at all about the rights and wrongs of Microsoft's conduct, which would not make any sense if IPRs are incapable of being abused. Other modes of exploitation involve imposing conditions on users which contractually bind them not to deal with the IP related product which the law would otherwise have left them free to exercise: for example, not to resell for export, or not to use (say in a student edition of a software program) the item in a commercial context. By these means, the IP rights are used to gain by voluntary agreement terms which may considerably extend the power of the IP holders and encroach on forms of access that are part of the participation rights of everyone. Questions about the equal right of each person to freedom and well-being arise; in particular, whether this is best respected by uphold-ing the voluntary bargains or abrogating them. Still other modes of exploitation leave the user of IP products little choice in that the use may be technologically controlled. An example of this is technological meas-ures for the protection of copyright and anti-circumvention laws to protect the protecting technology which will be briefly examined below at §7.4. It will suffice for the moment to note that – unless the law mandates technological access – technology that may restrict access, playing or printing by mode or number of occasions or to certain

---

[1]   Gewirth (1996), p. 45: 'When two rights are in conflict with one another, that right takes precedence whose object is more needed for action.' See above Ch. 2, §2.5.1.

machines and which limits or forbids editing of copyright material released in digital form, can be used to impose restrictions far more limiting than the terms of the IP laws' exceptions and limitations on protection. (Analogous biological controls for plants are 'GURTs' alluded to below at §7.4.1.) These modes of exploitation of IPRs are highlighted because such uses of IPRs and the issues they raise are the natural subject of moral discussion – both critique of the means of exercise of those rights as well as vigorous defence of them. There are laws which address many of these issues and, where there are not, or where the laws are inadequate or it is not at all clear what the correct legal rule on the subject is, there may be proposals for new laws to be made to resolve the questions. The moral dimension will be relevant because these laws invoke concepts which either call for moral evaluation, or are the grounds for reform. We must confront a kind of sceptic that is represented by a type that we may call 'the Legalist'. Rather than deny the existence of moral grounds, he uses those moral grounds to argue that, short of legal restrictions, he *ought* to have unfettered freedom in the exploitation of his IP rights. This criticism is interesting because it focuses on the nature of the moral argument (rather than the source of its grounds) once we concede the principle of an equal right to freedom and well-being. The Legalist seeks to make three arguments for unfettered exploitation. First, that the moral considerations have been built into the law; and if they have not, they ought to be, so there is no further scope of extra-legal moral constraints on how such rights are exploited.

Secondly, the value of liberty supports freedom in the exercise of one's property rights and respect for bargains that others have voluntarily made. Thirdly, that a free market tends to promote freedom and well-being by maximizing welfare and options, and free market principles support the idea that such exploitation should be unfettered. Addressing these contentions will help us to clarify the role of the moral dimension in the exercise of IPRs, and its relationship to the law, by throwing into relief the way this moral dimension functions. The first of these contentions seeks to treat the moral dimension as irrelevant (though not necessarily non-existent) by relying on the sufficiency of law. For this contention to succeed, it is not necessary to maintain that the intellectual property laws – that is, the laws that define the conditions of acquisition and extent of the rights – sufficiently encapsulate all the relevant moral considerations. The Legalist may concede that ancillary laws relating to their use – say, as regards anti-competitive agreements and conduct – are required. Nor is it necessary for him to maintain that the laws as they now stand do in fact successfully take into account all the relevant moral considerations. His point is that these considerations *can* and ought to be built into the laws. This is not a dictum drawn from a particular conception of law. The person making this point need not be committed to natural law. One may accept that law and morality are conceptually separate and yet maintain as a matter of socio-political policy that it is better that we look solely to the law for all the claims that we may have against one another about how we use our legal rights. The idea is captured most baldly and clearly in a dictum by Milton Friedman:

> [T]here is one and only one social responsibility of business – to use its resources and engage in activities designed to increase its profits as long as it stays within the rules of the game, which is to say, engages in open and free competition without deception and fraud.[2]

The critical premiss of the argument for this approach to the moral dimension of exercise is the assumption that laws *can* be, though not necessarily are, framed so as to incorporate every moral consideration. A fundamental problem for this objection is raised if it is correct that, though the equal right to freedom and well-being is objective, it is under-determinative as regards the precise consequential principles and rules by which it is worked out. This is why we have to commit to the principle of cooperation as one of the fundamental prescriptions (cf. §2.4.6). If morality, even the particular morality of the legal institution, is a continuing project whose rules are being refined, reformed and reformulated as we develop new technologies altering the balance of the relationships in the community, or new institutions and social practices which call for new moral responses, then it is not possible for us to make laws which encapsulate all the significant moral conclusions in rules in descriptive or technical language. One could, in a sense, incorporate the moral dimension by using moral language in provisos and conditions of the laws, as these would require us to revise our understanding of the law with that moral dimension in mind. But that kind of law making will not enable us to ignore the moral dimension; rather, it relies on a vibrant moral dimension as an active, if supporting, partner of the law. The second of the Legalist's contentions is that valuing liberty requires us to respect an individual's freedom to deploy his property however he (or she) wills, and to uphold the voluntary arrangements that others have made. That is certainly one understanding of liberty. It is not, however, consistent with the justification of IPRs as herein developed, which suggests that the property rights in ideas are also freighted with (moral)

---

[2]   Friedman (1970), quote at p. 55.

participation rights which require that some public domain aspects of our intellectual commons be protected.

The public's right to a participation interest, as part of the fundamental idea of justice that is the foundation of the right of property, is the condition upon which the property is acquired (cf. §§3.2.4 and 3.6.5). In Nozick's words, 'Each owner's title to his holding includes the historical shadow of the Lockean proviso on appropriation.'[3] He observes, 'Someone whose appropriation otherwise would violate the proviso still may appropriate *provided he compensates the others* so that their position is not thereby worsened; unless he does compensate these others, his appropriation will violate the principle of justice in acquisition and will be an illegitimate one'[4] (cf. §§3.2.2 and 3.2.4). Though the extent of the participation interests considered here may take the idea far beyond the limits envisaged by Nozick, this is because we have begun with a richer concept of justice – the equal right to freedom and well-being – that, it has been argued here, is necessarily foundational. Not all aspects of this participation right are fully embodied in the law. We can postulate some reasons for this. The right, being one that is to be collectively enjoyed by the public, is not conveniently cast in law as a Hohfeldian claim-right, or, quite simply, a 'right'[5] belonging to the collective, with a correlative duty *on all* to respect this freedom of participation, because that would mean that individuals cannot give up elements of the participatory elements if they so choose. The Legalist's second contention has a point in that respect for the freedom of individuals does require that we allow them to restrict themselves and alienate some of what they enjoy. Hence, the laws tend to reflect this moral right to participation as a legal privilege whose jural correlative are 'no-rights' of the owners; the public domain is more *IP's shadow in law*, rather than the reflection of positive claim-rights of the public, though they are positive *claim-rights in the moral dimension* (§4.8). The collective interest in the public domain that is founded on advancing and protecting *individual* freedom presents us with twin aims that pull in different directions: the freedom to give up interests and accept self-imposed restrictions; and the necessity of preserving the collective conditions of that freedom. This tension can be resolved by the criterion of needfulness for action:[6] most of the moral right to the public domain can be traded off by the individuals because such freedom is more necessary to their capacity to act; however, some aspects of those

---

[3] Nozick (1974), p. 180.
[4] *Ibid*, p. 178. Emphasis added.
[5] Hohfeld (1923); cf. §2.5.3 above.
[6] See n. 1 above.

rights of participation have to be entrenched in law, sometimes protected even against individual alienation because allowing that would too severely erode the basis of the freedom of all. The result is that, between the residual elements of the public domain that are positively protected, and perhaps entrenched, by law, and the property rights of IP owners, lies a gulf of public domain privilege (carved out by what, in law, would be an area where IP owners have 'no-rights') which is chiefly governed by the moral dimension. Just as there is a zone of public privilege (constituted by IP owners' lack of rights) where the participation interests are enjoyed (if not given away by contract or taken away by technological controls) but are not positively protected by law, there is a zone of exploitation covered by the IP rights which are justifiably the subject of legal intervention on behalf of the public domain, which may have been left within the sphere of the owners' legal right of exercise on the trust that this would not be abused – either because exercising those rights in this sphere will not be worth the owners' while, or because the appropriate restraint may be exerted by moral suasion.[7] Primary examples of this are the fields of the exercise of IPRs that are potentially subject to compulsory licences. Hence, there may be zones of the public domain which may become subject to IP owners' control, through market arrangements or technological means and of the IP owners' exclusivity, which may justifiably have been subject to legal limitations which have been left essentially to regulation by the morals and the market.

The justification from promotion and protection of freedom and well-being supports such an outcome because it advances liberty that there are zones of activity and cooperation that are left to be moulded by moral choice. This gives us a second answer to the Legalist's second contention in favour of a sceptical approach to the continued relevance of the moral dimension after the creation of legal institutions. It is not true, if our aim is to promote freedom and well-being, that we ought to incorporate all the moral considerations into the law. Freedom may require that some zones are not governed by law for morality to play a part. This may not necessarily be the only, or the dominant, part – for

---

[7]   This is the zone of IP rights not normally exercised or enforced, which the public practically enjoys as free, that Merges (2011) argues should be left to the operation of waivers by IP owners which should be encouraged by mechanisms to make this cheaper, simpler and more effective, as means of respecting the autonomy of both owners and users. Instead, the present chapter argues that the equal right to freedom and well-being favours the public having rights in the moral sphere which are in various ways given legal effect through the moral dimensions of the mechanisms mentioned here.

market mechanisms have a major role as well. The point here is not that morality is the primary consideration; instead, we are trying to understand why it has any kind of a role at all, and is not excluded once the law has said its piece. There are often differences in moral views. But this is the beginning of moral exploration and discourse, not the end of them. And this is a course which, if we take prescriptivism seriously (cf. §2.3), will lead to a debate about what the fundamental prescriptions are and how we should correctly express them. We do articulate such different moral views in the dimension of exercise, though without explicating the underpinning ideas very seriously. For example, sometimes corporations are accused of 'bio-piracy'[8] when a research laboratory or pharmaceutical company identifies a plant, organism, gene or biological extract from rainforest reserves, perhaps even already known to tribal groups, and manages to patent these, perhaps after enhancement, isolation of active elements or incorporation with other elements. These may be exploited in medicines or agricultural applications, with the potential being very profitable, but without compensating either the country with the rainforest or the tribal community concerned. Sometimes laws have been broken, but that is not really the point because the charge is made even if the activities leading to the patent are not subject to legal prohibition.

The point that the protestors seek to make is often a moral one: there ought to be respect for these reserves and compensation for their use and, if the laws do not ensure these, there ought to be reforms to provide these assurances.[9] The example is not raised here to defend one view or the other but to illustrate an essentially moral strand of the argument. IP holders make moral protests as well. When pharmaceutical companies are threatened with compulsory licences of their patented medicines or copyright owners of software are compelled under the competition law rulings to share aspects of their source codes, their defenders speak of

---

8   See e.g. review in Khor (2002), pp. 201–13 in Drahos and Mayne (eds.) (2002) at the section '(c) IPRs, biological materials and biopiracy', pp. 207–9; and Stenton (2004).

9   See Dutfield (2000) on the global IP and biodiversity regulatory framework. Some of the actors and proposed solutions are canvassed in Drahos and Mayne (eds.) (2002), amongst which: Blakeney (2002b), ch. 7, pp. 108–24, on the research and preservation role of the Consultative Group on International Agricultural Research and its IP concerns; and Sahai (2002), ch. 13, pp. 215–23, on India's implementation of the TRIPS requirement for extension of protection to plant varieties under either patents or a *sui generis* system or combination thereof (Art. 27(3)(b)) and its provisions for farmers' rights.

intellectual property 'theft'.[10] Again the point of the label is not a legal claim – for it is the law itself that is the object of the protest – but a moral one. It is true that the discourse is often not taken to any depth, and the mode is emotivist – designed to evoke and reinforce a conditioned response – rather than an appeal to moral reasoning. But that does not deny the moral nature of the claim and, hence, the potential for a transformation of the nature of the discourse from one that is doomed to deadlock and sterile labelling, to one that can more substantially generate solutions through a search for the principles that may unite us and resolve differences by an appeal to the common conditions of action that we all share an interest in at a more fundamental level. It may be that the particular participants in such exchanges of accusations are not particularly motivated to engage in such a transformative discourse, but that is no reason why the rest of the world should be hostages to those predilections.

The moral dimension is there: it can be stifled by denial, or we can realize its potential to transform reality by taking it seriously. Taking the moral dimension seriously requires one to confront the third of the Legalist's reasons for scepticism as to the relevance of the moral dimension: and that is the argument that, once the property rights have been fixed, the manner of their exercise is best left to the mechanism of the market if one's objective is to further liberty.[11] The argument is that the market is the best system for organizing distribution, and hence one should leave it to do its work if one is to maximize welfare (and hence the consequential overall enjoyment of freedom and well-being) and if one wants to respect each individual's freedom of choice. One response to this is that, assuming for the most part the premiss in that argument, the power of IPRs can in some cases be used to distort markets: that is the rationale for competition and antitrust laws and, where these are absent or inadequate, that premiss itself becomes the basis for a moral critique of certain conduct and calls for a reform of the laws to curb them. Another response, again largely accepting that premiss, is that the moral considerations are inputs which decision makers take into account in the market processes, and do not supplant the market. When IP owners

---

[10]   E.g. a news commentary described as 'patent theft' government compulsory licences for public sector use in Thailand (and Brazil) patented medicine for HIV/AIDS and heart disease, observing, 'Imagine that you are an inventor and the government steals your highly lucrative idea … you are informed that the government plans to mass-produce your invention and give it away for free'; see Pitts (2008) and Weisman (2008).

[11]   See Friedman (1970).

are deciding whether to make a cheaper student edition of a book available, or to grant a public licence on some copyright material or make a medicine available at lower prices in a certain jurisdiction, they will take many considerations into account: the marginal profit from the move certainly, but also matters like the overall strategy – whether it yields other long term advantages. In markets, people maximize their ends, whatever these may be, and not only profits (short or long term monetary gains or any combination of the two). Hence, a labourer will trade off wage and leisure, job satisfaction and pay increments. The presumption, in our normal understanding of how markets should work, is that there are other considerations, including moral claims, on consuming and production decisions, hence there is room for moral reflection and review, and a role for morality in the dimension of exercise. The various reasons we have for wanting to justify having the legal rights or respect for that property or enforcement of them will lead us to a clarification of the basis of that justification and a realization that it implies commitment to fundamental principles which now become grounds for a critique of these institutions.

This may result in obligations to seek and accept reform of these institutions and, pending this, recognize moral obligations regarding the way the rights are exercised even where the obligations do not translate into legal ones. This argument has been rather abstract but examples are not hard to find. One dramatic example is the problematic relationship of patent protection for medicines and medical technology to patients' interests in access to such inventions that are discussed in the next chapter (§8.4). We do criticize pharmaceutical companies when they do not provide lower priced versions of medicines that they supply else-where, in countries where they are widely needed but the people are too poor to afford them but the prices are kept up for fear of leakages (through parallel importing) to markets with higher price levels.[12] And we do criticize when they put up obstructions when national governments seek to obtain non-authorized versions through import of generics or production under compulsory licences.[13] Our criticism may be tempered

---

[12]   See: Mayne (2002), ch. 15, pp. 244–58, for an account of the advocacy at the height of the crisis before the Doha solutions; and Balasubramaniam (2002), ch. 6, pp. 90–107 for an account of patents and prices of medicine in that period.

[13]   See the news commentaries cited at n. 10 above and the reaction to litigation in South Africa brought by pharmaceutical companies in response to its Medicines and Related Substances Control Amendment Act of 1997 referred to in Chapter 8 at §8.4.

by the realization that, unless certain national and international safeguards are introduced, such acts might undermine the economic value of
the IPRs to the pharmaceuticals in countries where they are interested in
active exploitation, and this would undermine the work of IPRs in
promoting expansion of liberty by inducing innovation.[14] We recognize
the dilemma. But the dilemma is real. That is the point. The patients
whose health and whose very lives may be at stake have a real claim on
the rest of us for realistic access to medicines, even as we grapple with
the possibility that such technology would not be available if not for the
patent regime in the first place. The moral dimension accounts for the
reality of such claims, and the obligation to seek a solution, whether
through a reform of the patent system or through some other avenue. The
fact remains that, with medicines that are presently available and under
patent – notwithstanding that the possibility of such patents may have
played a role in making them available – some (in some countries, a
great many) of the poorer present patients are denied access because
patent restrictions make them too expensive or unmarketable.[15] They
have at least the claim that the basis of this denial ought to be fair. In this
regard, the reply that patents are property rights is not in itself a sufficient
answer unless the institution, in all respects, perfectly embodies all the
considerations of distributive justice. We have seen that it may not do so
because other motivations and forces also shape the institution; and, in
any case, it cannot do so because the scheme of justice – given that its
finer points are always being refined as we proceed – requires that moral
terms be built into its core rules, thus calling on an active accompanying
moral dimension, and a reliance on that moral dimension in the realm of
the exercise and continuing reform of that institution.

7.2.3   Enforcement of IPRs

Enforcement of IPRs embraces the assistance of officials and authorities
of the legal system in compelling observance of the IPRs and remedies
for breaches. At the very least, those who enjoy, enforce and exploit legal
rights want legal rules to operate as laws. The upshot of the previous
chapter is that at some point or other, we need morality and make moral
commitments for this purpose. The status of such rules as law requires an
aspiration towards legitimacy or claims be made that they have authority,
or recognition of their obligatory character. The people who enjoy the

---

[14]   See Abbott (2005).
[15]   See Stiglitz (2006), ch. 4, pp. 103–32.

rights may not themselves accept these elements, but they want the officials concerned to accept them, with all their implications. And he may want reform of enforcement rules nationally and internationally.[16] These wants compel them to enter the moral dimensions of IPRs and engage in moral discourse. This is the background against which the moral terms in the related laws draw their meaning.

7.3 LEGAL EXPRESSIONS OF THE MORAL DIMENSION OF EXERCISE

7.3.1 Legal Underpinnings of the Moral Dimension of Exercise

Moral sceptics are wrong when they suggest that morality is non-existent or irrelevant to the exercise of IPRs. But they have a point when they assert that our desire to abide by morality and create and maintain a moral world is weak in comparison with other things that we want, and may often be over-ridden in fact. This is why, though, there are legal rules reflecting, albeit imperfectly, this moral dimension: (i) in the common law rules limiting the extent of control by the means of implied licences (§7.3.2); (ii) competition laws for limiting the abuse of IPRs (§7.3.3); (iii) our rules for the enforcement of IPRs (§7.3.4); and (iv) compulsory licensing (§7.3.5). The enforcement provisions of TRIPS allow flexibility for such positive laws to be adopted or enacted by WTO members. Article 41(1) requires that 'enforcement procedures ... are available ... so as to permit effective action against any act of infringement of intellectual property rights covered by this Agreement'. As observed already at §5.3.1, the 'rights' for which effective enforcement procedures must be provided are those conferred by TRIPS read as a whole. The 'rights' as expressed in the rights conferring portions of that Agreement are meant to be understood as subject to and curtailed by expressly permitted exceptions and limitations[17] and the measures member countries may enact or exercise under Article 8 to protect public

---

[16] E.g. see Blakeney (2009), on various concerns raised by widespread counterfeiting and piracy – relating their impact on businesses, trade flows, revenue loss, foreign investment, competition, employment, consumer protection and public order – and proposals for strengthened ('TRIPS-Plus') enforcement regimes, including that by Japan, the US and the EU for a plurilateral agreement negotiated outside the WTO and WIPO for an Anti-Counterfeiting Trade Agreement (ACTA).

[17] Correa (2007), pp. 410–11.

health and nutrition and to promote the public interest, or to prevent the abuse of IPRs or the resort to practices which unreasonably restrain trade or adversely affect the international transfer of technology, bearing in mind the objectives of Article 7. Thus, in circumstances where the IPRs may be so curtailed, there would be no 'act of infringement' of the TRIPS rights. This understanding is fortified by the second sentence of Article 41(1) which specifies that 'These procedures shall be applied in such a manner as to avoid the creation of barriers to *legitimate* trade and to provide safeguards against their *abuse*' (emphasis added). Thus, these rules relating to the exploitation and enforcement of IPRs are important avenues for the expression of countervailing interests of non-right holders which are part of the balance of rights required by the moral dimension of IPRs. This section will identify the types of law that can fulfil this function.

7.3.2   Common Law Resources

The common law resources for the expression and efficacy of the moral dimension in the domain of exercise of IPRs include a variety of doctrines which are used to ameliorate the stringency of IPRs, to provide a measure of recognition of the right of the public to participation through a defence of the public domain. One of these, the role of public policy, restricted though it is, has been examined in Chapter 4 (§4.7.1). Another resource for the protection of the public domain is the underlying values and principles which the courts bring to bear on the interpretation of both common law and statutory rules in IPR regimes (§4.8.2). In addition to these, there are adjectival doctrines which the common law courts apply to these institutions. Amongst these are the device of the implied licence: such as implied licences of repair for legitimate purchasers of copyright or patented useful articles;[18] and the implied licence to use or import a patented product marketed by the patentee itself except where a clear and express embargo was attached,[19]

---

[18]   *Solar Thomson v. Barton* [1977] R.P.C. 537 (UK); however, the House of Lords in *United Wire Ltd v. Screen Repair Services (Scotland) Ltd.* [2001] F.S.R. 24, held that an article owner's right to repair was not an independent right but was a residual consequence of a finding that the exclusive act (making the patented item) has not occurred. Though this reasoning does limit the implied licence as an avenue for expanding the participation right, the line of decisions remains a latent resource for this should this rationale come to be re-appraised and questioned.

[19]   *Betts v. Willmott* (1871) L.R. 6 Ch. 239.

which the common law was perhaps developing as a form of attenuated exhaustion of rights doctrine before this was overtaken by statutory intervention.[20] An example of the courts shaping rules governing the exploitation of IPRs to give expression to participatory rights is the *Betts v. Willmott*[21] principle in UK patent law, which carves out a limited exhaustion of rights doctrine[22] by holding that when a patent holder manufactures and sells the patented article, a purchaser will acquire the article with an implied licence to use or sell or import that article free from the patent owner's rights in those respects unless the patent holder had obtained a clear and explicit agreement from the purchaser that those restrictions were not waived. The US equivalent is its longstanding judicially created exhaustion of rights doctrine which overcame attempts to restrict it when the Supreme Court in *Quanta Computer v. LG Electronics*[23] held that an unconditional sale of patented articles authorized by the patentee terminated all the patent owner's rights of subsequent control over the article.

The rights are exhausted even – and in this respect over-ruling the Federal Circuit Court of Appeals – when the claim is for a method which is embodied in the patented device, and even when the claimed invention will be fully implemented only when combined with other features, when what is supplied substantially embodies the patented invention. A dramatic example of the way the common law sometimes recognizes the participation right is the way the principle of non-derogation of grant was imported from the common law as to real property into copyright as the defence for makers of spare parts against copyright claims in the UK House of Lords decision in *British Leyland Motor Corp. v. Armstrong Patents Co.*[24] This example neatly illustrates how the implicit moral prescriptions of laws and judicial decisions may rationally require the further 'creation' of rules through judicial decisions, and support moral claims for legislative reform or clarification of the law. It built on earlier cases identifying implied licences of repair for legitimate purchasers of copyright or patented useful articles. It can be argued that the moral claim that justified the creation or acknowledgement of such licences was universalized and applied to the new question of whether third party

---

[20]   See Cornish and Llewelyn (2003), para. 6-15 and 6-16, pp. 249–50.
[21]   Cit. n. 19 above.
[22]   Cornish and Llewelyn (2003), para. 6-15.
[23]   *Quanta Computer, Inc. v. LG Electronics, Inc.* 128 S. Ct. 2109 (2008).
[24]   [1986] A.C. 577.

spare parts producers should also have a defence when making ready-made repair parts for consumers exercising such a right. This will explain Lord Scarman's contention that the justification for this defence was a

> principle latent in our law but not fully discussed or expressed until the present case that the manufacturer of an article such as a motor vehicle or other 'consumer durable' cannot by the exercise of copyright preclude the user of the article from access to a free market for spares necessary to maintain it in good working order.[25]

7.3.3 Competition and Antitrust Law Resources

Decisions about the exercise of IPRs, though they are ethical questions for the IPR owners, sometimes include matters which have legal implications. Some of these decisions involve matters that the law – if not that of IPRs, then some ancillary law – may regulate, like competition or antitrust law,[26] which often have critical roles in ameliorating the more negative effects of IPRs on the public domain.[27] When these laws require an assessment of the reasonableness or legitimacy of the exercise of the IPRs – for instance, whether the withholding of license would be an abuse of those IPRs – the background moral principles of the institutions that are implicitly shared by legislators, judges and IPR holders become legal principles also. An example is afforded by the EU rule (Article 82 of the EC Treaty) which prohibits any 'abuse ... of a dominant position within a common market or a substantial part of it'. This has been used by the European Commission to require TV broadcasters, who by virtue of arranging their own programme schedules were copyright owners of their programme lists – and would have been able under copyright law to refuse compilers of weekly TV guides permission to reproduce their lists – to permit the reproduction of those lists in magazine guides for a reasonable fee. This was upheld by the ECJ in the *Magill case*[28] on the ground that such refusals of licences would be, in such circumstances, an

---

25   *Ibid*, 613–14.

26   E.g. Art. 81 and 82 Treaty Establishing the European Community (1957), hereinafter, 'EC Treaty'; ref. Anderman (2000). For the US, Canadian and EU regulatory framework and competition policy esp. in relation to licensing arrangements for patents, see Gallini and Trebilcock (2004).

27   See e.g. Drexl (2005); Ullrich (2005); Fox (2005); Ghosh (2005).

28   *Radio Telefis Eirean (RTE) and Independent Television Publications Ltd (ITP) v. Commission of the European Communities* (Joint cases C-241/91P and C-242/91P–69/JO241) (1995) ECJ Celex Lexis 1716, applying Art. 82 (ex Art. 86) EC Treaty.

abuse of dominant position. As the primary right in copyright is the ability to withhold permission for the reproduction of one's copyright work, the notion that the exercise of that very right could in some circumstances be an 'abuse' would initially appear to be incoherent, especially if one were to adopt the Legalist's standpoint that the only thing that does matter to the exercise of IPRs is one's legal rights. Of course, a countervailing *legal* right or *legal* bar is introduced by Article 82. The Legalist may stand his ground and argue that it is still the case that only strict legal rights matter, it is just that sometimes two laws stand in tension, but it is still the legal outcome of that tension that matters. The point though, is that the countervailing law employs a term ('abuse') that requires for its elucidation that one develops a moral theory of the other institution (the IPR).

It is the legal provision and the interpretative decision of the relevant court or tribunal that gives recommendations of this moral theory legal force and the character of law; nevertheless, it is necessary, in order to give such a term meaningful content, to develop justificatory theories and rationales of the protection under which one may coherently speak of the abuse of the legal right as a moral idea. The moral dimension needs the law to have legal force, but the law needs the moral dimension to make sense. In fact, competition law assumes what the Legalist, as we have described him above (§7.2.2), denies – that the laws defining IPRs do not exhaustively encapsulate and embody all the relevant moral obligations regarding the subject matter of IPRs and should not be treated as if this is the case. It is only on the assumption that we do have moral obligations regarding how IPRs may be exercised that it makes sense for the competition law rules to speak of the exercise of such right (if the owner holds a dominant position) as being capable of being an 'abuse'. The ECJ (affirming the Court of First Instance) employed a triple condition test for the finding of an abuse where the IP right holder occupies a dominant position: (i) the refusal to license prevented the appearance of a new product for which there was a potential consumer demand; (ii) there was no justification for such refusal either in the right holder's main activity or in the ancillary activity pertaining to the licence; and (iii) the right holder by their conduct reserved to themselves the secondary market (of weekly television guides) by excluding all competition in that market.[29] (Even in this more specific test, the requirement that there be no *justification* for the refusal of the licence imports a reference to an

---

[29] *Ibid*, para. 54–6.

assumed moral background.) This test, then, defines one of the 'exceptional circumstances' where, for the court, the exercise of an exclusive right involves abusive conduct. Just what makes this set of circumstances 'exceptional' needs articulation.

The court was urged by the applicants to rule against the European Commission on the ground of conflict with Article 9 of the Berne Convention – and, therefore, that treating this refusal to license as an abuse conflicted with the right of reproduction in a way that did not fall within the exceptions and limitations permitted by the 'three-step test' in that provision. But the ECJ affirmed the Court of First Instance ruling that that Convention was not applicable in the case because the European Community was not a party to it and it did not apply as between the parties in this dispute or to limit the powers of the Community.[30] Although the Berne Convention provision on the reproduction right was, therefore, not examined, one may almost discern the ghostly after-image of the theory of that right in the reference to 'exceptional circumstances', because, without such a theory, one may not distinguish between normal and exceptional exercises of the right. A consequence of not explicitly articulating or exploring the basis for making any set of circumstances 'exceptional' is that this moral concept is relied upon but not examined. The Court of First Instance of the European Communities, in the later *Microsoft Corp. v. Commission of the European Communities*[31] refined the test in *Magill*, so that now a refusal to license an IPR would be an abuse of dominant position on the following three conditions: the refusal relates to a product or service indispensable to an activity on a neighbouring market; it is of such a kind as to exclude effective competition on that market; and it prevents the appearance of a new product for which there is potential consumer demand. Different terms may be used by the antitrust or competition laws in different countries, but the resort to the underlying moral dimension of the institution is the same whenever one seeks to curb the exercise of such rights because of the relationship between the two types of legal regime remains essentially the same. In the US, for example, the US Court of Appeals for the District of Columbia in *United States v. Microsoft*[32] could hold, amongst other findings, that the refusal by the defendant, which possessed a 'monopoly' in the market for the supply of operating systems for Intel based PC computers, engaged in anti-competitive 'monopolizing' in breach of

---

[30]   *Ibid*, para. 72–87.
[31]   [2007] 5 C.M.L.R. 11.
[32]   *United States of America v. Microsoft Corporation* 253 F. 3d 34 (CA D.C. 2001).

section 2 of the Sherman Act[33] by certain of the licence restrictions it placed on original equipment manufacturers which wanted to supply their machines with the defendant's 'Windows' operating system.

7.3.4 Resources under Legal Rules for Enforcement

Another resource which the courts may use to reflect the property and participation balance is the rules concerning remedies – especially, for common law systems, the equitable ones – in the enforcement of IPRs. The idea is to shift from a property based injunction approach to a liability based compensatory model of enforcement.[34] This was illustrated when the US Supreme Court over-ruled a Federal Circuit Court of Appeals holding that a permanent injunction should generally issue upon a finding of infringement of a valid patent, and that it should be denied only in unusual cases, in exceptional circumstances and in rare instances to protect the public interest.[35] The Supreme Court in *eBay v. Mercexchange*[36] over-ruled this holding, which strengthened the proprietary right. Instead, it restored the traditional four-factor test which it held applied to patent cases with equal force as in other cases. This test requires the party seeking the permanent injunction to satisfy the court that: (1) the plaintiff has suffered irreparable harm as a result of the breach; (2) monetary remedies, such as damages, are inadequate to compensate for the breach; (3) a permanent injunction is warranted considering the balance of hardship between plaintiff and defendant; and (4) the public interest would not be dis-served by the injunction. The consideration of the balance of hardship and the impact of the injunction on the public interest in factors (3) and (4) enables the court to give the participatory right weight in this remedy. This potential may not be used, but a concurring judgment[37] did point to the need to balance competition and property.[38]

---

[33] 15 U.S.C. §2.
[34] For property and liability rules in enforcement ref. Calabresi and Melamed (1972); see Reichman and Lewis (2005) for its application in respect of traditional knowledge protection.
[35] *Mercexchange v. eBay* 275 F.Supp. 2d 695 (2003).
[36] *eBay Inc. v. Mercexchange, L.L.C.* 547 U.S. 388 (2006).
[37] *Ibid*, 395–7, Kennedy J joined by Stevens, Souter and Breyer JJ.
[38] It cited *ibid* at 396, FTC (2003), ch. 3, pp. 38–9.

7.3.5   Compulsory Licensing

For WTO member countries, compulsory licences of patents are subject to the restrictions of Article 31 of TRIPS which sets conditions 'Where the law of a Member allows for *other use* of the subject matter of a patent without the authorization of the right holder'. A footnote to 'other use' in the Agreement clarifies that this refers to 'use other than that allowed under Article 30', the three-step test provision on exceptions to patent rights. Thus, subject to the Article 31 restrictions and conditions, compulsory licences for patents are allowed under TRIPS for situations even beyond those under which the public may generally enjoy access to the inventions on a non-paying basis. The moral dimension of IPRs is dramatically highlighted by the challenge of public health concerns which have centred around compulsory licensing (§8.4), though this is not the only aspect of the patent system that is challenged by such concerns. Our interest in health and the availability of services and technology that promote and preserve life and wealth is unquestionably a vital aspect of what Gewirth has called 'basic well-being';[39] the equal right to freedom and well-being would give strong support for a demand to access to medicines and medical technology.

The idea of compulsory licensing, though, is an acknowledgement of the rights the public has to participate in the benefits of IPRs. A direct attenuation of the property right by compulsory licensing is only one of several modes of satisfaction of these continuing claims. Others include taxation and public programmes. For example, in the area of promotion of health, this could include public funding for medical research and health programmes and subsidized medicines. The choice of solutions is a policy one, whose practical wisdom depends on pragmatic considerations about what works and what side effects are generated, which, in a well ordered state, is better left to democratic political processes. What the moral theory of the justification of IPRs explains is the nature of the moral argument in such political processes. It explains why there is a moral concern that some solution should be found and why it is not enough for those who object to compulsory licences to point to IPRs being property rights and to our obligations to respect property as an institution – the institution is morally subject to other claims.

---

[39]   Gewirth (1996); see discussion of this herein at §2.5.1.

7.4 TECHNOLOGICAL MEASURES AND THE MORAL DIMENSIONS OF IPRS

7.4.1 Technological Measures and the Moral Justification of IPRs

It has been earlier observed (at §7.2.2) that – unless the law mandates technological access – technology can be used to impose restrictions far more limiting than the terms of the IP laws' exceptions and limitations on protection. Such technological measures (TMs)[40] are a response to the threat to copyright posed by electronic digitization of media, a consequence of which is that text, graphics, sound recordings and all kinds of material that have been put in digital format have become subject to easy, cheap and virtually perfect copying with technology widely available and, with the Internet, capable of global dissemination.[41] TMs are the subject of Article 11 of the WCT and Article 18 of the WPPT. This section takes a quick look at TMs and, especially, the anti-circumvention laws we are enacting to protect them, with a view to the consequences for the moral dimensions of IPRs. The development of technological systems of control offers choices about whether these should be configured to include features that allow uses of the copyright material that the copyright law would ordinarily permit others to use without authorization. Technology with which copyright material is released may be configured to restrict access, playing or printing by mode or number of occasions or on certain machines and which limit or forbid editing of copyright material released in digital form. In response to threats in the digital environment, there appears to be a shift in the mode of protection: from legal controls (copyright) to a return to a physical form of control, now technologically assisted and extended. Analogous to this would be biological controls such as Genetic Use Restriction Technology ('GURTs') that enable producers of genetically engineered seeds and propagating materials to treat them to activate a gene that renders them sterile after the first propagation ('Variety-GURTs' or 'V-GURTs'), the so-called 'terminator' genes, or to bind a trait such that they are expressed only after the use of certain proprietory treatments ('Trait-GURTs' or

---

[40] A general introduction is a study for WIPO by Cunard, Hill and Barlas (2004).

[41] This digital challenge and copyright's response is encapsulated in Jones (2000).

'T-GURTs'), the so-called 'trait-or' genes. There are a variety of advantages and dangers to such technology.[42]

Some advantages include the possibility of restricting genetic pollution through uncontrolled spread of genetically modified plants and of supporting the IP protection of owners of patents over modified plants. However, a danger of such technology relevant to this discussion is that it may be used to frustrate whatever careful balance between property and participation rights IP laws may seek to establish. Should one engineer one's IP protected propagating material with genes to effectively defeat any possibility of purchasing farmers' exercising any privilege of replanting harvested material, or rebreeding livestock that the law may allow?[43] In this sense, 'Technological Measures' is an idea that has a breadth much wider than the electronic measures used to protect copyright materials to which this term usually refers. It is the technological measures to control access and use of copyright works, though, that is the primary concern of this section. Essentially, the file containing the work is encrypted and bundled with a program for use in conjunction with a machine with an appropriate program with the key that enables that machine to interact with the TM protected work to digitally unlock it and permit access and use only on the terms set by the person who applied the TM. These terms may grant access, or control use. Examples are: permit printing only, permit only low quality reproduction, allow a restricted number of reproductions to be made, or of limited clips, or use only with a specified machine (or type of machine), or re-use or replay for only a specified number of times or for a period of time from download or first use. The technology for such flexible forms of control of access exists already and can be refined to be ever more sophisticated if the will is present. The question TMs pose is: do they render the justification of IPRs moot?

---

[42] See Pendleton (2004) for these advantages and dangers, though generally positive about GURTs, especially T-GURTs.

[43] Cf. EU 'Biotechnology Directive', 98/44/EC of 6 July 1998, Art. 11. Compare UPOV 1991 Art. 14(1) which requires a mandatory protection of the breeder's exclusive right to '(i) production or reproduction (multiplication)', which is more expansive than the earlier UPOV 1978 Art. 5(1) where the right of authorization covered 'the production *for the purposes of commercial marketing*' (emphasis added). The restrictive formulation of the right in the latter implicitly allows a 'farmer's privilege' to replant their harvest on their own farms; instead, UPOV 1991 has broad exclusive rights but creates an optional farmer's privilege in Art. 15(2) that is 'subject to the safeguarding of the legitimate interests of the breeder'. See Greengrass (1991). (The idea of 'legitimate interests' is a moral concept.)

7.4.2   TMs and the Moral Dimensions of IPRs

Where TMs have been used to secure these digitally released works, copyright owners want laws to be enacted to protect these protection systems from circumvention. And they want these laws to be enforced. They claim that legislators and officials of the legal system have obligations in this regard. Thus, the ability to make such moral claims sincerely is dependent on their commitment to the moral dimension of IPRs and the underlying necessary moral prerequisites. Perhaps this is why Burrell and Coleman, in their study of the impact of digitization on the copyright and its responses, suggest the need for reforms for a more flexible and workable system that can be restyled as 'a system of users' rights' that allows for 'far more public participation'.[44] The necessary safeguards can be built into the law. Some laws mandating protection for TMs for protection of copyright works also vest in certain authorities the function of monitoring their use (to encroach on aspects that should have been accessible to the public under exceptions to copyright protection) and the power, albeit highly restricted and rather weak, to act to counter possible abuse.

Under the US Digital Millennium Copyright Act (DMCA), the Librarian of Congress has to review every three years whether the access control protection has adversely affected the ability of users to make non-infringing uses of any particular class of copyright works, and may, under certain conditions under a rule making procedure, on a positive determination that such adverse impact exists, publish a notice for that class of works with the effect that protection of access control provision will not apply to it for the ensuing three year period.[45] Under the EU 'Information Society Directive', it is envisaged that the copyright owners who use TMs protected by the Directive would undertake voluntary measures, including contracts, for making the benefits of certain exceptions available to their intended beneficiaries.[46] In the absence of such voluntary measures, the member states are

---

[44]   Burrell and Coleman (2005) at p. 276. Even more radically, Efroni (2011) envisions a possible re-orientation of copyright law in terms of 'access-right', especially as regards works in the digital realm.

[45]   Section 1201(a)(1)(C) & (D) Copyright Act, Title 17 USC (US).

[46]   EU Directive 2001/29/EC of 22 May 2001. Not every exception and limitation enumerated in that Directive but only Article 5(2)(a), (2)(c), (2)(d), (2)(e), (3)(b) and (3)(e) are subject to this limitation on the technological measures protection – see Art. 6(4). Most notably, not included in this list of preferred limitations and exceptions are the exceptions to the rights reproduction, and of communication to the public of works and the making available to the public other subject matter (covered by Art. 2 and 3), for quotations for purposes such as criticism or review in accordance with fair practice to the extent required

then required to 'take appropriate measures to make available' to users with legal access the 'means of benefiting from that exception or limitation, to the extent necessary to benefit from that exception or limitation'.[47] The role such devices play in facilitating reform is touched on in the next chapter (§8.3.1). An analogical comparison was made above between TMs for copyright works and GURTs for biological material. Like TMs, GURTs may be used to frustrate the public access that the law in theory allows to farmers, and to upset the balance between the proprietary and participatory rights in ideas that the IP regimes implicitly rely on for their justification. This explains the moral force behind some objections to GURT technology based on the idea of users abusing the technology by over-reaching in the extent of restrictions they impose. On this same analogy, we may look for voluntary measures by GURT users to ensure that a fair balance is maintained which is conditional on such voluntary measures being forthcoming and fair, failing which governmental intervention (perhaps an automatic suspension of the IP rights to enforcement) would be justifiable.

7.5   CONCLUSIONS ON THE MORAL DIMENSIONS OF EXERCISE

We have seen in this chapter why the moral dimensions of IPRs do not end with the justification of IPRs or the way we design and interpret the rules of these institutions. It remains a force when we consider how we ought to exercise the rights acquired under these institutions and, where these considerations can be overcome by other factors, the law can sometimes be used to recognize this moral dimension. Examples of this have been given in the common law devices that apply in an ancillary fashion to IPRs (§7.3.2), drawn from laws on competition and antitrust (§7.3.3), enforcement (§7.3.4) and compulsory licences (§7.3.5). But, as observed with the design of IPRs under national laws (Chapter 4) and in the international law relating to IPRs (Chapter 5), though the equal right to freedom and well-being provides the moral underpinnings of the legal rules and largely explicates their structure, they do not perfectly embody this right. It provides both a justification for them and grounds for critique of their limitations and imperfections. Hence, we turn finally to the dimension of reform.

---

by these purposes with due acknowledgement of source and authors (Art. 5(3)(d)), and for the purpose of caricature, parody or pastiche (Art. 5(3)(k)).

[47]   *Ibid*, Art. 6(4).

8. The moral dimension of reform of IPRs

8.1 REFORM AND THE MORAL DIMENSIONS OF IPRS

The dimension of reform is a concomitant result of the moral dimensions of IPRs heretofore developed. They each require and draw our attention to this one. The justification of IPRs casts a moral duty on owners to acknowledge the just claims of others to shared access, because it is only on the basis of acknowledgement of continuing rights to some degree of access to the subject matter of the property that we have conditions for the just acquisition of IPRs and other property rights (§§3.2.4, 3.6.1 and 3.6.5). This would mean that, so long as they do want to justify these institutions, and if the positive laws of IPRs (with their conditions for acquisition and limitations and exceptions) do not adequately reflect this obligation, the moral obligation would continue to operate when the owners come to exercise their IP rights (cf. §7.2) or when they are engaged in deliberations in the legislative forum regarding reform of the laws.

The dimension of reform is a concomitant of these notions for an even more basic reason, though. The idea of morality advanced here is that its principles and values are ever open to revision, reformulation and refinement of prescriptions which are universalized. If the aspiration towards legitimacy (a moral concept) is a necessary part of any justification of IPRs, then, as the character of this conception – even if it is the equal right to freedom and well-being defended herein – is under-determinative, our understanding of what a proper justification of IPRs requires for specific situations is always being revised, reformulated and refined (cf. §2.7). Yet another reason for reform being a concomitant companion of the justification of IPRs stems from the very character and purpose of IPRs themselves. They function to introduce innovation and change in the way our social world (and this includes technology) is constituted and conceived (§3.6.3); they expand the possibilities open to us and challenge the status quo. It is, therefore, not surprising that these institutions find change and adaptation a virtually constant challenge.

Hence, the reform aspect of the moral dimension is a constant, living companion with the justification of the institutions.

A part of this capacity for reform is built into the very design of IPRs through the moral concepts and terminology incorporated in some of the central rules defining the conditions for their existence or acquisition, the extent of the rights and the exceptions to them. These moral terms and concepts serve to express the intention that the institutions should be fair and just, and to enable adaptation towards that goal by facilitating a review, redefinition and re-invention of the institution (§4.1.2). They are transformational opportunities, albeit ones that are constrained by the other legal terms which provide their context, and are dependent on the willingness of the courts to use these as resources for reform. The imperative for reform derives also from the moral dimension of law itself. IPRs, being legal institutions which belong in the Rawlsian 'basic structure' of society, bear a burden in the general aspiration to serve a purpose that claims our allegiance (§6.3.1). And we found that resort to the institution's justification is an ineluctable part of the process of interpreting laws (§§6.2 and 6.4).

Although some of this underlying moral dimension is expressed through purely moral duties and considerations applying to the exercise of IP rights (cf. Chapter 7), sometimes supplemented by legal support through ancillary laws – such as those having to do with licensing, whether implied or compulsory, and competition or enforcement remedies – these cannot fully satisfy the imperative for reform. It was argued, when the exercise of IPRs was considered (§7.2.1), that claims to be entitled to enjoy the IPRs – that is, claims that those legal rights *ought* to be respected by others and enforced by legal officials – are freighted with an obligation to acknowledge the moral dimension of the institutions, and the fundamental principles that justify them. These provide the grounds for other claims as well, including the obligation to cooperate with claims for the reform of these institutions to make them consistent with their justificatory theory. In this regard, it is helpful to note that Correa's commentary on TRIPS suggests that 'Article 7 (and Article 8) may serve to justify exceptions to exclusive rights where the right-holder has failed to participate in social and economic development'[1] because Article 7 declares that the protection and enforcement of IPRs *should* contribute to the promotion of technological innovation *and* transfer and dissemination of technology to the mutual advantage of producers and users and in a manner conducive to social and economic

---

[1]   Correa (2007), p. 97.

welfare, and to a balance of rights and obligations. TRIPS itself makes this objective the basis for the rights it mandates, which provides the moral grounds for reform through interpretative avenues and legislated changes where its mandated institutions and how they are used do not live up to its promises.

It is, thus, fitting to round up with a chapter on the dimension of reform. This will explore in broad outline the avenues of reform: a reference to those resources internal to the IPR systems which we have already canvassed (§8.2.1), as well as a review of external judicial avenues for reform in the constitutional and human rights laws of states (§8.7.2); then, finally, the political avenues of reform (§8.3). An illustrative example of this would be the issue of access to medicines and patents and how this led to the amendment of Article 31 of TRIPS (§8.4).

8.2 JUDICIAL AVENUES FOR REFORM

8.2.1 Internal Resources of the IPR Systems

The way moral ideas and concepts can be, have been, interpretatively adapted to meet the imperative within IPR institutions towards legitimation consistent with a background principle of an equal right to freedom and well-being, has already been seen: in Chapter 4 in relation to the central rules defining the existence of, extent of and exceptions to, IPRs; and in Chapter 7 in relation to how they are exercised. Though there have been occasions when the courts have seized the interpretative opportunities,[2] they have also been hesitant in embracing this role.[3] Besides these internal resources for reform, there are the national constitutional and human rights laws as resources for reform.

8.2.2 Resources in National Constitutional and Human Rights Laws

Although reform is primarily the domain of legislature, it can result from applying the constitutional and human rights laws of the country. Not surprisingly, the key ideas in such laws are all essentially moral ones in

---

[2] E.g. the adaptation of the common law breach of confidence action for the protection of privacy discussed at §4.2.4; and the development of the US transformative use doctrine for fair use in copyright discussed at §4.3.4.

[3] We have seen this with *NOVARTIS/Transgenic plant G1/98* [2000] E.P.O.R. 303 (discussed heretofore at §§4.4.4 & 4.8.2), and the WTO Dispute Settlement Body Panel decision in *United States – Section 110(5) of the US Copyright Act* discussed at §§5.3.3–5.3.4.

that they are evaluative and require one to arrive at their meaning through a process of reflective search through competing prescriptions. These include: the European Convention of Human Rights enforced under the UK Human Rights Act 1998 which has already generated several cases relating to the juxtaposition of protection of IPRs with the protection of privacy and free speech;[4] and the US Constitution, notably Article 1 section 8 cl. 8[5] and the First Amendment.[6] All of these have key moral terms making direct references to the human rights values that are expressed in the equal right to freedom and well-being.

An obvious interface between such national over-riding laws and IPRs is the interplay between copyright and the right to free speech and expression.[7] Although the former enables the owner to prevent others from making infringing uses of copyright material in the exercise of expression, the two are not diametrically opposed. There is a tension between them, but copyright also facilitates speech by enabling one to control certain types of one's own expressions, and freedom of expression does not have to include the freedom to use the expression of others. In the US copyright regime, this potential conflict with the right to free speech and expression is largely avoided by the former developing within

---

[4]   See the *Douglas v. Hello! Ltd (No. 1)* and *Campbell v. Mirror Group Newspapers Ltd* discussed at §4.2.2, and others including: *Venables v. Newsgroup Newspapers* [2001] 1 All ER 908; *A v. B & C* [2002] EWCA Civ 337; *Ashdown v. Telegraph Group plc.* [2001] EWCA Civ 1142; *Cliberry v. Allan* [2001] 2 FCR 577; *Campbell v. Frisbee* [2002] EWCA Civ 1374 and [2002] EWHC 328 (Ch); *Murray v. Express Newspapers Plc* [2008] EWCA Civ 446 [2009] Ch. 481 reversing [2007] EWHC 1908 (Ch); see Ryan (2001).

[5]   E.g. for copyright, see *Eldred v. Ashcroft* 537 U.S. 186 (2003).

[6]   E.g. *Eldred v. Ashcroft, ibid*; *Harper & Row & Nation Enterprises* cit. below n. 10.

[7]   Especially in the US jurisprudence, see Patterson (1987) and Patterson and Birch Jr (1996). For the UK, see Angelopoulos (2008), who argues that the protection of freedom of expression through human rights laws enables the 'externalization' of an 'internal conflict' within copyright between the project of promoting freedom of the authors' expression and of the public through access and use of copyright works, which is inadequately resolved by rules 'internal' to copyright law. The Human Rights Act of 1998 thus enables us to correct this imbalance by resort to an external law (pp. 350–52). This line of argument is very much supported by this work. See also Couto (2008), who argues that conflict between copyright and the right to freedom of expression is unlikely because allowances made by the former accommodate the latter, but suggests that where the rare conflict arises, a liberal theory of justice would seek to resolve this by means of a 'qualitative analysis' which appeals to the value(s) which mutually ground both rights.

its rules the resources for finding a suitable accommodation of this tension. Thus, the idea–expression dichotomy already reflects the imperative under the free speech right that the subject matter of a work and substance of what is expressed remain available in the public domain, and it is only the expressive elements that reflect a modicum of the author's creativity that can be the object of the property right.[8] The fair use defence enables persons who do make transformative uses of the works of others, hence contributing a high degree of expression of their own, to take a fair amount of the copyright work.[9] But that defence may give way where, despite high public interest in a work of historical value such as the memoirs of an ex-President, the extracts go to the pith of what is most commercially valuable in the account.[10] It would be wrong to say that there is no free speech interest in another's copyright expression, because the latter's boundaries are determined by the former and vice versa.

In copyright regimes where the rules of the institution are less accommodating to free speech concerns, the tension between the two is more obtrusive. The UK copyright law provides a convenient contrasting illustration of this because, whereas the US regime has had to evolve alongside the free speech protection in its Constitution practically from its inception,[11] the UK's statutory copyright regime dates back (through various versions) to 1709 with the Statute of Anne, whilst it enacted its Human Rights Act, with its incorporation of the right to free speech and expression under the ECHR (Article 8) as fundamentally guiding interpretative principle for its courts in the development of law and interpretation of statutes, only in 1998. The relationship came before the UK Court of Appeal in *Ashdown v. Telegraph*[12] in a case regarding the use by the defendant newspaper of verbatim quotations from an unpublished confidential minute which the claimant Member of Parliament had made of a meeting with the Prime Minister and some others which appeared to contradict certain public declarations. Sir Andrew Morritt V-C granted a final injunction against the defendant and other directions. Although the Vice-Chancellor had held that the Article 10 freedom was engaged in such a case, he also ruled that the Copyright Act already provided for it:

---

8   *Feist Publications, Inc. v. Rural Telephone Service Co.* 499 U.S. 340.
9   *Campbell v. Acuff-Rose Music, Inc.* 510 U.S. 569.
10   *Harper & Row Publishers, Inc. v. Nation Enterprises* 471 U.S. 539.
11   The first federal Copyright statute, 1 Stat. 124, was enacted in 1790 and the First Amendment formed part of the Bill of Rights of 1791.
12   *Ashdown v. Telegraph Group plc.* [2001] EWCA Civ 1142, [2002] Ch. 149, affirming [2001] Ch. 685.

The balance between the rights of the owner of the copyright and those of the public which has been struck by the legislative organ of the democratic state itself in the legislation it has enacted. There is no room for any further defences outside the code which establishes the particular species of intellectual property in question.[13]

Having rejected the defence of fair dealing for the purpose of criticism or review (s 30(1)) on the ground that the minute itself was not the subject of criticism or review, and that for reporting of current events (s 30(2)) on the ground that there was no reasonable prospect of the defendant newspaper making good a case that there was fair dealing, bearing in mind the commercial competition with the owner's commercial exploitation (the claimant was intending to publish his memoirs including reference to the content of the minute), the fact that the minute was then unpublished and the amount and importance of the part that had been taken, and that he was bound by authority[14] to hold that the common law public interest defence (which is preserved by s 171(3)) was not applicable, the judge found himself then bound to find for the claimant.

The Court of Appeal upheld the High Court's judgment but, in the course of so holding, it considered ways in which the right of freedom of expression may conflict with copyright as a right of each legal or natural person 'to the peaceful enjoyment of his possessions'[15] and, where the balance between the two rights is inadequately reflected in the Copyright Act, how the courts may (under its obligation under s 3(1) of the Human Rights Act to give effect to the Charter rights where possible) give effect to the right to freedom of expression. It noted that, whilst the notion of a citizen's right to freely express ideas and convey (and receive) information would be stretched in a claim to be able to do so in the form of words (to which copyright protection is limited) devised by someone else,[16] there are occasions when protection of the right requires that a user be free to use copyright protected material. Most of these 'circumstances where freedom of expression trumped copyright protection'[17] are reflected in exceptions provided for in the Copyright Act (some 42 instances of which were identified by the Vice-Chancellor), including the fair dealing and public interest defence. But the Court of Appeal accepted the possibility that 'rare circumstances can arise where the right to

---

13   [2001] Ch. 685 (para. 20).
14   Cit. at n. 20 below.
15   [2001] EWCA Civ 1142, [2002] Ch. 149, para. 25 and 28.
16   *Ibid*, para. 31.
17   *Ibid*, para. 32; Article 1 to the First Protocol to the ECHR.

freedom of expression will come into conflict with the protection afforded by the Copyright Act, notwithstanding express exceptions to be found in the Act', where 'the Court is bound, insofar as it is able, to apply the Act in a manner that accommodates the right of freedom of expression'.[18]

This reopens an avenue for accommodating the right of freedom of expression closed by the Vice-Chancellor's holding that this right is fully exhausted by the balance of rights in the Copyright Act enacted by legislature. This may include declining the discretionary relief of an injunction. It went on to stress that '[T]he implications of the Human Rights Act must always be considered where the discretionary relief of injunction is sought, and this is true in the field of copyright quite apart from the ambit of the public interest defence.'[19] To accommodate the rare instance where copyright words should, in the public interest, be free for use without any sanction, the Court of Appeal has been at pains to hold that the categories of public interest preserved by section 171(3) are not closed and are not restricted to the three types of situation identified by Aldous LJ in the *Hyde Park Residence v. Yelland case*. The categories which Aldous LJ had identified as grounds on which a court may, in the public interest, refuse to enforce copyright were instances where 'the work is (i) immoral, scandalous or contrary to family life; (ii) injurious to public life, public health and safety or the administration of justice; (iii) incites or encourages others to act in a way referred to in (ii)'.[20] However, the Court of Appeal after reviewing the other judgments in that case and the other Court of Appeal decision of *Lion Laboratories v. Evans*,[21] preferred the conclusion that 'the circumstances in which public interest may override copyright are not capable of precise categorisation or definition' and that, 'Now that the Human Rights Act is in force, there is the clearest public interest in giving effect to the right of freedom of expression in those rare cases where this right trumps the right conferred by the Copyright Act'.[22]

---

[18] *Ibid*, para. 45.

[19] *Ibid*, para. 59.

[20] *Hyde Park Residence v. Yelland* [2001] Ch. 143, UK CA, per Aldous LJ at 168 (para. 66).

[21] [1985] QB 526.

[22] Cit. above n. 12, para. 58. For an argument that the Court of Appeal did not go far enough, in particular that its decision was wrong in that it did not give proper weight to the public's right to receive information that is part of the right to freedom of expression under Art. 10 ECHR when making the fair dealing assessment, see Griffiths (2002).

Limited though these avenues for expressing the idea of a participation right may be, the impact of the Human Rights Act of 1998 in the UK on the copyright jurisprudence does provide evidence for how human rights law may provide scope for reform of an IP institution even where the express statute or legal precedent may offer little encouragement. It is notable that the *Ashdown* judgment understands the right of freedom of expression (as it is required to by the jurisprudence developed by the European Court of Human Rights)[23] as protecting both 'the right to both publish information and receive it'.[24] This exemplifies the idea of a right of participation. The idea of a participatory right stems, as does the property right, out of the idea that protection and promotion of person-hood requires one to recognize a fundamental equal right to freedom and well-being. However, as the property right is explicitly advanced and entrenched in IP laws, it is the participatory right that struggles for recognition and expression through judicial interpretation of case based common law, moral terms and concepts built into the IP statutes and conventions, through the use of ancillary laws like those related to competition, and, in this case, through exercise of the court's power to review legislation for constitutionality. It can be frustrated by judicial reticence, but the potential for transformation remains.

8.3   REFORM IN THE ADMINISTRATIVE AND POLITICAL FORI

8.3.1   Various Administrative Loci for Reform

Whether this restraint reflects an overly timid understanding by the courts of their role or a due regard for the role of legislatures and the political process, the result is that most of the impetus for reform generated by the moral dimensions of IPRs tends to be channelled to administrative and legislative avenues for change that lie in *fori* that are characterized by political discourse (cf. §8.1).

Some examples of this have been noted already: the periodic review power of the Librarian of Congress under the US Digital Millennium Copyright Act to identify classes of works under a rule making procedure with the effect that its anti-circumvention of access control provision will not apply to TM used to protect them for the ensuing three year period

---

[23]   *Fressoz and Roire v. France* (1999) 5 BHRC 654; see *Ashdown v. Telegraph Group Ltd* cit. above n. 12, para. 41–3.

[24]   *Ashdown v. Telegraph Group Ltd*, cit. above n. 12, para. 43.

(§7.4.2);[25] the EU 'Information Society Directive'[26] envisages that the copyright owners who use TMs protected by the Directive would undertake voluntary measures, including contracts, for making the benefits of certain exceptions[27] available to their intended beneficiaries, in the absence of which, the member states are then required to 'take appropriate measures to make available' to users with legal access the 'means of benefiting from that exception or limitation, to the extent necessary to benefit from that exception or limitation'.[28]

Another example of facilitating access by means of administrative intervention is the device of compulsory licensing. It has been seen that the relatively rigid core rules of patent laws have meant that the judicial role in refining the institution to reflect the balance of the moral property and participatory rights is more restricted, and the system then relies for expression of that moral dimension on external avenues in some of the other dimensions of the institution (§4.4.5).

Compulsory licensing regimes allowed under Article 31 of TRIPS are an incentive for the IP right holder to consider voluntary market based negotiated terms of access – and normally requires the party seeking compulsory licences to first make a reasonable attempt at obtaining such access – and provides an avenue, when this is absent or inadequate, for non-owner authorization to be given on the 'individual merits' of each case (§7.3.5). This puts in the hands of the body entrusted with the power of considering and granting such authorization the responsibility of determining whatever counts as 'individual merits' for such applications. This would appear to be a discretionary power. But it is not one that may be exercised on an arbitrary whim because it must be subject to judicial review or some other means of oversight. Thus, the discretionary element allows and requires that body or official to make a determination that essentially reforms the institution, as it will shape the degree of access that others will enjoy despite a refusal by the right holder to provide that access voluntarily. However, the responsibility to make this determination on 'individual merits' means that that body or official must also be open to the moral considerations that underpin the institution and must inform such decisions. This allows the moral dimension to influence this aspect of the institution and, through its potential application, to influence the patent holders to consider forestalling such compulsory licences by voluntary means.

---

[25]   Section 1201(a)(1)(C) & (D) Copyright Act, Title 17 USC (US).
[26]   EU Directive 2001/29/EC of 22 May 2001.
[27]   *Ibid.* See §7.4.2 above and n. 46 in Chapter 7.
[28]   *Ibid*, Art. 6(4).

8.3.2   Legislative Routes to Reform and the Role of Morality in Politics

Reform of IPRs through new legislation or amending laws for existing regimes is purely a political matter. Even so, the moral dimension of the institution is not totally irrelevant, for moral arguments and considerations do play a role in the political process even though power and morality are often contrasted and politics is about the acquisition and wielding of power.

Some of the reasons for the persistent relevance of the moral dimension have already been canvassed in relation to its role in the development of the international regulatory framework for IPRs (§5.2). The interests of the powerful, even across different states, are not perfectly aligned, and the resulting cracks in unity provide interstitial spaces for use of moral arguments as a recourse as a means of forging consensus or, at least, enrolling sufficient support. At the level of domestic politics of national legislatures, governments – at least in democracies – have to answer to the broad voting population at the polls. Much of this may be by means of lobbying and means of persuasion that amount to no more than simplistic propaganda – such as 'copyright piracy is theft' – but this provides opportunities for more sustained critique and examination when these methods are called out. Thus, pure power requires the support of reason, allowing some room for the moral dimension of the IPRs to exert its force. Precisely because these institutions are abstruse in their details, they require what Braithwaite and Drahos call epistemic communities[29] – technical people in various industries, lawyers, academics – for their maintenance and formulation of new rules. Even as they represent opposing sides, these communities draw together to share some common language and values. The result is the need to develop some objective understanding of the nature and basis of the institutions and claims that are made about them that are the basis for such persons' claim to expertise and special qualifications. The self-conscious, discursive fori in which these qualifications are gained – the universities and professional academies – provide the basis of rational reflection on the various institutions of law they administer, including IPRs.

---

[29]   Braithwaite and Drahos (2000); see discussion herein at §5.2. An example of the academic and activist push-back against the proprietarian tide is the collection of responses the editors and contributors to Krikorian and Kapczynski (2010) have sought to describe (perhaps over-robustly) as an 'Access to Knowledge' ('A2K') movement.

Part of this discourse would include the ideas that are part of the moral dimension, though not always acknowledged as such, because the morality of justification is part of the interpretation and concept of law (Chapter 6) generally, and of IPRs in particular, given their nature (Chapters 3 and 4). Again, the self-consciously rational platform provided by these epistemic communities allows for these assumptions to be questioned and for any reform required by the moral dimension to be raised. As these epistemic communities provide both the framework of the institutions for policy adoption and the policy critique that accompanies the political process, moral grounds for reform exert a force, perhaps in an imperfect and weak form, on the outcome of the political process.

This suggests that the moral dimension may be elided by inattention and inadvertence, but it also points to its potential, if the systems are awakened to its possibilities and re-designed to take the prescriptivism in the moral dimension of such discourse seriously. Some of both the strengths and weaknesses of how this moral dimension works is illustrated by the way the patents system has, and is, responding to the problem of access to medicine.

8.4 THE CASE OF PATENTS AND MEDICINES

Patents and the provision of medicine are an example *par excellence*, where tension between the property imperative and the participatory claims of an IPR institution is exposed. The justification of patents, granting valuable rights of exclusion over the making or using or importing, amongst others, of a patented product or process, lies in the incentive such rights give to inventors to introduce new inventions. But the practice of medicine is a field where access to products and practices based on new ideas can be a matter of saving lives or vital difference to well-being. The advantage of exploring the moral dimensions of the core rules that go to the design of the patent institution and identifying the underlying justification in this same right is that – even if we conclude that the rules defining the conditions for protection should be essentially expansive – we are now able to consider the problem in terms of a common moral denominator and see a key link between the arguments for protection and the demands of others for access.

Even if one doubts that the principle of an equal right to freedom and well-being is fundamental, the approach that takes morality as a search for universalizable prescriptives would entail that whatever basic principles one uses to justify the property must hold as well, if relevant, for claims on behalf of patients for access to medicines. IP owners cannot assert their right to property and argue, if appropriate exceptions are not made to their property, that the problem of finding a solution for patients is a broader social concern purely for others to solve; they would be part of that society and the part of it with a special moral link to the issue (cf. §7.2.2).

If the fundamental principle supporting IPRs – as Chapter 3 argues – is one that requires the promotion and protection of liberty and well-being, the tradeoff between property and participation claims will depend on the relative weight of the impact of the attenuation of the property right in favour of participation access in terms of Gewirth's criterion of degree of necessity for action (or, which would be the same thing, for liberty).[30] Life and health being essential for action of all kinds, a grave and imminent threat to these must support an extremely powerful claim on the cooperation of others in the position to grant or deny access to anything that would remove or alleviate that threat. The liberty and well-being case for patent rights is indirect: in potentially generating a source of income for the inventors and, hence, supplying their needs for other actions, and by such incentive promoting further invention which contributes to the technological possibilities available to all, thereby increasing the potential liberty and well-being of all. The critical tradeoff is, thus, between the participatory interests of patients and the profit to the inventor and consequent potential inhibition of invention in this field.

Well known controversies of this kind include the public relations furore aroused when 39 pharmaceutical companies sued the South African government in response to its Medicines and Related Substances Control Amendment Act of 1997,[31] which made it possible for it to grant compulsory licences on, and to allow parallel import of, patented medicines used in the treatment of diseases including HIV/AIDS. Even before the litigation, the amending Act met with international pressure – notably from the US Trade Representative, which listed South Africa for possible trade sanctions, and the EU – suggesting that it violated South Africa's obligations under TRIPS. The pharmaceutical companies claimed in the 1998 lawsuit that the law was an interference with their patent rights because it violated the TRIPS Agreement. South Africa maintained that the enactment was necessary to address an urgent

---

[30]   Gewirth (1996), p. 45 and Ch. 2 above at §2.5.1.

[31]   See, for the worldwide patients' access campaign in response to this and other issues: Mayne (2002) and Smith and Duncan (2009); see also Drahos and Braithwaite (2002), ch. 1, esp. pp. 5–10. For an analysis of this Bill and an argument that it does not violate the TRIPS Agreement, see Bombach (2001).

national health emergency. By 2000, about 20 per cent of the South African population was infected with HIV.

The problem was a multi-faceted one, in which the price of AIDS related medicines is only one factor in denying adequate access to medicines to many. The healthcare infrastructure is another vital factor. But the role and impact of patent protected prices are dramatic. Prices of critical medicines for HIV/AIDS therapy, which can significantly delay the onset of AIDS in HIV infected persons, were said to fall from the US patented price of US$10,000 per patient per year, well beyond the reach of most African HIV/AIDS victims, to prices offered at a discount in African countries – after the eventual dropping of the litigation – of around US$900, though this still did not match generic rates, which reached about US$300 that year.[32]

The commencement of the trial on 5 March 2001 enabled AIDS and pro-patient activists to frame the issue in the public mind, perhaps over-simplistically, as a contest between globalized IP rights and patient rights to lifesaving medicines. They were able to fan popular outrage against the pharmaceutical companies in particular and patents for medicines in general. By April 2001 the litigation was settled when the pharmaceuticals withdrew their claim and cut drug prices in Africa. By this time, an issue about pricing and enforcement of patent rights for pharmaceutical companies had become one in the public consciousness about the legitimacy of globalized patent institutions, at least for medicines. The contest can be put as being between present and future patients. Although future patients do not tend to arouse our immediate sympathy, their claims will be no less urgent when their time of need comes. But the tradeoff is not starkly symmetrical: much will depend on the type of attenuation of the property interest required to promote the present patients' interests and the degree to which that reduces the profitability of the property and consequently inhibits innovation in medicine. This is where solutions may be found along the lines of compulsory licensing, especially where the products so authorized may be confined to markets that would be of relatively low interest to the patent holders.

This is why the moral dimension in the design of an IPR is important. Even if, as with patent systems, IPRs' central rules do not provide wide scope for its expression, it still operates at the margins and nevertheless provides the grounds for claims to access and sharing of the benefits by other means. And this lends weight to claims that, even if exclusion or

---

[32]   Source Mayne (2002) at p. 250, Smith and Duncan (2009) at p. 434.

limitation of patent rights over medicines is not the right solution, pharmaceutical companies, as the beneficiaries of an institution whose justification rests on a recognition of moral grounds which also support patients' claims to have affordable access to healthcare, have a special responsibility to support measures even in other fields of activity to help bring this about. This includes voluntary measures in the exercise of IPRs, such as the decision of GlaxoSmithKline and Merck to discount prices of their HIV/AIDS medicines to least-developed countries (LDCs) in the wake of the settlement of the South African litigation.[33] And it would also include infrastructure support and legal reform.

The furore over the role of IP protection, prices of medicines and public health issues, which was accompanied by concern at the UN with the apparent conflict between TRIPS implementation and international human rights law, especially as regards the right to health,[34] was part of a movement for reform which culminated in the 2001 Doha WTO Ministerial *Declaration on the TRIPS Agreement and Public Health*[35] ('the Doha Declaration') which recognized 'the gravity of the public health problems afflicting many developing countries and LDCs, especially those resulting from HIV/AIDS, tuberculosis, malaria and other epidemics',[36] and acknowledged the tension between IP protection 'important for the development of new medicines' and 'concerns about its effect on prices'.[37] The deadline for implementing the patent and undisclosed information section of TRIPS[38] was, with respect to pharmaceutical products, extended for LDCs to 1 January 2016. (The original deadline given LDCs for the implementation of the substantive protection provisions of TRIPS was to 2005.[39])

---

[33]   Source: Smith and Duncan (2009) at p. 434.

[34]   See U.N. Sub-Commission on Human Rights Resolution (2000/7) and the report of the High Commissioner for Human Rights (2001) which devoted a section to 'The TRIPS Agreement and the Right to Health', noting 'Article 12 of the ICESR [the UN International Covenant on Economic, Social and Cultural Rights] obliges States to respect, protect and fulfill the right of everyone to the highest attainable standard of physical and mental health' (para. 30) and that 'access to essential drugs is a human right' (para. 42). Later incidents raising such issues include those involving Thailand and Brazil that were the subject of an exchange between Pitts (2008) and Weisman (2008).

[35]   Adopted on 14 November 2001 (WT/MIN(01)/DEC/2 20 November 2001).

[36]   *Ibid*, para. 1.

[37]   *Ibid*, para. 3.

[38]   Sections 5 and 7 respectively of TRIPS.

[39]   Art. 66(1) TRIPS.

The Doha Declaration also attempted to find interpretative wiggle room in the TRIPS provisions, to enable member countries to accommodate (albeit in a limited manner) those concerns: '[W]e affirm that the Agreement can and should be interpreted and implemented in a manner supportive of WTO members' right to protect public health and, in particular, to promote access to medicines for all.'[40] This encapsulates the operation of the moral dimensions of IPRs: the moral participatory right exerts its force in the dimension of justification, in the debates occurring in political arenas at national and international levels, which find expression in rights' language – albeit the 'right' belongs to WTO member states – of legal material intended to influence the dimension of law through its interpretative resources.

The moral dimension is shaped by the decisions and commitments we make but is not an arbitrary artifice because the character of universality is required of the principles underpinning those commitments and, if Chapter 2 is correct, the implicit fundamental prescriptions which are required for the whole idea to work. As a result the moral dimensions of each sphere of activity – political discourse, international norm making, national legislation and legal interpretation – tend to become, as a result of universalization, a single moral dimension for our cooperative efforts in building a society, itself a foundation for and a product of this cooperative effort. As our efforts become globalized, perhaps in an effort to provide a global superstructure for societies, more and more we come to create a global moral dimension – albeit one which allows for local variations. Thus, the implicit goals and values which support IPRs can give rise to grounds for their limitation and critique which actually plays a role that shapes the political as well as legal processes which determine our IP laws.

Four interpretative outcomes were confirmed immediately in the Doha Declaration.[41] First, TRIPS objectives (Article 7) and principles (Article 8) are emphasized as the objects and purposes which provide guidance[42] for its interpretation under international law. Secondly, each member state has the right to grant, and determine the grounds for, compulsory licences. This confirms the discretion each member has to determine for itself what constitutes 'individual merits' of each case under Article 31(a)

---

[40] Cit. above n. 35, para. 4.

[41] *Ibid*, at para. 5.

[42] The Declaration itself also constitutes part of the context which is relevant to the interpretation of TRIPS, under Art. 31(3)(a) Vienna Convention on the Law of Treaties, 1969, because it is a 'subsequent agreement between the parties regarding the interpretation of the treaty or the application of its provisions'.

TRIPS. Thirdly, each member state has the right to determine 'what constitutes a national emergency or other circumstances of extreme urgency' which, under Article 31(b) of TRIPS, would release them from the obligation of requiring the party seeking the compulsory licence to make a prior attempt to obtain licensing from the patent owner at a commercial price. Fourthly, interpretation, of the rather Delphically phrased, exhaustion of rights provision (Article 6) and the rest of TRIPS that is adopted is that they leave each member state free 'to establish its own regime for exhaustion without challenge' subject to the principles of most favoured nation and national treatment embraced in Articles 3 and 4.

An important result is that patients' advocates may seek to reduce the price of patented medicines sold in their countries by sourcing from other markets where the products have been released by or with the consent of the patent owners. These provisions, though, do not allow the import of unlicensed generics. However, the somewhat paradoxical result of wide-spread adoption of universal exhaustion of rights principles is that producers will tend to price their products at a level higher than they otherwise would have for some of the poorer countries if they are able to segregate the countries as distinct markets. This is to prevent leakage by parallel importing into some of their more lucrative markets. Thus, permission for parallel importing is not the solution it appears to be. Hence, a vital antidote is the device of compulsory licensing, which serves to focus the minds of IP owners, when considering exploitation of their rights, on local needs and conditions; and provides an alternative solution by way of authorization of others if the IP owners' response is inadequate (§7.3.5). An important limitation to this solution was that Article 31(f) TRIPS restricted such compulsory licences to use which was predominantly for the supply of the domestic market. Hence, exports to other countries are not within the scope of such schemes. However, as the Doha Declaration recognizes, this means that 'WTO members with insufficient or no manufacturing capacities in the pharmaceutical sector could face difficulties in making use of compulsory licensing'.[43] That Declaration instructed the Council for TRIPS to seek a solution.

The solution that the Council for TRIPS adopted was a decision[44] regarding waivers of Article 31(f) and (h) (regarding the restriction to

---

[43]   Cit. above n. 35, para. 6.

[44]   Council of TRIPS Decision of 30 August 2003 *Implementation of Paragraph 6 of the Doha Declaration on the TRIPS Agreement and Public Health* (WT/L/540 2 September 2003), hereinafter referred to as 'the TRIPS Council Decision'. The references in the notes given below are to the TRIPS Council

domestic supply and the right of the patent owner to be paid an adequate remuneration in the case of compulsory licensing) within a system that seeks to balance protection of the interests of patent holders against leakage to other markets and the interest of countries in obtaining an adequate level of access for their patients. (This was later incorporated into a protocol to TRIPS pending ratification. See below.)

In this scheme, any LDC member and any member that has made a notification to the Council for TRIPS that it will use the system in a whole or limited way may become an 'eligible importing Member'.[45] The significance of being an 'eligible importing Member' is that 'exporting Members' may use this system to export the patented pharmaceutical products produced under compulsory licensing schemes to such countries under an exemption from the Article 31(f) restriction.[46] Exporting members granting a compulsory licence under this system must still ensure that the patent owner is paid an adequate remuneration pursuant to Article 31(h) of TRIPS. But this obligation is waived for 'eligible importing Members' granting compulsory licences under the scheme for those products for which such remuneration has already been paid in the exporting country.[47] There are several safeguards for the property interests of patent owners in requirements that medicines produced under these schemes should not be more than necessary to meet the needs of 'eligible importing Members', be distinguishable from the regular patented versions, and in arrangements to prevent their diversion to other territories.

This solution was later incorporated into a Protocol for the amendment of TRIPS by the addition of a new Article 31*bis* and an Annex,[48] which

---

Decision of 30 August 2003, but the corresponding references to the Art. 31*bis* and the Annex to the TRIPS Agreement introduced by an amending Protocol are also given in anticipation of its taking effect on the required proportion of acceptances. See nn. 48 & 49 below.

[45] *Ibid*, para. 1(b); when the Protocol comes into effect, Annex to the TRIPS Agreement para. 1(a).

[46] *Ibid*, para. 2; when the Protocol comes into effect, Art. 31*bis* para. 1.

[47] *Ibid*, para. 3; when the Protocol comes into effect, Art. 31*bis* para. 2.

[48] Adopted by the WTO General Council Decision on 'Amendment of the TRIPS Agreement' (WT/L/641 dated 8 December 2005), para. 1, and will take effect and enter into force, under Art. X, para. 3 of the WTO Agreement, when two-thirds of the WTO members have accepted the change.

is still awaiting the required number of acceptances to come into force.[49] Although this account illustrates the persistent relevance of the moral dimension of IPRs working to produce a reform of such institutions, it also shows up its limitations and weakness. This is a very obvious conflict of an IPR with an element essential for basic well-being (medicine for health and survival) and yet it took some egregious overplaying of its hand by the pharmaceutical industry in its lawsuit against the South African government before enough public outrage was stoked to put the issue of public health needs in relation to reform of TRIPS seriously on the WTO agenda. The requirements in the TRIPS Council's solution and the Amendment pending ratification are also so unwieldy as to be a serious impediment to countries without manufacturing capacity taking up the opportunity to be 'eligible importing Members'. This, of course, only reflects the reality of politics, and the dominant role of power in political relationships: the power of large business interests in shaping global regulation, and the more opportunistic power of weaker players, NGOs and individuals ready to provide alternative models,[50] when a crisis highlights a contradiction in the moral underpinnings of an institution. But such moral outrage is not merely a political ploy: it has power to move public opinion and put large business interests on the defensive because the morality that ignites the outrage is real, reasonable and rationally founded on commitments implicit in the justification for the institutions concerned.

---

[49]   The period for acceptances has been thrice extended: see Decisions of 18 December 2007 (WTO Document WT/L/711), 17 December 2009 (WTO Document WT/L/785) and 5 December 2011 (WTO Document WT/L/829) and currently expires on 31 December 2013.

[50]   On modelling and the role of model missionaries, mercenaries and mongers, see Braithwaite and Drahos (2000), ch. 25, pp. 578–601. For the implication of the right to health for IPRs, see Matthews (2010), who observes (p. 136): 'The deployment of human rights language also helped to frame the debate as a *moral* issue, and through the mobilization of moral outrage, thereby helped to generate a widespread sense that the TRIPS Agreement in its current form could not be justified'.

9. Conclusions on the moral dimensions of IPRs

9.1 THE MORAL DIMENSIONS *REDUX*

9.1.1 Answering the Riddles in the Rules

This work began by noting the presence of moral terms and concepts in some of the central and most critical rules of IP laws and exploring the riddles they pose (§1.1). It asked the questions: What do they mean? How do they get their meaning? And: What do they do in such systems? It noted several aspects of such institutions (dimensions) in which moral concepts and reasoning play a role, and asked: How are these interrelated? The central thesis of the work suggests that the idea of universal prescriptivism – developed by the moral philosopher R.M. Hare[1] – as a core characteristic of what is moral in moral precepts and principles may provide a key to answering these questions.

This idea was examined, critiqued and further developed in Chapter 2 to arrive at fundamental prescriptions as the basis of moral reasoning which sum up in the equal right to freedom and well-being (§2.4.7). This principle essentially restates Gewirth's Principle of Generic Consistency[2] in a new way to highlight the way moral terms work and the importance of the desire of participants in moral discourse to make claims that treat moral norms as having objective rational force (§2.5.1). It was also argued that the principle be identified as the prescriptive ground of the actual choices and commitments we have made as a global society through the idea of human rights as embodied in the Universal Declaration of Human Rights (§2.5.3).

These supply the basis for answering the riddles posed at the outset of this work (§§2.6 and 2.7). Moral terms mean what we would rationally prescribe in the context if we had to universalize that prescription to other situations as well, even if the positions of the parties are reversed,

---

[1] Hare (1952, 1963, 1981 and 1997).
[2] Gewirth (1978 and 1996).

as grounds for people making moral claims upon one another with objective rational force. We determine their meaning by so universalizing our prescriptions, but with the understanding that the grounds of universalization are also moral principles, fundamental ones, which (either as a result of *a priori* reasoning, or global commitments we have embraced as the grounds for international cooperation) are encapsulated in the idea of the principle of the equal right to freedom and well-being.

If we then turn to our first question (What do legislatures and other law makers mean when they use such moral terms, as they do in IP laws?) we get the perhaps surprising result that they must intend that these terms and concepts apply with objective moral force and, hence, must intend them to mean whatever a theory of morality that does account for such characteristics would assign to such words. That intention then takes us up the path of rational inquiry that leads to this thesis for the meanings of the words so used.

Finally, how, then, do they work? This right has to be refined and made more specific in each context, bearing in mind the commitments we have made and the other aspects of the institutions we want to maintain. Such moral terms provide an element of adaptability in the rules which employ them because this method would require that the outcomes they mandate would have to be reviewed and revised in the light of other developments in relation to the institution.

This, then, explains how the moral aspects of the different dimensions of IPRs are inter-related, and can have a persistent force and role despite the other more powerful forces of self-interest and economic imperatives that shape IP laws.

9.1.2   The Force of the Moral Dimensions of IPRs

The key to the practical force of morality in the various dimensions of IPRs lies in the fact that the central persons in each of these dimensions do have a desire, an objective, that makes the rationally required prerequisites of that objective necessary for such persons (cf. §§2.3.2 and 2.4.8). They want, even though this desire may be partial and weaker than the desire for other competing or conflicting objectives, to be able to make claims to cooperation from others which have a force which is rational and objective. They want morality as an institution that works. Therefore the different dimensions of IPRs are linked by morality as a necessary project – more properly speaking, a single moral dimension (§6.4).

In the dimension of justification of IPRs, this desire is plainly assumed because justification is about having moral supporting grounds. A consequence of the equal right to freedom and well-being is that property cannot be justly acquired without the owner assuming some residual burden to acknowledge just claims to participatory use of the matter over which one has property rights (§3.2.4). This idea of justice requires apportioning of the matter, even intellectual property, in a manner that satisfies the terms of just distribution (§§3.2.4 and 3.6.1). This is distribution in accordance with the principle of an equal right to freedom and well-being.

IPRs promote liberty because they enable people to have control, over what is otherwise uncontrollable, where the matter is related to their personhood and well-being; and because they serve to induce contributions that promote liberty and well-being generally for all others (§3.6.3). But that right of control is carved out of corresponding restrictions on the liberty of others to use the subject matter, who also have claims to liberty and well-being founded on the equal right to freedom and well-being. This tension is resolved by an idea of Gewirth's, of a criterion of degree of needfulness for action, in which one asks which distributive rule is more needful for promoting the action of individuals generally.[3]

This justification of IPRs informs and accounts for the structure of IPRs in the dimension of design. The rules define both property rights and exemptions and limitations that reflect a moral participation right, the essence of both of which is encapsulated in Article 27 of the Universal Declaration of Human Rights (§4.1.1).

The full implications of the equal right to freedom and well-being are evolving, being developed as we make various commitments that define it further (§4.1.2). Of particular pertinence to IPRs, this development is also driven by changes to society because of technological and cultural innovation that is in part the product of IPRs themselves, which make such contributions their *raison d'être* (§3.6). Although the principle of the equal right to freedom and well-being is foundational, its implications for the structure of IPRs, and how it distributes property and participatory access, is always and in principle subject to review and revision and, hence, always open to reform (§8.1). An important conclusion one may derive from this is that the moral terms and concepts in the core rules of IPRs, with their adaptability and sensitivity to the underlying justification

---

[3] Gewirth (1996), p. 45: 'When two rights are in conflict with one another, that right takes precedence whose object is more needed for action.' See also above Ch. 2, §2.5.1.

of the institutions, are present therein because this is a key part of the justification of IPRs (§3.6.1). They serve by their flexible prescriptivity and by the aspiration to justification that is part of the characteristic of universality, both to express the intention that the institution be justifiable and to, perhaps to a limited degree constrained by the context and other terms of the rule, enable that part of the institution to adapt to satisfy this justificatory imperative. They, thus, have a transformative role in these institutions (§4.1.2).

9.1.3   Implications for the Participation Right and Public Domain

Some important consequences for the way the moral participatory right is expressed and, hence, how the public domain is protected, stem from the observation that these moral terms and concepts tend to be present in the rules relating to the extent, exception and exercise of IPRs rather than those setting conditions for their existence (§§4.8.2 and 6.3). First, the expression of the public's moral right to participatory access depends on such rules and, thus, the burden of ensuring a just sharing of the resource falls in the main on these and, where these use moral terms, on the way they are interpreted. Secondly, whilst the property rights are clearly IP rights in *law*, the participatory 'right' is a *moral* one, implicit in the framework of the law adopted but the extent to which it acquires legal force depends on the willingness of the courts to interpret the provisions with this end in view. Thirdly, there are degrees to which it gains legal force or recognition: as a background principle which guides the inter-pretation of IP law but not itself a rule of law (§4.8.2); as rule or doctrine of IP law (such as the transformative use doctrine for fair use in American copyright law, cf. §4.3.4); as a consequence of a constitutional or human rights law (such as the right of free speech in the US and the UK) which over-rides or has some entrenched effect against ordinary national legislation (cf. §8.2.2). Fourthly, as the hard black letter rules tend to predominate amongst those establishing the property rights, and the institutions' aspiration towards a balance of property and participatory rights seems to depend on some of the rules which require interpretative activism by the courts, the thrust of reform required by appeals to this underlying balance in relation to these institutions would appear to be towards greater protection or extension of the public domain.

A major counter-example tends to confirm the theory. The extension of the common law action against breach of confidence by the UK courts to protect against certain forms of invasion of privacy is a major reversal of the direction of the law up to and including *Kaye v. Robertson*[4] (§4.2.5). This extended the control private persons have against the public right of access, even, in some circumstances, to photographs taken of persons in public view or on public streets.[5] However, this is an example from a law whose very basis and central rules for acquisition of protection are cast in terms appealing to moral concepts, and the underlying rationale is consistent with and justifiable under an appeal to the idea of an equal right to freedom and well-being. Where the existence of the property rights is firmly set out, and some of the major rules concerned with fleshing out how balancing participatory access is to be established are cast in ethical or evaluative language, the general thrust of reform tends to be concerned with protection of the public domain (§§6.3 and 8.1).

9.1.4   The Vulnerabilities of the Moral Dimensions

Fifthly, this moral dimension, and its potential role as a means of preserving and protecting the public domain, is vulnerable to a variety of tendencies or stratagems which restrict the relevance of these rules relating to the extent of, exceptions to, and exercise and enforcement of IPRs.

The dimension of reform was considered in the last chapter. This aspiration towards reform is part of the law's characteristic aspiration towards legitimacy, part of its Razian claim to authority, that was noted in Chapter 6 (§6.2). As noted, the principle of the equal right to freedom and well-being that underpins this tension between the property and participation right has a moral force for each category of participants in the various dimensions of IPRs because they each want, at least to some degree, to call on morality as a resource which has objective rational force. They must then be open to the rational basis of morality as an institution itself, and hence be open to any reforms required in the light of that fundamental principle. It was observed, however, that this potential for adapting towards and accommodating reform inherent in the moral dimensions of IPRs can be stifled or circumvented.

First, the judges and other officials with the responsibility of applying and interpreting IP laws may fail to seize the potential of such moral terms and concepts and give their role in the protection of the public domain its due weight. Examples of this include the proprietarian

---

[4]   [1991] F.S.R. 62.

[5]   *Campbell v. Mirror Group Newspapers* [2004] UK HL 22; [2004] 2 A.C. 457, *Murray v. Express Newspapers Plc* [2008] EWCA Civ 446, [2009] Ch. 481, [2007] EWHC 1908 (Ch); cf. §4.2.5.

assumptions brought to the WTO Dispute Settlement Body's Panel decision in *United States – Section 110(5) of the US Copyright Act*.[6]

Secondly, as the exemptions and limitations and other derogations from IPR protection in the international conventions, including TRIPS, are permissive provisions rather than mandatory requirements, they may not be fully enacted or embraced in the national laws.

Thirdly, they can be circumscribed by other developments in the international law for the protection of IPRs. TRIPS permits greater, but not a lessening of, protection under other international agreements, and FTA activity has been ratcheting up property rights with 'TRIPS-Plus' provisions (§5.4). Provisions permitting exemptions under one international regime can be avoided if effective overlapping (even if not identical) protection can be obtained by resort to another regime. Some of these areas of overlap include the relationship between patent protection for plants under patents and plant variety rights protection, where a different outcome in the *NOVARTIS II*[7] decision in the EPO might have put farmers relying on the farmers' privilege, of replanting their own seeds and other propagating material generated on their own farms, in a stronger position (§4.4.4).

A fourth vulnerability for the moral dimensions' potential for the protection of the public domain stems from the feature that what the public enjoys as a result of the exemptions and limitations is better characterized as a Hohfeldian privilege rather than a Hohfeldian right.[8] Those privileges can be surrendered by contract. They can be evaded by resort to another, overlapping, IPR regime. They can be nullified by resort to technological means (§7.4).

Fifthly, the force of the moral dimensions on owners and users as regards how the IPRs are exploited, and on administrators and politicians as regards the steps they take to modify IPRs or their impact, depends on whether there is rational discourse on these matters. This can be circumscribed if the various persons involved are not given the opportunity to, or if they fail to seize the opportunity to, engage in such discourse. It can be circumscribed if the decisions of the officials – such as those entrusted with the responsibility to prevent abuse of TMs used to protect copyright material, or to determine when a compulsory licence should be given – are not transparent and subject to rational examination; or if the law makers at national level or in international trade negotiations do not

---

6   WTO document no. WT/D160/R, 15 June 2000; see §§5.3.3–5.3.4.
7   *NOVARTIS/Transgenic plant G1/98* [2000] E.P.O.R. 303.
8   Hohfeld (1923); cf. discussion at §7.2.2.

take the various moral arguments they use to support their positions and claims seriously; or if the IP experts and academics are sceptical as to these moral dimensions.

9.2 THE FUTURE OF IPRS – TOWARDS RIGHTS IN THE PUBLIC DOMAIN?

This suggests that the structure of IPRs should be re-thought. Given the various ways that the moral dimensions, and hence the protection of the public domain, are vulnerable to being circumscribed and evaded, this re-thinking should be towards embodying and entrenching the moral right of participatory access, giving it recognition to varying degrees as legal rights.

The courts in particular may take on the activist role suggested by David Lange[9] using various means to protect the public domain (§4.8). They may use the flexibilities of common law policy (§7.3.2), competition law restrictions (§7.3.3) and conditions for enforcement (§7.3.4) to shape a more balanced outcome. Administrative authorities have certain powers to resist encroachment on the public domain or reduction of participatory access: for example, through the exercise of powers to grant compulsory licences (§7.3.5) or to exempt over-reaching TMs from protection against circumvention (§7.4.2). In these cases, the moral rights of participatory access do not become legal rights in themselves but are background moral rights relevant to how the rules are interpreted and wielded. They can also become expressly embodied in the rules: to give the courts authority to make the appropriate adaptations to the law, an example of which is the American style fair use defence[10] (§4.3.4). That moral right may also be entrenched through constitutional and human rights laws protection, in some countries, of the right to freedom of expression and speech, which may over-ride or operate to limit the width of some copyright laws (§8.3.2).

Even more ambitiously, perhaps it is time to consider at the international stage, making some of the exemptions and limitations mandatory on the grounds that some access is critical to the enjoyment of liberty and well-being as a human right. This, though, requires international consensus. We are far from such a consensus at this stage. But, perhaps, the observations of this work are a start in getting there.

---

[9] Lange (1981); cf. §4.8.2.
[10] Copyright Act (US) Title 17 USC, s 107, cf. §4.3.4.

9.3   A PARTING WORD

The moral dimension of IPRs is an absurd thing: it points to a potential reality we aspire towards because of various circumstances in which we want to be able to make moral claims for cooperation from one another, but never quite fulfils that aspiration because other aims and pressures cause us to betray its promise.

Yet we are never quite able to fully abandon it. This, though, gives us a reason to pay attention to the way our institutions sustain and support this moral dimension or stifle it. IPRs are a product of conflicting interests and aims and objectives and do not quite embody fully the principles their moral dimensions imply. But, if we can never quite abandon these moral dimensions, and these dimensions themselves contain the potential for accommodating reform, then this absurdity is a basis for hope.

Bibliography

Abbott, Frederick M., 2005, 'Managing the Hydra', in Keith E. Maskus and Jerome H. Reichman (eds.), *International Public Goods and Transfer of Technology: Under a Globalized Intellectual Property Regime*, Cambridge University Press: Cambridge, 393–424

Allan, James, 1998, *A Sceptical Theory of Morality and Law*, Peter Lang Publishing: New York, N.Y.

Anderman, Steven D., 2000, *EC Competition Law and Intellectual Property Rights*, Oxford University Press: Oxford

Ang, Steven, 1994, 'The Idea–Expression Dichotomy and Merger Doctrine in the Copyright Laws of the U.S. and the U.K.', *International Journal of Law and Information Technology*, Vol. 2, No. 2, 111–53

Angelopoulos, Christina J., 2008, 'Freedom of Expression and Copyright', [2008] *I.P.Q.*, Issue 3, 328–53

Aoki, Keith, 1993, 'Authors, Inventors and Trademark Owners: Private Intellectual Property and the Public Domain. Part I', *Columbia–VLA Journal of Law and the Arts*, Vol. 18, 1–73

Aoki, Keith, 1994, 'Authors, Inventors and Trademark Owners: Private Intellectual Property and the Public Domain. Part II', *Columbia–VLA Journal of Law and the Arts*, Vol. 18, 191–267

Aristotle, 1976, *Ethics* ('The Nicomachean Ethics'), J.A.K. Thomson (trans.1953) (Rev. Ed.), Penguin Books: London

Austin, John, 1998, *The Province of Jurisprudence Determined; and, The Uses of the Study of Jurisprudence* (with Introduction by H.L.A. Hart, orig. pub. by Weidenfeld and Nicolson, 1954), Hackett Publishing Company: Indianapolis

Ayer, Alfred Jules, 2006, *Language, Truth and Logic*, Penguin Books: London (orig. pub. 1936)

Balasubramaniam, Kumariah, 2002, 'Access to Medicines: Patents, Prices and Public Policy – Consumer Perspectives', in P. Drahos and R. Mayne (eds.), *Global Intellectual Property Rights*, Palgrave Macmillan: Basingstoke, ch. 6, 90–107

Barthes, Roland, 1977, 'Death of the Author', in *Images–Music–Text*, S. Heath (trans.) (ed.), London: Fontana, 142

Becker, Lawrence C., 1977, *Property Rights: Philosophic Foundations*, Routledge & Kegan Paul: London

Bently, Lionel, and Maniatis, Spyros M., 1998, *Intellectual Property and Ethics*, Sweet & Maxwell: London

Berlin, Isaiah, 2002, *Liberty*, Henry Hardy (ed.), Oxford University Press: Oxford

Beyleveld, Deryck, 1991, *The Dialectical Necessity of Morality: An Analysis and Defense of Alan Gewirth's Argument to the Principle of Generic Consistency*, The University of Chicago Press: Chicago and London

Beyleveld, Deryck, and Brownsword, Roger, 1993, *Mice, Morality and Patents*, The Common Law Institute of Intellectual Property: London

Blakeney, Michael, 2002a, 'Protection of Plant Varieties and Farmers' Rights' [2002], *E.I.P.R.*, 9–19

Blakeney, Michael, 2002b, 'Agricultural Research: Intellectual Property and the CIAR System', in P. Drahos and R. Mayne (eds.), *Global Intellectual Property Rights*, Palgrave Macmillan: Basingstoke, ch. 7, 108–24

Blakeney, Michael, 2005, 'Stimulating Agricultural Innovation', in Keith E. Maskus and Jerome H. Reichman (eds.), *International Public Goods and Transfer of Technology: Under a Globalized Intellectual Property Regime*, Cambridge University Press: Cambridge, 367–90

Blakeney, Michael, 2009, 'International Proposals for the Criminal Enforcement of Intellectual Property Rights', [2009] *I.P.Q.*, No. 1, 1–26

Bombach, Kara M., 2001, 'Can South Africa Fight AIDS? Reconciling the South African Medicines and Related Substances Act with the TRIPS Agreement', *B.U. International L.J.*, Vol. 19, 273–306

Boyle, James, 1996, *Shamans, Software & Spleens: Law and the Construction of the Information Society*, Harvard University Press: Cambridge, MA

Boyle, James, 2003, 'The Second Enclosure Movement and the Construction of the Public Domain', *Law and Contemporary Problems*, Vol. 66 (Winter/Spring), 33–74

Boyle, James, 2008, *The Public Domain: Enclosing the Commons of the Mind*, Yale University Press: New Haven and London

Braithwaite, John, and Drahos, Peter, 2000, *Global Business Regulation*, Cambridge University Press: Cambridge

Burrell, Robert, and Coleman, Alison, 2005, *Copyright Exceptions: The Digital Impact*, Cambridge University Press: Cambridge

Caenegem, William Van, 2002, 'The Public Domain: Scientia Nullius?' [2002] *E.I.P.R.*, 324–30

Calabresi, Guido, and Melamed, A. Douglas, 1972, 'Property Rules, Liability Rules, and Inalienability: One View of the Cathedral', *Harv. L. Rev.*, Vol. 85, 1089

Canadian Biotechnology Advisory Committee (June 2002), *Patenting of Higher Lifeforms and Related Issues: Report to the Government of Canada Biotechnological Ministerial Coordinating Committee*, http:// publications.gc.ca/collections/Collection/C2-598-2001-2E.pdf (last accessed 1 August 2013)

Chevalier, Michel, and Mazzalovo, Gérald, 2004, *ProLogo: Brands as a Factor of Progress*, Palgrave Macmillan: Houndsmill

Coombe, Rosemary J., 1998, *The Cultural Life of Intellectual Properties*, Duke University Press: Durham and London

Cornish, William, 1989, *Intellectual Property: Patents, Copyright, Trade Marks and Allied Rights* 2nd ed., Sweet & Maxwell: London

Cornish, William, and Llewelyn, David, 2003, *Intellectual Property: Patents, Copyright, Trade Marks and Allied Rights* 5th ed., Sweet & Maxwell: London

Correa, Carlos M., 2007, *Trade Related Aspects of Intellectual Property Rights: A Commentary on the TRIPS Agreement*, Oxford University Press: Oxford

Couto, Alexandra, 2008, 'Copyright and Freedom of Expression: A Philosophical Map', in A. Grosseries, A. Marciano and A. Strowel (eds.), *Intellectual Property and Theories of Justice*, Palgrave Macmillan: Basingstoke, 160–87

Cunard, J.P., Hill, K. and Barlas, C., 2004, *Current Developments in the Field of Digital Rights Management*, SCCR/10/2 Rev. 4 May 2004 (a study for WIPO's Standing Committee on Copyright and Related (10th Session, Geneva, November 2003)), http://www.wipo.int/edocs/mdocs/ copyright/en/sccr_10/sccr_10_2_rev.pdf (last accessed 1 August 2013)

De George, Richard T., 2005, 'Intellectual Property and Pharmaceutical Drugs', originally pub. in *Business Ethics Quarterly*, Vol. 15, No. 4, reprinted in Beauchamp, T.L., Bowie, N.E. and Arnold, D.G. (eds.), *Ethical Theory and Business* 8d, Pearson Prentice Hall: Upper Saddle River, N.J., 2008, 465–76

De Greiff, P. and Cronin, C. (eds.), 2002, *Global Justice & Transnational Politics*, The MIT Press: Cambridge, MA

Demsetz, Harold, 1967, 'Towards a Theory of Property Rights', *The American Economic Review*, Vol. 57, No. 2 (May 1967), 347–59

Drahos, Peter, 1996, *A Philosophy of Intellectual Property*, Dartmouth: Aldershot

Drahos, Peter, 1998, 'The Universality of Intellectual Property Rights: Origins and Development', paper delivered at the Panel Discussion on Intellectual Property and Human Rights, Geneva, 9 November 1998, organized by WIPO and the Office of the United Nations High Commissioner for Human Rights, quotes from sect. 5.

Drahos, Peter, with Braithwaite, John, 2002, *Information Feudalism*, The New Press: New York, N.Y.

Drahos, Peter, and Mayne, Ruth (eds.), 2002, *Global Intellectual Property Rights*, Palgrave Macmillan: Basingstoke

Drexl, Josef, 2005, 'The Critical Role of Competition Law in Preserving Public Goods in Conflict with Intellectual Property Rights', in K.E. Maskus and J.H. Reichman (eds.), *International Public Goods and Transfer of Technology: Under a Globalized Intellectual Property Regime*, Cambridge University Press: Cambridge, 709–25

Dreyfuss, Rochelle Cooper, 2010, 'Patents and Human Rights: Where is the Paradox?', in Willem Grosheide (ed.), *Intellectual Property and Human Rights: A Paradox*, Edward Elgar: Cheltenham, 72–6

Dufay, Julien, and Pican, Xavier, 'The Erosion of the Moral Right: Comparison of France–United States', [2004] *I.B.L.J.*, Issue 4, 461–88

Dutfield, Graham, 2000, *Intellectual Property Rights, Trade and Biodiversity*, Earthscan: London

Dworkin, Ronald, 1977, *Taking Rights Seriously*, Harvard University Press: Cambridge, MA

Dworkin, Ronald, 1986, *Law's Empire*, Harvard University Press: Cambridge, MA

Dworkin, Ronald, 1996, 'Objectivity and Truth: You'd Better Believe It', *Philosophy and Public Affairs*, Vol. 25, No. 2, 87–139

Efroni, Zohar, 2011, *Access-Right: The Future of Digital Copyright Law*, Oxford University Press: Oxford

European Group on Ethics in Science and New Technologies, 2002, *Opinion No. 16: Ethical Aspects of Patenting Involving Human Stem Cells* (Rap.: Nielsen, and Whittaker), available at: http://ec.europa.eu/european_group_ethics/docs/avis16_en.pdf (last accessed 4 April 2011)

FAO, 2001, *Report of the Commission on Genetic Resources for Food and Agriculture*, 6th Extraordinary Session, 25–30 June 2001, FAO Doc. CGFRA-Ex 6/01/REP

Foot, Phillippa, 1978, 'Morality as a System of Hypothetical Imperatives', *Virtues and Vices and Other Essays in Moral Philosophy*, Basil Blackwell: Oxford, ch. XI, 157–73. Originally published in *The Philosophical Review*, Vol. 81, No. 3 (July 1972)

Fox, Eleanor M., 2005, 'Can Antitrust Policy Protect the Global Commons from the Excesses of IPRs?', in K.E. Maskus and J.H. Reichman (eds.), *International Public Goods and Transfer of Technology: Under a Globalized Intellectual Property Regime*, Cambridge University Press: Cambridge, 758–69

Friedman, Milton, 1970, 'The Social Responsibility of Business Is to Increase Its Profits', *New York Times Magazine*, 13 September 1970; reprinted in T.L. Beauchamp, N.E. Bowie and D.G. Arnold, *Ethical*

Theory and Business 8d, Pearson Prentice Hall: Upper Saddle River, N.J., 2009, ch. 2, 51–5

FTC, 2003, *To Promote Innovation: The Proper Balance of Competition and the Patent Law and Policy*, ch. 3, 38–9 (Oct. 2003)

Gallini, Nancy T. and Trebilcock, Michael J., 2004, 'Intellectual Property Rights and Competition Policy', in K.E. Maskus (ed.), *The WTO, Intellectual Property Rights and the Knowledge Economy*, Edward Elgar Publishing: Cheltenham, 198–242

Gewirth, Alan, 1978, *Reason and Morality*, University of Chicago Press: Chicago

Gewirth, Alan, 1982, *Human Rights: Essays on Justification and Applications*, University of Chicago Press: Chicago and London

Gewirth, Alan, 1984, 'Replies to My Critics', in *Gewirth's Ethical Rationalism*, Edward Regis Jr (ed.), University of Chicago Press: Chicago and London

Gewirth, Alan, 1996, *The Community of Rights*, University of Chicago Press: Chicago

Ghosh, Shubha, 2005, 'Comment: Competitive Baselines for Intellectual Property Rights' in K.E. Maskus and J.H. Reichman (eds.), *International Public Goods and Transfer of Technology: Under a Globalized Intellectual Property Regime*, Cambridge University Press: Cambridge, 793–813

Gordon, Wendy, 1982, 'Fair Use as Market Failure', *Columbia Law Review*, Vol. 82, 1600

Gordon, Wendy, 1992, 'On Owning Information: Intellectual Property and the Restitutionary Impulse', *Virginia Law Review*, Vol. 78, 149

Gordon, Wendy, 2010, 'Current Patent Laws cannot Claim the Backing of Human Rights', in Willem Grosheide (ed.), *Intellectual Property and Human Rights: A Paradox*, Edward Elgar: Cheltenham, 155–71

Greengrass, Barry, 1991, 'The 1991 Act of the UPOV Convention' [1991] 12 *E.I.P.R.*, 466

Griffiths, Jonathan, 2002, 'Copyright Law after Ashdown', [2002] *I.P.Q.*, Issue 3, 240–64

Grosheide, Willem (ed.), 2010a, *Intellectual Property and Human Rights: A Paradox*, Edward Elgar: Cheltenham

Grosheide, Willem, 2010b, 'General Introduction', in *Intellectual Property and Human Rights*, Edward Elgar: Cheltenham, ch. 1, 3–36

Grosseries, Axel, Marciano, Alain, and Strowel, Alain, 2008, *Intellectual Property and Theories of Justice*, Palgrave Macmillan: Basingstoke

Gurry, Francis, 1984, *Breach of Confidence*, Clarendon Press: Oxford

Habermas, Jürgen, 2002, 'On Legitimation Through Human Rights', in P. De Greiff and C. Cronin (eds.), *Global Justice & Transnational Politics*, The MIT Press: Cambridge, MA, ch. 6, 197–214

Hare, Richard Mervyn, 1952, *The Language of Morals*, Clarendon Press: Oxford

Hare, Richard Mervyn, 1963, *Freedom and Reason*, Clarendon Press: Oxford

Hare, Richard Mervyn, 1981, *Moral Thinking: Its Levels, Method, and Point*, Clarendon Press: Oxford

Hare, Richard Mervyn, 1997, *Sorting Out Ethics*, Clarendon Press: Oxford

Hare, Richard Mervyn, 1999, *Objective Prescriptions and Other Essays*, Clarendon Press: Oxford

Harman, Gilbert, 2000, *Explaining Value: And Other Essays in Moral Philosophy*, Clarendon Press: Oxford

Harmon, Shawn H.E., 2006, 'From Engagement to Re-engagement: The Expression of Moral Values in European Patent Proceedings, Past and Future', *E. L. Rev.*, Issue 31, No. 5, 642–66

Hart, H.L.A., 1994, *The Concept of Law* (2nd ed.), P.A. Bulloch and J. Raz (eds.), Oxford University Press: Oxford

Hart, H.L.A., 1984, 'Are There Any Natural Rights?', in Jeremy Waldron (ed.), *Theories of Rights*, Oxford: Oxford University Press

Hegel, G., 1967, *Hegel's Philosophy of Right* (1952, Knox trans.), Oxford: Oxford University Press

High Commissioner for Human Rights report, 2001, 'The Impact of the Agreement on Trade-Related Aspects of Intellectual Property Rights on Human Rights', Economic and Social Council document E/CN.4/Sub.2/2001/13

Hobbes, Thomas, 1996, *Leviathan*, Oxford University Press: Oxford (orig. pub. 1651)

Hohfeld, Wesley N., 1923, 'Fundamental Legal Conceptions As Applied in Judicial Reasoning', *Yale Law Journal*, Vol. 23, No. 1, 16–59

Hudson, W.D., 1983, *Modern Moral Philosophy* (2nd ed.), Macmillan Press: London and Basingstoke

Hudson, W.D., 1988, 'Development of Hare's Moral Philosophy', in D. Seanor and N. Fotion (eds.), *Hare and His Critics: Essays on Moral Thinking*, Clarendon Press: Oxford, ch. 2, 9–23

Hughes, Justin, 1988–89, 'The Philosophy of Intellectual Property', *The Georgetown Law Journal*, Vol. 77, 287

Hume, David, 2000, *A Treatise on Human Nature* (Oxford Philosophical Text edition). D.F. Norton and M.J. Norton (eds), Oxford University Press, Oxford

Jones, Lucinda, 2000, 'An Artist's Entry into Cyberspace: Intellectual Property on the Internet' [2000] *E.I.P.R.*, 79–92

Kant, Immanuel, 1996, *The Groundwork of the Metaphysics of Morals* (1785) in *Immanuel Kant: Practical Philosophy*, Mary J. Gregor (trans.) (ed.), Cambridge University Press: Cambridge (the cross ref. to the pagination of the Royal Prussian Academy of Sciences edition of Kant's works is given in square brackets)

Khor, Martin, 2002, 'Rethinking Intellectual Property Rights and TRIPS', in P. Drahos and R. Mayne (eds.), *Global Intellectual Property Rights*, Palgrave Macmillan: Basingstoke, ch.12, 201–13

Krikorian, G., and Kapczynski, A., 2010, *Access to Knowledge: In the Age of Intellectual Property*, Zone Books: New York, 8.3.2

Laddie, H.I.L., Prescote, P. and Vitoria, M., 1995, *The Modern Law of Copyright & Designs* 2d, London: Butterworths

Landes, William M., and Posner, Richard A., 2003, *The Economic Structure of Intellectual Property Law*, The Belknap Press: Cambridge, MA

Lange, David, 1981, 'Recognizing the Public Domain', *Law and Contemporary Problems*, Vol. 44, No. 4, 147

Laurie, Graeme, 2004, 'Patenting Stem Cells of Human Origin', [2004] *E.I.P.R.*, Issue 26(2), 59–66

Lehmann, Michael, 1985, 'The Theory of Property Rights and the Protection of Intellectual and Industrial Property', *IIC*, Vol. 16, No. 5, 525–40

Lemley, Mark A., 1997, 'Romantic Authorship and the Rhetoric of Property', *Texas Law Review*, Vol. 75, 873–906, reprinted in P. Drahos (ed.), *Intellectual Property* 2d, Ashgate, Dartmouth: Aldershot, 1999, 307–40

Lessig, Lawrence, 1999, *Code: And other Laws of Cyberspace*, Basic Books: New York, N.Y.

Lessig, Lawrence, 2001, *The Future of Ideas*, Random House: New York, N.Y.

Litman, Jessica, 1990, 'The Public Domain', *Emory Law Journal*, Vol. 39, Fall, 965

Locke, John, 1986, *The Second Treatise on Civil Government*, Prometheus Books: New York (orig. pub. in *Two Treatises Of Government*, 1690)

MacCormick, Neil, 1994, *Legal Reasoning and Legal Theory* (in paperback with corrections), Oxford University Press: Oxford

MacCormick, Neil, and Weinberger, Ota, 1986, *An Institutional Theory of Law: New Approaches to Legal Positivism*, D. Reidel Publishing Co.: Dordrecht

Machiavelli, N., 1961, *The Prince* (George Bull, trans.), Penguin Books: Harmondsworth

Machlup, Fritz, 1999, 'An Economic Review of the Patent System', a report prepared for the US Senate Judiciary Committee's Subcommittee on Patents, Trademarks and Copyrights; reference is to the excerpts of this report in *The International Intellectual Property System: Commentary and Materials*, Frederick Abbott, Thomas Cottier and Francis Gurry (eds), Kluwer Law International: The Hague, 224–46

Mackie, John Leslie, 1990, *Ethics: Inventing Right and Wrong*, Penguin Books: London (orig. pub. 1977)

Marmor, Andrei, 1992, *Interpretation and Legal Theory*, Clarendon Press: Oxford

Marmor, Andrei, 2001, *Positive Law and Objective Values*, Clarendon Press: Oxford

Matthews, Duncan, 2010, 'Intellectual Property Rights, Human Rights and the Right to Health', in W. Grosheide (ed.), *Intellectual Property and Human Rights: A Paradox*, Edward Elgar: Cheltenham, 118–39

Max Planck Institute for Intellectual Property and Competition Law, 2011, *Declaration: A Balanced Interpretation of the 'Three-Step Test' in Copyright Law*, 5 January, available at: http://www.ip.mpg.de/ww/en/pub/news/declaration_on_the_three_step_.cfm (last accessed 15 November 2011)

May, Christopher, 2000, *A Global Political Economy of Intellectual Property Rights: The New Enclosures?*, Routledge: New York, N.Y.

Mayne, Ruth, 2002, 'The Global Campaign on Patents and Access to Medicines', in P. Drahos and R. Mayne (eds.), *Global Intellectual Property Rights,* Palgrave Macmillan: Basingstoke, ch. 15, 244–58

Merges, Robert P., 2011, *Justifying Intellectual Property*, Harvard University Press: Cambridge, MA

Mills, Oliver, 2010, *Biotechnological Inventions: Moral Restraints and Patent Law* (Rev. Ed.), Ashgate Publishing: Farnham

Moore, Adam D., 2001, *Intellectual Property and Information Control*, Transaction Publishers: New Brunswick and London

Moore, George Edward, 1959, *Principia Ethica*, Cambridge University Press: Cambridge (orig. pub. 1903)

Moufang, Rainer, 1994, 'Patenting Genes, Cells and Parts of the Human Body?' [1994] *I.I.C.*, Issue 25, No. 4, 487–515

Narveson, Jan, 1985, 'The How and Why of Universalizability', in N.T. Potter and M. Timmons (eds.), *Morality and Universalizability*, D. Reidel Publishing Co.: Dordrecht

National Conference of Commissioners on Uniform State Laws, (U.S.), 1985, *Commissioners' Comment to the Uniform Trade Secrets Act* (1979, amended 1985)

Nozick, Robert, 1974, *Anarchy, State and Utopia*, Basic Books: New York

Nussbaum, Martha, 2002, 'Capabilities and Human Rights', in P. De Greiff and C. Cronin (eds.), *Global Justice & Transnational Politics*, The MIT Press: Cambridge, MA, ch. 4, 117–50

Overwalle, Gertrui Van, 2010, 'Human Rights Limitations in Patent Law', in W. Grosheide (ed.), *Intellectual Property and Human Rights: A Paradox*, Edward Elgar: Cheltenham, 236–71

Patterson, L. Ray, 1987, 'Free Speech, Copyright, and Fair Use', *Vanderbilt L. Rev.*, Vol. 40, No. 1, 7, 1–66

Patterson, L. Ray, and Birch Jr, Stanley F., 1996, 'Copyright and Free Speech Rights', *J. Intell. Prop. L.*, Vol. 4, No. 1

Pendleton, Cullen N., 2004, 'The Peculiar Case of "Terminator" Technology', *Biotechnology Law Report*, Vol. 23, No. 1 (February), 1–29

Penrose, Edith Tilton, 1951, 'The Economics of the International Patent System', reference is to the excerpts of this report in *The International Intellectual Property System: Commentary and Materials*, F. Abbott, T. Cottier and F. Gurry (eds), Kluwer Law International: The Hague, 1999, 255–64

Phillips, Jeremy, 2003, *Trade Mark Law: A Practical Anatomy*, Oxford University Press: Oxford

Pitts, Peter, 2008, 'We're Taking Your Medicine, Literally', in River Cities' Reader, Wednesday, 5 March 2008, available at http://www.essentialaction.org/access/index.php?/archives/130-Response-to-Peter-Pitts-River-Cities-Reader-Iowa.html (last accessed 12 December 2011)

Pogge, Thomas, 2002, 'Human Rights and Human Responsibilities', in P. De Greiff and C. Cronin (eds.), *Global Justice & Transnational Politics*, The MIT Press: Cambridge, MA, ch. 5, 151–96

Radin, Margaret Jane, 1993, *Reinterpreting Property*, University of Chicago Press: Chicago and London

Rawls, John, 1993, *Political Liberalism*, Columbia University Press: New York

Rawls, John, 1999, *A Theory of Justice* (Rev. Ed.), The Belknap Press: Cambridge, MA (original pub. 1971)

Raz, Joseph, 1979, *The Authority of Law*, Oxford University Press: Oxford

Reichman, J.H. and Lewis, T., 2005, 'Using Liability Rules to Stimulate Local Innovation in Developing Countries: Application to Traditional Knowledge', in Keith E. Maskus and Jerome H. Reichman (eds.), *International Public Goods and Transfer of Technology: Under a Globalized Intellectual Property Regime*, Cambridge University Press: Cambridge, 337–66

Resnik, David B., 2004, *Owning the Genome: A Moral Analysis of DNA Patenting*, State University of New York Press: Albany

Ricketson, Staniforth, 1984, *The Law of Intellectual Property*, The Law Book Company Ltd: Sydney

Ridley, Matt, 1996, *The Origins of Virtue*, Penguin Books: London

Rousseau, Jean Jacques, 1762, *The Social Contract*, G.D.H. Cole (trans.), available at: http://www.constitution.org/jjr/socon.htm (last accessed 28 October 2011)

Ryan, Chris, 2001, 'Human Rights and Intellectual Property', [2001] *E.I.P.R.*, 521–7

Ryan, Michael P., 1998, *Knowledge Diplomacy: Global Competition and the Politics of Intellectual Property*, Brookings Institution Press: Washington, D.C.

Sahai, Suman, 2002, 'India's Plant Variety Protection and Farmers' Right Legislation', in P. Drahos and R. Mayne (eds.), *Global Intellectual Property Rights*, Palgrave Macmillan: Basingstoke, ch. 13, 215–23

Scanlon, Thomas, 1982, 'Contractualism and Utilitarianism', in Amartya Sen and Bernard Williams (eds.), *Utilitarianism and Beyond*, Cambridge University Press: Cambridge, reprinted in James Rachels (ed.), *Ethical Theory 2: Theories About How We Should Live*, Oxford University Press: Oxford, 1998, ch. VI, 102–28

Schechter, Frank I., 1927, 'The Rational Basis of Trademark Protection', *Harvard Law Review*, Vol. 40, 813

Seanor, Douglas, and Fotion, N., 1988, *Hare and His Critics*: *Essays on Moral Thinking*, Clarendon Press: Oxford

Searle, John R., 1995, *The Construction of Social Reality*, The Free Press: New York, N.Y.

Sen, Amartya, 1999, *Freedom as Development*, Alfred A. Knopf: New York, N.Y.

Sen, Amartya, 2009, *The Idea of Justice*, Allen Lane: London

Sherman, Brad, and Bently, Lionel, 1999, *The Making of Modern Intellectual Property Law*, Cambridge University Press: Cambridge

Shifrin, Seana Valentine, 2001, 'Lockean Arguments for Private Intellectual Property', in Stephen R. Munzer (ed.), *New Essays in the Legal and Political Theory of Property*, Cambridge University Press: Cambridge, ch. 5, 138–67

Singer, Joseph W., 2000, *Entitlement: The Paradoxes of Property*, Yale University Press: New Haven and London

Singer, Marcus G., 1984, 'Gewirth's Ethical Monism', in Edward Regis Jr. (ed.), *Gewirth's Ethical Rationalism*, University of Chicago Press: Chicago, ch. 2, 23–38

Singer, Peter, 1986, 'All Animals are Equal', (originally published in *New York Review of Books*, 5 April 1973) reprinted in *Applied Ethics*, Peter Singer (ed.), Oxford University Press: Oxford, 1986, ch. XIII, 215–28

Smith, Adam, 1790, *The Theory of Moral Sentiments*, T. Cadell: London (extended version), republished Clarendon Press: Oxford, 1976, III, i, 2.

Smith, N. Craig, and Duncan, Anne, 2009, 'GlaxoSmithKline and Access to Essential Medicines', case study for the London Business School, in N.C. Smith and G. Lenssen (eds.), *Mainstreaming Corporate Responsibility*, John Wiley & Sons: Chichester, 417–36

Sommer, Tine, 2008, 'Patenting the Animal Kingdom? From Cross-breeding to Genetic Make-up and Biomedical Research', [2008] *IIC*, Issue 39, No. 2, 139–72

Spector, Horacio M., 1989, 'An Outline of a Theory Justifying Intellectual and Industrial Property Rights', [1989] 8 *EIPR* 270–73

Stenton, Gavin, 2004, 'Biopiracy within the Pharmaceutical Industry: A Stark Illustration of how Abusive, Manipulative and Perverse the Patenting Process can be towards Countries of the South', [2004] *E.I.P.R.*, Issue 26, No. 1, 17–26

Sterling, J.A.L., 2003, *World Copyright Law* 2d, Sweet & Maxwell: London

Stiglitz, Joseph, 2006, *Making Globalization Work*, W. W. Norton & Co.: New York, N.Y.

Thomas, D., and Richards, G.A., 2004, 'The Importance of the Morality Exception under the European Patent Convention: The Oncomouse Case Continues', [2004] *E.I.P.R.*, Issue 26, No. 3, 97–104

Trerise, Jonathan, 2008, 'Liberty and the Rejection of Strong Intellectual Property Rights', in A. Grosseries, A. Marciano and A. Strowel (eds.), *Intellectual Property and Theories of Justice*, Palgrave Macmillan: Basingstoke, 122–37

Ullrich, Hanns, 2005, 'Expansionist Intellectual Property Protection and Reductionist Competition Rules', in K.E. Maskus and J.H. Reichman (eds.), *International Public Goods and Transfer of Technology*, Cambridge University Press: Cambridge, 726–56

U.N. Sub-Commission on the Promotion and Protection of Human Rights, 2000, Sub-Commission on Human Rights Resolution 2000/7 'Intellectual property rights and human rights', http://www.unhchr.ch/Huridocda/Huridoca.nsf/0/c462b62cf8a07b13c12569700046704e (last accessed 1 August 2013) 8.4

Waldron, Jeremy, 1988, *The Right to Private Property*, Clarendon Press: Oxford

Waldron, Jeremy, 1993, 'From Authors to Copiers', *Chicago-Kent Law Review*, Vol. 68, 841

Waldron, Jeremy, 1999, *Law and Disagreement*, Oxford University Press: Oxford

Walzer, Michael, 1983, *Spheres of Justice*, Basic Books: New York, N.Y.

Warren, Amanda, 1998, 'A Mouse in Sheep's Clothing: The Challenge to the Patent Morality Criterion Posed by "Dolly"', [1998] *E.I.P.R.*, Issue 20, No. 2, 445–52

Warren-Jones, Amanda, 2006, 'Identifying European Moral Consensus', [2006] *E.I.P.R.*, Issue 28, No. 1, 26–37

Weis, Rick, 2005, 'U.S. Denies Patent for a Too-Human Hybrid', *Washington Post*, 13 February, p. A03, available at: http://www.washingtonpost.com/wp-dyn/articles/A19781-2005Feb12.html (last accessed 31 May 2011)

Weisman, Robert, 2008, 'Stronger Patent Protection Will Take Lives, Not Save Them', in *River Cities' Reader*, Thursday, 20 March, available at: http://www.essentialaction.org/access/index.php?/archives/130-Response-to-Peter-Pitts-River-Cities-Reader-Iowa.html (last accessed 31 May 2011)

Werhane, Patricia H., and Gorman, Michael E., 2005, 'Intellectual Property Rights, Moral Imagination, and Access to Life-Enhancing Drugs', original pub. in *Business Ethics Quarterly*, Vol. 15, No. 4, reprinted in T.L. Beauchamp, N.E. Bowie and D.G. Arnold (eds.), *Ethical Theory and Business* 8d, Pearson Prentice Hall: Upper Saddle River, N.J., 2008, 477–85

WIPO, 1994, *Protection Against Unfair Competition: Analysis of the Present World Situation*, WIPO: Geneva

Wright, Robert, 1994, *The Moral Animal: Evolutionary Psychology and Everyday Life*, Abacus: London, reprinted 1996

Yu, Peter K., 2009, 'The Objectives and Principles of the TRIPS Agreement', *Houston Law Rev.*, Vol. 46, No. 4, 979–1046

Zemer, Lior, 2007, *The Idea of Authorship in Copyright*, Ashgate Publishing Ltd: Aldershot

Index

Aoki, Keith 177
Aristotle 78
Austin, John 231
Ayer, Alfred Jules 25, 35, 59

Beyleveld, Deryck 15, 192, 219
biotechnological inventions, protection
    of 153, 155–167, 190–209, 232,
    237–238, 261–262, 263–264
Braithwaite, John 217–218, 274, 282
Brownsword, Roger 15, 192
Burrell, Robert 263

Categorical Imperative see Kant,
    Immanuel
Coleman, Alison 263
competition law and intellectual
    property 5, 221–222, 238–239,
    256–258, 289
compulsory license of patents 259–260,
    273, 276–282, 289
confidence, action for breach of
    free speech and expression, and 129,
        187, 189
    nature of 2, 4, 5, 19, 116–122
    privacy protection under 118, 121,
        122–129, 130, 235, 268,
        286–287
    public policy exception 187–189
constitutional law, U.S.
    First Amendment 5, 268–269
    legislative power of Congress 4, 76,
        268
Coombe, Rosemary 169, 177, 179
copyright
    competition law, and 244, 249,
        256–258, 289
    exceptions 3–4, 222–228, 239,
        269–272

    see also copyright, fair use or
        dealing; copyright, public
        policy exception
    fair use/dealing 59, 144–155, 235,
        238, 286, 289
    free speech and expression 72, 148,
        151, 189, 268–269, 286, 289
    history 132–134, 269
    ideas, non-protection of 131,
        134–138
    nature of 1–2, 19, 130–134, 229
    originality requirement 134, 138–144
    public policy exception 187–189,
        269–272, 289
    see also technological measures

database protection 210
designs, protection of 222–223
Drahos, Peter 16, 79, 217–219, 274, 282
Dworkin, Ronald
    constructive model of law 17
    interpretivist approach to law as
        integrity 232, 234–235
    objectivity of morality 43
    rights as 'trumps' 211

equal right to freedom and well-being
    alienability of IPRs, and 185
    concept of 44–45, 106, 109, 124, 192,
        283
    confidence, action for breach of, and
        119–122
    consequentialism, and 76–79, 112
    copyright protection and 131, 140
    design of IPRs, and 99–102
    economic justification for IPRs, and
        79–80
    exercise or exploitation of IPRs, and
        242–252